Fashion Doll
Price Guide Annual
2000-2001

Incorporating *MILLER'$ 1999 Price Guide Pocket Annual*

Portfolio Press

To purchase additional copies of this book, please contact:
Portfolio Press, 130 Wineow Street, Cumberland, MD 21502
877-737-1200

ISBN 0-9242620-41-0

Design and Production: Tammy S. Blank
Cover Design: Kourtney Mills
Printed and bound in Korea
•

Contents

continued

3

USING THIS PRICE GUIDE

The authors of the *Fashion Doll Price Guide* are merely acting as "Reporters" of prices by surveying active dealers and collectors. The figures are a compilation of prices realized from the Internet, dealers' lists, sales tables at shows, and reports of purchases by collectors. We do our best to eliminate questionable data.

Wherever possible we have quoted a high, a low and an average or median price for each item. That way, collectors and dealers can see the entire spectrum and decide for themselves what range they feel comfortable buying and selling in. Please keep in mind that some items are so rare or infrequently traded that we could not find any data whatsoever.

The prices reflect a geographic diversity, the prices originally paid by the sellers, and how motivated the sellers were at the time of sale. Condition, rarity, and demand are all contributing factors in the pricing of a particular item.

We have chosen to report only items in "Never Removed From Box" or "Mint in Box" form and in mint and complete condition. *Any item in near mint or excellent condition would be priced accordingly lower* as would repaired or repainted items. (No standard exists for a percentage reduction for non-mint items.)

The prices quoted are retail selling prices from within the hobby (dealer to collector or collector to collector). When selling into the hobby, it is not uncommon to be offered a wholesale price (20%-50% less than the quoted prices). The percentage of the discount can depend upon the buyer, the rarity, and the condition of the item. This is standard practice with almost any collectible.

As authors we do not have anything to gain by influencing the direction (either up or down) of collectible fashion doll prices. As with any collectible, the law of supply and demand would ultimately override any attempt to manipulate market prices. Our goal is to "tell it like it is" by providing our readers with the BEST AVAILABLE price information for fashion dolls, outfits and accessories. The *Fashion Doll Price Guide* should facilitate buying and selling through education of what a fair price might be for a particular item.

At the risk of stating the obvious, we'd like to make two final points. *First, no one is obligated to buy or sell on the basis of the prices we quote.* Second, although every effort is made to insure the accuracy of the information in this book, common sense tells us that when dealing with such a large amount of data, errors and omissions are bound to occur at some point.

These price listings should be considered as guides only, not as absolute, fixed prices. The published prices are also not an offer to buy or sell on the part of the authors, publishers or any other party.

— Barbara Miller
— Sue Mauro
Editors

DEFINITIONS

NRFB:	Never Removed From Box
MIB:	Factory Mint Doll in Original Box
MINT & COMPLETE:	Pristine, flawless outfit and all accessories in mint condition
MINT (LOOSE DOLL):	Pristine, flawless doll – generally includes original mint swimsuit and shoes
OT:	Open Toe
CT:	Closed Toe
N/A:	Not applicable
– :	No data available
LE:	Limited Edition

NRFB dolls and fashions with flawless contents and packaging will command a price on the higher end of the scale. For example, an NRFB vintage fashion in a perfect box with sticker should fetch a higher price than one in a damaged box.

A GUIDE TO VINTAGE DOLLS

A blonde No.1 with lips fading toward orange.

A brunette No. 2 with dark red lips.

No. 1 Ponytail (1959)
Stock No. 850

1. Blonde or Brunette, soft hair with tiny ringlets for bangs.
2. White irises with dark blue eyeliner.
3. Red lips (*may have faded toward orange*).
4. High arched eyebrows.
5. Has holes in bottoms of feet and copper tubing in legs.
6. Heavy, solid body dressed in black/white striped swimsuit.
7. Vinyl has often turned very white.
8. Markings: Barbie™/Pats. Pend./©MCMLVIII/by Mattel/Inc.

No. 2 Ponytail (1959)
Stock No. 850

Identical features as the No. 1 except that the copper tubing was removed, and there are no longer the holes in the feet.

A GUIDE TO VINTAGE DOLLS

A brunette No. 3 with blue eyeliner.

A blonde No. 4

No. 3 Ponytail (1960)
Stock No. 850

1. Blonde or Brunette, same type hair as first two issues.
2. Blue irises.
3. Red lips (*may have faded toward orange*).
4. More gently curved eyebrows than with first two issues.
5. Eyeliner can be brown or blue.
6. Heavy, solid body, same as a No. 2, dressed in black and white swim suit.
7. Vinyl has often turned very white.
8. Same markings as first two issues.

No. 4 Ponytail (1960)
Stock No. 850

1. Blonde or Brunette, same type hair as first two issues.
2. Blue irises.
3. Red lips.
4. Same gently curved eyebrows as the No. 3.
5. Blue eyeliner only.
6. Heavy, solid body dressed in black and white swimsuit.
7. Different type vinyl retains its tan tone.
8. Same markings as first three issues.

A GUIDE TO VINTAGE DOLLS

A redheaded No.5

No. 5 Ponytail (1961)
Stock No. 850

1. Wider variety in hair color – first issue available with red hair.
2. Firmer hair texture than first four – bangs have larger curls.
3. Red lips.
4. Blue irises, blue eye liner, same gently curved brows.
5. New hollow, lighter-weight body retains its pinkish color.
6. Dressed in black and white swimsuit.
7. First issue to have a wrist tag.
8. Same markings as first four issues except Barbie™ is now Barbie®

An ash blonde No. 6 with coral lips.

No. 6 Ponytail (1962) & Ponytail (1963-1964)
Stock No. 850

1. Identical features and markings as No. 5 except for wider variety of hair and lip color.
2. Wears a different red jersey swimsuit.
3. A somewhat "chubbier" appearance to the face.
4. ***Ponytail (1963) only:*** Identical to No. 6 except new markings on torso: "Midge™/ © 1962/Barbie®/©1958/ by/Mattel, Inc."

A GUIDE TO VINTAGE DOLLS

Bubble Cut (1961-1967)
Stock No. 850

1. Wide variety of hair colors.
2. Blue irises.
3. Red lips most often available in 1961 – many lip colors from 1962-1967.
4. Same gently curved eyebrows.
5. Dressed in black/white striped swimsuit in 1961 only – available in red one-piece swimsuit from 1962-1967.
6. Markings in 1961 and 1962: Barbie®/Pats. Pend./©MCM-LVIII/by Mattel/Inc. Markings in 1963-1967: Midge™/©1962/Barbie®/©1958/by/Mattel, Inc./Patented.

A redheaded 1961 Bubble Cut.

Fashion Queen (1963-1964)
Stock No. 870

1. Molded dark brown hair with a blue vinyl headband.
2. Blue irises.
3. Available with coral lips.
4. Same gently curved eyebrows.
5. Dressed in a gold lamé and white striped swimsuit and turban.
6. Included three interchangeable wigs and a white wig stand.
7. '63 Markings: Midge™/©1962/Barbie®/©1958/by/Mattel, Inc. '64 Markings: Midge™/©1962/Barbie®/©1958/by/Mattel, Inc./Pat.

Fashion Queen

A GUIDE TO VINTAGE DOLLS

Lemon Blonde Swirl Ponytail.

Miss Barbie®, also known as Sleep-Eye.

Swirl Ponytail (1964-1965)
Stock No. 850
1. Wide variety of hair colors in a new side-swept ponytail tied with a yellow ribbon and attached with a miniature bobby pin.
2. Blue irises.
3. Wide variety of lip colors.
4. Same gently curved eyebrows.
5. Dressed in a red one-piece swimsuit.
6. Markings: Midge™/©1962/ Barbie®/©1958/by/Mattel, Inc./Patented.

Miss Barbie® (Sleep-Eye) 1964
Stock No. 1060
1. Molded dark brown hair with an orange vinyl headband.
2. Eyes that open and close.
3. Coral lips.
4. Gently curved eyebrows.
5. Dressed in one-piece pink, finge-skirted swimsuit with matching swimcap.
6. Includes 3 wigs (blonde, brunette and titian) and a wig stand. Also includes lawn swing and potted plant.
7. First doll with bendable knees.
8. Markings: ©1958/Mattel. Inc./ U.S. Patented/U.S. Pat. Pend

A GUIDE TO VINTAGE DOLLS

Bendable Leg (1966).

An ash blonde Side Part.

Bendable Leg (1965-1966)
Stock No. 1070
1. New bendable legs at the knees.
2. Variety of hair colors in Dutch boy style parted down the middle '65 version had short, coarse hair, and '66 had longer, silkier hair.
3. Blue irises and somewhat brighter, heavier makeup, especially with the 1966 version.
4. Wide variety of lip colors.
5. Same gently curved eyebrows.
6. Dressed in new multi-striped top swimsuit with aqua bottom.
7. Markings in 1965: ©1958/ Mattel, Inc./U.S. Patented/U.S. Pat. Pend. (all indented). Markings in '66: Same as 1965 but with raised "Made in Japan," or later in '66 — all raised markings.

Bendable Leg Side Part (1966)
Stock No. 1070
1. Bendable legs at the knees.
2. Variety of hair colors in a flip hairstyle parted down the side and held in place with an aqua headband.
3. Blue irises and make-up similar to above Bendable Leg.
4. Same gently curved eyebrows.
5. Dressed in multi-striped top swimsuit with aqua bottom.
6. Markings same as above Bendable Leg 1965 but with raised "Made in Japan," or later in '66 — all raised markings.
7. Wide variety of lip colors.

A GUIDE TO VINTAGE DOLLS

Golden Blonde Color Magic.

Color Magic (1966-1967)
Stock No. 1150

1. New hair with the ability to change between two colors. Two versions were available – Golden Blonde or Midnight Black.
2. Blue irises and very heavy eye makeup.
3. Available with red or coral lips.
4. Same gently curved eyebrows.
5. Dressed in a multi-colored diamond print swimsuit and head-band that also changed color. Also came with an aqua hair clip.
6. Markings: Same as 1966 Bendable Leg dolls.
7. Has bendable legs.

Twist 'N Turn (1967-1968)
Stock No. 1160

1. Bendable legs.
2. New waist that could twist back and forth.
3. Totally new face mold with a gently opened mouth.
4. New rooted eyelashes.
5. Four hair colors — Summer Sand, Sun Kissed, Go Go Co Co, and Chocolate Bon Bon, but variations exist. Hair long and straight with pulled back section affixed with a rubber band and ribbon.
6. Blue irises and new, more rounded eyebrows.
7. Dressed in orange two-piece swimsuit with white fishnet cover-up and orange hair ribbon in '67. In '68, dressed in pink block print belted top swimsuit and pink bottom with pink hair ribbon.
8. Markings: ©1966/Mattel, Inc./U.S. Patented./U.S. Pat Pend. /Made in/Japan.

American Stories Collection

American Indian

American Stories Collection

Civil War Nurse
Colonial, First Edition
Patriot
Pilgrim, First Edition
Pioneer, Second Edition
Pioneer, First Edition

14

American Beauties Collection

Ballroom Beauties Collection

Army
Mardi Gras

Starlight Waltz
Midnight Waltz

Bob Mackie Series

Gold Mackie

Starlight Splendor
Empress Bride

Bob Mackie Series

Neptune Fantasy
Fantasy Goddess of Asia
Goddess of the Sun
Madame Du

Masquerade Ball
Moon Goddess
Platinum
Queen of Hearts

Bob Mackie Series — Jewel Essence Collection

Amethyst
Diamond Dazzle
Emerald Embers
Ruby Radiance
Sapphire Splendor

Career

Astronaut, Toys R Us
Astronaut 1986

Travel and Career

International Travel
International Travel
Paleontologist, Toys R Us
Police Officer, Toys R Us
President 2000, Toys R Us
Skating Star, Wal-Mart

Dr. Barbie, Brunette, Mattel Festival
Dr. Barbie, Toys R Us
Fire Fighter, Toys R Us
Fire Fighter, black version, Toys R Us
Flight Time, brunette, Toys R Us
Flight Time Ken

Space Camp, Toys R Us
Stars 'n Stripes, Air Force Thunderbirds
Stars 'n Stripes, Air Force
Stars 'n Stripes, Air Force Barbie & Ken Gift Set

Stars 'n Stripes, Army
Stars 'n Stripes, Army Ken
Stars 'n Stripes, Navy
Stars 'n Stripes, Navy, black version
Teacher

Children's Collector Series

Barbie as Cinderella   Barbie as Little Bo Peep
Barbie as Rapunzel
Barbie as Sleeping Beauty   Barbie as Snow White

City Seasons Collection

Autumn in Paris
Spring in Tokyo
Summer in San Francisco, FAO, blonde
Winter in New York

Classic Ballet Series

Sugar Plum Fairy (Nutcracker)   Swan Lake

Classique Collection

Benefit Ball   City Style

Evening Extravaganza
Midnight Gala
Opening Night
Starlight Dance,
  black version
Uptown Chic

Dolls of the World

Arctic, 2nd Edition
Australian
Brazilian
Canadian
Chinese, Dutch, Kenyan Gift Set
Chinese, 2nd Edition

Czechoslovakian
Dutch
English
Eskimo
French Barbie, 2nd Edition
German

31

Dolls of the World

Ghanian
German, 2nd Edition
Greek
Icelandic
Indian, 2nd Edition
Irish, German, Polynesian Gift Set

Italian, 2nd Edition Reissue   Japanese Barbie

Japanese, 2nd Edition Reissue   Jamaican Barbie   Kenyan Barbie

Dolls of the World

Korean
Malaysian
Mexican
Mexican, 2nd Edition Reissue
Native American, 2nd Edition
Native American, Toys R Us,
   4th Edition

Native American, 1st Edition
Native American, 5th Edition
Nigerian
Norwegian
Parisian
Peruvian

Dolls of the World

Polynesian   Russian   Russian, 2nd Edition Reissue

Scottish   Spanish   Swiss

Enchanted Seasons Collection

Autumn Glory

Snow Princess

Spring Bouquet

Summer Splendor

Evening Elegance Series

Golden Winter
Night Dazzle
Winter Renaissance

Gift Sets

35th Anniversary
Ballet Recital Barbie & Kelly
Barbie and Friends
Barbie and Nibbles
Barbie's Sharin' Sisters

Gift Sets

Barbie's Sharin' Sisters
Barbie Winter Ride, FAO Schwarz
BillyBoy Feelin' Groovy
Dream Wedding
Flight Time Barbie
Flight Time Barbie, black version

Holiday Sisters
Hollywood Hair
Hot Skatin' Barbie
  and Mustang
Ocean Friends
  Barbie & Keiko
Olympic Skater
Rollerblade Snack
  and Surf

Gift Sets

Sparkle Eyes Barbie
Travelin' Sisters
Wedding Fantasy
Western Stampin'
Western Stampin', black version
Western Stampin'
Winter Holiday Vacation

Great Eras Collection

Gibson Girl

Great Eras Collection

Flapper

Egyptian Queen

Elizabethan Queen

Chinese Empress

Grecian Goddess

Medieval Lady

Southern Belle

Victorian Lady

Happy Holidays

1988 Happy Holidays

Happy Holidays

1989 Happy Holidays
1991 Happy Holidays versions
1992 Happy Holidays versions

Happy Holidays

1992 Happy Holidays versions

1993 Happy Holidays versions

1994 Happy Holidays versions

1995 Happy
Holidays versions

1996 Happy
Holidays
versions

1997
Happy
Holidays
versions
Different
box back-
grounds

Happy Holidays

1997 Happy Holidays versions Different box backgrounds

1998 Happy Holidays Barbie versions

Happy Holidays — International

1994 Happy Holidays

1995 Happy Holidays

1996 Happy Holidays

Holiday Theme

Make-A-Valentine
Make-A-Valentine,
   black version

Caroling Fun
Holiday Hostess
Holiday Dreams

Holiday Theme

Holiday Seasons, black version
Holiday Seasons
Holiday Treats
Festive Season
Holiday Treasures, Mattel Club doll

Easter Barbie   Easter Basket Barbie   Easter Fun Barbie   Easter Party Barbie

Easter Style Barbie   Sweet Spring   Spring Bouquet

Holiday Theme

| Valentine Barbie | Valentine Barbie | Valentine Barbie | Valentine Barbie |

Valentine Date Barbie   BMine   Pretty Hearts   Make-A-Valentine

Valentine Fun   Valentine Fun, black version   Valentine Romance   Valentine Sweetheart

Valentine Style,   Valentine Style,   XXXOOO Barbie   With Love
Target   Target, black version

Hollywood Legends Collection

Barbie as Scarlett O'Hara in Gone With the Wind, Green Velvet

Scarlett O'Hara, black and white (New Orleans)

Scarlett O'Hara, red

Scarlett O'Hara, green and white picnic

Rhett Butler

Hollywood Legends Collection

My Fair Lady, Ascot

Professor Higgins

My Fair Lady, pink

My Fair Lady, Flowers

My Fair Lady, Embassy Ball

Barbie as Dorothy in
the Wizard of Oz
Barbie as Maria in the
Sound of Music
Barbie as Glinda in the
Wizard of Oz
Ken as the Scarecrow in
the Wizard of Oz
Ken as the Tin Man in
the Wizard of Oz

Miscellaneous

Andalucia

Sweet Daisy, Military Series
Making Friends, Military Series
Barbie Had a Little Lamb, Nursery Rhymes Collection
Oshogatsu, 1995, Oshogatsu Collection
Oshogatsu, 1996, Oshogatsu Collection
My Very Own Watch Barbie, Philippine Exclusive

Miscellaneous

Blue Rhapsody,
  Service Merchandise Series
Trailblazin', Supermarket/Drug
  Store Series
Rose, A Garden of Flowers Series
Barbie Style, Applause
Holiday, Applause
Birthday Wishes, white version,
  Birthday Wishes Collection
Birthday Surprise, Supermarket/Drug
  Store Series

Happy Birthday, 1984, Regular
  Edition
Cool Collecting
Illusion, Masquerade Galla Collection
  from direct mail services
Empress Sissy
Tangerine Twist, Fashion Savvy
  Collection
Friendship, 1990
Friendship, 1991
Friendship (Berlin Wall), 1992

Miscellaneous

Secret of the Three Teardrops - Grolier
Evening Flame, Home Shopping Club
Tale of Peter Rabbit, Keepsake Treasures Series
City Shopper, Macy's
Special Occasion, 1996, Mercantile Stores Co. Inc. Series
Special Occasion, 1999, Mercantile Stores Co. Inc.

Bedtime
Pretty Dreams
Tean Talk
Tahiti

Millennium Collection

Nostalgic Series/Vintage Reproductions

Poodle Parade
Fashion Luncheon
Silken Flame,
   brunette
Wedding Day,
   redhead

Commuter Set
Midge 35th Anniersary Gift Set
Far Out, Twist 'n Turn

35th Anniversary, blonde
35th Anniversary, brunette
Busy Gal

Solo In The
 Spotlight, blonde
Solo In The
 Spotlight, brunette
Francie Gad-About
Enchanted Evening,
 blonde

Porcelain Collection

Enchanted Evening

Solo In The Sportlight

Sophisticated Lady

30th Anniversary Ken

School

Back To School
Back to School
Becky, School Photographer

Graduation, 1998
Graduation, 1996
Graduation, 1997
Millennium Grad, black gown
Millennium Grad, blue gown
School Spirit
Schooltime Fun

Sports

Bowling Champ
DH Sport Barbie
Gymnast Barbie
Horse Riding Barbie

NASCAR Barbie,
  50th Anniversary
NBA Barbie, Seattle Sonics
Show 'n Ride, Toys R Us
WNBA
WSU University

Store Exclusives and Special Editions

Ice Cream
Party in Pink
Ladybug Fun

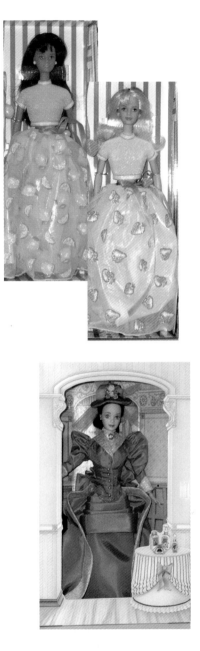

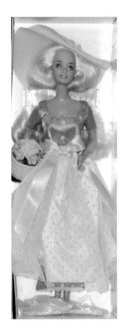

Lemon-Lime Sorbet
Strawberry Sorbet
PFE Albee #2
PFE Albee #1
Spring Blossom #1
Spring Blossom #1, black version

Spring Petals #2
brunette

Spring Petals #2
blonde

Spring Tea Petals #3,
brunette

Winter Rhapsody #2
Winter Splendor
Winter Velvet #1

Barbie at Bloomingdale's

Calvin Klein, Donna

Karan brunette, Savvy

Shopper by Nicole Miller

Circus Star
Statute of Liberty
Madison Avenue

FAO Schwarz — Store Exclusives and Special Editions

Winter Fantasy
Silver Screen
Night Sensation
Shopping Spree

Store Exclusives and Special Editions

GAP

Gap Gift Set, Barbie and Kelly

Gap Barbie
Gap Barbie, black version

General Mills

Hamleys

1997 Winter Dazzle,
black version

1997 Winter Dazzle

West End Barbie

Victorian Elegance

Holiday Memories

Yultide Romance

Sweet Valentine

Sentimental Valentine

Fair Valentine

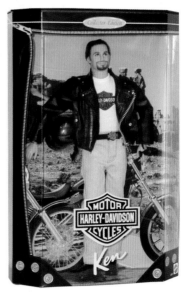

Barbie #2
Harley Davidson #3
Harley Davidson #4
Harley Davidson Ken

Hills

JC Penney

Party Lace

Polly Pocket

Foam 'n Color

JC Penney

Arizona Jeans, #1

Arizona Jeans #2

Enchanted Evening

Evening Sensation

Store Exclusives and Special Editions — K-Mart

March of Dimes Walk America
Pretty In Purple
Peach Pretty

Koolaid (Premiums)

Kool-Aid #1
Kool-Aid #2
Kool-Aid #3

Kraft (Premiums)

Kraft Treasures

Little Debbie Snacks (Premiums)

Little Debbie Figurine Set

Store Exclusives and Special Editions

Little Debbie (Premiums)

Little Debbie, #1
Little Debbie 40th Anniversary
Little Debbie Snacks, #2

Little Debbie, #3

NAF NAF

NAF NAF

Osco

Picnic Pretty

Radio Shack

Earring Magic
Software Pak

Russell Stover

Russell Stover
Russell Stover

Sears

100th
Anniversary
Celebration

Blossom
Beautiful

Blue Starlight
Dream Princess
Evening Enchantment
Royal Enchantment

Lavender Surprise
Lavender Surprise, black version
Enchanted Princess
Pink Reflections
Ribbons & Roses

Moonlight Magic
Southern Belle
Silver Sweetheart

Sidewalk Chalk
Blossom Beauty

Regal Reflections
Royal Invitation
Shopping Chic
Sterling Wishes

Store Exclusives and Special Editions — Spiegel

Theatre Elegance
Summer Sophisticate
Winner's Circle

Summit

Summit, white
Summit, Asian
Summit, black version

101 Dalmations
Charity Ball
Got Milk?
Cool 'n Sassy
Crystal Splendor
Spots 'n Dots
Spring Parade
Spring Parade, black version

Malt Shoppe
Pen Friend
Quinceanera Teresa
Radiant in Red,
  white version
Radiant in Red,
  black version
Sweet Romance

White version

Asian version

Black version

Hispanic version

Country Bride
Country Western Star
Dream Fantasy
Pretty Choices
Super Star
Sweet Magnolia
Toothfairy

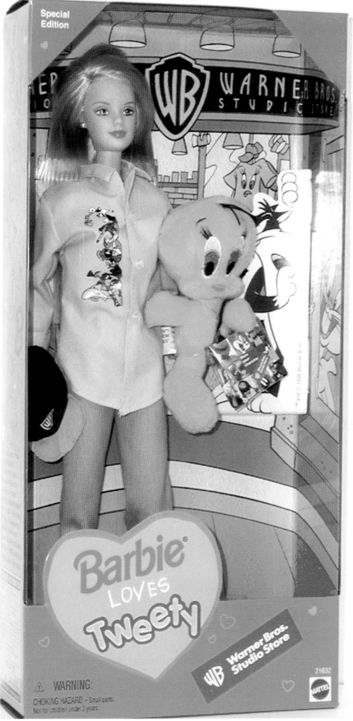

Barbie Loves
Tweetie

Special
Expressions,
1989

Special
Expressions,
1990

Special
Expressions,
1990

Special
Expressions,
1991

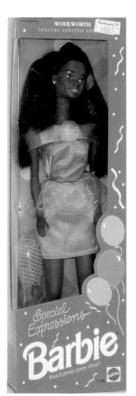

Special Expressions, 1992
Special Expressions, 1992
Sweet Lavender, 1992

Regular Edition – Rappin' Rockin'

Barbie
Christie
Teresa
Ken

Regular Edition – Barbie and the Rockers

Winter Princess Collection

Winter Princess, first in the series

Jewel Princess
Midnight Princess
Peppermint Princess
Evergreen Princess

Wizard of Oz Collection

Barbie as Glinda
Barbie as Dorothy
Ken as the Tin Man
Ken as the Cowardly Lion.

Ken as Scarecrow
Kelly as Lullaby Munchkin
Tommy™ as Mayor Munchkin
Tommy™ as Lollipop Munchkin

Wholesale Club

Party Sensation
Juewl Jubilee
Festiva
Season's Greetings

Winter's Eve
Silver Royale
Winter Fantasy, blonde
Winter Fantasy, brunette

VINTAGE BARBIE & FAMILY

STOCK NO.	YEAR OF ORIGIN	DOLL NAME/DESCRIPTION	NRFB HIGH	LOW	AVG	MINT HIGH	LOW	AVG
		Barbie						
850	1959	#1 PONYTAIL - Blonde	7800	5465	7115	4620	3450	3980
850	1959	#1 PONYTAIL - Brunette	8400	5850	7580	5250	4020	4594
850	1959	#2 PONYTAIL - Blonde	7480	5168	6510	4210	3090	3750
850	1959	#2 PONYTAIL - Brunette	7700	5015	6330	4200	3252	3785
850	1960	#3 PONYTAIL - Blonde**	1295	875	1100	780	640	735
850	1960	#3 PONYTAIL - Brunette**	1485	925	1138	940	660	785
850	1960	#4 PONYTAIL	895	575	665	395	250	312
850	1961	#5 PONYTAIL	615	400	560	335	185	285
850	1961	#5 PONYTAIL - Redhead	800	490	642	425	320	365
850	1962	#6 PONYTAIL	590	440	525	330	250	286
850	1964	SWIRL	850	475	622	400	200	300
850	1964	SWIRL - Platinum	1600	1000	1215	550	400	475
850	1961	BUBBLE CUT - Brownette	1200	850	1026	575	450	552
850	1961	BUBBLE CUT - White Ginger	1100	600	880	500	300	400
850	1961	BUBBLE CUT - other hair colors	580	320	435	275	150	200
850	1962	BUBBLE CUT - Side Part	1200	700	760	600	350	450
850	1965	BUBBLE CUT - Japanese Side-Part	4000	3500	3950	3200	2900	3000
870	1963	FASHION QUEEN (Wigs and wig stand included)	535	320	350	180	130	156
870	1963	FASHION QUEEN (No wigs included)	N/A	N/A	N/A	85	50	65
871	1964	WIG WARDROBE (Molded Barbie Head Only w/3 Wigs)	595	400	480	N/A	N/A	N/A
1060	1964	MISS BARBIE - SLEEP-EYE (Accessories included)	1600	995	1390	600	325	475
1060	1964	MISS BARBIE - SLEEP-EYE (No accessories included)	N/A	N/A	N/A	295	200	255
4038/9	1965/66	COLOR 'N CURL SET* (Molded Barbie Head Only)	795	485	590	N/A	N/A	N/A
1070	1965	BEND-LEG - AMERICAN GIRL	1875	1310	1580	795	550	595
1070	1966	BEND-LEG - AMERICAN GIRL	3000	2200	2500	2000	1200	1500
1070	1966	BEND-LEG - AMERICAN GIRL Color Magic Face	3600	2900	300	2500	1750	1900
1070	1966	BEND-LEG - AMERICAN GIRL - Side-Part	3700	2500	3050	2600	1995	2115
1070	1966	AMERICAN GIRL - Japanese Side-Part Straight Leg pink Skinned Body	3600	3000	3250	2900	2250	2675
1070	1966	BEND-LEG - AMERICAN GIRL - Side-Part (High Color - American Vinyl)	4100	3750	3990	3700	3225	3475
1070	1966	BEND-LEG - AMERICAN GIRL - Japanese Side-Part (High Color - Rare Pink-toned Vinyl)	5000	4350	4885	4200	3990	4185
1150	1966	COLOR MAGIC - Blonde (Plastic Box)	2000	1300	1700	550	385	420
1150	1966	COLOR MAGIC - Blonde (Cardboard Box)	3200	2500	2995	550	385	420
1150	1966	COLOR MAGIC - Midnight (Plastic Box)	3500	2700	3125	1900	1450	1700
1150	1966	COLOR MAGIC - Midnight (Cardboard Box)	4500	3650	3945	1900	1450	1700

VINTAGE BARBIE & FAMILY CONTINUED

STOCK NO.	YEAR OF ORIGIN	DOLL NAME/DESCRIPTION	NRFB HIGH	LOW	AVG	MINT HIGH	LOW	AVG
Barbie (CONTINUED)								
1160	1967	TWIST-N-TURN	685	475	526	300	175	240
1160	1967	TWIST-N-TURN - Redhead	1200	840	880	750	490	548
1190	1967	STANDARD	670	395	520	295	170	255
1190	1967	STANDARD - Redhead	1195	850	886	795	500	645
4043	1967	HAIR FAIR (Mint price includes body)	295	185	200	155	90	111
1115	1968	TALKING	500	300	385	200	125	138
1116	1970	LIVING	358	200	288	150	95	120
1067	1971	MALIBU (SUNSET)	90	60	75	50	35	45
3269	1972	MALIBU (Forget Me Not/Baggie)	160	150	155	50	35	45
1144	1971	GROWIN' PRETTY HAIR	430	295	352	250	150	178
1152	1971	LIVE ACTION ON STAGE (Includes stage)	350	198	270	200	160	190
1155	1971	LIVE ACTION (Stage not included)	195	138	170	125	75	100
1174	1971	HAIR HAPPENIN'S	1250	900	1140	545	415	485
1182	1972	WALK LIVELY	290	190	250	100	85	95
1195	1972	BUSY (Talking)	395	330	370	275	195	235
3311	1972	BUSY	300	235	265	140	118	130
3210	1972	WARD'S #1 REPLICA (Cardboard shipping carton)	795	595	700	595	440	505
—	1972	WARD'S #1 REPLICA (rare pink window box)	900	800	850	595	440	505
Ken								
750	1961	STRAIGHT LEG (flocked hair)	320	185	240	140	100	130
750	1961	STRAIGHT LEG (flocked hair - Brownette)	375	295	325	225	155	195
750	1962	STRAIGHT LEG (molded hair)	225	125	154	100	55	75
750	1963	STRAIGHT LEG (molded hair-¼" shorter doll)	250	150	185	125	75	95
1020	1965	BENDABLE LEG	495	350	412	185	125	170
1111	1969	TALKING	275	140	165	75	50	60
1124	1970	BENDABLE LEG (Talking Ken head mold)	140	100	120	75	50	65
1088	1971	MALIBU (SUNSET)	70	50	60	50	30	40
1159	1971	LIVE ACTION (stage not included)	135	80	95	60	40	50
1172	1971	LIVE ACTION ON STAGE (includes stage)	190	140	152	145	95	110
1184	1972	WALK LIVELY	195	125	138	75	50	60
1196	1972	BUSY (Talking)	240	160	175	90	65	78
3314	1972	BUSY	250	150	180	90	60	75
1111	1973	BAGGIE (same as Talking, but doesn't talk)	75	55	65	45	35	40
1159	1973	BAGGIE (Live Action)	70	50	60	60	40	50
4224	1973	MOD HAIR	135	95	100	55	40	45
1111	1974	BAGGIE (Talking Body/Live Action Head)	75	50	56	40	30	35
4234	1974	MOD HAIR (Ward's Exclusive)	185	138	150	90	70	80
7809	1974	SUN VALLEY - The Sports Set	140	90	105	70	40	48
7261	1975	GOLD MEDAL SKIER	110	75	96	60	35	45
7280	1975	FREE MOVING	85	45	60	40	25	34

*Cannot authenticate if not NRFB

STOCK NO.	YEAR OF ORIGIN	DOLL NAME/DESCRIPTION	NRFB			MINT		
			HIGH	LOW	AVG	HIGH	LOW	AVG

Ken (CONTINUED)

1088	1975	SUNSET MALIBU (white box)	90	75	84	50	30	40
9342	1976	NOW LOOK	90	60	75	50	32	44

Skipper

950	1964	STRAIGHT LEGS	295	175	205	110	65	85
5950	1964	STRAIGHT LEGS (Japan)	550	400	500	395	300	375
1030	1965	BENDABLE LEGS	395	250	330	115	70	88
1030	1967	BENDABLE LEGS (RE-ISSUE)	495	300	440	N/A	N/A	N/A
1105	1968	TWIST 'N TURN	400	195	200	195	135	160
1105	1969	TWIST 'N TURN (new 2 curl hairstyle)	395	185	230	195	150	165
1117	1970	LIVING (Dramatic)	140	98	110	85	55	68
1147	1970	TRADE-IN SPECIAL LIVING	150	100	125	N/A	N/A	N/A
950	1971	STRAIGHT LEGS (re-issue)	550	325	450	350	195	285
1069	1971	MALIBU SUNSET	75	50	65	40	30	35
1179	1972	POSE 'N PLAY (MIB includes gym)	295	250	265	110	90	98
1117	1973	POSE 'N PLAY (Baggie)	100	75	88	N/A	N/A	N/A
4223	1973	QUICK CURL	100	80	95	52	30	44
4223	1973	QUICK CURL (box w/side flap)	125	100	110	N/A	N/A	N/A
7259	1975	GROWING UP (2 box versions)	120	80	110	65	40	50
1069	1975	SUNSET MALIBU	60	50	55	40	30	35

Midge

860	1963	STRAIGHT LEGS	285	175	240	150	90	125
860	1963 only	STRAIGHT LEGS (w/teeth)	395	195	340	240	165	220
860	1963 only	STRAIGHT LEGS (freckleless w/teeth)	560	390	480	320	225	290
860	1963	STRAIGHT LEGS (freckleless)	570	385	475	325	225	286
860	1965	STRAIGHT LEGS (Hard Curl Butterscotch)	345	206	275	165	105	135
1080	1965	BENDABLE LEGS	695	500	596	420	285	356
1080	1965	BENDABLE LEGS (Long hair)	795	550	675	480	320	400
1080*	1965	BENDABLE LEGS (Flip hairstyle)	865	625	745	N/A	N/A	N/A
1009	1965	WIG WARDROBE (Head put on Straight Leg Body)	595	400	495	250	150	220
N/A	1965	MOLDED no wigs (Head put on Straight Leg Body)	N/A	N/A	N/A	135	90	110
N/A	1965	MOLDED High Color, no wigs (Head put on Straight Leg Body)	N/A	N/A	N/A	160	105	136
N/A	1965	MOLDED w/wigs and stand (Head put on Straight Leg Body)	N/A	N/A	N/A	385	270	345
N/A	1965	MOLDED High Color, w/wigs and stand (Head put on Straight Leg Body)	N/A	N/A	N/A	435	300	370

Allan

1000	1964	STRAIGHT LEGS	175	120	150	90	60	75

VINTAGE BARBIE & FAMILY CONTINUED

STOCK NO.	YEAR OF ORIGIN	DOLL NAME/DESCRIPTION	NRFB HIGH	LOW	AVG	MINT HIGH	LOW	AVG
Allan (CONTINUED)								
1010	1965	BENDABLE LEGS	680	430	525	295	195	255
Francie								
1130	1966	BENDABLE LEGS	525	300	375	175	120	160
1140	1966	STRAIGHT LEGS	550	320	415	200	125	180
—	1966	FRANCIE (Japanese Exclusive)	2500	1450	1795	1190	900	1050
1100	1967	BLACK TWIST 'N TURN	1750	1500	1695	1375	900	1295
1170	1967	TWIST 'N TURN	595	385	460	300	175	250
1122	1970	HAIR HAPPENIN'S	475	300	400	175	140	150
1129	1970	GROWIN' PRETTY HAIR	385	200	290	165	95	130
1068	1971	MALIBU (SUNSET)	70	60	65	50	40	45
1074	1971	GROWIN' PRETTY HAIR (extra hair pieces)	375	250	310	275	150	198
1170	1971	"NO BANGS" TWIST 'N TURN	1995	1400	1650	1080	800	895
3313	1972	BUSY	465	300	400	330	200	275
—	1972	FRANCIE (European Exclusive)	1650	1500	1575	1395	1200	1300
4222	1974	QUICK CURL	200	150	165	100	75	90
7699	1975	"BAGGIE"	150	100	135	100	75	94
1068	1975	SUNSET MALIBU (white box)	150	100	125	50	40	45
1067	1976	MALIBU (pink box)	70	50	62	50	40	45
Skooter								
1040	1965	STRAIGHT LEGS	165	125	140	100	65	85
1120	1966	BENDABLE LEGS	350	290	305	160	100	138
Ricky								
1090	1965	STRAIGHT LEGS	200	135	160	85	55	62
Fluff								
1143	1971	LIVING	350	175	250	175	100	132
Tiff								
1199	1972	POSE 'N PLAY	450	300	390	250	150	205
Ginger								
9222	1976	GROWING UP	250	130	160	120	65	92
Casey								
1180	1967	TWIST 'N TURN	400	275	300	200	150	174
9000	1975	BAGGIE	185	125	140	110	75	92
Twiggy								
1185	1967	TWIST 'N TURN	475	320	395	250	165	200

VINTAGE BARBIE & FAMILY CONTINUED

STOCK NO.	YEAR OF ORIGIN	DOLL NAME/DESCRIPTION	NRFB HIGH	LOW	AVG	MINT HIGH	LOW	AVG
P.J.								
1113	1969	TALKING	375	225	295	190	110	146
1118	1970	TWIST 'N TURN	325	195	265	160	100	125
1153	1971	LIVE ACTION ON STAGE (includes stage)	295	185	255	200	150	180
1156	1971	LIVE ACTION (no stage included)	N/A	N/A	N/A	115	90	110
1087	1972	MALIBU (SUNSET)	85	60	78	60	40	55
1113	1973	BAGGIE (same as Talking, but doesn't talk)	125	100	108	50	40	45
1156	1973	BAGGIE (same as Live Action, but no stand)	150	120	135	115	90	110
7263	1975	GOLD MEDAL GYMNAST	130	90	100	75	50	62
7281	1975	FREE MOVING	120	85	98	60	45	54
1087	1975	SUNSET MALIBU (white box)	125	100	115	60	40	55
9218	1976	DELUXE QUICK CURL	165	100	135	60	40	50
2323	1978	FASHION PHOTO	100	75	85	50	35	40
Stacey								
1125	1968	TALKING	500	300	400	285	150	210
1165	1968	TWIST 'N TURN	500	325	410	275	160	200
1165	1969	TWIST 'N TURN (short flip)	550	395	485	275	170	238
1125	1970	TALKING (blue/silver suit)	565	400	495	295	168	245
1165	1970	TWIST 'N TURN (aqua/rose suit)	495	350	425	295	155	250
Christie								
1126	1968	TALKING	375	235	325	240	150	195
1119	1970	TWIST 'N TURN	475	310	375	285	150	210
1175	1971	LIVE ACTION	300	220	285	180	135	150
7745	1973	MALIBU (SUNSET)	75	65	70	60	50	58
7745	1975	SUNSET MALIBU (white box)	115	80	95	60	50	58
Brad								
1114	1970	TALKING	250	150	185	125	85	98
1142	1970	BENDABLE LEGS	275	170	220	120	80	95
Curtis								
7282	1975	FREE MOVING	225	150	165	80	52	65
Tutti								
3550	1966	BENDABLE/POSEABLE (pink/white gingham suit & hat, white shoes)	195	145	180	135	90	98
3580	1967	BENDABLE/POSEABLE (2 dress variations)	185	125	160	100	75	88
Todd								
3590	1967	BENDABLE/POSEABLE (red/white/blue checkered shirt & cap, blue shirt & socks, red shoes)	275	180	195	140	90	102

116

VINTAGE BARBIE & FAMILY CONTINUED

STOCK NO.	YEAR OF ORIGIN	DOLL NAME/DESCRIPTION	NRFB HIGH	LOW	AVG	MINT HIGH	LOW	AVG
Chris								
3570	1967	BENDABLE/POSEABLE (multi-print dress, 2 green hair ribbons, barrette, orange shoes)	320	185	245	135	90	108
Jamie								
1132	1970	WALKING	475	385	415	345	185	210
Steffie								
1183	1972	WALK LIVELY	400	265	340	215	130	178
1186	1972	TALKING BUSY	460	295	370	270	160	212
3312	1972	BUSY	425	290	370	180	100	165
7888	1974	BABS (Baggie Busy Steffie)	190	145	175	N/A	N/A	N/A
Cara								
7283	1975	FREE MOVING	155	95	105	75	50	58
7291	1975	QUICK CURL	120	90	100	65	45	55
9220	1976	DELUXE QUICK CURL	100	75	88	60	45	50
9528	1976	BALLERINA	100	75	86	55	38	42
Kelley								
4221	1973	QUICK CURL	200	150	170	95	65	80
7808	1974	YELLOWSTONE	375	275	320	185	150	176
Julia								
1127	1969	TWIST 'N TURN	375	245	315	185	125	150
1128	1969	TALKING	325	215	270	175	120	145
1128	1971	TALKING (new hairstyle)	220	220	250	160	110	135
Truly Scrumptious								
1107	1969	TALKING	585	475	525	320	250	275
1108	1969	STANDARD	585	450	500	345	225	250
Miss America								
3194-9991	1972	KELLOGG'S SPECIAL	315	165	220	135	90	120
3200	1972	WALK LIVELY	270	180	216	140	85	110
8867	1973	QUICK CURL	175	100	150	90	65	74
Buffy & Mrs. Beasley								
3577	1968	BUFFY & MRS. BEASLEY	250	195	220	155	120	132
Pretty Pairs								
1133	1970	LORI 'N RORI	360	200	275	180	120	155
1134	1970	NAN 'N FRAN	325	185	235	150	110	135
1135	1970	ANGIE 'N TANGIE	320	175	226	150	108	134

DRESSED BOXED VINTAGE DOLLS

STOCK NO.	YEAR OF ORIGIN	OUTFIT	MINT/COMPLETE		
			HIGH	LOW	AVG
		BARBIE			
934	1963	AFTER FIVE (1964)	725	525	625
984	1963	AMERICAN AIRLINES STEWARDESS	825	650	740
931	1963	GARDEN PARTY	675	525	620
940	1963	MOOD FOR MUSIC	725	600	663
965	1963	NIGHTY NEGLIGEE (1964)	650	525	590
987	1963	ORANGE BLOSSOM	725	550	638
991	1963	REGISTERED NURSE	825	700	765
982	1963	SOLO IN THE SPOTLIGHT	950	750	850
941	1963	TENNIS ANYONE?	675	550	615
874	1964	ARABIAN NIGHTS	1500	1050	1275
823	1964	BARBIE IN HOLLAND	900	750	825
820	1964	BARBIE IN MEXICO	900	750	825
822	1964	BARBIE IN SWITZERLAND	900	750	825
1609	1964	BLACK MAGIC ENSEMBLE	950	775	865
947	1964	BRIDE'S DREAM	1050	775	915
954	1964	CAREER GIRL	950	775	863
872	1964	CINDERELLA	950	775	863
1603	1964	COUNTRY FAIR	675	525	600
946	1964	DINNER AT EIGHT	675	525	600
961	1964	EVENING SPLENDOUR	700	575	640
1606	1964	GARDEN TEA PARTY	675	525	600
873	1964	GUINIVERE	725	575	650
942	1964	ICE BREAKER	750	650	700
957	1964	KNITTING PRETTY (pink version)	1650	875	1270
957	1964	KNITTING PRETTY (royal version)	700	575	638
944	1964	MASQUERADE	700	575	638
951	1964	SENIOR PROM	1350	950	1150
955	1964	SWINGIN' EASY	725	550	642
959	1964	THEATRE DATE	725	600	665

DRESSED BOXED VINTAGE DOLLS CONTINUED

STOCK NO.	YEAR OF ORIGIN	OUTFIT	MINT/COMPLETE		
			HIGH	LOW	AVG
	KEN				
770	1963	CAMPUS HERO	450	300	375
782	1963	CASUALS	450	300	375
790	1963	TIME FOR TENNIS	450	300	375
774	1964	ARABIAN NIGHTS	500	300	400
793	1964	DR. KEN	550	325	440
1408	1964	FRATERNITY MEETING	500	300	400
777	1964	KEN IN HOLLAND	525	325	425
778	1964	KEN IN MEXICO	525	325	425
776	1964	KEN IN SWITZERLAND	525	325	425
773	1964	KING ARTHUR	600	350	475
772	1964	PRINCE, THE	625	350	488
796	1964	SAILOR	500	300	400
799	1964	TOUCHDOWN	450	300	375
	SKIPPER				
1904	1964	FLOWER GIRL	450	250	350
1903	1964	MASQUERADE	425	250	338
1901	1964	RED SENSATION	395	225	305
1921	1964	SCHOOL DAYS	400	250	325
1902	1964	SILK 'N FANCY	385	250	315
1908	1964	SKATING FUN	400	275	338

VINTAGE GIFT SETS

STOCK NO.	YEAR OF ORIGIN	GIFT SET/DESCRIPTION	MINT/COMPLETE		
			HIGH	LOW	AVG
856	1960	PARTY SET #3 or #4 Ponytail	2600	1900	2350
857	1960	MIX 'N MATCH SET	2250	1500	1810
858	1960	TROUSSEAU SET #4 Ponytail	3500	2500	2900
857	1962	Mix 'N Match Set Slightly different	2200	1500	1850
861	1962	BARBIE MIX 'N MATCH SET Ponytail or Bubble Cut Wards	1850	1350	1605
892	1962	BARBIE & KEN TENNIS SET *Wards, Spiegel*	1500	1000	1300
—	1962	BARBIE & KEN MIX 'N MATCH SET *Wards, Spiegel*	1700	1000	1360
863	1963	FASHION QUEEN BARBIE & HER FRIENDS			
		Barbie, Ken, Midge	2500	1800	2256
864	1964	FASHION QUEEN BARBIE & KEN TROUSSEAU	3000	2000	2615
1011	1964	BARBIE SPARKLING PINK GIFT SET Bubble Cut	3000	1700	2600
1012	1964	MIDGE ENSEMBLE GIFT SET	3200	3000	3150
1013	1964	BARBIE 'ROUND THE CLOCK Bubble Cut	5500	4000	4995
1014	1964	BARBIE, KEN & MIDGE ON PARADE SET	2600	1850	2355
1017	1964	BARBIE WEDDING PARTY GIFT SET Barbie,			
		Ken, Midge, Skipper	3250	2600	3000
1018	1964	BARBIE & KEN LITTLE THEATRE SET	6500	4500	5500
1022	1964	BARBIE, KEN, MIDGE PEP RALLY SET	1750	1000	1400
3807	1964	MIDGE MIX 'N MATCH SET *Sears*	3250	2500	2810
1021	1965	SKIPPER HOLIDAY PARTY SET Bend Leg doll	900	750	800
1021	1965	SKIPPER PARTY TIME SET Straight Leg	650	450	550
1032	1965	SKIPPER ON WHEELS SET *Sears*	650	450	550
1034	1965	BARBIE HOSTESS SET	5000	4500	4750
4035	1965	COLOR 'N CURL SET Molded Barbie & Midge Heads	1350	950	1150
4038/9	1965/66	COLOR 'N CURL SET* Molded Barbie Head Only	795	500	600
1042	1966	FRANCIE & HER SWINGIN' SEPARATES SET *Sears*	1800	1000	1350
1043	1966	COLOR MAGIC BARBIE GIFT SET Sears	4500	3500	4000
1044	1966	FRANCIE'S SPORTIN' SET Bend Leg doll *JCPenney*	5000	4000	4500
1021	1966	SKIPPER PARTY TIME SET re-issue	650	450	550
3552	1966	TUTTI "WALKIN' MY DOLLY" PLAYSET	495	300	400
		Blonde Tutti, includes baby & buggy			
3553	1966	TUTTI "NIGHT-NIGHT SLEEP TIGHT" PLAYSET	400	250	335
		Titian Tutti, includes bed			
3554	1966	TUTTI "ME AND MY DOG" PLAYSET Dark brown			
		Tutti, includes dog	385	275	350
3555	1966	TUTTI "MELODY IN PINK" PLAYSET	395	285	370
		Pale Blonde Tutti, includes piano/stool			
3556	1966	TUTTI & TODD "SUNDAE TREAT" PLAYSET	450	350	398
		Titian Tutti, includes Titian Todd, table, chairs, accessories			
4040	1966	COLOR MAGIC FASHION DESIGNER SET	850	600	725
1036	1967	SKOOTER CUT 'N BUTTON *Sears*	850	650	750

VINTAGE GIFT SETS CONTINUED

STOCK NO.	YEAR OF ORIGIN	GIFT SET/DESCRIPTION	MINT/COMPLETE		
			HIGH	LOW	AVG
3301	1967	CHRIS FUN-TIMERS SET *Sears*	1000	850	950
3303	1967	BARBIE BEAUTIFUL BLUES SET TNT doll *Sears*	3600	3000	3310
3304	1967	CASEY GOES CASUAL SET *Sears*	2000	1500	1715
3559	1967	TUTTI "COOKIN' GOODIES" PLAYSET	375	275	328
		Upswept black hair, stove, pot			
3560	1967	TUTTI "SWING-A-LING" PLAYSET Blonde, includes swing	350	275	335
1544	1968	BARBIE TRAVEL IN STYLE SET Standard *Sears*	2900	2000	2420
1545	1968	STACEY STRIPES ARE HAPPENING SET TNT *Sears*	3000	2500	2900
1546	1968	SKIPPER PERFECTLY PRETTY SET TNT *Sears*	1000	950	975
1551	1968	BARBIE DINNER DAZZLE SET Talking *Sears*	1700	1200	1550
1552	1968	BARBIE SILVER 'N SATIN SET Talking JCPenney	1600	1200	1450
1590	1969	BRIGHT 'N BREEZY SET *Sears*	1000	850	950
1591	1969	STACEY NITE LIGHTNING SET TNT *Sears*	2250	1900	2110
1593	1969	BARBIE GOLDEN GROOVE SET Talking *Sears*	1700	1100	1505
1595	1969	BARBIE & KEN FABULOUS FORMAL SET Talking *Sears*	1750	1200	1350
1596	1969	BARBIE PINK PREMIER SET Talking JCPenney	1700	1200	1600
1866	1969	BARBIE TWINKLE TOWN SET Standard *Sears*	1750	1200	1500
1594	1969	SIMPLY WOW Talking Julia Gift Set *Sears*	1600	1100	1350
1584	1970	WALKING JAMIE FURRY FRIENDS SET *Sears*	1200	850	1050
1585	1970	BARBIE ACTION ACCENTS SET Living *Sears*	1200	900	1100
1586	1970	SKIPPER VERY BEST VELVET SET Living *Sears*	750	500	555
1588	1970	P.J. SWINGIN' IN SILVER SET TNT *Sears*	1500	1000	1300
1589	1970	KEN RED, WHITE & WILD SET Bend Leg *Sears*	650	450	575
1587	1970	TALKING BARBIE MAD ABOUT PLAID GIFT SET	1350	1000	1250
		Plaid Coat & Dress *Sears*			
1193	1971	BARBIE PERFECTLY PLAID Talking *Sears*	1500	1100	1258
1194	1971	FRANCIE RISE 'N SHINE Growin' Pretty *Sears*	1250	950	1150
1248	1971	KEN SURF'S UP SET Malibu *Sears*	550	385	450
1249	1971	FLUFF SUNSHINE SPECIAL SET Living *Sears*	1000	850	975
1508	1971	P.J. FASHION 'N MOTION SET Live Action *Sears*	1000	750	850
1179	1972	SKIPPER & HER SWING-A-ROUNDER GYM Pose 'N Play	395	295	360
1247	1972	WALKING JAMIE STROLLIN' IN STYLE *Sears*	1200	1000	1100

BARBIE 800 SERIES FASHIONS

STOCK NO.	FASHION	NRFB			MINT		
		HIGH	LOW	AVG	HIGH	LOW	AVG
874	**ARABIAN KNIGHTS** - Pink blouse, skirt & sari, gold slippers, gold/aqua bead necklace, 3 bracelets, gold earrings, lamp, program.	495	325	410	250	175	216
823	**BARBIE IN HOLLAND** - Blue blouse, multi-striped skirt, apron, hat, long socks, plastic "wooden shoes," pamphlet.	375	220	265	140	85	118
821	**BARBIE IN JAPAN** - Red kimono, obi, 3 hair ornaments, red thongs, socks, fan, saismen, travel pamphlet.	500	375	435	285	185	200
820	**BARBIE IN MEXICO** - White dress, red/green skirt, black mantilla, crystal necklace, crystal/pearl earrings, red OT shoes, pamphlet.	285	200	252	120	80	100
822	**BARBIE IN SWITZERLAND** - Pink/white dress w/attached apron, white bonnet, white OT shoes, flower bouquet, pamphlet.	265	175	225	145	95	115
889	**CANDY STRIPER VOLUNTEER** - Red & white striped pinafore, white blouse, white hat, tennies, washcloth, hot water bottle, Kleenex box, soap, knife, fork, spoon, blue plate w/watermelon, glass of orange juice w/straw.	375	300	360	250	175	200
876	**CHEERLEADER** - White sweater w/letter "M," red skirt, socks, red tennies, red/white pompons, megaphone.	250	150	175	100	65	84
872	**CINDERELLA** - "Rich" gown, long white gloves, headpiece, clear OT shoes w/silver glitter, "poor" dress, broom, program.	550	400	458	275	175	222
875	**DRUM MAJORETTE** - Red jacket, white skirt, nylons, red hat, short white gloves, white boots, baton.	265	175	200	98	70	84
873	**GUINIVERE** - Royal blue gown w/chain belt, hat w/snood, armlets, cloth shoes, program.	295	200	265	175	150	160
819	**IT'S COLD OUTSIDE** - Brown coat w/tan fur collar.	185	100	115	55	30	42
	VARIATION: Red coat w/black fur collar.	300	200	255	100	50	78
880	**LITTLE RED RIDING HOOD** - Blue dress, black corset, long socks, black shoes, straw basket, cloth napkin, rolls, wolf, cap, bonnet, program.	625	500	580	295	185	252

BARBIE 900 SERIES FASHIONS CONTINUED

STOCK NO.	FASHION	NRFB HIGH	NRFB LOW	NRFB AVG	MINT HIGH	MINT LOW	MINT AVG
934	**AFTER FIVE** - Black dress, white hat, black OT shoes.	200	120	150	70	40	58
984	**AMERICAN AIRLINES STEWARDESS** - Royal blue jacket & skirt, white bodysuit, hat w/medal, flight bag, black OT shoes, black shoulder purse.	195	150	180	90	60	80
917	**APPLE PRINT SHEATH** - Black dress w/apple print, black OT shoes.	275	150	190	80	60	72
989	**BALLERINA** - Silver tutu, black leotard & tights, paper tiara, shoe bag, ballet shoes, poster.	195	135	150	75	55	65
953	**BARBIE BABYSITS** (1st Version) - Apron, baby, 2 diapers, sacque, bassinet, blanket, pillow, baby bottle, soda bottle, pretzel box, 3 books w/strap, glasses, clock, white phone, phone numbers.	295	195	250	130	85	100
	(2nd Version)	475	400	430	265	185	235
923	**BARBIE DOLL ACCESSORIES** - Coral swimsuit, straw bag w/flowers, pearl necklace/bracelet, glasses, hoop earrings, short white gloves, OT shoes in black, white & light pink.	475	425	450	N/A	N/A	N/A
962	**BARBIE-Q** - Dusty rose cotton sundress w/white crochet-style trim, white apron w/3 pockets, white chef's hat, rolling pin, red/white checked potholder, large spoon, knife & spatula utensils, white OT shoes.	180	150	168	65	50	58
947	**BRIDE'S DREAM** - Gown, pearl veil, long white gloves, white OT shoes, blue garter, pearl necklace, bouquet.	350	200	300	175	100	145
981	**BUSY GAL** - Red jacket & skirt, red/white striped bodysuit, straw hat & belt, glasses, navy OT shoes, portfolio, 2 pages of sketches.	450	395	438	220	150	190
956	**BUSY MORNING** - Reddish orange/white dress, straw hat & fruit basket, white OT shoes, white phone.	295	200	250	160	90	112
954	**CAREER GIRL** - Black/white tweed jacket, skirt & hat, red bodysuit, long black gloves, black OT shoes.	375	300	350	155	100	135
916	**COMMUTER SET** - 2 piece navy suit, white bodysuit, blue & white bodysuit, red hat, hat box, crystal necklace & bracelet, short white gloves, navy OT shoes.	1400	1000	1195	600	495	575
912	**COTTON CASUAL** - Navy & white striped dress, white OT shoes.	150	95	130	45	28	36
918	**CRUISE STRIPES** - Dress w/navy skirt & red & white striped bodice, white belt, black OT shoes.	175	100	150	75	50	62
946	**DINNER AT EIGHT** - Persimmon jumpsuit, gold net hostess coat, gold/cork wedgies.	275	195	240	95	65	78

BARBIE 900 SERIES FASHIONS CONTINUED

STOCK NO.	FASHION	NRFB HIGH	NRFB LOW	NRFB AVG	MINT HIGH	MINT LOW	MINT AVG
971	**EASTER PARADE** - Dress, black coat, black hat, black purse, black OT shoes, short white gloves, pearl necklace & earrings.	4800	4000	4450	1750	1450	1600
983	**ENCHANTED EVENING** - Pink gown w/sequins at waist, fur stole, long white gloves, clear OT shoes w/gold glitter, pearl choker & drop earrings.	380	300	350	195	150	175
	ALTERNATE VERSION w/rose at waist.	400	350	380	250	200	225
961	**EVENING SPLENDOUR** - Gold & white dress & coat, fur hat, aqua purse, brown OT shoes, hanky, pearl necklace & earrings.	325	275	300	195	135	158
943	**FANCY FREE** - Red & navy dress w/white rick-rack trim.	125	85	98	30	20	25
921	**FLORAL PETTICOAT** - Slip, bra, panties, pink comb, brush & mirror.	150	85	95	35	20	25
979	**FRIDAY NIGHT DATE** - Blue jumper, white under-dress, black OT shoes, tray, 2 glasses, 2 straws.	325	220	285	110	75	90
931	**GARDEN PARTY** - Pink/white floral & dot dress, short white gloves, white OT shoes.	225	150	175	65	45	55
964	**GAY PARISIENNE** - Navy dress, white fur stole, navy hat, long white gloves, navy OT shoes, pearl necklace & earrings, gold purse.	6000	4200	5000	1200	975	1098
992	**GOLDEN ELEGANCE** - Red/gold sheath & coat, fur hat, red purse, brown OT shoes, hanky, pearl necklace & earrings.	395	310	350	200	150	176
911	**GOLDEN GIRL** - Gold & white sheath, short white gloves, aqua purse, brown OT shoes, pearl necklace, pearl bracelet.	200	150	180	95	70	82
945	**GRADUATION** - Black robe, mortar board, white collar, diploma tied w/ribbon.	75	50	65	38	25	32
942	**ICE BREAKER** - Red bodysuit, red skirt, white fur jacket, nylons, skates w/blades.	185	130	150	60	50	54
957	**KNITTING PRETTY** - Royal blue or pink shell & skirt, royal or pink OT shoes, yarn bowl w/needles, scissors, book.						
	PINK	450	350	410	290	200	250
	ROYAL	350	275	290	125	90	100
978	**LET'S DANCE** - Blue dress, white purse, black OT shoes, pearl on chain necklace.	225	165	180	115	75	92
944	**MASQUERADE** - Yellow/black costume, felt hat, black tights, mask, black OT shoes w/yellow pompons, invitation.	250	165	195	90	70	82

STOCK NO.	FASHION	NRFB			MINT		
		HIGH	LOW	AVG	HIGH	LOW	AVG
940	**MOOD FOR MUSIC** - Light blue sweater w/white collar, white halter top, blue pants, gold/cork wedgies, pearl choker.	260	150	210	115	85	98
933	**MOVIE DATE** - Blue/white striped dress w/organdy overskirt.	140	95	125	35	25	30
965	**NIGHTY NEGLIGEE** - Pink nightgown, robe, pink OT shoes w/pompons, stuffed dog.	165	100	130	65	45	50
985	**OPEN ROAD** - Beige coat, beige sweater, pants, straw hat w/red scarf, red glasses, red/cork wedgies, road map.	385	295	350	240	170	200
987	**ORANGE BLOSSOM** - Yellow dress, lace overskirt, yellow hat, short or long white gloves, white OT shoes, bouquet.	250	175	200	65	50	56
958	**PARTY DATE** - White dress w/gold glitter, gold belt & purse, clear OT shoes w/gold glitter.	305	200	285	180	110	152
915	**PEACHY FLEECY COAT** - Beige coat, brown felt hat, brown OT shoes, white plastic gloves, mustard purse.	175	100	150	95	68	82
967	**PICNIC SET** - Red/white check bodysuit, jeans, straw hat & basket, white/cork wedgies, fishing pole, fish.	365	300	345	165	105	152
966	**PLANTATION BELLE** - Pink dress, white slip, pink hat, short white gloves, pink OT shoes, pink pearl necklace, bracelet, earrings, straw purse.	600	525	560	345	250	298
949	**RAINCOAT** - Yellow coat, hat & umbrella, white boots.	125	85	92	45	30	40
939	**RED FLARE** - Red velvet coat, hat, purse, long white gloves, red OT shoes.	185	150	165	65	48	58
991	**REGISTERED NURSE** - White uniform, navy cape, hat, glasses, white OT shoes, diploma, water bottle, medicine bottle, spoon.	275	250	260	100	75	90
963	**RESORT SET** - Red jacket, black & white striped shirt, white shorts, white hat, white/cork wedgies, charm bracelet.	200	150	175	85	60	75
968	**ROMAN HOLIDAY** - Dress w/white belt, coat, white purse, red hat, short white gloves, black OT shoes, pearl on chain necklace, hanky, glasses w/case, compact w/puff, comb.	5000	4000	4500	1995	1450	1750
951	**SENIOR PROM** - Blue & green gown, green OT shoes w/pearls.	295	185	225	110	85	92
986	**SHEATH SENSATION** - Red dress, white straw hat, short white gloves, white OT shoes.	175	125	150	75	50	62
977	**SILKEN FLAME** - Dress, gold belt, gold purse, black OT shoes.	250	175	215	85	60	78

BARBIE 900 SERIES FASHIONS CONTINUED

STOCK NO.	FASHION	NRFB HIGH	NRFB LOW	NRFB AVG	MINT HIGH	MINT LOW	MINT AVG
988	**SINGING IN THE SHOWER** - Yellow robe & slippers, blue towel & wash cloth, shower cap, powder & puff, bath brush, soap.	150	100	125	48	30	40
948	**SKI QUEEN** - Blue parka, turquoise pants, red mittens, black boots, brown skis, poles, goggles.	250	185	220	70	55	65
982	**SOLO IN THE SPOTLIGHT** - Black gown, pink scarf, long black gloves, black OT shoes, crystal necklace, microphone.	375	295	340	200	145	175
993	**SOPHISTICATED LADY** - Pink gown w/silver trim, rose velvet coat, long white gloves, light pink OT shoes, pink pearl necklace, tiara.	420	375	390	200	150	180
937	**SORORITY MEETING** - Brown dress, brown sweater, brown hat, brown OT shoes, pearl necklace & earrings.	300	220	275	90	70	78
949	**STORMY WEATHER** - Yellow coat, hat, umbrella, white boots.	125	85	92	45	30	40
969	**SUBURBAN SHOPPER** - Blue/white dress, straw hat & fruit basket, pearl on chain necklace, white OT shoes, pink phone.	350	200	275	150	90	106
976	**SWEATER GIRL** - Orange cardigan, orange shell, grey skirt, black OT shoes, knitting bowl w/yarn & needles, scissors, book.	200	150	175	85	65	75
973	**SWEET DREAMS** - Yellow or pink 2-piece shortie PJ's, hair ribbon, blue OT shoes w/pompons, apple, clock, diary.						
	PINK	475	350	420	285	200	250
	YELLOW	195	140	150	68	45	52
955	**SWINGIN' EASY** - Green dress, white purse, black OT shoes, pearl on chain necklace.	245	175	225	90	65	80
941	**TENNIS ANYONE?** - Tennis dress, cardigan, socks, tennis shoes, racket, 2 balls, rulebook, sunglasses.	150	90	120	50	35	42
959	**THEATRE DATE** - Green jacket, skirt & hat, white shell, green OT shoes.	250	175	225	100	70	86
919	**UNDERGARMENTS** - Blue bra, panties, slip, girdle.	100	70	85	40	20	30
972	**WEDDING DAY SET** - Gown, pearl veil, short white gloves, blue garter, white OT shoes, pearl necklace, bouquet.	450	350	400	175	125	150
975	**WINTER HOLIDAY** - White coat w/belt, striped T-shirt, black pants, red plastic gloves, zipper bag, white/cork wedgies.	295	240	270	100	80	90

BARBIE 1600 SERIES FASHIONS (1964-67)

STOCK NO.	FASHION	NRFB			MINT		
		HIGH	LOW	AVG	HIGH	LOW	AVG
1631	**ABOARD SHIP** - Nautical dress, vest, red belt, red CT shoes, camera, 3 brochures, poster.	550	395	475	185	125	162
1605	**BARBIE IN HAWAII** - Grass skirt, red/white 2-piece swimsuit, lei, ankle lei, pineapple, travel pamphlet.	180	140	168	100	75	86
1634	**BARBIE LEARNS TO COOK** - Dress, belt, blue CT shoes, potholder, 3 pots w/lids, double boiler, tea kettle, toaster, 2 pieces of toast, cookbook.	575	460	500	265	155	190
1651	**BEAU TIME** - Red/navy checked dress w/big red bow.	425	295	375	150	100	140
1698	**BEAUTIFUL BRIDE** - Gown, underskirt w/dotted tulle, dotted tulle w/bow veil, white CT shoes, short white gloves, blue garter, bouquet.	2100	1750	1900	1385	900	1150
1667	**BENEFIT PERFORMANCE** - Red velvet tunic w/2 rhinestones, white underskirt w/12 bows, long white gloves, red OT shoes.	1400	1200	1300	750	500	550
1609	**BLACK MAGIC ENSEMBLE** - Black dress, black tulle cape, black OT shoes, short black gloves, gold purse.	420	325	374	150	100	135
1628	**BRUNCH TIME** - Butterfly print dress, orange CT shoes, 3 casserole dishes w/lids, handle, coffee pot.	395	300	325	150	108	128
1616	**CAMPUS SWEETHEART** - Gown, long white gloves, red OT shoes, pink pearl necklace, rose bouquet, trophy.	1750	1395	1550	695	500	600
1687	**CARIBBEAN CRUISE** - Wide-leg yellow halter jumpsuit w/ruffles, yellow flats.	295	175	200	110	75	86
1672	**CLUB MEETING** - Turquoise sheath w/print bodice, jacket w/flowers, turquoise CT shoes.	450	300	375	175	140	150
1670	**COFFEE'S ON** - Butterfly print dress, casserole dish w/lid, coffee pot w/lid.	195	165	185	110	75	92
1627	**COUNTRY CLUB DANCE** - White/gold metallic dress, long white gloves, white CT shoes, pearl necklace, gold purse.	490	395	455	320	215	260
1603	**COUNTRY FAIR** - Yellow bodysuit, orange/multi skirt, orange purse.	175	140	160	75	50	55
1604	**CRISP 'N COOL** - White blouse w/3 red buttons & attached scarf, red skirt, white OT shoes, short white gloves, red/white purse.	195	160	175	80	55	68
1626	**DANCING DOLL** - Pink/white checked dress, pink belt, white CT shoes, record player, 2 records.	525	350	450	360	225	250
1666	**DEBUTANTE BALL** - Blue/aqua gown, fur stole w/aqua sash, long white gloves, clear OT shoes w/gold glitter, gold purse, pearl on chain necklace.	1300	1000	1185	700	515	610

BARBIE 1600 SERIES FASHIONS (1964-67) CONTINUED

STOCK NO.	FASHION	NRFB HIGH	NRFB LOW	NRFB AVG	MINT HIGH	MINT LOW	MINT AVG
1633	**DISC DATE** - White bodysuit, fuchsia skirt, fuchsia CT shoes, record player, 2 records.	350	225	290	140	110	125
1613	**DOG 'N DUDS** - Grey poodle, 2 leashes, red velvet coat w/gold, pink tulle mask, hat, white collar, pink/black coat, earmuffs, dog food, bowl of food, bone.	350	250	298	150	100	130
1669	**DREAMLAND** - Peach nightgown, white OT shoes w/pink pompons, white comb & brush.	275	150	198	120	75	90
1695	evening enchantment - Red dress w/chiffon overdress w/white feather trim, red cape w/feather collar, red CT shoes.						
1695	**EVENING ENCHANTMENT** - Red dress w/chiffon overdress w/white feather trim, red cape w/feather collar, red CT shoes.	595	475	525	375	250	298
1660	**EVENING GALA** - Gold lamé long dress, turquoise long skirt, turquoise pants, clear OT shoes w/gold glitter.	475	350	400	195	115	162
1676	**FABULOUS FASHION** - Pink/red gown w/white flocked flowers & glitter, red fur trimmed coat, clear OT shoes w/silver glitter.	595	475	525	365	300	325
1635	**FASHION EDITOR** - Turquoise sheath w/printed bodice, jacket w/flowers, aqua CT shoes, camera.	950	600	750	300	200	275
1656	**FASHION LUNCHEON** - Pink sheath, pink jacket, pink hat w/flowers, long white gloves, light pink CT shoes.	1400	1000	1250	795	595	680
1691	**FASHION SHINER** - Pink/blue/white striped halter dress, red vinyl raincoat & purse, short white gloves, red OT shoes.	300	200	255	120	90	100
1696	**FLOATING GARDENS** - Multi-brights print dress, red hooded cape w/rhinestone "button," red CT shoes, pink/red earrings, 1 fuchsia bracelet, 1 red bracelet.	550	425	500	325	185	275
1697	**FORMAL OCCASION** - White long dress w/gold lamé, fuchsia hooded gold lamé cape, white CT shoes.	550	450	510	350	260	295
1638	**FRATERNITY DANCE** - Gown w/lace bodice & jewel, long white gloves, fuchsia OT shoes, pearl on chain necklace.	650	550	610	300	200	256
1624	**FUN AT THE FAIR** - Bodysuit, skirt, scarf, red tennies cotton candy.	345	250	295	130	85	96
1619	**FUN 'N GAMES** - Multi-striped dress, 2 wickets, 2 stakes, mallet, ball.	375	250	300	120	90	102
1606	**GARDEN TEA PARTY** - Red dress w/floral print & white eyelet panel, short white gloves, white OT shoes.	250	185	225	70	60	66

STOCK NO.	FASHION	NRFB			MINT		
		HIGH	LOW	AVG	HIGH	LOW	AVG
1658	**GARDEN WEDDING** - Rose strapless dress, white lace overdress w/rose waist band & bow, rose CT shoes.	575	425	500	300	180	252
1647	**GOLD 'N GLAMOUR** - Blue/gold lamé dress, jacket w/fur trimmed scarf, hat w/fur trim, long brown gloves, brown CT shoes.	1750	1350	1600	975	785	865
1610	**GOLDEN EVENING** - Gold skirt w/gold glitter, gold shirt, gold belt, mustard OT shoes, charm bracelet.	300	200	250	138	90	100
1645	**GOLDEN GLORY** - Gold lamé gown w/green scarf, coat w/fur collar, short white gloves, clear OT shoes w/gold glitter, green purse.	495	325	395	235	180	200
1665	**HERE COMES THE BRIDE** - Satin & lace gown, veil, long white gloves, white CT shoes, blue garter, orchid bouquet.	1200	795	995	395	300	350
1639	**HOLIDAY DANCE** - White/gold striped gown, orange sash w/gold beads, white long gloves, white CT shoes, gold purse.	625	500	595	425	300	350
1653	**INTERNATIONAL FAIR** - White blouse w/6 gold buttons, red/white striped skirt, white CT shoes, camera.	500	400	475	275	180	230
1632	**INVITATION TO TEA** - Pink jumpsuit, pink lamé tunic w/silver belt, clear OT shoes w/silver glitter, 2 cups/saucers, teapot.	600	400	525	285	150	232
1620	**JUNIOR DESIGNER** - Turquoise sheath, floral appliques, green belt, green CT shoes, iron, book.	389	250	325	120	80	90
1614	**JUNIOR PROM** - Red gown, white stole w/white lining, long white gloves, red OT shoes, pearl on chain necklace.	695	500	615	385	300	350
1621	**KNIT HIT** - Sweater, navy skirt, red flats, newspaper.	225	150	185	98	75	82
1602	**KNIT SEPARATES** - Multi-brights top w/deep blue sash, deep blue skirt, mustard pants, deep blue OT shoes.	175	135	160	60	40	50
1661	**LONDON TOUR** - Cream vinyl coat, hat & purse, bone CT shoes, turquoise scarf.	475	350	400	250	150	178
1600	**LUNCH DATE** - Red/yellow print dress w/organdy overlay & 2 red bows.	175	120	145	60	40	50
1649	**LUNCH ON THE TERRACE** - Green/white check dress w/multi dot bodice, matching hat, white CT shoes.	350	275	300	195	130	160
1673	**LUNCHTIME** - "Barbie" print dress w/pink belt, saucepan w/lid, teakettle, coaster, 2 pieces of toast.	350	220	295	145	105	130
1646	**MAGNIFICENCE** - Red/pink gown, red jacket w/fur collar, pink slip, clear (no glitter) or pink OT shoes.	625	500	595	395	295	355
1640	**MATINEE FASHION** - Red sheath, red jacket w/leopard fur trim, red hat w/scarf, red CT shoes.	575	475	500	450	300	385
1617	**MIDNIGHT BLUE** - Blue gown, blue cape, long white gloves, deep blue OT shoes, pearl necklace, silver purse.	850	750	800	550	385	450

STOCK NO.	FASHION	NRFB			MINT		
		HIGH	LOW	AVG	HIGH	LOW	AVG
1699	**MINK COAT** (Sears) - Tan genuine mink short jacket w/satin lining.	3900	2500	3250	2250	1850	1995
1641	**MISS ASTRONAUT** - Silver spacesuit, brown plastic gloves & boots, white helmet, American flag on stick.	700	540	645	425	325	370
1625	**MODERN ART** - Green dress, green CT shoes, painting, program.	620	475	535	305	250	265
1663	**MUSIC CENTER MATINEE** - Red tunic w/pin, red skirt, rose hat, long white gloves, red CT shoes.	725	525	595	425	295	345
1644	**ON THE AVENUE** - Dress, jacket w/gold belt, short white gloves, white CT shoes, pearl necklace, gold purse.	575	450	500	400	250	300
1650	**OUTDOOR ART SHOW** - Multi-floral sheath w/red trim, turquoise felt hat w/red band & bow.	600	485	550	285	200	250
1637	**OUTDOOR LIFE** - Blue/white checked jacket, blue shirt, blue/white houndstooth pants, white hat, tennis shoes.	385	275	350	135	90	105
1601	**PAJAMA PARTY** - Light blue pajama top & bottom, clock.	100	75	90	45	25	34
1678	**PAN AMERICAN AIRLINES STEWARDESS** - Blue/grey suit jacket & skirt, white blouse, hat, Pan-Am emblem, short white gloves, black shoulder bag, black CT shoes.	5000	4000	4500	1700	1100	1550
1692	**PATIO PARTY** - Floral print hostess jumpsuit, blue/green long dress, royal CT shoes, navy/gold earrings.	400	295	350	168	110	135
1648	**PHOTO FASHION** - Turquoise sweater, dickey & pants, turquoise flats, camera.	500	350	450	195	150	175
1694	**PINK MOONBEAMS** - Hot or light pink nightgown, matching robe w/pink feather trim, light pink OT shoes.						
	HOT PINK	400	295	360	150	90	132
	LIGHT PINK	350	250	315	115	80	98
1643	**POODLE PARADE** - Green sheath, pink dickey, green w/white check coat, pink scarf, tote bag, trophy, glasses, green CT shoes, certificate.	985	695	840	595	438	540
1652	**PRETTY AS A PICTURE** - Black/white checked dress w/black bodice, black/white checked hat, black CT shoes.	495	395	450	285	195	250
1686	**PRINT A PLENTY** - Multi-block print dress, fuchsia drop earrings, fuchsia CT shoes.	325	275	265	125	95	110
1654	**RECEPTION LINE** - Blue dress w/sheer overskirt, blue hat, blue CT shoes.	600	500	550	400	295	340
1668	**RIDING IN THE PARK** - Brown/white checked jacket, yellow jodhpurs, white bodysuit, brown plastic hat & boots, crop.	625	525	595	395	290	350
1611	**SATIN 'N ROSE** - Rose bolero jacket, blouse, skirt, hat, pink OT shoes w/silver glitter, rhinestone earrings.	395	350	376	225	175	195

STOCK NO.	FASHION	NRFB			MINT		
		HIGH	LOW	AVG	HIGH	LOW	AVG
1615	**SATURDAY MATINEE** - Brown jacket w/brown fur, hat, short brown gloves, brown CT shoes, gold purse w/fur trim.	950	750	875	600	450	500
1681	**SEARS PINK FORMAL** - Light pink halter overdress w/glitter & tulle, pink underskirt, clear OT shoes, boa.	2450	1800	2125	900	700	810
1664	**SHIMMERING MAGIC** - Silver lamé sheath, red coat, hat w/6 red roses, red CT shoes.	1750	1200	1595	875	695	785
1629	**SKATER'S WALTZ** - Pink skating dress, pink collar & mittens, nylons, skates w/blades.	450	350	400	220	165	182
1608	**SKIN DIVER** - Orange hooded sweatshirt, 2 piece swimsuit, yellow top, orange bottom, green fins, snorkel & mask w/plastic window.	145	85	120	65	45	55
1636	**SLEEPING PRETTY** - Blue nightgown, robe, blue OT shoes w/pompons, pillow & blue brush.	375	300	350	135	90	110
1674	**SLEEPY TIME GAL** - Pink robe, pink 2 piece PJ's, pink OT shoes w/blue pompons, 6 curlers, 6 bobby pins, blue brush & comb, "Lose Weight" book.	300	250	265	140	85	100
1642	**SLUMBER PARTY** - Pink robe, pink 2 piece PJ's, pink OT shoes w/blue pompons, scale, 6 curlers, 6 bobby pins, blue brush & comb, "Lose Weight" book.	300	250	265	140	85	100
1671	**SPORTING CASUALS** - Turquoise sweater & pants, turquoise flats.	350	225	315	120	85	105
1622	**STUDENT TEACHER** - Dress, red CT shoes, glasses, globe, pointer, geography book.	475	350	410	225	160	180
1690	**STUDIO TOUR** - Red, green & yellow dress & hat w/black dots, red CT shoes.	275	235	255	120	90	104
1675	**SUNDAY VISIT** - Dress w/gold bodice, jacket w/gold belt, white CT shoes, gold purse.	595	450	525	250	135	186
1683	**SUNFLOWER** - Halter dress, fuchsia CT shoes, pink/navy earrings, 2 pink bracelets.	350	250	300	140	100	125
1612	**THEATRE DATE** - Green satin jacket, skirt w/peplum, white shell, green OT shoes.	250	175	225	100	75	86
1688	**TRAVEL TOGETHERS** - Yellow/red floral print jacket, skirt & matching hat, red CT shoes.	300	250	270	95	70	86
1655	**UNDER FASHIONS** - Pink corselet, slip, bra, panties, textured nylons.	750	500	625	350	295	325
1685	**UNDERPRINTS** - Hot pink print slip, bra, girdle w/supporters, aqua mirror, brush, comb & phone.	300	225	275	130	90	100
1623	**VACATION TIME** - Pink sweater, pink/white checked shorts, pink flats, camera.	285	200	235	125	80	92
1607	**WHITE MAGIC** - White satin coat w/2 rhinestone "buttons," hat, short white gloves, silver purse.	395	230	315	210	130	165

BARBIE SEW FREE FASHIONS 1700'S (1965-66)

STOCK NO.	FASHION	NRFB HIGH	NRFB LOW	NRFB AVG	MINT HIGH	MINT LOW	MINT AVG
1723	DAY 'N NIGHT				95	70	82
1712	DAY IN TOWN				65	55	60
1711	DEBUTANTE PARTY				75	65	70
1724	GOLDEN BALL				85	65	75
1707	HOOTENANNY				58	55	56
1721	MOONLIGHT 'N ROSES				85	65	75
1701	NINE TO FIVE				65	55	62
1708	PATIO PARTY				60	55	58
1706	PRETTY TRAVELERS				65	55	60
1713	SIGHTSEEING				65	55	60
1703	SORORITY TEA				56	55	55
1722	STARDUST				85	65	75

❖❖❖❖❖❖❖❖❖❖❖❖❖❖❖

BARBIE 1800 SERIES FASHIONS (1967-69)

STOCK NO.	FASHION	NRFB HIGH	NRFB LOW	NRFB AVG	MINT & COMPLETE HIGH	MINT & COMPLETE LOW	MINT & COMPLETE AVG
1848	ALL THAT JAZZ - Multi-striped dress, coat, flesh hose, orange bow shoes.	350	195	285	185	120	168
1810	BERMUDA HOLIDAYS - Multi-flowered tunic, matching hat, green Bermuda shorts, pink flats.	350	250	295	190	140	170
1805	BOUNCY FLOUNCY - Multi-floral ruffled dress, matching purse, orange CT shoes.	300	225	270	150	90	125
1864	CLOSE-UPS - Pink bra w/yellow rose, yellow slip w/pink ruffles, pink pantyhose w/yellow rose.	150	95	120	58	35	40
1862	COUNTRY CAPERS - Orange/yellow striped turtleneck, yellow shorts, yellow flats.	125	90	110	50	35	42
1843	DANCING STRIPES - Pink/burgundy/gold-striped dress, matching coat, hot pink CT shoes.	250	175	195	100	75	86 ·
1807	DISCO DATER - Orange satin dress, orange lace overblouse, bright orange CT shoes.	285	220	265	150	100	126
1867	DREAM-INS - Fuchsia/peach peignoir, fuchsia fur robe.	125	85	100	56	35	45
1857	DREAMY PINK - Pink nylon nightgown w/pink raindrops, robe, pink felt slippers w/flowers.	125	95	110	50	35	42
1808	DRIZZLE DASH - Orange/fuchsia diamond print raincoat, matching scarf, orange rainboots.	220	150	185	75	55	62

STOCK NO.	FASHION	NRFB			MINT & COMPLETE		
		HIGH	LOW	AVG	HIGH	LOW	AVG
1844	**EXTRAVAGANZA** - Pink dress w/net overdress w/silver polka-dots & roses, long pink gloves, silver clutch, clear OT shoes w/silver glitter or hot pink CT shoes.	395	325	385	250	175	195
1874	**FAB CITY** - Gown w/silver bodice & skirt w/black flowers & pink puffs, silver shawl, short hot pink gloves, hot pink pilgrim or CT shoes.	450	295	375	250	185	200
1858	**FANCY-DANCY** - Dress w/chartreuse skirt & fuchsia bodice, chartreuse coat w/fuchsia lace trim, flowered hose, pink bow shoes.	250	125	140	115	75	90
1547	**GLIMMER GLAMOUR** (Sears) - Aqua dress w/metallic gold polka-dots, gold lamé swing coat, gold belt, gold hose, clear OT shoes w/gold glitter.	5000	—	5000	1850	1350	1630
1865	**GLO-GO** - Halter dress w/burgundy lamé top, belt, & chiffon overskirt w/swirls & dots, red CT shoes.	275	150	200	85	60	72
1868	**HAPPY GO PINK** - Dress w/hot pink top & white ruffled skirt w/pink-flowered trim, pink hose, hot pink CT shoes or pilgrim shoes.	200	120	165	85	65	75
1823	**JUMP INTO LACE** - Pink satin jumpsuit w/white lace overlay, hot pink OT shoes.	150	95	125	70	45	62
1804	**KNIT HIT** - Knit dress w/aqua top & hot pink bottom, light blue CT shoes.	150	85	120	60	40	52
1879	**LET'S HAVE A BALL** - Gown w/turquoise velvet bodice, chiffon overskirt w/painted flowers, turquoise velvet jacket w/white fur, gold belt w/flower & stone, aqua pilgrim or CT shoes.	325	275	300	180	120	160
1881	**MADE FOR EACH OTHER** - Orange/yellow plaid coat w/orange fur & orange belt, orange skirt, yellow ribbed top, orange fur hat, orange boots, bead necklace.	275	185	245	140	100	120
1861	**MAKE MINE MIDI** - White blouse w/self stripes w/2 gold buttons & lace trimmed cuffs & front placket, hot pink cotton midi skirt w/yellow velour wasteband & bow, 3 white sheer nylon poufs & 2 pink nylon poufs on green nylon stars, hot pink lace-trimmed half slip, hot pink sheer hose, hot pink pilgrim or bow shoes.	350	295	325	135	98	125
1869	**MIDI-MAGIC** - Midi dress w/white lace bodice, black taffeta skirt w/velvet belt, black hose, black pilgrim, CT or bow shoes.	185	150	165	130	85	105
1870	**MIDI-MARVELOUS** - White dress w/white eyelet lace overlay & pink ribbon, matching hat, white hose, white pilgrim, CT or bow shoes.	185	135	160	105	75	90

STOCK NO.	FASHION	NRFB			MINT & COMPLETE		
		HIGH	LOW	AVG	HIGH	LOW	AVG
1809	**MINI PRINTS** - Multi-print jersey mini dress, matching hose, royal blue bow shoes.	275	195	245	125	90	108
1866	**MOVIE GROOVIE** - Silver lamé blouse w/sheer pink sleeves, pink satin skirt, pink hose, hot pink pilgrim or bow shoes.	190	110	165	75	55	68
1841	**NIGHT CLOUDS** - Peignoir w/yellow bodice & orange/pink/yellow ruffles, yellow robe, yellow OT shoes.	120	75	98	40	28	34
1853	**NOW WOW!** - Aqua corduroy mini w/crocheted trim, matching bonnet, chartreuse-patterned hose, light blue boots w/chartreuse trim.	165	95	135	110	78	86
1806	**PAJAMA POW** - Multi-print, bell-bottomed jumpsuit, red/pink/gold dangle earrings, yellow flats.	300	200	260	125	75	128
1873	**PLUSH PONY** - Black/white pony-print fur coat w/orange trim, gold chain belt, dress w/fur skirt/orange bodice, orange boots.	200	100	160	75	50	65
1863	**PRETTY POWER** - Dress w/white blouse w/lace trim, pink skirt w/white/black flower pattern, black pilgrim, CT or bow shoes.	150	100	130	60	45	55
1817	**RED FANTASTIC** (Sears) - Deep pink long dress w/white crepe & gold trim, marabou cape, hot pink CT shoes.	850	795	825	495	450	475
1871	**ROMANTIC RUFFLES** - Long ruffled dress w/silver bodice & pink skirt, silver lamé purse, pink rosette-on-chain earrings, hot pink pilgrim, CT or bow shoes.	250	200	235	150	85	125
1845	**SCENE STEALERS** - Sheer pink coat, ruffled pink skirt w/lime trim, lime lamé top, hot pink CT shoes.	275	200	250	120	85	96
1872	**SEE-WORTHY** - Aqua sailor dress w/yellow trim, matching hat w/pompon, aqua stockings, aqua tennis shoes, camera.	325	200	285	140	100	128
1885	**SILVER SPARKLE/SALUTE TO SILVER** - Silver lamé long-sleeved mini dress w/textured stripe patterned bodice, clear OT or T-strap shoes.	120	100	112	55	45	50
1860	**SMASHEROO** - Red cotton striped dress w/chain, yellow fur jacket & hat, yellow lace hose, red boots.	275	195	235	135	85	102
1824	**SNAP DASH** - Lime nylon dress w/yellow trim, lime felt hat, yellow knee socks, yellow bow shoes or ankle boots.	195	125	160	85	60	72
1813	**SNUG FUZZ** - Silver lamé sweater & stockings, pink fur jacket w/white belt, fur skirt, grey ankle boots.	275	165	250	130	85	120

STOCK NO.	FASHION	NRFB			MINT & COMPLETE		
		HIGH	LOW	AVG	HIGH	LOW	AVG
1814	**SPARKLE SQUARES** - Pink/yellow/silver checked coat w/white lace trim, matching dress w/white ruffles & silver belt, white hose, silver clutch, white bow shoes.	350	275	325	140	110	126
1822	**SWIRLEY-CUE** - Multi-swirl dress, green/pink dangle earrings, hot pink CT shoes.	300	200	260	125	90	120
1855	**TEAM UPS** - Pink jacket, dress w/multi-striped top & pink bottom, attached gold belt, hot pink CT shoes.	225	150	185	85	55	75
1842	**TOGETHERNESS** - Aqua knit dress w/floral stripes, matching bonnet & hose, hot pink bow shoes.	185	100	150	80	60	70
1846	**TRAILBLAZERS** - Pink/green/orange striped jacket, matching pants, yellow blouse w/design, goggles, green ankle boots.	250	165	200	120	80	100
1859	**TUNIC 'N TIGHTS** - Pink/yellow striped turtleneck & tights, yellow vinyl tunic & shorts, yellow ankle boots.	300	200	275	150	120	130
1854	**TWINKLE TOGS** - Blue lamé dress w/striped net bottom, lime hose, blue CT shoes.	275	200	250	125	85	100
1821	**UNDERLINERS** - Green floral bodysuit w/pink lace trim, matching garter belt, flesh hose, pink OT shoes.	165	100	130	80	50	65
1818	**VELVETEENS (Sears)** - Pantsuit w/red velvet flared legs & white crepe top w/red trimmed ruffles, red velvet jacket, hot pink flats.	850	650	750	450	350	400
1849	**WEDDING WONDER** - White satin gown w/white dot overdress, veil, bouquet, white CT shoes.	375	300	350	175	125	145
1815	**WEEKENDERS (Sears)** - Pink/burgundy/green print top w/attached green belt, matching pants & cap, matching striped jacket, hot pink flats.	950	795	895	475	400	440
1856	**WILD 'N WONDERFUL** - Multi-print top & matching mini, orange high strapped sandals.	300	200	275	125	95	118
1880	**WINTER WEDDING** - White brocade gown w/fur trim, cap veil w/fur, pink bouquet, white pilgrim or CT shoes.	295	225	270	150	90	110
1816	**YELLOW GO, THE (Sears)** - Yellow raincoat, matching hat w/attached checked scarf & blue pompon, yellow lace hose, blue shoulder bag, blue bow shoes.	850	795	825	550	425	495
1820	**ZOKKO!** - Silver/blue lamé sheath dress w/orange belt, grey boots w/orange stripe, orange dangle earrings.	250	165	195	110	85	96

BARBIE 1400 SERIES FASHIONS (1969-70)

STOCK NO.	FASHION	NRFB			MINT & COMPLETE		
		HIGH	LOW	AVG	HIGH	LOW	AVG
1464	ANTI-FREEZERS - Orange knit coat, yellow blouse, orange/yellow/white plaid blouse & scarf, yellow boots.	135	95	120	75	50	68
1469	BLUE ROYALTY - Blue lamé gown w/silver/gold trim, white fur jacket, blue pilgrim or T-strap shoes.	275	175	230	120	90	98
1457	CITY SPARKLER - Lime dress w/lamé top & chiffon bottom, lime pilgrim or T-strap shoes.	135	90	120	75	50	60
1489	CLOUD 9 - Blue satin robe w/pink shawl collar, blue peignoir w/pink top, pink slippers w/blue ruffle.	165	120	150	65	40	54
1476	DREAM WRAP - Pink cotton robe w/white lace trim, ribbon tie, panties, pink felt slippers w/white soles & flowers.	95	65	75	40	26	32
1456	DREAMY BLUES - Aqua satin dress w/lime & aqua ruffles, blue pilgrim or T-strap shoes.	150	75	100	70	50	60
1493	FAB FUR - Tan/white fur jacket & skirt, pink shell w/gold trim, gold lamé boot tights.	300	195	265	185	105	140
1481	FIRELIGHTS - Aqua/silver lamé brocade jumpsuit, blue OT shoes.	185	125	160	85	60	74
1453	FLOWER WOWER - Multi-floral print organdy dress, lime pilgrim or T-strap shoes.	85	60	70	45	30	35
1494	GOLDSWINGER - Orange/gold lamé brocade coat, orange chiffon dress w/gold top, gold belt, orange CT shoes.	295	195	245	150	90	112
1459	GREAT COAT - Yellow coat w/fur trim, matching hat, yellow pilgrim, T-strap or bow shoes.	95	70	85	50	30	40
1458	GYPSY SPIRIT - Pink bodysuit, aqua vest & skirt w/knit loop trim, blue or hot pink pilgrim or T-strap shoes.	100	75	82	55	35	45
1477	HURRAY FOR LEATHER - Orange knit top w/fur trim, yellow vinyl mini w/orange fur trim, yellow pilgrim or bow shoes.	95	65	80	50	30	40
1482	IMPORTANT IN-VESTMENT - Green knit mini-dress, gold chain belt w/felt flower, white fleece vest w/felt flower, green pilgrim shoes.	125	85	95	55	35	46
1470	INTRIGUE - Gold belted lamé dress w/white fishnet-type top, gold coat, separate gold belt w/square buckle, white or bone CT shoes.	425	350	395	275	175	195
1467	LAMB 'N LEATHER - White fur coat w/black vinyl trim, white matching hat, pink/black belt, purse & boots, short black gloves.	295	200	275	150	100	132
1479	LEISURE LEOPARD - Leopard print/yellow nylon leisure suit, yellow pilgrim or OT shoes.	90	65	76	48	30	40

STOCK NO.	FASHION	NRFB			MINT & COMPLETE		
		HIGH	LOW	AVG	HIGH	LOW	AVG
1465	LEMON KICK - Yellow pleated chiffon top & pants, opt. yellow shorts, yellow pilgrim, T-strap or bow shoes.	150	100	120	70	50	60
1483	LITTLE BOW-PINK - Pink satin dress w/ruffle trim, pink hose, hot pink pilgrim or bow shoes.	175	120	150	85	60	70
1454	LOOP SCOOP - Yellow cotton dress w/multi-colored crochet trim, yellow pilgrim or T-strap shoes.	85	65	75	50	28	40
1463	LOVELY SLEEP-INS - Pink lace robe w/fur trim, pink nightgown, pink fur slippers.	100	75	95	48	30	42
1452	NOW KNIT - Lime dress w/blue/silver stripes, lime fur hat, blue tie scarf, royal blue pilgrim or T-strap shoes.	125	95	115	55	40	48
1440	PINK SPARKLE - Pink sheath w/lamé dot-swirl pattern, pink chiffon cape, hot pink OT shoes.	275	185	245	160	85	110
1462	RARE PAIR - Yellow/orange knit dress, matching jacket, yellow hose, yellow pilgrim or bow shoes.	150	100	126	85	65	75
1491	RED, WHITE, 'N WARM - White vinyl coat w/fur trim, white belt, pink/orange colorblock dress, white vinyl hat & boots w/fur & chains.	265	185	245	135	98	120
1478	SHIFT INTO KNIT - Knit dress w/navy bottom & red top, red fringed scarf, red pilgrim or bow shoes.	95	75	85	55	35	45
1487	SHIRTDRESSY - Yellow dress w/white lace overskirt, yellow slip, yellow hose, yellow pilgrim shoes.	170	115	150	75	55	65
1492	SILVER POLISH - Silver lamé jumpsuit, yellow long coat w/silver trim, yellow pilgrim shoes.	200	150	184	125	85	100
1468	SPECIAL SPARKLE - Pink/gold brocade coat, pink gathered blouse, gold lamé skirt, hot pink pilgrim or T-strap shoes.	225	150	180	95	80	85
1451	TANGERINE SCENE - Orange vinyl bodysuit, orange/white plaid wrap skirt, orange pilgrim or flat shoes.	85	65	74	40	24	34
1460	TROPICANA - Orange/yellow/white sheath w/daisy, orange CT shoes.	175	100	150	75	55	65
1488	VELVET VENTURE - Pink/gold lamé dress, lime velvet coat, acid green pilgrim shoes.	195	125	165	85	60	70
1486	WINTER WOW - Orange jacket w/brown fur trim, orange pleated skirt, brown fur hat & muff, gold metallic belt & boots.	250	185	235	115	80	90
1484	YELLOW MELLOW - Yellow velvet dress w/pink rick-rack trim, yellow hose, yellow pilgrim shoes.	160	100	135	85	65	75

BARBIE 1700 SERIES FASHIONS (1970-71)

STOCK NO.	FASHION	NRFB HIGH	NRFB LOW	NRFB AVG	MINT & COMPLETE HIGH	MINT & COMPLETE LOW	MINT & COMPLETE AVG
1786	**BRIGHT 'N BROCADE** - Pink/green/gold lamé brocade blouse, pink sheer pants w/brocade cuffs, pink bow shoes.	150	95	125	75	55	65
1794	**CHECK THE SUIT** - Hot pink/yellow herringbone plaid jacket, matching pants, yellow knit shell, yellow vinyl belt, yellow pilgrim or T-strap shoes.	135	95	110	65	40	52
1789	**FIERY FELT** - Orange felt coat w/orange fringe trim, matching hat, orange boots.	85	60	75	50	34	42
1796	**FUR SIGHTED** - Orange cotton jacket w/yellow fur trim, matching hat w/strap, orange pants, yellow/orange lamé zig-zag knit top, yellow pilgrim shoes.	200	125	176	100	75	88
1784	**HAREM-M-M'S** - Reddish-orange nylon jumpsuit w/gold/silver cord tie belt.	70	50	60	38	25	30
1791	**LACE CAPER, THE** - White lace blouse & pants, pink sheer cape, pink pilgrim or T-strap shoes.	160	100	130	80	60	70
1799	**MAXI 'N MINI** - Blue lamé coat w/blue fur trim, blue/pink/gold lamé mini dress w/gold cord belt, blue lamé thigh boots.	375	285	340	200	165	175
1792	**MOOD MATCHERS** - Pink/aqua/yellow/orange print mini-dress w/aqua nylon bow waist, matching print long pant skirt, aqua blouse w/aqua vinyl belt, aqua pilgrim or T-strap shoes.	200	100	150	85	60	70
1787	**PRIMA BALLERINA** - Fuchsia satin tutu w/pink/yellow net ruffle, fuchsia pantyhose, pink toe shoes w/ties.	75	50	60	38	25	34
1798	**RAINBOW WRAPS** - Green/blue/pink geometric print formal w/green lamé bodice & reddish-orange bow waist, matching shawl w/pink fringe, pink petticoat, blue pilgrim or T-strap shoes.	350	275	315	170	125	150
1783	**RUFFLES 'N SWIRLS** - Pink/aqua ruffled wrap dress, pink vinyl belt, aqua pilgrim or T-strap shoes.	100	70	86	65	40	50
1788	**SCUBA-DO'S** - Yellow hooded bodysuit, orange/yellow/blue 2-piece swimsuit, orange fins, mask, snorkel.	70	50	60	30	20	26
1782	**SHAPE-UPS** - Red leotard, red hose, 2 black weights, stretch rope, twist platform, exercise booklet, red Francie soft buckle flats.	100	75	86	65	40	56
1793	**SKATE MATES** - Coral pink skating dress w/white fleece trim, matching hat & mittens, coral pink tights, skates w/blades.	140	100	120	65	45	55
1797	**SKI SCENE, THE** - Orange vinyl jacket, hood & mask, fuchsia knit sweater, yellow vinyl pants, orange boots, skis w/"baskets," poles.	180	120	165	80	60	70
1781	**TENNIS TEAM** - White tennis dress w/2 red bows, white tennis shoes, racket, tennis ball.	75	60	70	40	25	34

JULIA FASHIONS (1969-70)

STOCK NO.	FASHION	NRFB HIGH	LOW	AVG	MINT & COMPLETE HIGH	LOW	AVG
1752	**BRR FURRR** - Aqua weave coat w/lime fur trim & aqua belt, matching hat, aqua weave dress w/lime bodice, aqua pilgrim shoes.	250	175	210	100	85	95
1753	**CANDLELIGHT CAPERS** - Orange lamé & yellow velvet mini-dress, yellow velvet cape, yellow hat w/yellow fur trim, yellow platform shoes.	250	175	200	110	70	90
1751	**LEATHER WEATHER** - Red vinyl coat, matching purse, pink knit shell, red/pink/blue/ brown/white woven plaid skirt.	225	160	180	100	80	90
1754	**PINK FANTASY** - Hot pink chiffon nightgown w/lace bodice, 3-tiered peignoir w/multi-shaded pink ruffles, rosette & ribbons, gold lamé ankle booties w/pink pompons, pink pilgrim shoes.	225	175	195	100	80	90

❖❖❖❖❖❖❖❖❖❖❖❖❖❖❖

COLOR MAGIC FASHIONS (1967)

STOCK NO.	FASHION	NRFB HIGH	LOW	AVG	MINT & COMPLETE HIGH	LOW	AVG
1778	**BLOOM BURSTS** - Multi-brights ruffled floral print dress, pink chiffon bonnet w/ties, changers A & B, sponge applicator w/yellow or red handle.	550	400	480	360	225	295
1779	**MIX 'N MATCHERS** - Multi-brights stripe/floral print blouse & skirt, pink pants w/print cuffs & pocket, straw hat w/yellow scarf tie, pink flats, changers A & B, yellow Corningware-type dish, 2 applicators w/red & yellow handles.	475	300	405	175	130	150
1777	**PRETTY WILD!** - Multi-brights block print sheath w/floral border, block print hat w/yellow brim, floral bag w/yellow handles, changers A & B, sponge applicator w/red or yellow handle.	500	325	450	350	250	295
1776	**SMART SWITCH** - Fuchsia/yellow/blue striped skirt, matching scarf, yellow sleeveless top w/striped belt, changers A & B, sponge applicator w/red or yellow handle.	550	400	475	350	220	285
1775	**STRIPES AWAY** - Olive green long dress w/orange & fuchsia stripes, matching scarf, 2 pink snake bracelets, changers A & B, sponge applicator w/red or yellow handle.	500	350	420	250	200	225

BARBIE 3400 SERIES FASHIONS (1971-72)

STOCK NO.	FASHION	NRFB HIGH	NRFB LOW	NRFB AVG	MINT & COMPLETE HIGH	MINT & COMPLETE LOW	MINT & COMPLETE AVG
3433	**ALL ABOUT PLAID** - Lime/orange plaid dress w/lime bodice & fringe, orange vinyl belt, matching plaid shawl & shoulder bag, lime pilgrim or T-strap shoes.	165	125	150	70	50	64
3403	**BABY DOLL PINKS** - Pink ruffled short nightie w/coral red straps & bow, pink fuzzy slippers.	125	95	100	50	38	45
3417	**BRIDAL BROCADE** - White brocade gown w/white fur trim, brocade cap veil w/fur trim, short white gloves, green lace fan/white flowers bouquet, white T-strap shoes.	285	200	260	195	125	165
3421	**BUBBLES 'N BOOTS** - Purple/orange/green dot print peasant dress, purple suede belt & boots.	165	100	130	85	50	66
3429	**COLD SNAP** - Red cotton knit coat w/white fur collar, red plastic boots.	90	60	70	45	30	36
3422	**COLOR KICK, THE** - Multi-brights striped jumpsuit, yellow fur wrap skirt w/3 reddish-orange buttons.	160	125	140	70	50	62
3437	**DANCING LIGHTS** - Fuchsia/orange/blue swirl print dress w/ruffled tiers & pink lamé waist, pink lamé shawl, hot pink T-strap shoes, black butterfly choker.	350	250	300	195	135	180
3427	**DREAM TEAM, THE** - White lace robe w/blue ribbon tie waist, white nylon short nightie w/lace trim, white felt slippers w/lace trim.	175	100	140	65	50	58
3406	**EVENING IN** - Pink nylon overdress w/gold medallion waist, pink/green print nylon pants 2 "Casey" earrings, pink snake bracelet, hot pink pilgrim or T-strap shoes.	160	100	128	85	55	68
3401	**FRINGE BENEFITS** - Fuchsia knit mini-dress w/orange suede trim & orange suede fringed tie belt, orange suede fringed boots.	100	75	90	50	35	45
3412	**FUN FLAKES** - White knit top & pants w/hot pink snowflake design hot pink shell, hot pink pilgrim or T-strap shoes.	120	85	100	50	30	45
3434	**FUN FUR** - Sable-colored fur coat w/brown suede collar, matching suede belt w/gold buckle, brown corduroy hat w/suede brim or tan crocheted cap, brown plastic boots.	225	175	195	115	75	96
3436	**GAUCHO GEAR** - Multi-floral print bodyblouse & skirt, orange vinyl gauchos w/suede trim, brown suede fringed vest, purse, & boots, orange felt hat.	275	198	225	165	110	138
3404	**GLOWIN' OUT** - Sleeveless dress w/pink satin bodice & gold lamé brocade skirt, hot pink pilgrim or T-strap shoes.	120	85	100	65	45	58

BARBIE 3400 SERIES FASHIONS (1971-72) CONTINUED

STOCK NO.	FASHION	NRFB HIGH	NRFB LOW	NRFB AVG	MINT & COMPLETE HIGH	MINT & COMPLETE LOW	MINT & COMPLETE AVG
3413	GOLFING GREATS - Yellow nylon bodyblouse, blue/red/yellow plaid wrap skirt & cap, matching plaid golf bag, 2 clubs, 2 balls, aqua cotton knee-socks, red round sunglasses, aqua tennis shoes.	275	185	240	165	120	146
3424	IN BLOOMS - Lime/fuchsia/aqua print nylon leisure dress, optional royal blue wedge or hot pink flat shoes.	90	70	80	55	35	45
3432	IN STITCHES - Yellow nylon blouse w/scarf tie, red/green/pink patterned wool vest, pants, & bag, yellow ankle boots.	185	130	170	95	70	85
3418	MAGNIFICENT MIDI - Red velvet coat w/black fur & vinyl trim, sleeveless dress w/black rib knit bodice & velvet skirt, black vinyl belt, red velvet hat w/black fur trim, black vinyl boots w/fur trim.	350	275	315	250	185	220
3407	MIDI MOOD - Yellow cotton blouse w/3 buttons, turquoise wrap skirt w/pink/yellow rose print, yellow pilgrim or T-strap shoes.	100	70	85	45	30	38
3423	NIGHT LIGHTER - Red nylon jumpsuit W/purple/lime accents, purple suede belt w/gold buckle, red ankle boots.	185	100	140	75	50	62
3438	PEASANT DRESSY - Multi-floral print velvet midi dress w/lace-up purple bodice, white eyelet petticoat & camisole, purple T-strap shoes.	200	150	175	130	85	98
3411	PONCHO PUT-ON - Yellow/orange plaid knit jumpsuit, w/chain belt, yellow vinyl poncho w/orange trim, yellow knit hood w/orange vinyl visor, yellow ankle boots.	165	100	140	80	55	70
3409	RED FOR RAIN - Red cotton belted trench coat, red hat w/scarf tie, white rain boots.	85	50	70	35	20	28
3414	SATIN SLUMBER - Aqua satin 2-piece pajamas, aqua velour robe w/satin trim & belt, aqua satin ankle slippers.	175	100	150	75	50	65
3419	SILVER SERENADE - Turquoise/silver lamé gown, turquoise fur boa, turquoise hose, silver lamé long gloves, silver microphone, aqua T-strap shoes.	485	365	440	300	195	275
3408	SUPER SCARF - Red wool knit sweater, matching fringed scarf, navy/red/white herringbone plaid skirt w/gold chain belt, red plastic boots.	125	85	100	50	30	42
3426	TURTLE 'N TIGHTS - Blue nylon knit turtleneck, matching tights, orange suede belt & fringed skirt, blue soft flats.	225	150	170	100	80	92
3402	TWO-WAY TIGER - Lime/orange swirl patterned sleeveless tunic w/orange bow & trim, matching pants, lime pilgrim or T-strap shoes.	120	85	98	50	35	45

141

STOCK NO.	FASHION	NRFB			MINT & COMPLETE		
		HIGH	LOW	AVG	HIGH	LOW	AVG
3431	**VICTORIAN VELVET** - Purple velvet maxi dress w/white lace sleeves & trim, purple or rose T-strap shoes.	200	135	175	85	65	75
3416	**WILD 'N WINTERY** - Hot pink felt hooded coat w/faux leopard sleeves & trim, hot pink felt mini-skirt, pink knit shell, pink hose, white vinyl belt & thigh-high boots.	350	285	320	225	180	200
3439	**WILD THINGS** - Lime ribbed-knit jumpsuit, white fur long vest w/floral trim, royal blue vinyl belt, royal blue ankle boots.	295	250	275	195	120	178
3428	**ZIG-ZAG BAG, THE** - Red/white/navy/gold zig-zag-striped blouse, red velour vest, red/gold zig-zag-striped knit pants, red tennis shoes.	185	135	155	95	75	85

❖❖❖❖❖❖❖❖❖❖❖❖❖❖❖

BARBIE 3400 SERIES FASHIONS (1971-72) - PART TWO

STOCK NO.	FASHION	NRFB			MINT & COMPLETE		
		HIGH	LOW	AVG	HIGH	LOW	AVG
3337	**ALL AMERICAN GIRL** - Royal blue mock T-neck top w/gathered waist & sleeves, royal blue tights, royal blue/white/orange miniskirt w/4 white buttons, orange or red pilgrim shoes.	95	75	85	55	45	50
3362	**FANCY THAT PURPLE** - Gold lamé maxi skirt w/multi colored brocade pattern, purple shell, purple hose, gold lamé shorts, purple pilgrim or T-strap shoes.	125	100	115	80	60	70
3492	**FLYING COLORS** - Hot pink/yellow/orange/ turquoise striped full-length skirt with hot pink vinyl waist, yellow long-sleeved blouse, orange plush vest with hot pink vinyl trim, hot pink vinyl flowered choker, hot pink pilgrim shoes.	385	295	365	200	150	185
3480	**FUN SHINE** - Silver lamé "brick" patterned skirt w/orange tie at waist, orange sheer blouse w/matching silver "brick" lining, orange nylons, orange pilgrim or soft bow shoes.	200	150	180	110	80	94
3336	**FURRY 'N FUN** - Red midi coat w/white plush collar & cuffs, red belt w/gold buckle, white boots w/"laces."	120	85	100	50	35	45
3354	**GLOWIN' GOLD** - Gold metallic bell bottoms w/2 gold buttons, turquoise shell, blue pilgrim or aqua or royal blue low hard shoes.	95	60	70	45	35	40

BARBIE 3400 SERIES FASHIONS
(1971-72) - PART TWO CONTINUED

STOCK NO.	FASHION	NRFB			MINT & COMPLETE		
		HIGH	LOW	AVG	HIGH	LOW	AVG
3340	GOLDEN GLITTER - Marigold sleeveless satin dress w/3 gold buttons, gold lamé waistband and chiffon ruffles, matching purse w/gold lamé handle, matching hose, gold low hard shoes.	145	100	120	85	60	70
3351	GOOD SPORTS - Dark denim bell bottoms w/white stitching, red mock T-neck shell, red bandana w/daisy pattern, brown wide belt w/2 gold beads, red sunglasses, white tennis shoes.	95	65	80	55	35	45
3339	LIGHT 'N LAZY - White short penoir w/white lace trim & lavender bow, matching short robe w/white ties, matching white underpants, white slippers w/lace trim.	85	65	75	50	40	42
3341	LONG 'N FRINGY - Orange/black/yellow/red plaid midi wrap skirt w/3 gold buttons, yellow bodysuit w/neck tie, black pilgrim or low hard shoes.	125	70	90	70	45	55
3358	LOVELY 'N LAVENDER - Light silvery pink nighty w/ruffled hem, matching robe w/white plush collar, textured polka dot pattern & lace trim, white pitcher, white glass.	175	140	160	95	70	85
3485	MADRAS MAD - Red/white/navy plaid maxi coat-dress w/red suede-like collar, cuffs, & belt w/gold buckle, matching plaid purse, red pilgrim or square-toes heels shoes.	175	100	145	80	50	60
3338	MAINLY FOR RAIN - Dark blue/orange/green houndstooth A-line coat w/dark blue trim & 3 dark blue buttons, matching hat, dark blue boots w/"laces."	75	50	62	40	30	35
3486	O-BOY CORDUROY - Red maxi corduroy jumper, royal blue peasant blouse w/white choker, white boots w/"laces."	100	75	88	65	50	56
3488	OVERALL DENIM - Dark indigo denim overalls, red jersey tee w/1 lavender sleeve & 1 blue sleeve, blue/white striped backpack w/red vinyl straps, white tennis shoes.	135	95	120	85	50	74
3359	PANTS-PERFECT PURPLE - Rust knit long-sleeved mock T-neck, matching bell bottom pants, gold chain belt, tiger-print fur purse w/black vinyl trim & black strap, black pilgrim, low hard or soft bow shoes.	95	75	85	60	45	52
3490	PARTY LINES - Black granny midi dress w/red rose pattern & white lace trim, white hose, black wrap shoes.	210	160	186	135	100	128
3482	PEASANT PLEASANT - Orange shirt with 3/4 bell sleeves & ecru braided trim on sleeves & peplum waist, ecru skirt w/orange rick-rack trim, orange wrap wedge shoes.	150	100	115	90	65	78

BARBIE 3400 SERIES FASHIONS
(1971-72) - PART TWO CONTINUED

STOCK NO.	FASHION	NRFB			MINT & COMPLETE		
		HIGH	LOW	AVG	HIGH	LOW	AVG
3355	**PICTURE ME PRETTY** - Peasant-style mini-dress w/purple/rose panels, multi-floral pattern & white eyelet trim, white underpants w/lace trim, white half slip w/lace trim, fuchsia pilgrims shoes.	100	75	85	55	45	48
3360	**PLEASANTLY PEASANTY** - Granny-style red midi dress w/floral pattern & white lace trim, midi-length half slip w/white eyelet trim, black wide tie belt, black pilgrim or low hard shoes.	95	70	80	55	40	48
3483	**PURPLE PLEASERS** - Purple gathered peasant shirt w/peplum waist, purple/gold/blue/white patterned peasant maxi skirt, white pilgrim shoes or square-toed heels.	80	60	70	40	20	30
3493	**SATIN 'N SHINE** - Wedding gown w/satin bodice, lace overlay on skirt & sheer lace gathered, peasant-style sleeves, sheer hat veil, single flower bouquet w/white ribbon, white pilgrim or square-toed heels.	350	250	300	175	100	160
3481	**SHORT SET, THE** - White/multi-diamond patterned white, long-sleeved shirt, matching shorts, red belted purse, red boots w/"laces."	150	100	125	60	48	55
3357	**SILVER BLUES** - Gold lamé long coat w/multi-floral colored brocade pattern w/1 gold button at waist, purple chiffon scarf, purple pilgrim or T-strap shoes.	120	85	95	55	35	45
3487	**SLEEPY SET** - Light pink robe w/tiny pink & green floral "embroidery" & green ribbon tie, pink sheer, short nighty w/matching floral top, pink/white felt slippers.	150	125	135	75	50	65
3353	**SPORT STAR** - Red bodysuit w/gathered waits & cuffs w/white star & dot pattern, chambray wrap mini-jumper w/white stitching & 3 white buttons, aqua low hard shoes.	75	55	65	45	30	36
3491	**SUEDE 'N FUR** - Brown "suede" & faux fur coat w/3 latch buttons, brown suede mini skirt w/3 gold buttons, red jersey catsuit, brown boots.	260	180	215	160	100	130
3350	**SWEET DREAMS** - 2-piece pajama set w/white background, pink polka-dot & yellow/pink poppy pattern, pink felt slippers w/gold beads.	65	55	60	35	25	30
3361	**SWEETHEART SATIN** - Ecru satin wedding gown w/ecru lace trimmed bell sleeves & hem, ecru lace cap veil w/netting & white satin ribbon trim, ecru lace bouquet w/pink flowers & white ribbon, white pilgrim, T-strap or low hard shoes.	195	150	175	140	100	125
3352	**WHITE 'N WITH IT** - White A-line coat w/red stitching, small gold lamé attached belt w/buckle, gold lamé drawstring-type bag w/gold chain handle, white pilgrim shoes or low hard heels.	75	65	60	50	35	42

MISS AMERICA FASHIONS (1972-1973)

STOCK NO.	FASHION	NRFB HIGH	LOW	AVG	MINT & COMPLETE HIGH	LOW	AVG
3216	**MAJESTIC BLUE** - Turquoise taffeta sleeveless gown w/organdy overlay, white plush fur stole w/gold trim, long white gloves, "Miss America" banner w/3 red roses bouquet, blue pilgrim shoes.	550	500	525	380	285	365
3217	**REGAL RED** - Halter gown w/gold lamé bodice & reddish rose satin skirt, matching reddish rose cape w/yellow fur trim, long yellow gloves, gold lamé purse & belt w/gold bead, red square-toed shoes.	595	525	570	475	400	445
3215	**ROYAL VELVET** - Red velvet gown w/white plush fur-trimmed collar, fuchsia full slip, white plush fur muff, rose pilgrim shoes.	575	500	550	425	350	400

❖❖❖❖❖❖❖❖❖❖❖❖❖❖❖❖

BARBIE 1000 SERIES FASHIONS - PUT-ONS & PETS (1972)

STOCK NO.	FASHION	NRFB HIGH	LOW	AVG	MINT & COMPLETE HIGH	LOW	AVG
1063	**HOT TOGS** - Red/black/olive houndstooth plaid bolero jacket, red hot pants, brown belt & attached purse w/red stitching, olive knit stockings & matching hat, lime hose, brown boots w/"laces," Afghan dog w/collar & leash.	850	695	750	475	350	395
1062	**KITTY KAPERS** - Yellow/blue/melon color blocks w/white polka dot & daisy patterned bolero top w/white rick-rack trim, matching shorts, matching skirt, white boots w/"laces," white cat, yellow food bowl.	900	750	840	500	375	435
1061	**POODLE DOODLES** - Mini-dress w/red roll collar top & black/multi floral print skirt, matching floral vest w/turquoise collar & waistband w/button closure, matching black/floral boots, black poodle w/collar & gold chain leash.	800	700	760	475	350	386

❖❖❖❖❖❖❖❖❖❖❖❖❖❖❖❖

BARBIE 1000 SERIES FASHIONS 'N SOUNDS (1971-1972)

STOCK NO.	FASHION	NRFB HIGH	LOW	AVG	MINT & COMPLETE HIGH	LOW	AVG
1055	**COUNTRY MUSIC** - Red/white dot & floral-patterned peasant blouse & skirt w/rick-rack trim, white lace shawl, white boots, record.	385	300	325	180	130	155
1056	**FESTIVAL FASHION** - White lace peasant blouse, multi-brights abstract-patterned skirt, hot pink vest w/3 gold buttons, matching bandana, brown cummerbund, brown vinyl w/"laces" or suede boots, record.	400	310	360	200	140	165
1057	**GROOVIN' GAUCHOS** - Hot pink peasant blouse, multi-brights abstract-patterned gauchos & vest, hot pink "suede" fringed purse, hot pink "suede" choker, orange or hot pink suede or hot pink or lime vinyl boots, record.	375	295	320	195	135	160

VINTAGE OUTFIT ACCESSORIES
BARBIE 800 SERIES FASHIONS

STOCK NO.	OUTFIT	MINT COMPLETE		
		HIGH	LOW	AVG
874	**ARABIAN KNIGHTS**			
	Earrings	45	28	37
	Gold Bracelet	32	22	27
	Gold Slippers	28	18	23
	Lamp	38	28	33
	Necklace	24	15	20
	Pamphlet	50	35	43
	Sari	25	18	22
	Turquoise Bracelet	32	22	27
823	**BARBIE IN HOLLAND**			
	Apron	18	10	14
	Hat	18	10	14
	Pamphlet	50	35	43
	Shoes	25	12	19
	Stockings	30	20	25
821	**BARBIE IN JAPAN**			
	Fan	55	38	47
	Flower Buds	40	28	34
	Flower Hair Piece w/metal dangles	45	28	37
	Orange on Stick	95	65	80
	Pamphlet	95	55	75
	Saismen (Banjo)	40	28	34
	Sandals	95	45	70
820	**BARBIE IN MEXICO**			
	Earrings	45	28	37
	Mantilla (Shawl)	25	18	22
	Necklace	40	22	31
	Pamphlet	50	35	43
822	**BARBIE IN SWITZERLAND**			
	Bouquet	25	15	20
	Hat	18	10	14
	Pamphlet	50	35	43
889	**CANDY STRIPER VOLUNTEER**			
	Blue Plate	15	10	13
	Fork	28	20	24
	Hat	28	18	23
	Hot Water Bottle	10	5	8
	Kleenex Box	24	15	20
	Knife	28	20	24
	Orange Juice Glass	15	9	12

STOCK NO.	OUTFIT	MINT COMPLETE		
		HIGH	LOW	AVG
889	**CANDY STRIPER VOLUNTEER (continued)**			
	Soap w/"B"	15	10	13
	Spoon	24	15	20
	Straw	20	12	16
	Tennis Shoes	10	6	8
	Washcloth	28	16	22
	Watermelon Slice	20	10	15
	White Tray	18	12	15
876	**CHEERLEADER**			
	Megaphone	20	13	17
	Pom Pom ea.	24	15	20
	Red/White Tennis Shoes	20	15	18
	White Cotton Socks	20	10	15
872	**CINDERELLA**			
	Broom	24	15	20
	Long White Gloves	18	15	17
	Pamphlet	50	35	43
	Veil	75	45	60
875	**DRUM MAJORETTE**			
	Baton	25	15	20
	Boots	20	10	15
	Hat	18	10	14
	Pantyhose	25	15	20
	Short White Gloves	18	13	16
873	**GUINIVERE**			
	Armlets	45	35	40
	Hat	40	28	34
	Slippers	45	35	40
819	**IT'S COLD OUTSIDE**			
	Hat	20	15	18
880	**LITTLE RED RIDING HOOD**			
	Basket	35	22	29
	Corset	35	22	29
	Granny Cap	30	18	24
	Hunter's Cap	18	10	14
	Napkin	35	22	29
	Pamphlet	95	45	70
	Rolls	45	25	35
	Shoes	75	45	60
	White Knee High Socks	28	22	25
	Wolf Head	50	35	43

VINTAGE OUTFIT ACCESSORIES BARBIE 900 SERIES FASHIONS

STOCK NO.	OUTFIT	MINT COMPLETE		
		HIGH	LOW	AVG
934	**AFTER FIVE**			
	Hat	35	10	23
984	**AMERICAN AIRLINES STEWARDESS**			
	Black Shoulder Bag	22	12	17
	Blue Flight Bag	15	5	10
989	**BALLERINA**			
	Ballet Program	25	12	19
	Ballet Slippers	10	3	7
	Pink Ballet Bag	8	2	6
	Silver Crown	22	12	17
953	**BARBIE BABYSITS**			
	Alarm Clock	10	6	8
	Baby	18	13	16
	Baby Bottle20	10	15	
	Bassinet w/liner	15	5	10
	Black Glasses	35	15	25
	Blanket	10	5	7
	Bookstrap	15	5	10
	Coke Bottle	10	5	7
	Diaper	12	8	10
	How to Get A Raise	12	6	9
	How to Lose Weight	12	6	9
	How To Travel Book	12	6	9
	Pillow	10	3	7
	Pretzel Box	15	10	13
	Telephone List	20	13	17
	White Telephone	12	8	10
962	**BARBIE-Q**			
	Chef's Hat	15	10	13
	Knife w/red handle	12	7	10
	Red/White Checked Potholder	5	1	3
	Rolling Pin	5	1	3
	Spatula w/red handle	10	7	9
	Spoon w/red handle	10	4	7
947	**BRIDE'S DREAM**			
	Blue Garter	20	13	17
	Bouquet	18	13	16
	Elbow Length White Gloves	25	18	22
	Graduated Pearl Necklace	38	25	32
	Veil	24	15	20
981	**BUSY GAL**			
	Belt	25	18	22

VINTAGE OUTFIT ACCESSORIES
BARBIE 900 SERIES FASHIONS CONTINUED

STOCK NO.	OUTFIT	MINT COMPLETE		
		HIGH	LOW	AVG
981	**BUSY GAL** (continued)			
	Glasses	35	15	25
	Hat	25	18	22
	Portfolio	48	32	40
	Sketch	20	15	18
956	**BUSY MORNING**			
	Fruit Tote	22	13	18
	Hat	35	22	29
	Pearl Drop Necklace	95	55	75
	White Phone	12	8	10
954	**CAREER GIRL**			
	Hat	25	15	20
	Long Black Gloves	22	12	17
916	**COMMUTER SET**			
	Bracelet	50	25	38
	Hat	225	125	175
	Hatbox	275	125	200
	Necklace	50	25	38
	Short White Gloves	18	13	16
946	**DINNER AT EIGHT**			
	Gold/Cork Wedgies	24	15	20
971	**EASTER PARADE**			
	Black Patent Purse	12	9	11
	Graduated Pearl Necklace	38	25	32
	Hat	450	250	350
	Pearl Earrings	30	15	23
	Short White Gloves	18	13	16
983	**ENCHANTED EVENING**			
	Earrings	58	35	47
	Long White Gloves	18	10	14
	Three Strand Choker	60	38	49
	White Stole w/pink lining	18	10	14
961	**EVENING SPLENDOUR**			
	Aqua Envelope Purse	15	10	13
	Graduated Pearl Necklace	38	25	32
	Hat w/pearls	40	25	33
	Pearl Earrings	30	20	25
	Short White Gloves	18	13	16
	White Hankie	48	28	38
921	**FLORAL PETTICOAT**			
	Pink Brush or Comb ea.	3	1	2

VINTAGE OUTFIT ACCESSORIES
BARBIE 900 SERIES FASHIONS CONTINUED

STOCK NO.	OUTFIT	MINT COMPLETE HIGH	LOW	AVG
979	**FRIDAY NIGHT DATE**			
	Black Tray	14	8	11
	Orange Juice Glass	12	8	10
	Straw	20	14	17
931	**GARDEN PARTY**			
	Short White Gloves	18	13	16
964	**GAY PARISIENNE**			
	Gold Velvet Purse	275	125	200
	Graduated Pearl Necklace	38	25	32
	Hat	225	125	175
	Long White Gloves	18	15	17
992	**GOLDEN ELEGANCE**			
	Fur Hat w/pearls	50	25	38
	Graduated Pearl Necklace	38	25	32
	Pearl Earrings	30	20	25
	Red Velvet Purse	45	25	35
	Short White Gloves	18	13	16
	White Hankie	48	28	38
911	**GOLDEN GIRL**			
	Aqua Envelope Purse	15	10	13
	Graduated Pearl Necklace	38	25	32
	Short White Gloves	18	13	16
945	**GRADUATION**			
	Cap	15	5	10
	Diploma	20	12	16
	White Collar	18	10	14
942	**ICE BREAKER**			
	Ice Skates	15	10	13
	Pantyhose	25	15	20
957	**KNITTING PRETTY** (Pink or Royal)			
	Bowl w/yarn and needles	12	7	10
	How to Knit Book	18	13	16
	Metal Scissors	24	15	20
978	**LET'S DANCE**			
	Pearl Drop Necklace	95	55	75
	White Vinyl Purse	10	5	8
944	**MASQUERADE**			
	Black Mask	20	15	18
	Black Pantyhose	25	13	19
	Clown Hat	10	5	8
	Party Invitation	25	18	22

VINTAGE OUTFIT ACCESSORIES
BARBIE 900 SERIES FASHIONS CONTINUED

STOCK NO.	OUTFIT	MINT COMPLETE		
		HIGH	LOW	AVG
940	**MOOD FOR MUSIC**			
	3-Strand Pearl Choker	60	25	43
	Gold/Cork Wedgies	24	15	20
965	**NIGHTY NEGLIGEE**			
	Pink Dog	12	8	10
985	**OPEN ROAD**			
	Hat w/red chiffon scarf	55	30	43
	Map	25	15	20
	Red/Cork Wedgies	30	22	26
	Red Sunglasses w/blue lenses	135	95	115
987	**ORANGE BLOSSOM**			
	Bouquet	15	13	14
	Hat	22	15	19
	Short White Gloves	18	13	16
958	**PARTY DATE**			
	Gold Dimple Belt	18	13	16
	Gold Dimple Purse	10	5	8
915	**PEECHY FLEECY COAT**			
	Hat w/feather & bead	28	18	23
	Purse	10	5	8
	White Vinyl Gloves	12	8	10
967	**PICNIC SET**			
	Basket	20	10	15
	Fish on Pole	110	75	93
	Straw/Cork Wedgies	35	22	29
966	**PLANTATION BELLE**			
	Graduated Pink Pearl Necklace	48	25	37
	Pink Pearl Earrings	75	25	50
	Pink Snake Bracelet	55	35	45
	Short White Gloves	18	13	16
949	**RAINCOAT** (aka Stormy Weather)			
	Boots	12	5	9
	Hat	10	5	8
	Umbrella w/tassel	18	10	14
939	**RED FLARE**			
	Long White Gloves	18	15	17
	Pillbox Hat	24	12	18
	Purse	15	8	12
991	**REGISTERED NURSE**			
	Black Glasses	35	15	25
	Diploma	25	18	22
	Hat	20	10	15

STOCK NO.	OUTFIT	MINT COMPLETE HIGH	LOW	AVG
991	**REGISTERED NURSE** (continued)			
	Hot Water Bottle	10	5	8
	Medicine Bottle	25	15	20
	Metal Spoon	24	15	20
963	**RESORT SET**			
	Gold Charm Bracelet	45	38	42
	Visor	15	10	13
	White/Cork Wedgies	22	12	17
968	**ROMAN HOLIDAY**			
	Black Glasses	35	15	25
	Brass Compact w/puff	950	550	750
	Hat	395	225	310
	Pearl Drop Necklace	95	55	75
	Pink Comb	8	5	7
	Short White Gloves	18	13	16
	Vinyl w/plastic window Eyeglass Case	250	125	188
	White Hankie	48	28	38
	White Vinyl Clutch	10	5	8
986	**SHEATH SENSATION**			
	Hat	38	25	32
	Short White Gloves	18	13	16
977	**SILKEN FLAME**			
	Gold Dimple Belt	18	13	16
	Gold Dimple Purse	10	5	8
988	**SINGING IN THE SHOWER**			
	Back Brush w/sponge	12	5	9
	Blue "Hers" Towel	8	5	7
	Blue Washcloth	7	3	5
	Powder Puff	8	3	6
	Shower Cap	10	3	7
	Slippers	8	2	5
	Soap	7	2	5
	Talc Box w/lid	10	5	8
948	**SKI QUEEN**			
	Blue Glasses	18	13	16
	Red Nylon Gloves pr.	15	10	13
	Skis pr.	15	10	13
	Ski Poles pr.	20	12	16
982	**SOLO IN THE SPOTLIGHT**			
	Long Black Gloves	22	12	17
	Microphone	110	50	80
	Necklace	48	38	43
	Scarf	35	22	29

VINTAGE OUTFIT ACCESSORIES
BARBIE 900 SERIES FASHIONS CONTINUED

STOCK NO.	OUTFIT	MINT COMPLETE HIGH	LOW	AVG
993	**SOPHISTICATED LADY**			
	Long White Gloves	18	15	17
	Pink Pearl Necklace	48	35	42
	Tiara	110	75	93
937	**SORORITY MEETING**			
	Graduated Pearl Necklace	38	25	32
	Hat	18	10	14
	Pearl Earrings	35	20	28
969	**SUBURBAN SHOPPER**			
	Fruit Tote	32	15	24
	Hat	48	24	36
	Pearl Drop Necklace	95	55	75
	Pink Phone w/metal dial	20	14	17
976	**SWEATER GIRL**			
	Bowl of Yarn w/needles	10	5	8
	How to Knit Book	12	8	10
	Metal Scissors	22	15	19
973	**SWEET DREAMS** (Pink or Yellow)			
	Blue Hair Ribbon w/ring	18	12	15
	Brass Clock	10	6	8
	Dear Diary	12	8	10
	Pink Hair Ribbon w/ring	25	18	22
	Wax Apple	25	10	18
955	**SWINGIN' EASY**			
	Pearl Drop Necklace	95	55	75
	White Clutch	12	7	10
941	**TENNIS ANYONE?**			
	Blue Glasses	18	3	16
	Tennis Ball	13	5	9
	Tennis Racket	10	2	6
	Tennis Rules Book	15	10	13
	Tennis Shoes	10	6	8
	White Cotton Socks	20	10	15
959	**THEATRE DATE**			
	Green Pillbox Hat	25	15	20
972	**WEDDING DAY SET**			
	Blue Garter	20	12	16
	Bouquet	18	13	16
	Short White Gloves	18	13	16
	Veil	24	15	20
975	**WINTER HOLIDAY**			
	Plaid Bag	12	4	8
	Red Vinyl Gloves	12	10	11
	White/Cork Wedgies	20	15	18

VINTAGE OUTFIT ACCESSORIES
BARBIE 1600 SERIES FASHIONS

STOCK NO.	OUTFIT	MINT COMPLETE		
		HIGH	LOW	AVG
1631	**ABOARD SHIP**			
	Camera	40	28	34
	Hawaii Travel Brochure	25	20	23
	How to Travel Book	12	6	9
	Mexico Travel Brochure	25	20	23
	Niagra Travel Brochure	28	24	26
	Red Belt	30	24	27
	Travel Poster	55	45	50
1605	**BARBIE IN HAWAII**			
	Ankle Lei	75	45	60
	Neck Lei	15	10	13
	Pineapple	20	15	18
1634	**BARBIE LEARNS TO COOK**			
	Double Boiler	25	18	22
	Easy As Pie Cookbook	22	15	19
	Large Pan w/lid	18	13	16
	Medium Pan w/lid	18	13	16
	Pink Belt	28	22	25
	Potholder	25	20	23
	Small Pan w/lid	15	10	13
	Toast ea.	15	10	13
	Toaster	15	10	13
1698	**BEAUTIFUL BRIDE**			
	Blue Garter	20	13	17
	Bouquet	155	95	125
	Short White Gloves	18	13	16
	Veil	145	95	120
1667	**BENEFIT PERFORMANCE**			
	Long White Gloves	18	15	17
1609	**BLACK MAGIC ENSEMBLE**			
	Gold Dimple Purse	10	5	8
	Short Black Gloves	65	45	55
1628	**BRUNCH TIME**			
	Casserole Handle	55	35	45
	Coffee Pot w/lid	15	10	13
	Large Casserole w/lid	15	10	13
	Medium Casserole w/lid	15	10	13
	Small Casserole w/lid	15	8	12
1616	**CAMPUS SWEETHEART**			
	Bouquet	250	195	223
	Long White Gloves	18	15	17
	Pink Pearl Necklace	50	38	44
	Trophy	250	195	223
1687	**CARIBBEAN CRUISE**			
	Yellow Soft Pointed Flats	35	24	30

STOCK NO.	OUTFIT	MINT COMPLETE HIGH	LOW	AVG
1627	**COUNTRY CLUB DANCE**			
	Gold Dimple Purse	10	5	8
	Graduated Pearl Necklace	38	25	32
	Long White Gloves	18	15	17
1603	**COUNTRY FAIR**			
	Orange Envelope Purse	10	5	8
1604	**CRISP 'N COOL**			
	Purse	22	14	18
	Short White Gloves	18	13	16
1626	**DANCING DOLL**			
	Blue Label Record	15	10	13
	Blue Record Player	15	13	14
	Pink Belt	50	38	44
	Red Label Record	15	10	13
1666	**DEBUTANTE BALL**			
	Gold Dimple Purse	10	5	8
	Long White Gloves	18	15	17
	Pearl Drop Necklace	95	55	75
1633	**DISC DATE**			
	Blue Label Record	15	10	13
	Blue Record Player	15	12	14
	Red Label Record	15	10	13
1613	**DOG 'N DUDS**			
	Black Mask	20	15	18
	Black/White Collar	15	10	13
	Clown Hat	10	5	8
	Dog Bone	20	15	18
	Dog Food Bowl	20	15	18
	Dog Food Box	18	14	16
	Ear Muffs	15	10	13
	Gray Poodle	55	38	47
	Plaid Coat	10	3	7
	Red Collar w/chain leash	18	12	15
	Red Collar w/stretch leash	18	12	15
	Red Velvet Coat	10	3	7
	Tutu	18	10	14
1669	**DREAMLAND**			
	White Brush	5	3	4
	White Comb	5	3	4
1635	**FASHION EDITOR**			
	Camera	40	28	34
	Hat	145	95	120
1656	**FASHION LUNCHEON**			
	Hat	275	225	250
	Long White Gloves	18	15	17

STOCK NO.	OUTFIT	MINT COMPLETE		
		HIGH	LOW	AVG
1691	**FASHION SHINER**			
	Purse	28	18	23
	Short White Gloves	18	15	17
1696	**FLOATING GARDENS**			
	Bracelet ea.	45	28	37
	Earrings	55	25	40
1638	**FRATERNITY DANCE**			
	Long White Gloves	18	15	17
	Pearl Drop Necklace	95	55	75
1619	**FUN 'N GAMES**			
	Ball	15	10	13
	Mallet	15	10	13
	Metal Wickets	27	18	23
	Stake	24	18	21
1624	**FUN AT THE FAIR**			
	Cotton Candy	115	45	80
	Head Scarf	25	18	22
	Red/White Tennis Shoes	20	15	18
1606	**GARDEN TEA PARTY**			
	Short White Gloves	18	13	16
1647	**GOLD 'N GLAMOUR**			
	Graduated Pearl Necklace	38	25	32
	Long Brown Gloves	245	165	205
1610	**GOLDEN EVENING**			
	Charm Bracelet	45	28	37
	Gold Dimple Belt	18	13	16
1645	**GOLDEN GLORY**			
	Purse	95	65	80
	Short White Gloves	18	13	16
1664	**HERE COMES THE BRIDE**			
	Blue Garter	24	15	20
	Bouquet	225	175	200
	Long White Gloves	18	12	15
1639	**HOLIDAY DANCE**			
	Gold Dimple Purse	10	5	8
	Long White Gloves	18	15	17
	Orange Sash	135	95	115
	White CT Heels	55	45	50
1653	**INTERNATIONAL FAIR**			
	Camera	40	28	34
1632	**INVITATION TO TEA**			
	Pink Cup	25	20	23
	Pink Saucer	25	20	23
	Silver Belt	35	25	30
	Silver Tea Pot	25	15	20

STOCK NO.	OUTFIT	MINT COMPLETE		
		HIGH	LOW	AVG
1620	**JUNIOR DESIGNER**			
	Appliques ea.	25	18	22
	Belt	50	35	43
	How to Design Fashions Book	25	18	22
	Iron	22	15	19
1614	**JUNIOR PROM**			
	Long White Gloves	18	15	17
	Pearl Drop Necklace	95	55	75
1621	**KNIT HIT**			
	Mattel Newspaper	65	45	55
	Soft Red Pointed Flats	30	24	27
1661	**LONDON TOUR**			
	Hat	40	28	34
	Purse	40	28	34
	Scarf	95	55	75
1649	**LUNCH ON THE TERRACE**			
	Hat	75	50	63
1646	**MAGNIFICENCE**			
	Slip	95	45	70
1640	**MATINEE FASHION**			
	Hat w/chiffon scarf	150	110	130
1617	**MIDNIGHT BLUE**			
	Graduated Pearl Necklace	38	25	32
	Silver Dimple Purse	27	18	23
1641	**MISS ASTRONAUT**			
	Boots	85	65	75
	Flag	95	35	65
	Gloves	85	65	75
	Helmet	225	145	185
1625	**MODERN ART**			
	Painting	110	45	78
	Program	120	75	98
1663	**MUSIC CENTER MATINEE**			
	Hat	95	55	75
1644	**ON THE AVENUE**			
	Gold Dimple Purse	10	5	8
	Graduated Pearl Necklace	38	25	32
	Short White Gloves	18	13	16
1650	**OUTDOOR ART SHOW**			
	Hat	150	110	130
1637	**OUTDOOR LIFE**			
	Hat	35	28	32
	White Tennis Shoes	10	6	8
1601	**PAJAMA PARTY**			
	Alarm Clock	10	6	8

VINTAGE OUTFIT ACCESSORIES
BARBIE 1600 SERIES FASHIONS CONTINUED

STOCK NO.	OUTFIT	MINT COMPLETE		
		HIGH	LOW	AVG
1678	**PAN AMERICAN AIRLINES STEWARDESS**			
	Black Shoulder Bag	22	12	17
	Hat w/emblem	600	395	498
	Short White Gloves	18	13	16
1692	**PATIO PARTY**			
	Earrings	45	25	35
1648	**PHOTO FASHION**			
	Camera	40	28	34
	Soft Pointed Turquoise Flats	25	18	22
1643	**POODLE PARADE**			
	Brown Sunglasses	195	125	160
	Certificate	120	95	108
	Dickey	50	35	43
	Head Scarf	45	32	39
	Purse	75	45	60
	Trophy	150	110	130
1652	**PRETTY AS A PICTURE**			
	Hat	95	75	85
1686	**PRINT A PLENTY**			
	Hot Pink Earrings	48	35	42
1654	**RECEPTION LINE**			
	Hat	145	110	128
1668	**RIDING IN THE PARK**			
	Boots	28	20	24
	Crop	145	110	128
	Hat	28	20	24
1611	**SATIN 'N ROSE**			
	Hat	25	20	23
	Rhinestone Earrings	65	25	45
1615	**SATURDAY MATINEE**			
	Hat	125	95	110
	Purse	245	195	220
	Short Brown Gloves	150	125	138
1664	**SHIMMERING MAGIC**			
	Hat	395	295	345
1629	**SKATER'S WALTZ**			
	Collar	65	45	55
	Mittens	65	45	55
	Pantyhose	25	15	20
	Skates	15	10	13
1608	**SKIN DIVER**			
	Flippers	8	3	6
	Mask	7	3	5
	Snorkel	5	3	4

VINTAGE OUTFIT ACCESSORIES
BARBIE 1600 SERIES FASHIONS CONTINUED

STOCK NO.	OUTFIT	MINT COMPLETE		
		HIGH	LOW	AVG
1636	**SLEEPING PRETTY**			
	Blue OT Heels w/Blue Poms	25	18	22
	Blue Satin Pillow	25	15	20
	White Brush	7	3	5
	White Comb	7	3	5
1642	**SLUMBER PARTY**			
	Blue Brush	7	3	5
	Blue Comb	7	3	5
	How to Lose Weight Book	12	6	9
	Rollers (6) ea.	7	4	6
	Scale	12	8	10
1622	**STUDENT TEACHER**			
	Black Glasses	35	15	25
	Geography Book	20	12	16
	Globe	40	35	38
	Pointer	75	55	65
1690	**STUDIO TOUR**			
	Hat no ties	38	30	34
	Hat w/ties	45	35	40
	Red CT Heels	35	25	30
1683	**SUNFLOWER**			
	Earrings	75	45	60
	Hot Pink Bracelets ea.	65	35	50
1688	**TRAVEL TOGETHERS**			
	Hat	20	15	18
1685	**UNDERPRINTS**			
	Turquoise "B" Mirror	8	5	7
	Turquoise Brush	8	5	7
	Turquoise Comb	5	3	4
	Turquoise Princess Phone	12	8	10
1625	**VACATION TIME**			
	Camera	40	28	34
	Soft Pink Pointed Flats	25	18	22
1607	**WHITE MAGIC**			
	Hat	25	18	22
	Short White Gloves	18	13	16
	Silver Dimple Purse	27	18	23
	Black Socks	5	3	4
	Striped Tie	15	10	13
	Brown Dress Shoes	5	3	4
	Long Olive Socks	8	6	7

MOD ERA BARBIE® ACCESSORIES

STOCK NO.	OUTFIT	MINT COMPLETE		
		HIGH	LOW	AVG
1055	**COUNTRY MUSIC**			
	45 RPM Record "Here in Nashville"	75	35	55
	White Open Weave Shawl	46	30	38
	White Soft Lace Up Boots w/red painted laces	24	12	18
1056	**FESTIVAL FASHION**			
	45 RPM Record "Fly, Children, Fly"	75	35	55
	Brown Soft Lace Up Boots	15	5	10
	Brown Suede Corset w/laces	48	24	36
	Brown Suede Boots w/pink cord laces	38	18	28
	Coral Nylon Head Scarf	46	30	38
1057	**GROOVIN' GAUCHOS**			
	45 RPM Record "Rapping in Rhythm"	75	35	55
	Hot Pink Neck piece w/round gold buckle	72	24	48
	Hot Pink Soft Lace Up Boots	24	12	18
	Hot Pink Suede High Heeled Boots	29	15	22
	Hot Pink Suede Shoulder Bag	30	18	24
	Lime Green Soft Lace Up Boots	11	5	8
	Orange Suede Boots w/fringe	24	12	18
1061	**POODLE DOODLES**			
	Aqua Suede Dog Collar on chain w/aqua suede hand grip	125	65	95
	Black Poodle	225	125	175
	Black w/multicolored floral print Boots	75	35	55
1062	**KITTY CAPERS**			
	Yellow Plastic Food Bowl	65	25	45
	White Fuzzy Cat	225	125	175
	White Vinyl Lace Up Boots	12	8	10
1063	**HOT TOGS**			
	Beige fuzzy Acrylic Afghan Dog	125	65	95
	Brown Cotton Suede Belt	62	38	50
	Brown Cotton Suede Dog Collar w/Brown Cotton Suede Leash	75	35	55
	Lime Green Sheer Pantyhose	48	28	38
	Olive Green Knit Cap	30	18	24
	Olive Green Knit Thigh High Stockings	56	24	40
	Soft Brown Lace Up Boots	12	8	10
1193	**PERFECTLY PLAID**			
	Fuzzy White Hat	250	105	145
	Red Soft Pointed Flats	33	15	24
	White Vinyl Clutch w/white bead	35	15	25
1247	**STROLLIN' IN STYLE**			
	Blue Cotton Suede dog Collar w/silver buckle	96	55	75
	Blue Sheer Nylon Head Scarf	35	15	24
	Blue/Yellow Hollow Plastic Ball	46	30	38

MOD ERA BARBIE® ACCESSORIES

STOCK NO.	OUTFIT	MINT COMPLETE		
		HIGH	LOW	AVG
1247	STROLLIN' IN STYLE (continued)			
	Red Vinyl Boots (Twiggy style)	33	15	24
	White Fuzzy Poodle	275	95	180
	White Panties w/scalloped edge	24	12	18
	Yellow Plastic Bowl w/red food	65	25	45
1440	PINK SPARKLE			
	Cape	96	55	75
1452	NOW KNIT			
	Green Furry Hat w/royal blue ribbon	18	10	14
	Royal Blue Nylon Neck Scarf	46	30	38
1459	GREAT COAT			
	Yellow Vinyl Hat w/leopard Trim	28	15	22
1462	RARE PAIR			
	Yellow Sheer Nylon Hose	46	30	38
1463	LOVELY SLEEP-INS			
	Plush Fuzzy Slippers	15	5	10
1464	ANTI-FREEZERS			
	Orange/White Plaid Scarf	24	12	18
	Yellow Soft Boots (Twiggy style)	33	15	24
1465	LEMON KICK			
	Thin Yellow Vinyl Shorts	35	15	25
1467	LAMB 'N LEATHER			
	Pink Boots w/black trim	46	24	35
	Pink Purse w/black trim	46	30	38
	Shiny Black/Pink Belt	55	35	45
	Short Black Gloves	65	45	55
	White Furry Hat	36	24	30
1470	INTRIGUE			
	Gold Foil Belt	45	28	36
1476	DREAM WRAP			
	Pink Felt Slippers w/flower accent	18	12	15
1478	SHIFT INTO KNIT			
	Gold Chain Belt w/gold disk accent	33	15	24
	Orange Knit Scarf w/fringe tips	36	24	30
1483	LITTLE BOW-PINK			
	Hot Pink Cotton Mesh Hose	46	30	38
1484	YELLOW MELLOW			
	Yellow Lacy Fishnet Hose	46	30	38
1486	WINTER WOW			
	Brown Plush Bonnet	28	15	22
	Brown Plush Muff	28	15	22

STOCK NO.	OUTFIT	MINT COMPLETE		
		HIGH	LOW	AVG
1486	**WINTER WOW** (continued)			
	Gold Foil Belt w/square buckle	24	12	18
	Gold Thigh High Boots	36	24	30
1487	**SHIRTDRESSY**			
	Yellow Sheer Nylon Hose	46	30	38
1489	**CLOUD 9**			
	Coral/Blue Satin Booties	18	12	15
1491	**RED, WHITE, 'N WARM**			
	Boots w/gold chain w/gold bead	48	32	40
	Hat	40	24	32
	White Belt with oval gold buckle	33	15	24
1493	**FAB FUR**			
	Gold Lamé Pantyhose style boots	40	24	32
1508	**FASHION 'N MOTION**			
	45 RPM Record	75	35	55
	Orange Cotton Suede Boots w/scallop edge	40	24	32
1544	**TRAVEL IN STYLE**			
	Green/Blue/White Hatbox	62	42	52
	Royal Blue Sheer Nylon Hose	115	55	85
1545	**STRIPES ARE HAPPENIN'**			
	Multicolored Striped Knee Socks	125	75	100
1547	**GLIMMER GLAMOUR**			
	Gold Dimple Belt	24	12	18
	Shimmery Butterscotch Sheer Hose	325	265	295
1551	**DINNER DAZZLE**			
	Pink Sheer Nylon Hose	55	30	45
1552	**SILVER 'N SATIN**			
	Hot Pink Nylon Petticoat	35	15	25
	Hot Pink Sheer Nylon Hose	52	38	45
	Silver Foil Belt w/silver buckle	55	38	45
1584	**FURRY FRIENDS**			
	Dog Bone	14	10	12
	Dog Food Box	12	8	10
	Gray Poodle	55	30	45
	Hot Pink Vinyl Collar w/leash	96	55	75
	Orange Boots (Twiggy style)	33	15	24
	Orange Plush Hat	35	15	25
	Yellow Dog Food Bowl	46	24	35
	Yellow Nylon Panty w/scallop edge	24	12	18
1588	**SWINGIN' IN SILVER**			
	Silver Lamé Boots w/white fur trim at top	165	135	150

STOCK NO.	OUTFIT	MINT COMPLETE		
		HIGH	LOW	AVG
1591	**NITE LIGHTNING**			
	Royal Blue Sheer Nylon Hose	325	265	295
	—Twinkle Town			
	Hot Pink Sheer Nylon Hose	52	38	45
	Hot Pink Soft Bow Heels	18	12	15
1592	**GOLDEN GROOVE**			
	Gold Lamé Thigh High Boots	36	24	30
1595	**FABULOUS FORMAL**			
	Silver Knit Purse lined in yellow	55	35	45
	Yellow Nylon Flower Earrings	62	42	52
1596	**PINK PREMIERE**			
	Gold Lame Gloves	35	15	25
	Hot Pink Nylon Pantyhose w/mesh panty	34	22	28
	Pink Satin Purse w/gold trim	35	15	25
1751	**LEATHER WEATHER**			
	Red Vinyl Purse	45	28	36
1753	**CANDLELIGHT CAPERS**			
	Yellow Velour Hat	45	28	36
1754	**PINK FANTASY**			
	Gold Lamé Booties w/pink nylon poufs	34	22	28
1775	**STRIPES AWAY**			
	Color Changer Applicator w/sponge	18	12	15
	Color Change Packet A & B ea.	35	15	25
	Pink Snake Bracelet (2) ea.	45	28	36
1776	**SMART SWITCH**			
	Color Changer Applicator w/sponge	18	12	15
	Color Change Packet A & B ea.	35	15	25
	Head Scarf	85	45	65
1777	**PRETTY WILD!**			
	Hat	96	55	75
	Color Changer Applicator w/sponge	18	12	15
	Color Change Packet A & B ea.	35	15	25
	Tote Bag	85	45	65
1778	**BLOOM BURSTS**			
	Color Changer Applicator w/sponge	18	12	15
	Color Change Packet A & B ea.	35	15	25
	Pink Silk Organza Hat	145	95	120
1779	**MIX 'N MATCHERS**			
	Color Change Packet A & B ea.	35	15	25
	Hot Pink Soft Pointed Flats	28	15	22
	Metal Spoon w/red handle tip	11	3	7
	Red or Pink Color Changer Applicator	25	15	20

STOCK NO.	OUTFIT	MINT COMPLETE		
		HIGH	LOW	AVG
1779	MIX 'N MATCHERS (continued)			
	Straw Hat w/yellow silk scarf	55	35	45
	Yellow Color Changer Applicator w/sponge	18	12	15
	Yellow Plastic Bowl	15	10	13
1781	TENNIS TEAM			
	Plastic Tennis Racket	7	1	4
	White Plastic Tennis Ball	10	2	6
	White Vinyl Sneakers	10	2	6
1782	SHAPE-UPS			
	Black Plastic Dumbell	3	1	2
	Black Elastic Exercise Cord	18	12	15
	Paper Living Barbie Exercise Book	20	8	14
	Red Sheer Nylon Hose	28	15	22
	Red Soft Buckle Flats	36	20	28
	Twist Board with or without stirrups	14	10	12
1783	RUFFLES 'N SWIRLS			
	Pink Vinyl Belt w/silver oval buckle	24	12	18
1787	PRIMA BALLERINA			
	Hot Pink Sheer Nylon Pantyhose (tights)	24	12	18
	Hot Pink Soft Ballet Slipers	11	5	8
1788	SCUBA-DO'S			
	Orange Plastic Snorkle	6	2	4
	Orange Vinyl Mask w/elastic strap	9	3	6
	Orange Vinyl Swim Fins	6	2	4
1789	FIERY FELT			
	Orange Felt Hat w/fringe	33	15	24
	Orange Soft Vinyl Rain Boots	18	12	15
1792	MOOD MATCHERS			
	Aqua Vinyl Belt w/silver oval buckle	30	18	24
1793	SKATE MATES			
	Hot Coral Plush Mittens	28	15	22
	Hot Coral Sheer Nylon Pantyhose (tights)	28	15	22
	Hot Coral Suede Bonnet w/plush trim	24	12	18
	White Skates w/gray plastic blades	18	12	15
1796	SKI SCENE, THE			
	2 Orange Plastic Skis	14	10	12
	2 Wood Ski Poles w/orange grips/snowflakes	18	12	15
	Orange Soft Ski Boots	11	5	8
	Orange Vinyl Hood w/gray lining	24	12	18
	Orange Vinyl Ski Mask w/clear plastic lense	28	15	22
1798	RAINBOW WRAPS			
	Hot Coral Sheer Nylon Petticoat	51	45	48

MOD ERA BARBIE® ACCESSORIES CONTINUED

STOCK NO.	OUTFIT	MINT COMPLETE HIGH	LOW	AVG
1799	**MAXI 'N MINI**			
	Blue Lamé Hip Length Boots	38	22	30
1805	**BOUNCY FLOUNCY**			
	Tote	55	35	45
1806	**PAJAMA POW**			
	Pink/Red/Gold Metallic Dangle Earrings	150	100	125
	Yellow Soft Pointed Heels	33	15	24
1808	**DRIZZLE DASH**			
	Hot Pink/Orange Vinyl Head Scarf	35	15	25
	Orange Rain Boots	18	12	15
1809	**MINIPRINTS**			
	Multicolored Abstract Hose	82	42	62
1810	**BERMUDA HOLIDAYS**			
	Hot Pink Soft Pointed Flats	28	15	22
	Multicolored Abstract Hat	55	35	45
1813	**SNUG FUZZ**			
	Shiny White Vinyl Belt	35	15	25
	Silver Mesh Hose	33	15	24
1814	**SPARKLE SQUARES**			
	Silver Dimple Purse	33	15	24
	White Sheer Nylon Hose	48	32	40
1815	**WEEKENDERS**			
	Hot Pink/Burgundy/Green Hat w/green visor	185	125	155
	Hot Pink Soft Pointed Flats	28	15	22
1816	**YELLOW GO, THE**			
	Light Blue Vinyl Purse w/gold Chain Strap	150	100	125
	Pale Yellow Lacy Textured Hose	96	55	75
	Yellow Hood w/attached scarf	175	95	135
1817	**RED FANTASTIC**			
	Coral Pink Closed Toe Heels	46	24	35
	Coral Pink Satin Cape w/white marabou	300	265	285
1820	**ZOKKO!**			
	Orange Plastic Dangle Earrings	55	35	45
	Silver Boots w/orange trim	28	15	22
1821	**UNDERLINERS**			
	Beige Sheer Nylon Hose	48	32	40
1822	**SWIRLY-CUE**			
	Pink/Green Plastic Dangle Earrings	55	35	45
1824	**SNAP DASH**			
	Green Felt Cowboy-style Hat	33	15	24
	Yellow Cotton Knee Socks	28	15	22

165

STOCK NO.	OUTFIT	MINT COMPLETE HIGH	LOW	AVG
1842	**TOGETHERNESS**			
	Aqua Knit Bonnet w/floral print	25	15	20
	Aqua Knit Stockings w/floral print	24	12	18
1844	**EXTRAVAGANZA**			
	Long Hot Pink Gloves	75	35	55
	Silver Dimple Purse	33	15	24
1846	**TRAILBLAZERS**			
	Green Plastic Sunglasses w/pink stripes	125	65	95
1848	**ALL THAT JAZZ**			
	Beige Sheer Nylon Hose	48	32	40
	Thin Gold Foil Belt (rare)	140	45	95
1849	**WEDDING WONDER**			
	Bouquet	85	45	65
	Circular Net Veil	95	55	75
1853	**NOW WOW!**			
	Blue Majorette Boots trimmed in yellow	24	12	18
	Corduroy Bonnet	30	18	24
	Pale Blue Sheer Nylon Hose	36	24	30
1854	**TWINKLE TOGS**			
	Lime Green Sheer Nylons	48	32	40
1856	**WILD 'N WONDERFUL**			
	Orange Vinyl Panty	33	15	24
	Orange Vinyl Roman-style Sandals	55	35	45
1857	**DREAMY PINK**			
	Hot Pink Felt Slippers	18	12	15
1858	**FANCY-DANCY**			
	Pale Pink Sheer Hose w/floral pattern	55	35	45
1859	**TUNIC 'N TIGHTS**			
	Hot Pink/Yellow Striped Tights	45	28	36
1860	**SMASHEROO**			
	Gold Chain Belt w/hook closure	36	20	28
	Red Soft Riding Boots	24	12	18
	Yellow Plush Hat	28	15	22
	Yellow Textured Hose	34	22	28
1861	**MAKE MINE MIDI**			
	Hot Pink Half Slip	24	12	18
	Hot Pink Sheer Nylon Hose	36	24	30
1862	**COUNTRY CAPERS**			
	Yellow Soft Pointed Flats	30	18	24
1864	**CLOSE-UPS**			
	Hot Pink Cotton Mesh Bra	16	8	12
	Pink Nylon Pantyhose w/mesh panty	12	8	10

MOD ERA BARBIE® ACCESSORIES CONTINUED

STOCK NO.	OUTFIT	MINT COMPLETE HIGH	LOW	AVG
1866	**MOVIE GROOVIE**			
	Hot Pink Sheer Nylon Hose	52	38	45
1868	**HAPPY GO PINK**			
	Hot Pink Sheer Nylon Hose	52	38	45
	Pink Sheer Nylon Hose	52	38	45
1869	**MIDI-MAGIC**			
	Black Sheer Nylon Hose	56	40	48
1870	**MIDI-MARVELOUS**			
	White Nylon Hat w/eyelet & pink trim	35	15	25
	White Sheer Nylon Hose	48	32	40
1871	**ROMANTIC RUFFLES**			
	Pink Nylon Rosette on Chain Earrings	62	42	52
	Silver Purse lined in pink	36	24	30
1872	**SEE-WORTHY**			
	Aqua Knit Knee Socks	36	24	30
	Aqua Ribbed Hat w/gold pom	35	15	25
	Aqua Sneakers	25	15	20
	Black/Gray Camera	36	20	28
	Gold Satin Neck Tie	115	55	85
1873	**PLUSH PONY**			
	Orange Soft Rain Boots	18	10	14
1874	**FAB CITY**			
	Short Hot Pink Gloves	68	48	58
	Silver Thread Stole	25	15	20
1880	**WINTER WEDDING**			
	Bouquet	36	20	28
	Veil	28	15	22
1881	**MADE FOR EACH OTHER**			
	Orange Vinyl Belt w/round buckle	28	15	22
	Orange Plush Hat	36	20	28
	Yellow/Orange Double Strand Necklace	46	24	35
	Orange Soft Riding Boots	36	24	30
3215	**ROYAL VELVET**			
	White Fuzzy Muff w/deep rose handle	155	125	140
	Hot Pink Sheer Nylon Petticoat	165	135	150
3216	**MAJESTIC BLUE**			
	White Plush Jacket	95	55	75
	Red Satin Roses w/Miss America Streamer	160	110	135
3217	**REGAL RED**			
	Hot Coral Cape line w/pale yellow fur	145	95	120
	Gold Foil Belt	36	20	28

STOCK NO.	OUTFIT	MINT COMPLETE HIGH	LOW	AVG
3217	**REGAL RED** (continued)			
	Bright Yellow Long Gloves	145	95	120
	Gold Dimple Purse	8	2	5
3303	**BEAUTIFUL BLUES**			
	Shiny Blue Vinyl Clutch	175	95	135
3335	**FURRY 'N FUN**			
	Red Vinyl Belt w/square buckle	46	24	35
	White Soft Lace Up Boots	15	5	10
3336	**FURRY 'N FUN**			
	Red Vinyl Belt w/square buckle	36	20	28
	White Lace Up Boots	12	8	10
3337	**ALL AMERICAN GIRL**			
	Royal Blue Nylon Tights	18	12	15
3338	**MAINLY FOR RAIN**			
	Red/Blue/Green/Black Houndstooth Hat	18	12	15
	Royal Blue Soft Lace Up Boots	11	5	8
3339	**LIGHT 'N LAZY**			
	White Nylon Panty	18	12	15
	White Nylon Booties	18	12	15
3340	**GOLDEN GLITTER**			
	Butterscotch Gold Satin Purse	18	12	15
	Yellow Sheer Nylon Pantyhose	33	15	24
	Butterscotch Gold Low Hard Heels	18	12	15
3350	**SWEET DREAMS**			
	Pink Felt Booties w/gold button	14	10	12
	Pink Mirror	8	2	5
	Pink Comb	8	2	5
	Pink Brush	8	2	5
3351	**GOOD SPORTS**			
	Purple Scarf w/floral print	18	10	14
	Brown Vinyl Belt	24	12	18
	Red Plastic Sunglasses	14	10	12
	White Sneakers	10	2	6
3352	**WHITE 'N WITH IT**			
	Gold Lamé Duffle Bag-style Purse	24	12	18
3355	**PICTURE ME PRETTY**			
	White Half Slip trimmed w/lace	16	8	12
	White Panty trimmed w/lace	18	10	14
3357	**SILVER BLUES**			
	Purple Sheer Nylon Scarf	28	18	24
3358	**LOVELY 'N LAVENDER**			
	White Plastic Tumbler	24	12	18

STOCK NO.	OUTFIT	MINT COMPLETE		
		HIGH	LOW	AVG
3358	**LOVELY 'N LAVENDER (continued)**			
	White Plastic Pitcher	28	15	22
3359	**PANTS-PERFECT PURPLE**			
	Double Gold Chain Belt w/hooks	24	15	18
	Plush "cat print" Purse w/black braid strap	18	12	15
3360	**PLEASANTLY PEASANTY**			
	Half Slip with eyelet trim	26	18	22
	Black Velvet Mini Corset w/braid ties	18	12	15
3361	**SWEETHEART SATIN**			
	Veil w/lace Cap w/white satin bow/streamers	75	35	55
	Bouquet	62	34	48
3362	**FANCY THAT PURPLE**			
	Purple Cotton Suede Shell	36	28	32
	Gold Lame Hot Pants	24	12	18
	Purple Sheer Pantyhose	30	18	24
3401	**FRINGE BENEFITS**			
	Orange Cotton Suede Boots w/fringe	28	15	22
3403	**BABY DOLL PINKS**			
	Pink Plush Slippers	25	15	20
3406	**EVENING IN**			
	Triangle Earrings (Casey)	28	15	22
	Pink Plastic Snake Bracelet	30	18	24
3408	**SUPER SCARF**			
	Red Knit Scarf w/fringe	30	18	24
	Red Soft Vinyl Rain Boots	16	8	12
3409	**RED FOR RAIN**			
	Red Cotton Twill Bonnet	24	12	18
	White Soft Vinyl Rain Boots	6	4	5
3411	**PONCHO PUT-ON**			
	Yellow Knit Hood w/orange visor	36	20	28
3413	**GOLFING GREATS**			
	Multicolored Cap w/aqua vinyl visor	18	12	15
	Aqua Knit Knee Socks	25	15	20
	Red Plastic Sunglasses	28	15	22
	2 White Plastic Golf Balls	6	2	4
	Aqua Sneakers	24	12	18
	Black/Silver Putter	11	5	8
	Black/Silver and brown plastic Golf Club	11	5	8
	Multicolored Golf Bag w/yellow vinyl trim	14	10	12
3414	**SATIN SLUMBER**			
	Ice Blue Satin Belt w/sheet nylon trim	25	15	20
	Ice Blue Satin Booties	30	18	24

MOD ERA BARBIE® ACCESSORIES CONTINUED

STOCK NO.	OUTFIT	MINT COMPLETE		
		HIGH	LOW	AVG
3416	**WILD 'N WINTERY**			
	Pink Sheer Nylon Pantyhose	38	25	32
	White Vinyl "Alligator" Textured Belt	88	48	68
	White Vinyl "Alligator" Textured Boots	145	75	110
3417	**BRIDAL BROCADE**			
	Net Veil made of the gown material	52	38	45
	Bouquet	52	38	45
3418	**MAGNIFICENT MIDI**			
	Red Cotton Suede Hat w/fur trim	46	30	38
	Black Shiny Vinyl Boots w/fur trim	88	48	68
3419	**SILVER SERENADE**			
	Aqua Boa	46	24	35
	Aqua Sheer Nylon Pantyhose	46	30	38
	Gray Plastic/Silver Metal Microphone	125	65	95
3421	**BUBBLES 'N BOOTS**			
	Purple Cotton Suede Belt w/gold foil back	52	32	42
	Purple Cotton Suede High Heeled Boots	30	18	24
3423	**NIGHT LIGHTER**			
	Purple Cotton Suede Belt	46	30	38
3426	**TURTLE 'N TIGHTS**			
	Orange Cotton Suede Belt	38	25	32
	Blue Soft Pointed Flats	25	15	20
3427	**DREAM TEAM, THE**			
	White Felt Slippers w/blue satin straps trimeed with beige lace	35	15	25
3432	**IN STITCHES**			
	Multicolored "Indian" Print Purse	38	25	32
3433	**ALL ABOUT PLAID**			
	Green/Orange/Yellow/White Shawl	36	20	28
	Green/Orange/Yellow/White Purse	30	18	24
3434	**FUN FUR**			
	Honey Gold Cotton Suede Belt	36	20	28
	Beige Crocheted Hat w/pouf	96	55	75
	Corduroy Cap w/vinyl bill	96	55	75
	Honey Gold Soft Lace Up Boots	12	8	10
3436	**GAUCHO GEAR**			
	Orange Felt Hat w/gold cord trim	46	24	35
	Honey Colored Fringe Vest	30	18	24
	Honey Colored Shoulder Bag	33	15	24
	Honey Colored Fringed Boots	24	12	18
3437	**DANCING LIGHTS**			
	Rose Thread Stole line in pink	30	18	24
	Black Plastic Adjustable Necklace w/butterfly	125	65	95

STOCK NO.	OUTFIT	MINT COMPLETE		
		HIGH	LOW	AVG
3438	**PEASANT DRESSY**			
	White Petticoat w/eyelet trim	85	45	65
	White Camisole w/yellow nylon cord straps	115	55	85
3439	**WILD THINGS**			
	Royal Blue Textured Vinyl Belt	85	45	65
3480	**FUN SHINE**			
	Orange Sheer Nylon Pantyhose	46	30	38
3481	**SHORT SET, THE**			
	Red Vinyl Belt w/brass ring closure	24	12	18
	Red Vinyl Double Pocket Purse	24	12	18
	Red Soft Lace Up Boots	15	5	10
3482	**PEASANT PLEASANT**			
	Orange Plastic Wedgies w/long ankle ties	46	30	38
3485	**MADRAS MAD**			
	Red/Navy Blue/White/Gold Plaid Purse	35	15	25
3487	**SLEEPY SET**			
	White Felt Slippers w/pink sheer poufs	18	12	15
3488	**OVERALL DENIM**			
	White and Blue Striped Backpack	46	24	35
	White Sneakers	10	2	6
3490	**PARTY LINES**			
	White Sheer Nylon Stockings	48	32	40
3491	**SUEDE 'N FUR**			
	Red Nylon Full Body Suit	125	65	95
	Grayish-Brown Lace Up Boots	14	10	12
3492	**FLYING COLORS**			
	Deep Orange Plush Vest w/hot pink vinyl trim	46	30	38
	Hot Pink Vinyl Neckband with hot pink flower	125	45	65
3493	**SATIN 'N SHINE**			
	White net veil over ivory white satin headband	125	65	95
	Bouquet with one large flower w/bead center	85	45	65

OPEN TOE SHOES

DESCRIPTION	MINT PAIR	
	HIGH	LOW
AQUA	25	15
CLEAR	25	15
CLEAR WITH SILVER GLITTER	30	15
CLEAR WITH GOLD GLITTER	25	15
BLACK	10	5
BLACK WITH BLACK POMS	35	20
BLACK WITH YELLOW POMS	35	20
BROWN	15	10
EMERALD GREEN	15	10
EMERALD GREEN WITH PEARLS	35	25
GINGER ALE WITH GLITTER FLECKS	25	15
HOT PINK (3 variations)	20	10
LIGHT BLUE WITH LIGHT BLUE POMS	25	15
LIGHT PINK	10	5
LIGHT PINK WITH GLITTER	35	25
LIGHT PINK WITH PINK POMS	25	15
LIGHT PINK WITH BLUE POMS	35	25
MEDIUM BLUE	10	5
MIDNIGHT BLUE	50	40
MUSTARD	10	5
NAVY BLUE	40	25
ORANGE	8	5
RED	10	5
ROSE	25	15
ROSE WITH SILVER GLITTER	50	35
ROYAL BLUE	15	10
WHITE	12	10
WHITE WITH SILVER GLITTER	45	25
WHITE WITH WHITE POMS	35	20
WHITE WITH MELON POMS	95	75
YELLOW	10	5

PUMPS

DESCRIPTION	MINT PAIR	
	HIGH	LOW
APPLE GREEN (JCPenney)	200	175
ACID GREEN	250	200
BLACK	35	25
BLUE	30	20
BONE	30	25
BROWN	200	125
CLEAR	125	100
CLEAR WITH GLITTER	300	200
DEEP NAVY BLUE	N/A	N/A
HOT PINK (various shades)	25	20
JADE GREEN	35	25
LAVENDER	N/A	N/A
LIGHT PURPLE	N/A	N/A
OLIVE	125	75
ORANGE	25	15
PALE BLUE	30	20
PALE PINK	35	30
PURPLE (JCPenney)	175	150
RED	25	15
ROSE	45	35
ROYAL BLUE	30	20
TURQUOISE	30	20
WHITE	75	50
YELLOW (JCPenney)	200	150

❖❖❖❖❖❖❖❖❖❖❖❖❖❖❖

PILGRIMS (SHOES)

DESCRIPTION	MINT PAIR	
	HIGH	LOW
ACID GREEN	6	3
AQUA	6	3
BLACK	6	3
BROWN	20	15
BLUE	6	3
FUSHCIA	6	3
GREEN	6	3
HOT PINK	6	3
LIGHT BLUE	6	3
LIME	6	3
NAVY BLUE	6	3
NEON ORANGE	6	3
ORANGE	6	3
PALE PINK	40	25
PINK	6	3
PURPLE	10	8
RED	6	3
ROSE	6	3
ROYAL BLUE	15	10
WHITE	6	3
YELLOW	6	3

BARBIE® SPIKE HEELS

DESCRIPTION	MINT PAIR	
	HIGH	LOW
BROWN	250	200
CLEAR (Put-together set from Ken's outfit "The Prince")	200	150
JADE	150	100
OLIVE	250	150
PALE BLUE	100	50
RED	75	50
TURQUOISE	75	50
WHITE	125	100

❖❖❖❖❖❖❖❖❖❖❖❖❖❖❖

T-STRAP SHOES

DESCRIPTION	MINT PAIR	
	HIGH	LOW
AQUA	12	5
BLACK	40	25
BLUE	12	5
CLEAR	30	20
HOT PINK	12	5
LIME GREEN (darker)	12	5
LIME GREEN (lighter)	12	5
ORANGE	12	5
PURPLE	12	5
ROYAL BLUE	12	5
ROSE	12	5
WHITE	12	5
YELLOW	12	5

HARD LOW HEELS

DESCRIPTION	MINT PAIR	
	HIGH	LOW
AQUA (Barbie)	5	3
AQUA (Francie)	5	3
BLACK (Barbie)	5	3
BLACK (Francie)	5	3
BLACK WITH ANKLE TIES (Barbie)	75	50
GOLD (Barbie)	10	6
GREEN (Francie)	5	3
HOT PINK (Francie)	5	3
LIGHT BLUE (Francie)	75	50
LIGHT BROWN (Francie)	15	10
LIGHT PINK (Francie)	5	3
LIME GREEN (Barbie)	5	3
LIME GREEN (Francie)	5	3
MINT GREEN (Francie)	5	3
NAVY BLUE (Barbie)	6	4
ORANGE (Barbie)	5	3
ORANGE (Francie)	5	3
PEACH (Barbie & Francie)	5	3
PURPLE (Barbie)	20	10
RED (Barbie)	5	3
RED (Francie)	5	3
ROYAL BLUE (Barbie)	5	3
TERRA COTTA RED (Francie)	5	3
WHITE (Barbie)	5	3
WHITE (Francie)	5	3
YELLOW (Francie)	5	3
OTHER COLORS	5	3

SOFT ANKLE BOOTS

DESCRIPTION	MINT PAIR	
	HIGH	LOW
ACID GREEN	15	10
APPLE GREEN	12	8
BLACK	30	20
GRAY	12	8
LIME GREEN	12	8
ORANGE	12	8
PINK	12	8
RED	12	8
ROYAL BLUE	15	10
WHITE	50	25
YELLOW	12	8

❖❖❖❖❖❖❖❖❖❖❖❖❖❖

SOFT BOW SHOES

DESCRIPTION	MINT PAIR	
	HIGH	LOW
ACID GREEN	12	8
APPLE GREEN	15	10
AQUA	95	50
BLACK	12	8
LIGHT BLUE	8	5
LIME GREEN	15	10
ORANGE	12	8
PINK	12	8
RED	12	8
ROYAL BLUE	12	8
WHITE	25	15
YELLOW	12	8

BARBIE® SIZE LUGGAGE

DESCRIPTION	YEAR	MINT & COMPLETE	NRFP
BONE WHITE, Overnight case, Pullman case, ladies wardrobe, activity case Payton Products, Inc. #1201	1963	25	260
CHARCOAL GRAY, Overnight case, Pullman case, ladies wardrobe, activity case, Payton Products, Inc. #1201	1963	25	260
TEAL BLUE, Overnight case, Pullman case, ladies wardrobe, activity case Payton Products, Inc. #1201	1963	25	260
APPLE GREEN Payton Products, Inc.	1974	43	173
APPLE GREEN Payton Products Inc. #5751 United FriendShip 1974	53	173	
Luggage Set Mattel (4 piece)			
BUBBLE GUM PINK Payton Products, Inc.	1974	43	N/A
CANARY YELLOW Payton Products, Inc.	1974	43	N/A
LIME GREEN (United Airlines) Payton Products, Inc.	1974	43	N/A
RED (United Airlines) Payton Products, Inc.	1974	43	N/A
GREEN/WHITE VINYL ZIPPERED "BOWLING BAG" Payton Products knockoff	—	10	95
TAN BAG MARKED SAMSONITE Payton Products knockoff	—	10	95
VARIOUS COLORED SOFT VINYL FLIGHT BAGS with logos and names of different airlines	—	10	225
WHITE W/RAISED STAR Shoulder bag, hat box & one suiter Payton Products knockoff	—	17	195

SWIMSUIT

DESCRIPTION	MINT/COMPLETE		
	HIGH	LOW	AVG
BLACK/WHITE ZEBRA	25	12	15
RED/WHITE ZEBRA (Premier)	25	12	15
NAVY/WHITE ZEBRA (Premier)	25	12	15
PINK/WHITE ZEBRA (Premier)	25	12	15
LIGHT BLUE/WHITE ZEBRA (Premier)	25	12	15
CORAL	48	20	28
RED JERSEY	30	10	20
BLACK JERSEY	30	10	20
NAVY BLUE JERSEY	25	10	15
LIGHT BLUE JERSEY	25	10	15
ORANGE JERSEY	34	14	20
PINK JERSEY	22	10	12
FASHION QUEEN Gold/White	40	15	25
MISS BARBIE w/glitter	48	20	28
MISS BARBIE w/gold painted on	40	18	22
COLOR MAGIC	60	20	40
AMERICAN GIRL Pink/Turquoise/Green/Red Stripe Top	60	20	40
AMERICAN GIRL Red/White/Turquoise/Green/Orange Stripe Top (variation)	110	60	85
AMERICAN GIRL same stripes as Allan's Swimsuit Jacket	100	50	75
SL MIDGE BRUNETTE Green Top/Orange Bottom 2-piece	30	10	20
SL MIDGE REDHEAD Pink Top/Red Bottom 2-piece	30	10	20
SL MIDGE BLONDE Light Blue Top/Darker Blue 2-piece	30	10	20
BL MIDGE Multi-Stripe	60	20	40
1967 TNT BARBIE Orange Vinyl Bikini Top and Bottom	25	10	15
1968 TNT BARBIE Pink/Red/Green/Chartreuse Checked Shell/Pink Vinyl Bottoms	45	15	30
1969 TNT BARBIE Multicolored Diamond Check	25	10	15
1970 TNT BARBIE Pink/White Nylon w/Cross on Front	25	10	15
1971 TNT BARBIE Pink/Multicolored Abstract Geometric Print	30	15	20
1968 TALKING BARBIE Hot Pink Knit Coverup w/yellow yarn trim/ Pink Vinyl Bottoms	25	10	15
1970 TALKING BARBIE Red Orange Vinyl Top/Bottom, Silver/ White Lacy Cover up	25	10	15
1971 TALKING BARBIE White Vinyl Top and Bottom, Gold Mesh Coverup	55	20	35
1967 STANDARD STRAIGHT LEG BARBIE 2-pc. Hot Pink Helenca 40	15	25	
1970 STANDARD BARBIE Hot Pink/Lime Green Nylon Suit w/pink 48 plastic flower at hip	18	30	
1968 TALKING STACEY Navy Blue/Hot Pink/White/Green Stripe 27	12	15	

SWIMSUIT CONTINUED

DESCRIPTION	MINT/COMPLETE		
	HIGH	LOW	AVG
1970 TALKING STACEY Blue/Silver Lamé (HTF)	40	15	25
1968 TNT STACEY Red Stretch w/Midriff Cutout	27	12	15
1969 TNT STACEY Multicolored Abstract Print	30	10	20
1970 TNT STACEY Pink/Blue/Green Floral Nylon	100	35	65
1970 LIVING BARBIE Gold/Silver Lamé w/Orange Mesh Coverup	40	15	25
1971 LIVING BARBIE White Nylon Swimsuit w/red/pink/purple polka dots	55	20	35
TNT PJ Hot Pink Nylon w/hot pink crocheted skirt	27	12	15
TNT CHRISTIE Pink/Yellow/White Abstract Nylon (HTF)	40	15	25
1968 TALKING CHRISTIE Green Knit coverup w/pink trim, pink vinyl bottoms	40	15	25
1970 TALKING CHRISTIE Orange Vinyl Strapless Swimsuit,Multicolored Abstract Cover	55	20	35
1972 MALIBU P.J. Lavender Nylon Swimsuit	30	10	20
1966 SL FRANCIE White w/red dots cotton top, red/white checked bottom	60	20	40
1966 BL FRANCIE Aqua Stretch Helenca Swimsuit w/green/fuchsia block and floral print	55	20	35
1967 BL FRANCIE White Stretch Helenca Top w/green/fuchsia blocks, floral print, solid green bottom	55	20	35
1967 TNT FRANCIE Multicolored Stripe Top w/pink nylon bottom	27	12	15
1969 TNT FRANCIE Hot Pink Knit w/yellow diagonal stripes	27	12	15
1967 TNT BLACK FRANCIE White Sheer Nylon w/sewn in 2-piece swimsuit multicolor abstract print	100	35	65
OR White Sheer Nylon w/sewn in 2-piece swimsuit in Pajama Pow print	100	35	65
1969 TNT FRANCIE Hot Pink Knit Top w/yellow diagonal striped bottom27	12	15	
1970 TNT FRANCIE Yellow Floral print beach type dress and pink nylon shorts	40	15	25
1971 MALIBU FRANCIE Hot Pink Nylon Top w/yellow attached belt and red bottom	27	12	15
1975 BAGGIE FRANCIE Yellow Nylon Bikini Top and Bottom	30	10	20
1967 TNT CASEY White/Gold Knit Top w/gold lamé bottom	28	10	18
1975 BAGGIE CASEY Rose OR Hot Pink Nylon Bikini Top and Bottom	30	10	20

VINTAGE PAKS

DESCRIPTION	HIGH	LOW	AVG
EARLY HANGER PAKS			
ACCESSORY PAK	270	190	230
PURSE PAK	75	40	58
SILK SHEATH (white)	95	50	73
SILK SHEATH (yellow)	80	40	60
SILK SHEATH (gold)	75	40	58
SILK SHEATH (blue)	80	35	58
SILK SHEATH (green)	80	40	60
SILK SHEATH (red)	80	40	60
SILK SHEATH (black)	100	55	78
BRA, PANTIES, SLIP	85	50	68
HELENCA SWIMSUIT (red)	200	130	165
HELENCA SWIMSUIT (navy)	175	120	148
HELENCA SWIMSUIT (black)	180	120	150
SHEATH w/GOLD BUTTONS (red)	55	35	45
SHEATH w/GOLD BUTTONS (green)	60	40	50
SHEATH w/GOLD BUTTONS (blue)	70	50	60
TWO-PIECE PAJAMAS (yellow)	30	20	25
TWO-PIECE PAJAMAS (pink)	30	20	25
TWO-PIECE PAJAMAS (blue)	30	20	25
SCOOP NECK PLAYSUIT (white w/orange belt)	75	50	63
SCOOP NECK PLAYSUIT (pink w/black belt)	65	35	50
SCOOP NECK PLAYSUIT (red w/yellow belt)	70	40	55
SCOOP NECK PLAYSUIT (floral w/red belt)	80	45	63
SCOOP NECK PLAYSUIT (black /blue belt)	85	45	65
SHEATH SKIRT (white w/black telephone)	55	35	45
SHEATH SKIRT (pink w/black telephone)	55	35	45
SHEATH SKIRT (orange w/black telephone)	50	30	40
SHEATH SKIRT (floral w/white telephone)	70	45	58
SHEATH SKIRT (black w/white telephone)	70	45	58
PLAIN BLOUSE (white w/red purse)	55	35	45
PLAIN BLOUSE (pink w/white purse)	50	30	40
PLAIN BLOUSE (orange w/pink purse)	55	30	43
PLAIN BLOUSE (red w/yellow purse)	50	30	40
PLAIN BLOUSE (floral w/blue purse)	55	35	45
SLACKS (white w/red belt)	35	25	30
SLACKS (pink w/pink belt)	35	25	30
SLACKS (red w/yellow belt)	35	25	30
SLACKS (floral w/red belt)	35	30	33
SLACKS (black w/blue belt)	40	30	35
GATHERED SKIRT (pink w/pink mules)	55	35	45
GATHERED SKIRT (orange w/orange mules)	55	35	45

VINTAGE PAKS CONTINUED

DESCRIPTION	HIGH	LOW	AVG
EARLY HANGER PAKS (contined)			
GATHERED SKIRT (redw/red mules)	50	35	43
GATHERED SKIRT (floral w/black mules)	60	40	50
GATHERED SKIRT (black w/black mules)	60	40	50
WOOL CARDIGANS W/KNITTED WAISTBAND			
CARDIGAN (white w/white collar)	45	25	35
CARDIGAN (pink w/white collar)	45	25	35
CARDIGAN (blue w/white collar)	45	25	35
CARDIGAN (black w/white collar)	50	30	40
COTTON CARDIGANS W/SEWN WAISTBAND			
CARDIGAN (white w/white collar)	30	20	25
CARDIGAN (pink w/white collar)	30	20	25
CARDIGAN (blue w/white collar)	30	20	25
CARDIGAN (black w/white collar)	35	25	30
LINGERIE PAK (white)	180	110	145
LINGERIE PAK (pink)	175	100	138
LINGERIE PAK (blue)	175	105	140
LINGERIE PAK (black)	200	160	180
BARBIE-Q APRON (white)	65	40	53
BARBIE-Q APRON (red)	65	40	53
BARBIE-Q APRON (blue)	65	40	53
BELLE DRESS (pink)	115	75	95
BELLE DRESS (blue)	120	75	98
BELLE DRESS (red)	140	100	120
WOOL SWEATERS W/KNITTED WAISTBAND			
SQUARE NECK SWEATER (white)	45	25	35
SQUARE NECK SWEATER (pink)	45	25	35
SQUARE NECK SWEATER (black)	50	30	40
COTTON SWEATERS W/SEWN WAISTBAND			
SQUARE NECK SWEATER (white)	30	20	25
SQUARE NECK SWEATER (pink)	30	20	25
SQUARE NECK SWEATER (black)	35	25	30
FUR STOLE WITH BAG	75	40	58
SATIN BLOUSE (white)	60	40	50
SATIN BLOUSE (pink w/glitter)	60	50	55
SATIN BLOUSE (rose)	55	40	48
SATIN BLOUSE (black)	75	50	63
SATIN SLACKS (white w/clear mules)	110	75	93

VINTAGE PAKS CONTINUED

DESCRIPTION	HIGH	LOW	AVG
COTTON SWEATERS W/SEWN WAISTBAND (continued)			
SATIN SLACKS (pink w/glitter pink mules)	100	70	85
SATIN SLACKS (rose w/pink mules)	85	65	75
SATIN SLACKS (black w/clear mules)	115	75	95
SATIN BOLERO JACKET & HAT (white)	105	75	90
SATIN BOLERO JACKET & HAT (pink w/glitter)	110	80	95
SATIN BOLERO JACKET & HAT (rose)	100	75	88
SATIN BOLERO JACKET & HAT (black)	105	65	85
SATIN SKIRT (white)	55	35	45
SATIN SKIRT (pink w/glitter)	60	40	55
SATIN SKIRT (rose)	55	35	45
SATIN SKIRT (black)	60	40	50
SATIN COAT (white)	100	70	85
SATIN COAT (pink w/glitter)	115	75	95
SATIN COAT (rose)	105	65	85
SATIN COAT (black)	115	75	95
SATIN WRAP SKIRT (white)	105	65	85
SATIN WRAP SKIRT (pink w/glitter)	120	75	98
SATIN WRAP SKIRT (rose)	110	70	90
SATIN WRAP SKIRT (black)	115	75	95
KNIT TOP & SUNGLASSES (gold)	65	40	53
KNIT TOP & SUNGLASSES (blue)	65	40	53
KNIT TOP & SUNGLASSES (striped)	70	45	58
KNIT SKIRT (gold w/glitter)	60	45	53
KNIT SKIRT, blue w/glitter	60	45	53
KNIT SKIRT (striped)	65	50	58
KNIT SLACKS (gold w/red wedge shoes)	45	30	38
KNIT SLACKS (blue w/blue wedge shoes)	45	35	40
KNIT SLACKS (striped w/red wedge shoes)	50	40	45
KNIT DRESS (gold)	55	40	48
KNIT DRESS (blue)	55	45	50
KNIT DRESS (striped)	65	50	58
KNIT TOP & SHORTS (gold top/striped shorts)	45	35	40
KNIT TOP & SHORTS (blue top/gold shorts)	45	35	40
KNIT TOP & SHORTS (striped top/gold shorts)	45	35	40
KNIT TOP & SHORTS (striped top/blue shorts)	45	35	40
KNIT SKIRT & SUNGLASSES (gold)	45	35	40
KNIT SKIRT & SUNGLASSES (blue)	45	35	40
KNIT SKIRT & SUNGLASSES (striped)	60	40	50
KNIT ACCESSORIES	160	85	123
SQUARE NECK SWEATER & PINK SCARF (white)	35	30	33
SQUARE NECK SWEATER & PINK SCARF (pink)	35	30	33

DESCRIPTION	HIGH	LOW	AVG
COTTON SWEATERS W/SEWN WAISTBAND (continued)			
SQUARE NECK SWEATER & PINK SCARF (black)	55	35	45
PEACHY FLEECY COAT	75	45	60
LAMÉ SHEATH	270	180	225
LATER T-SHAPED PAKS			
BATHROBE	55	40	48
SHOE PAK (12 pairs mules & wedges)	265	220	243
JEANS	60	45	53
FUR HAT & BAG	550	—	550
IN THE SWIM (red)	450	275	363
IN THE SWIM (blue)	450	275	363
SHOE WARDROBE (13 pairs mules & wedges) #1833	275	230	253
FOR BARBIE DRESSMAKERS #1831	30	20	25
FOR RINK AND COURT	85	45	65
GOING TO THE BALL	145	80	113
COSTUME COMPLETERS	165	115	140
DRESS UP HATS	130	80	105
FASHION ACCENTS	275	200	238
SWEET DREAMS	150	90	120
COLOR COORDINATES	115	80	98
BARBIE'S BOUDOIR	140	90	115
LEISURE HOURS	180	105	143
ON THE GO (blue)	90	65	78
ON THE GO (green)	105	65	85
ON THE GO (red)	105	65	85
ON THE GO (floral print)	155	105	130
JUMPIN' JEANS	105	70	88
SPECTATOR SPORT (gold)	70	65	68
SPECTATOR SPORT (blue)	70	65	68
SPECTATOR SPORT (striped)	75	70	73
FASHION FEET	90	55	73
CAMPUS BELLE (blue)	185	135	160
CAMPUS BELLE (red)	180	135	158
LOVELY LINGERIE (white)	185	120	153
LOVELY LINGERIE (pink)	180	120	150
LOVELY LINGERIE (blue)	180	120	150
LOVELY LINGERIE (black)	210	170	190
RUFFLES 'N LACE	140	100	120
WHAT'S COOKING (white apron, hat)	120	80	100
WHAT'S COOKING (blue apron, white hat)	120	80	100
WHAT'S COOKING (red apron, white hat)	120	80	100

VINTAGE PAKS CONTINUED

DESCRIPTION	HIGH	LOW	AVG
LATER T-SHAPED PAKS (continued)			
LUNCH DATE (variations exist)	185	125	155
RED DELIGHT	165	130	148
MATCH MATES	280	210	245
TAILORED TOPS (variations exist)	120	70	95
PERT SKIRTS (variations exist)	220	125	173
SET 'N SERVE	400	280	340
HAVE FUN	360	280	320
KITCHEN MAGIC	260	145	203
GLAMOUR HATS	425	325	375
FLATS 'N HEELS (12 pr. pumps, mules, wedges)	375	310	343
BEST BOW (many variations)	210	125	168
SKIRT STYLES	125	85	105
TOP TWOSOME	130	80	105
FANCY TRIMMINS (Blonde braid)	245	165	205
FANCY TRIMMINS (Brunette braid)	255	175	215
COOK UPS	285	180	233
DRESSED UP (many variations of dresses)	185	130	158
EXTRA CASUALS	165	115	140
PEDAL PUSHERS	135	100	118
CHANGE ABOUTS	185	135	160
ADD-ONS	190	135	163
FLATS 'N HEELS (13 pr. pumps, mules, wedges)	260	160	210
SUN SHINER	165	130	148
TERRIFIC TWOSOMES	175	125	150
PETTI - PINKS	155	130	143
FINISHING TOUCHES	190	135	163
TOUR INS	190	135	163
FLATS 'N HEELS, MOD PILGRIMS	155	110	133
SHARP SHIFT (many variations)	140	80	110
COOL CASUALS (many variations)	165	115	140
PERFECT BEGINNINGS	140	70	105
STITCH 'N STYLE	30	15	23
ALL THE TRIMMINGS	205	165	185
FOOTLIGHTS	140	115	128
SOFT 'N SNUG	195	140	168
PLUSH 'N WARM	95	35	65
FASHION FIRSTS	145	65	105
WALKING PRETTY	155	85	120
THE SEW IN	30	10	20

SKIPPER PAKS

DESCRIPTION	YEAR	HIGH	LOW	AVG
BEAUTY BATH	1965	135	65	100
HATS 'N HATS	1965	50	35	43
JUST FOR FUN	1965	135	80	108
PARTY PINK	1965	50	35	43
SHOE PARADE	1965	55	35	45
WOOLY P.J.'S	1965	65	50	58
HAPPY TIMES	1970	125	70	98
NIGHTY NIGHT	1970	55	40	48
SIDE LIGHTS	1970	75	60	68
SUMMER SLACKS (several variations)	1970	60	45	53
TOE TWINKLES	1970	55	40	48
UNDER TONES	1970	55	40	48
ACTION FASHION	1971	80	55	68
CHECK THE SLACKS	1971	50	35	43
SKIMMER 'N SCARF	1971	40	30	35
SPORTY SHORTY	1971	45	30	38
SOME SHOES	1971	50	35	43

KEN (1961-64)
700 SERIES FASHIONS - PART ONE

STOCK NO.	FASHION	NRFB			MINT & COMPLETE		
		HIGH	LOW	AVG	HIGH	LOW	AVG
797	**ARMY AND AIR FORCE** - Khaki shirt & pants, matching cap, beige belt & socks, navy cap, belt, socks & tie, brown tie, brown shoes, navy shoes, metal "wings."	160	135	150	95	70	86
770	**CAMPUS HERO** - Red/white/charcoal sweater, white pants, yellow felt "U," "STATE" pennant, red socks, white shoes. *(Rarer "M" commands a higher price.)*	100	75	95	35	25	30
782	**CASUALS** - Yellow knit shirt, khaki pants, red cap, multi-striped socks, brown/white shoes.	75	55	65	45	30	38
793	**DR. KEN** - White coat & pants, white hat & mask, black doctor's bag, stethoscope, forehead "Light," white socks, white shoes.	150	120	140	65	50	55
785	**DREAMBOAT** - Olive blazer, dark green pants, grey/green/olive patterned shirt, straw hat w/orange/black hatband 7 red feather, yellow socks, brown shoes.	145	95	130	65	30	48
791	**FUN ON THE ICE** - Black/blue/mustard V-neck sweater, mustard cords, mustard scarf, mittens, & hat w/blue pompon, black skates w/silver blades.	130	85	108	50	35	40
795	**GRADUATION** - Black robe, black mortar board w/black tassel, diploma w/white ribbon.	75	50	66	35	25	28
780	**IN TRAINING** - White knit mock tee, red/white polka-dot boxers, white briefs, training manual, 2 black hand weights.	65	40	50	28	16	22
794	**MASQUERADE** - Black yellow costume w/ruffled collar, cuffs & sleeves, white knit hood, black/yellow clown hat w/orange yarn, mask, invitation, black shoes.	150	100	130	75	60	64
792	**PLAY BALL** - Grey/white pinstripe 2-piece baseball uniform w/red felt trim & "M" & black attached belt, red plastic mitt, bat, ball, black cleats.	130	95	115	55	40	48
788	**RALLY DAY** - Khaki coat w/red tartan lining, red cap, road map, car keys on chain w/engraved "K."	100	75	85	55	40	46

KEN (1961-64)
700 SERIES FASHIONS - PART ONE CONTINUED

STOCK NO.	FASHION	NRFB			MINT & COMPLETE		
		HIGH	LOW	AVG	HIGH	LOW	AVG
796	**SAILOR** - White sailor top, white bell bottoms, black tie, white plastic cap, blue denim draw-string bag, white socks, black shoes.	130	100	118	60	45	50
786	**SATURDAY NIGHT DATE** - Charcoal suit jacket, slacks, white dress shirt, red/grey/navy striped tie, black socks, black shoes.	125	90	106	60	40	50
798	**SKI CHAMPION** - Red jacket, black stirrups, black stocking cap w/red pompon, black mittens, brown skis, wooden poles w/brown "baskets," green goggles, black boots.	135	95	125	65	50	60
781	**SLEEPER SET** - Brown/white striped 2-piece paja-mas w/brown collar, wax cinnamon roll, glass of milk, alarm clock.	85	60	70	35	20	26
783	**SPORT SHORTS** - Olive/red/blue/black figured short-sleeved shirt topped yellow fly-front Bermuda shorts, olive knee-high knit socks & brown shoes.	65	45	55	25	12	18
784	**TERRY TOGS** - Blue terrycloth robe w/tie belt, yellow towel marked "His," white briefs, blue sponge, bar of soap, black comb, grey razor, w/cord, blue terry slippers.	95	70	85	40	25	35
790	**TIME FOR TENNIS** - White polo w/button closure, white cardigan w/navy/red trim, white shorts, tennis racquet, 2 tennis balls, tennis rulebook, green sun-glasses, white socks, white tennis shoes.	125	95	110	50	30	38
799	**TOUCHDOWN** - Red football jersey w/white No. 7, red football pants w/white trim, red shoulder pads, red helmet, football, red w/navy striped knee-socks, black cleats.	135	85	110	50	35	44
787	**TUXEDO** - Black tux w/white boutonniere, black slacks white tux shirt, burgundy cummerbund & bow tie, corsage, black socks, black shoes.	185	110	165	70	55	65
789	**YACHTSMAN, THE** - Light blue zippered jacket w/navy trim, light blue pants, red/white striped tee, sailing manual, white socks, black shoes. *(Rare cap included commands a higher price.)*	130	85	115	50	25	40

KEN (1964-65)
700 SERIES FASHIONS - PART TWO

STOCK NO. FASHION	NRFB			MINT & COMPLETE		
	HIGH	LOW	AVG	HIGH	LOW	AVG
0779 **AMERICAN AIRLINES CAPTAIN** - Navy blue blazer w/silver braid trim & captain's wings, navy pants, navy cap w/silver braid & emblem, (with or without AA flight bag), black socks, black shoes, flight log.	350	250	300	200	150	170
0774 **ARABIAN NIGHTS** - Red velour coat w/braided trim & tie belt, gold/white lamé pants & matching turban w/jewel, red velour slippers w/gold braid trim, theatre program.	295	175	225	160	110	140
0770 **CAMPUS HERO** - Red/white/charcoal sweater, white pants, yellow felt "M" pennant, red socks, white shoes.	175	125	150	80	55	68
0782 **CASUALS** - Multi-striped knit shirt, khaki pants, red cap, multi-striped socks, brown/white shoes, car keys w/"K."	95	85	90	60	40	48
0775 **DRUM MAJOR** - White band jacket w/red/gold braided trim & epaulettes, red pants w/white stripe trim, white plush hat w/gold plume & neck strap, gold baton, white socks & shoes.	200	150	175	90	70	85
0777 **KEN IN HOLLAND** - White shirt w/8 silver buttons, blue felt cap, red patterned scarf, bouquet, white knee-socks, wooden shoes, travel pamphlet.	200	150	180	100	75	85
0778 **KEN IN MEXICO** - Brown felt bolero jacket w/black braid & white loop trim, matching pants, matching sombrero w/green rick-rack trim & neckband, white short-sleeved shirt, green cummerbund, ribbon necktie, black cowboy boots, travel pamphlet.	260	175	225	150	98	125
0776 **KEN IN SWITZERLAND** - White short-sleeved shirt, grey flannel shorts w/red suspenders & 8 silver buttons, black felt hat w/white hatband & feather, stein, pipe, white knee-socks, black ankle boots, travel pamphlet.	200	150	175	125	90	110
0773 **KING ARTHUR** - Silver lamé shirt, tights & hood, red satin vest w/gold crest, gold belt, sword, sheath, spurs, silver helmet, shield w/crest, theatre program.	395	300	350	200	175	185
0772 **PRINCE, THE** - Dark green velour cape w/gold satin lining, dark green/gold lamé brocade jacket w/diamond buttons & lace cuffs, white lace collar, dark green velour pantaloons w/gold nylon tights, gold velour hat w/jewel & feather, dark green slippers, theatre program, maroon pillow, clear "glass slipper" (clear spike).	425	350	395	325	200	285
0781 **SLEEPER SET** - Blue/white striped 2-piece pajamas, glass of milk, Danish, alarm clock.	135	100	115	50	40	45
0789 **YACHTSMAN, THE** - Light blue zippered jacket w/navy trim, light blue pants, red/white striped tee, sailing manual, white socks, black shoes, cap.	475	395	440	295	250	280

KEN (1964-66)
1400 SERIES FASHIONS - PART ONE

STOCK NO.	FASHION	NRFB HIGH	NRFB LOW	NRFB AVG	MINT & COMPLETE HIGH	MINT & COMPLETE LOW	MINT & COMPLETE AVG
1425	**BEST MAN** - White tux jacket, white tux shirt w/3 pearl buttons, black pants w/braid trim, red bow tie & cummerbund, black knit socks, black shoes.	1295	950	1100	800	695	755
1424	**BUSINESS APPOINTMENT** - Dark navy tweed coat, black felt hat, black vinyl gloves, black briefcase, newspaper.	1300	995	1150	850	700	795
1410	**CAMPUS CORDUROYS** - Tan corduroy sportcoat w/brown elbow patches, tan corduroy pants.	80	55	64	35	20	28
1416	**COLLEGE STUDENT** - Multi-plaid blazer w/green partial lining, white short-sleeved shirt, brown pants, brown tie, brown socks, brown shoes, typewriter.	600	500	550	295	200	250
1400	**COUNTRY CLUBBIN'** - Black/white houndstooth jacket w/red partial lining, black pants.	175	100	135	60	45	50
1407	**FOUNTAIN BOY** - White uniform shirt w/KEN on pocket, white cap w/red trim, brown tray, order pad, 2 pencils (1 yellow, 1 brown), 2 napkins, 1 chocolate soda, 1 strawberry soda each w/straw.	195	160	180	120	80	94
1408	**FRATERNITY MEETING** - Brown/white patterned cardigan w/4 silver buttons & white trim, brown pants, white polo shirt w/button closure.	120	75	85	45	30	38
1403	**GOING BOWLING** - Red short-sleeved shirt w/ white stitching (with or without white socks & white tennis shoes).	95	70	80	40	20	26
1409	**GOING HUNTIN'** - Red/white/navy plaid cotton shirt, jeans, red vinyl cap, black/brown rifle, (with or without black hunting boots & red socks).	135	95	118	55	40	45
1426	**HERE COMES THE GROOM** - Grey flannel coat & tails w/white boutonniere, white tux shirt w/3 pearl buttons, grey flannel vest w/6 clear buttons, black w/white pinstriped pants, grey ascot w/pearl, grey gloves, light grey plastic top hat, black socks, black shoes.	1695	1200	1395	825	695	740
1412	**HIKING HOLIDAY** - Olive green cowl-neck sweater, khaki hiking shorts, white socks, brown shoes.	295	200	250	130	90	110
1414	**HOLIDAY** - White nylon polo w/blue collar, cuffs, & 3 white buttons, blue textured-weave pants, blue/white houndstooth cap, white socks, black/white shoes.	285	190	230	135	100	118
1420	**JAZZ CONCERT** - Blue/taupe patterned polo w/6 "pearl" buttons, taupe pants, white socks, white tennis shoes.	325	275	295	160	120	140
1423	**KEN A GO GO** - Red/blue/yellow striped polo w/red collar & sleeves & 6 blue buttons, gold pants, black fur wig, orange ukulele w/black strap, silver microphone, red socks, white tennis shoes.	795	650	705	520	425	485

STOCK NO.	FASHION	NRFB HIGH	NRFB LOW	NRFB AVG	MINT & COMPLETE HIGH	MINT & COMPLETE LOW	MINT & COMPLETE AVG
1404	**KEN IN HAWAII** - Blue/aqua/white floral patterned sarong, tan straw hat w/flowered hatband, yellow lei, orange ukulele, cork sandals w/orange straps, travel pamphlet.	225	150	190	100	75	88
1427	**MOUNTAIN HIKE** - Red cowl-neck sweater, khaki walking shorts, white socks, white shoes.	275	250	250	125	95	110
1415	**MR. ASTRONAUT** - Silver spacesuit, brown plastic gloves & boots, white helmet w/clear plastic window, American flag on stick.	850	600	745	385	325	365
1413	**OFF TO BED** - Royal blue pajama top w/red/white/blue houndstooth pattern & red trim, royal pajama bottoms w/red cuffs, red fuzzy slippers, red telephone, glass of milk, "How to Get a Raise" book.	200	135	150	90	75	80
1405	**ROLLER SKATE DATE** - Orange/brown/white V-neck argyle sweater w/orange trim, brown skates w/white rollers, (with or w/out white pants & orange knit hat w/green pompon).	150	100	125	60	40	46
1417	**ROVIN' REPORTER** - Red blazer w/3 buttons, white short-sleeved shirt, navy pants, red socks, black shoes, camera.	375	275	310	180	150	165
1421	**SEEIN' THE SIGHTS** - Red/navy tweed sport coat w/checkerboard lining, white short-sleeved shirt, navy pants, red tie, red socks, black shoes.	495	400	455	225	150	190
1406	**SKIN DIVER** - Orange hooded sweatshirt w/white tie, multi-striped swimming trunks, green fins, green mask w/clear plastic window & elastic tie, green snorkel.	65	40	50	30	15	24
1401	**SPECIAL DATE** - Dark blue suit jacket, matching pants, white long-sleeved shirt, red tie, red socks, black shoes.	185	140	160	85	70	78
1422	**SUMMER JOB** - Grey suit jacket, matching pants, olive pinstripe short sleeved shirt, olive tie, olive socks, black shoes.	595	395	480	300	185	250
1419	**T.V.'s GOOD TONIGHT** - Red cotton robe, w/navy braided trim & pocket crest, self belt, cork sandals w/red straps, television w/antenna.	260	185	230	110	85	95
1418	**TIME TO TURN IN** - Navy 2-piece pajamas w/red polka-dots, red collar, cuffs, & 3 red buttons, grey electric razor.	175	130	140	65	50	60
1411	**VICTORY DANCE** - Navy knit blazer w/pocket crest, white long-sleeved shirt, white pants, red vest w/plaid back & 3 gold buttons, red socks, black/white shoes.	155	100	138	60	48	55

KEN (1969-72)
1400 SERIES FASHIONS - PART TWO

STOCK NO.	FASHION	NRFB			MINT & COMPLETE		
		HIGH	LOW	AVG	HIGH	LOW	AVG
1434	**BIG BUSINESS** - Black/white houndstooth 2-piece suit, blue short-sleeved shirt, multi-pastel striped tie, black socks, black loafers.	85	55	66	35	20	28
1436	**BOLD GOLD** - Gold/yellow/burgundy plaid blazer, yellow nylon shirt, gold pants, gold socks, brown loafers.	80	50	72	40	26	34
1428	**BREAKFAST AT 7** - Yellow/orange plaid 2-piece pajamas, orange knit robe w/matching plaid collar & tie belt, orange boxers, shaver, brown slippers.	75	45	60	38	25	32
1472	**CASUAL SCENE** - Blue felt jacket w/4 white buttons, white nylon dickey, red/blue patterned knit pants, blue socks, black loafers.	75	50	62	40	20	34
1431	**GURUVY FORMAL** - Red Nehru jacket, red/gold brocade vest w/white back, white long-sleeved shirt w/attached gold lamé tie, white pants, white socks, white loafers.	140	100	118	75	50	65
1496	**NIGHT SCENE** - Burgundy velour jacket w/satin shawl collar, boutonniere, matching velour pants w/satin stripe, white ruffled dickey w/burgundy trim & black bow tie, burgundy cummerbund, burgundy socks, black loafers.	100	75	86	75	45	60
1433	**PLAY IT COOL** - Tan felt double-breasted coat w/4 buttons, red knit turtleneck, gold/red/black argyle print knit pants, red socks, brown loafers.	85	65	75	40	25	30
1429	**RALLY GEAR** - Brown vinyl jacket w/8 buttons, reddish-orange/yellow/blue plaid cotton shirt, tan cotton pants, brown cowboy boots.	95	80	85	55	40	45
1449	**SEA SCENE** - Red/white blue bold striped jacket w/red stitching & 2 white buttons, matching striped pants, white vinyl belt w/gold buckle, blue nylon shirt, white vinyl sandals.	70	45	56	40	28	34
1435	**SHORE LINES** - Blue plastic jacket w/yellow zippered front, multi-brights abstract-patterned pants w/attached red belt, blue swim trunks w/vinyl trim, yellow vinyl mask, snorkel & fins.	65	40	55	35	25	32

KEN (1964-66)
1400 SERIES FASHIONS - PART TWO CONTINUED

STOCK NO.	FASHION	NRFB HIGH	NRFB LOW	NRFB AVG	MINT & COMPLETE HIGH	MINT & COMPLETE LOW	MINT & COMPLETE AVG
1438	**SKIING SCENE, THE** - Red/yellow/navy striped sweater, matching hat w/red pom, navy cotton pants, red gloves, black ski boots, yellow skis, wooden ski poles w/black "baskets."	100	75	88	50	38	44
1439	**SUEDE SCENE** - Brown fringed suede vest, self belt w/gold buckle, matching brown suede pants, red medallion-print shirt, brown socks, brown loafers.	70	50	62	40	22	30
1430	**TOWN TURTLE** - Blue cotton double-breasted blazer w/6 buttons, white cotton shirt, blue plaid pants, blue socks, black loafers.	85	50	68	45	30	38
1473	**V.I.P. SCENE** - Red/black plaid blazer w/4 buttons, matching plaid pants, orange shirt, white tie w/black dots, black socks, black loafers.	90	65	78	45	30	35

❖❖❖❖❖❖❖❖❖❖❖❖❖❖❖❖

KEN (1972) FASHION ORIGINALS

STOCK NO.	FASHION	NRFB HIGH	NRFB LOW	NRFB AVG	MINT & COMPLETE HIGH	MINT & COMPLETE LOW	MINT & COMPLETE AVG
1718	**BROWN ON BROWN** - Brown cotton blazer, yellowish-green shirt w/stripe & tan flowers, light brown pants, yellow tie, brown loafers.	95	75	85	60	40	50
1717	**CASUAL CORDS** - Royal blue vest w/self belt & gold buckle, multi-floral print shirt, gold cords, brown loafers.	80	65	72	55	35	40
1719	**MIDNIGHT BLUES** - Navy blue cotton blazer & pants, white cotton shirt, ribbon bow tie, black loafers.	125	95	112	75	55	65
1828	**MOD MADRAS** - Gold cotton shirt w/2 buttons & belt w/gold buckle, maroon dickey, maroon, gold, white, dark blue madras plaid pants, brown plastic sandals.	120	85	105	70	52	65
1829	**RED, WHITE & WILD** - Red nylon shirt w/white stars, blue pinstriped vest w/buckles, blue/white awning-striped pants, white tennis shoes.	80	50	65	30	20	26
1720	**WAY OUT WEST** - Dark denim jacket & jeans, red nylon bandana, brown cowboy boots.	80	50	65	40	20	28

VINTAGE OUTFIT ACCESSORIES KEN 700 SERIES FASHIONS

STOCK NO.	OUTFIT	MINT/COMPLETE HIGH	LOW	AVG
779	**AMERICAN AIRLINES CAPTAIN**			
	Black Shoes	5	3	4
	Black Socks	5	3	4
	Flight Log	35	15	25
	Hat	55	35	45
774	**ARABIAN NIGHTS**			
	Slippers	28	15	22
	Turban	25	15	20
797	**ARMY AND AIR FORCE**			
	Beige Cap	8	5	7
	Beige Socks	10	7	9
	Beige Tie	14	10	12
	Blue Cap	8	5	7
	Blue or Beige Belt ea.	10	6	8
	Blue Tie	15	12	14
	Navy Blue Socks	14	10	12
	Poster	18	12	15
770	**CAMPUS HERO**			
	Pennant	13	5	9
	Red Socks	5	3	4
	White Dress Shoes	5	3	4
782	**CASUALS**			
	Brown Shoes w/white tops	8	5	7
	Hat	10	3	7
	Keys	45	25	35
	Striped Socks	8	5	7
793	**DR. KEN**			
	Doctor Bag	15	10	13
	Hat	8	5	7
	Head Mirror	10	5	8
	Mask	14	10	12
	Stethoscope	14	10	12
	White Shoes	5	3	4
	White Socks	5	3	4
785	**DREAMBOAT**			
	Brown Dress Shoes	5	3	4
	Hat	18	12	15
	Yellow Socks	5	3	4
775	**DRUM MAJOR**			
	Baton	28	15	22

VINTAGE OUTFIT ACCESSORIES
KEN 700 SERIES FASHIONS CONTINUED

STOCK NO.	OUTFIT	MINT/COMPLETE		
		HIGH	LOW	AVG
775	**DRUM MAJOR** (continued)			
	Hat	18	10	14
	Socks	5	3	4
	White Shoes	5	3	4
791	**FUN ON THE ICE**			
	Gloves	14	10	12
	Hat	8	3	6
	Scarf	15	12	14
	Skates	15	10	13
795	**GRADUATION**			
	Cap	10	5	8
	Diploma	20	15	18
780	**IN TRAINING**			
	Bar Bells	5	1	3
	How to Build Muscles Book	12	8	10
777	**KEN IN HOLLAND**			
	Bouquet	35	22	29
	Hat	25	14	20
	Socks	18	12	15
	"Wooden" Shoes	24	18	21
778	**KEN IN MEXICO**			
	Black Cowboy Boots	12	10	11
	Black Tie	24	15	20
	Green Cummerbund	24	15	20
	Hat	15	10	13
776	**KEN IN SWITZERLAND**			
	Boots	10	5	8
	Ceramic Stein	50	38	44
	Hat	18	13	16
	Pipe	50	38	44
	Socks	20	12	16
773	**KING ARTHUR**			
	Gold Belt	24	15	20
	Gray Plastic Sword	22	15	19
	Shield	40	28	34
	Spurs	95	45	70
794	**MASQUERADE**			
	Black Shoes	5	3	4
	Hat	10	5	8
	Invitation	25	15	20

STOCK NO.	OUTFIT	MINT/COMPLETE		
		HIGH	LOW	AVG
794	**MASQUERADE** (continued)			
	Mask	15	10	13
	Skull Cap	15	10	13
792	**PLAY BALL**			
	Baseball	10	7	9
	Bat	12	7	10
	Cap	5	2	4
	Cleats	8	5	7
	Mitt	12	7	10
	Socks	14	10	12
772	**PRINCE, THE**			
	Green Slippers	32	18	25
	Hat	35	18	27
	White Collar	35	22	29
788	**RALLY DAY**			
	Cap	10	3	7
	Keys	45	25	35
	Map	25	15	20
796	**SAILOR**			
	Black Shoes	5	3	4
	Blue Tie	20	14	17
	Cap	5	2	4
	Duffle Bag w/string	14	6	10
	White Socks	5	3	4
786	**SATURDAY NIGHT DATE**			
	Black Dress Shoes	5	3	4
	Black Socks	5	3	4
	Striped Tie	15	10	13
798	**SKI CHAMPION**			
	Gloves	12	8	10
	Green Glasses	15	12	14
	Knit Cap	10	4	7
	Ski Boots	8	5	7
	Ski Poles w/grips and snowflakes	18	12	15
	Skis	14	10	12
781	**SLEEPER SET**			
	Alarm Clock	15	10	13
	Cinnamon Bun	15	10	13
	Glass of Milk	15	13	14

VINTAGE OUTFIT ACCESSORIES
KEN 700 SERIES FASHIONS CONTINUED

STOCK NO.	OUTFIT	MINT/COMPLETE		
		HIGH	LOW	AVG
782	**SLEEPER SET** (Blue)			
	Alarm Clock	10	6	8
	Glass of Milk	15	10	13
	Honey Bun	18	12	10
783	**SPORT SHORTS**			
	Brown Dress Shoes	5	3	4
	Long Olive Socks	8	6	7
784	**TERRY TOGS**			
	Black Comb	10	4	7
	Blue Washcloth	5	3	4
	"His" Yellow Towel	8	3	6
	Razor w/cord	14	10	12
	Terry Slippers	8	5	7
	White Briefs	10	5	8
	White Soap	8	3	6
790	**TIME FOR TENNIS**			
	Green Glasses	15	12	14
	Tennis Ball ea.	5	3	4
	Tennis Racket	10	5	8
	Tennis Rules Book	14	10	12
	White Socks	5	3	4
	White Tennis Shoes	8	5	7
799	**TOUCHDOWN**			
	Cleats	8	5	7
	Football	15	8	12
	Helmet	10	5	8
	Shoulder Pads	12	5	9
	Socks	14	10	12
787	**TUXEDO**			
	Black Dress Shoes	5	3	4
	Black Socks	5	3	4
	Bow Tie	28	20	24
	Corsage in clear plastic box	35	18	27
	Corsage - no box	32	15	24
	Cummerbund	15	12	9
789	**YACHTSMAN, THE**			
	Black Dress Shoes	5	3	4
	How to Sail Book	15	10	13
	Rare Cap	250	125	188
	White Socks	5	3	4

VINTAGE OUTFIT ACCESSORIES
KEN 1400 SERIES FASHIONS

STOCK NO.	OUTFIT	MINT/COMPLETE		
		HIGH	LOW	AVG
1425 BEST MAN				
	Black Shoes	5	3	4
	Black Socks	5	3	4
	Red Bow Tie	125	95	110
	Red Cummerbund	195	115	155
1424 BUSINESS APPOINTMENT				
	Briefcase	295	195	245
	Gloves	250	175	213
	Hat	225	95	160
	Mattel Daily Newspaper	85	45	65
1416 COLLEGE STUDENT				
	Brown Shoes	5	3	4
	Brown Socks	30	20	25
	Brown Tie	25	10	18
	Typewriter	125	35	80
1407 FOUNTAIN BOY				
	Brown or Yellow Pencil ea.	25	18	22
	Brown Tray	18	10	14
	Chocolate Soda	15	12	14
	Hat	18	12	15
	Napkins ea.	18	12	15
	Order Pad	25	18	22
	Spoons ea.	25	15	20
	Strawberry Soda	15	12	14
	Straws ea.	25	15	20
1409 GOING HUNTIN'				
	Boots	12	5	9
	Cap	8	3	6
	Rifle	18	12	15
	Red Socks	5	3	4
1426 HERE COMES THE GROOM				
	Ascot	125	75	100
	Black Shoes	5	3	4
	Black Socks	5	3	4
	Gloves	250	175	213
	Hat	295	195	245
1414 HOLIDAY				
	Black Shoes w/white tops	15	8	12
	Cap	25	15	20
	White Socks	5	3	4
1420 JAZZ CONCERT				
	White Socks	5	3	4
	White Tennis Shoes	12	6	9
1423 KEN A GO GO				
	Guitar w/black Strap	45	25	35
	Microphone	125	75	100
	Red Socks	5	3	4

VINTAGE OUTFIT ACCESSORIES
KEN 1400 SERIES FASHIONS CONTINUED

STOCK NO.	OUTFIT	MINT/COMPLETE		
		HIGH	LOW	AVG
1423 KEN A GO GO (continued)				
	White Tennis Shoes	12	6	9
	Wig	275	125	200
1404 KEN IN HAWAII				
	Hat	15	10	13
	Neck Lei	12	8	10
	Orange/Cork Sandals	18	15	17
	Ukulele	15	8	12
1415 MR. ASTRONAUT				
	Boots	85	45	65
	Flag	50	35	43
	Gloves	75	45	60
	Helmet	150	65	108
1413 OFF TO BED				
	Glass of Milk	15	10	13
	How to Get a Raise Book	10	5	8
	Red Fuzzy Slippers	25	15	20
	Red Telephone	15	10	13
1417 ROVIN' REPORTER				
	Black Shoes	5	3	4
	Camera	40	25	33
	Red Socks	5	3	4
1421 SEEIN' THE SIGHTS				
	Black Shoes	5	3	4
	Red Socks	5	3	4
	Red Tie	20	10	15
1406 SKIN DIVER				
	Green Face Mask	5	1	3
	Green Fins	5	1	3
	Green Snorkel	6	3	5
1401 SPECIAL DATE				
	Black Shoes	5	3	4
	Red Socks	5	3	4
	Red Tie	20	10	15
1422 SUMMER JOB				
	Black Shoes	5	3	4
	Olive Knit Socks	65	40	53
	Olive Tie	75	48	62
1418 TIME TO TURN IN				
	Gray Razor w/cord	10	5	8
1419 T.V.'S GOOD TONIGHT				
	Brown T.V.	10	5	8
	Red/Cork Slippers	15	8	12
1411 VICTORY DANCE				
	Black Shoes w/white tops	15	8	12
	Red Socks	5	3	4
	Red Tie	20	10	15

SKIPPER 1900 SERIES FASHIONS (1964-66) - PART ONE

STOCK NO.	FASHION	NRFB HIGH	LOW	AVG	MINT & COMPLETE HIGH	LOW	AVG
1905	**BALLET LESSONS** - Pink lamé/tulle tutu, black leotard & tights flower & ribbon headband, pink satin bag, program, white toe shoes.	125	100	120	70	45	60
1923	**CAN YOU PLAY?** - Blue sleeveless dress w/red spots & tiny white dots w/ruffled collar & hem, matching red w/white dotted scarf & panties, white ball, jump rope, red flats.	175	125	150	70	40	58
1926	**CHILL CHASERS** - White faux fur coat w/red lining & buttons, red felt beret, white socks, red flats.	90	75	82	60	38	48
1912	**COOKIE TIME** - Red/white/blue sleeveless dress w/red belt & 5 red buttons, cookie mix, cookbook, rolling pin, mixing spoon, pot, red flats.	150	95	120	75	50	64
1933	**COUNTRY PICNIC** - Pink/lime/blue sleeveless dress w/appliqued butterflies, matching tote, red/white checked tablecloth, matching napkin, aqua plate, ice cream cone, glass w/pink drink, hamburger, hotdog on fork, watermelon slice, red or blue thermos, ball, butterfly net, butterfly, pink flats.	475	400	450	295	225	250
1911	**DAY AT THE FAIR** - "Barbie" - print bodysuit, matching scarf, red cotton wrap skirt w/red vinyl belted closure, miniature Barbie doll, red flats.	225	175	190	125	95	110
1929	**DOG SHOW** - Sleeveless top w/pink knit trim & Scottie design, pink skirt w/red pleats, white Scottie w/red leash, dog food box, red flats.	375	265	300	200	100	152
1909	**DREAMTIME** - Pink dotted Swiss 2-piece pajamas w/white lace trim, pink robe w/ribbon tie, stuffed cat, blue phone, phonebook, alarm clock, hot pink felt slippers w/fringe trim.	125	85	98	45	35	40
1906	**DRESS COAT** - Red velvet coat w/3 gold buttons, matching bowed hat & purse w/gold handle & button, white short gloves & anklets, white flats.	150	100	125	65	40	54
1904	**FLOWER GIRL** - Yellow cotton sleeveless dress w/white lace overskirt & straps, yellow-flowered headband w/ribbon, multi-pastel bouquet, short white gloves, white anklets, white flats.	175	120	150	60	45	55
1920	**FUN TIME** - Royal blue jacket w/lime accents & buttons, matching royal pants, madras plaid blouse, sleeveless embroidered blouse, croquet mallet, ball, stake, 2 wickets, royal flats.	175	110	130	85	60	76
1919	**HAPPY BIRTHDAY** - Sleeveless dress w/periwinkle bodice & white skirt w/periwinkle embroidery, white underslip w/periwinkle eyelet trim, white straw hat w/periwinkle ribbon, birthday cake, 6 candles, doily, present, invitation, 4 napkins, 2 pink snappers, short white gloves, white anklets, white flats.	550	495	520	300	185	245

SKIPPER 1900 SERIES FASHIONS (1964-66) - PART ONE CONTINUED

STOCK NO.	FASHION	NRFB HIGH	LOW	AVG	MINT & COMPLETE HIGH	LOW	AVG
1934	**JUNIOR BRIDESMAID** - Pink nylon dress w/white dotted-tulle overlay & pink satin waistband, white organdy slip, pink tulle & flowered hat, pink flower basket w/pink ribbon, short white gloves, white anklets, pink flats.	500	450	475	260	195	240
1917	**LAND & SEA** - Light blue denim jacket & clam-diggers w/red stitching, matching denim hat, red/white striped shirt, red sunglasses, white flats.	165	125	135	95	80	88
1935	**LEARNING TO RIDE** - Black/white checked riding jacket, yellow jodhpurs, red sleeveless shirt, short black gloves, crop, black plastic hat & boots.	350	265	300	195	160	180
1932	**LET'S PLAY HOUSE** - White dress w/blue heart & flower design w/turquoise collar & cuffs, turquoise pinafore w/heart print pockets & 3 handkerchiefs (yellow/lime/pink), baby in diaper, cradle, nursery rhymes book, turquoise flats.	295	200	265	150	100	138
1930	**LOUNGIN' LOVELIES** - Light aqua 2-piece pajamas w/white lace & ribbon trim, matching robe, matching felt slippers.	150	100	130	60	50	52
1903	**MASQUERADE** - Yellow/black short dress w/black tulle trim, black panties, yellow/black felt hat, black mask, invitation, black flats w/yellow pompons.	175	135	155	80	60	70
1913	**ME 'N MY DOLL** - Pink/white cotton gingham dress w/flower applique & ribbon straps, pink nylon slip w/white lace trim, miniature Barbie doll w/matching gingham skirt, white anklets, white flats.	295	250	270	155	125	138
1915	**OUTDOOR CASUALS** - Turquoise roll-collared sweater, matching pants, matching dickey, short white gloves, red yo-yo, white flats.	100	85	94	60	45	54
1914	**PLATTER PARTY** - Maxi dress w/navy bodice & red/green/blue plaid skirt w/red pompon hem, record player, 2 records (1 red, 1 blue), red flats.	135	95	120	65	55	60
1916	**RAIN OR SHINE** - Yellow cotton trench coat w/gold buckle, matching hat, yellow umbrella w/yellow tassel, white boots.	100	80	90	45	28	34
1928	**RAINY DAY CHECKERS** - White/red/navy/green plaid dress w/white lace collar & cuffs, red vest w/4 gold buttons, checkerboard, set of 20 checkers, red tights, black flats.	350	265	300	150	120	138
1901	**RED SENSATION** - Red sleeveless dress w/red rickrack trim & 4 gold buttons, white straw hat w/red ribbon, short white gloves, white anklets, red flats.	165	100	130	60	50	55

SKIPPER 1900 SERIES FASHIONS (1964-66) - PART ONE CONTINUED

STOCK NO.	FASHION	NRFB HIGH	NRFB LOW	NRFB AVG	MINT & COMPLETE HIGH	MINT & COMPLETE LOW	MINT & COMPLETE AVG
1907	**SCHOOL DAYS** - Pink knit cardigan w/4 gold buttons, pink flannel skirt, white blouse, bowl of yarn (green, red, pink) w/2 needles, pink or white kneesocks, black flats.	175	120	145	80	60	70
1921	**SCHOOL GIRL** - Red blazer w/crest, red/white houndstooth pleated skirt, white sleeveless blouse w/red stitching & 2 red buttons, felt hat w/houndstooth hatband & white feather, apple, black patent bookstrap, 3 books (Arithmetic, English, Geography), 2 pencils (red & tan), brown glasses, white anklets, red flats.	250	195	225	140	110	120
1918	**SHIP AHOY** - Dress w/navy/red/white striped knit top & navy pleated skirt, navy nautical vest w/6 gold buttons, sail boat, camera, 2 brochures (Hawaii & Mexico), white anklets, red flats.	225	145	165	125	95	118
1902	**SILK 'N FANCY** - Short-sleeved dress w/red velvet bodice & white satin skirt & gold braid waistband, gold elastic headband, white anklets, black flats.	165	100	130	62	40	52
1908	**SKATING FUN** - Leotard w/white turtleneck top & red tights, red velvet skirt w/floral print suspenders, white fur bonnet w/matching floral print ties & red pompon, white fur muff, white skates w/grey blades.	185	125	150	60	45	56
1936	**SLEDDING FUN** - White fur-collared jacket w/red/navy floral & diamond print, red sleeveless turtleneck, navy bonnet w/matching print ties, navy pants w/attached red socks, white fur/red knit mittens, red sled w/white string, red boots.	325	295	310	180	140	156
1910	**SUNNY PASTELS** - Multi-pastel striped shift w/tree print & 6 gold sequins, matching purse, white anklets, pink flats.	130	100	120	60	46	52
1924	**TEA PARTY** - Yellow sleeveless dress w/white/black daisy pattern & ruffled hem, 2 placemats, 2 turquoise plates, 2 turquoise cups & saucers, 2 spoons, 2 cake slices, yellow flats.	300	235	280	135	90	125
1922	**TOWN TOGS** - Green felt coat w/belted waist & gold buckle, matching jumper w/2 gold buttons at straps, yellow knit turtleneck, black/white checked cap & tights, black flats.	150	110	120	95	55	70
1900	**UNDER-PRETTIES** - White dotted lace half slip w/ruffled hem, white panties, 4 pink curlers, pink comb, brush, hand mirror.	60	50	55	32	22	28
1925	**WHAT'S NEW AT THE ZOO?** - Red sleeveless dress w/white loop trim & 3 red buttons, white cotton sweater w/red trim, red flats.	150	100	125	65	45	55

SKIPPER 1900 SERIES FASHIONS (1966-70) - PART TWO

STOCK NO.	FASHION	NRFB HIGH	NRFB LOW	NRFB AVG	MINT & COMPLETE HIGH	MINT & COMPLETE LOW	MINT & COMPLETE AVG
1949	**ALL PRETTIED UP** - Pink party dress w/white crochet overskirt & lace-trimmed cuffs, white lace nylons, white flats.	175	130	160	90	65	80
1941	**ALL SPRUCED UP** - Black/white tweed dress w/black buttons, white collar & cuffs, orange ribbon tie, white hat w/orange ribbon trim, white shoulder purse, white lace nylons, black flats.	165	120	140	60	40	50
1957	**BABY DOLLS** - Pink 2-piece shortie pajamas w/white lace trim & hot pink bow, pink or yellow comb & brush, hot pink slippers.	115	75	95	50	30	40
1939	**BEACHY-PEACHY** - Yellow dress w/large daisy print & yellow rick-rack trim, yellow shirt/short set w/smaller daisy pattern & rick-rack trim, pink vinyl tote w/large daisy, yellow headband, yellow flats.	160	130	148	110	85	94
1973	**CHILLY CHUMS** - Pink coat w/brass-buckled attached belt, matching hood, pink/yellow ruffled-front dress, pink nylons, yellow flats.	145	100	120	60	45	50
1592	**CONFETTI CUTIE** (Sears) - Yellow mini-skirted jumper w/2 gold buttons & gold chain belt, turquoise/yellow checked mock knit turtleneck, matching checked knee socks, turquoise riding hat, yellow ankle boots.	—	—	—	285	225	258
1972	**DRIZZLE SIZZLE** - Hot pink/lime knit dress w/2 orange flowers, clear raincoat w/orange trim, matching hood, clear boots w/orange trim.	160	120	138	60	40	50
1974	**EENY, MEENY, MIDI** - Yellow midi dress w/white ruffled lace overlay, yellow pantaloons w/white lace trim, hand mirror w/face, wrapped present, yellow flats.	150	115	125	70	50	60
1939	**FLOWER SHOWERS** - Royal blue raincoat w/light blue daisy pattern & self belt w/gold buckle, matching hood, hot pink galoshes.	150	120	135	60	48	52
1949	**GLAD PLAIDS** - White/yellow/pink plaid coat w/pink buttons & belt w/gold buckle, matching plaid skirt, hot pink knit sleeveless shirt, hot pink knit cap w/vinyl bill, matching plaid purse w/gold chain, yellow lace nylons, white ankle boots.	175	125	150	90	70	80
1945	**HEARTS 'N FLOWERS** - Lime print dress w/suspenders & yellow ribbed top, lime print jacket, matching cap, yellow ribbed knee socks, yellow vinyl shoulder purse, black glasses, black book strap w/l red pencil & 1 tan pencil, Arithmetic book, English book, yellow ankle boots. (Variation: Pink/blue/white/green floral pattern fabric - less common.)	325	250	275	160	120	140

STOCK NO.	FASHION	NRFB			MINT & COMPLETE		
		HIGH	LOW	AVG	HIGH	LOW	AVG
1990	**HOPSCOTCHINS** - Hot pink/lime/yellow/blue striped blouse w/gold buttons, lime shorts w/yellow/hot pink vinyl belt & gold buckle, blue flats.	150	100	125	60	40	50
1970	**ICE CREAM 'N CAKE** - White ruffled blouse w/lace trim, light blue full skirt, pink vinyl belt, blue panties w/white lace trim, white lace nylons, white flats.	175	150	160	70	58	65
1944	**'JAMAS 'N JAUNTIES** - One piece, full length lime/hot pink/orange floral print pajamas w/white lace trim & lime bows, matching print cap, white w/hot pink/orange floral print panties & half slip, 4 pink rollers, 4 hairpins, hot pink felt slippers.	150	125	135	70	50	60
1967	**JAZZY JAMYS** - Coral two-piece ruffled baby doll pajamas with chiffon overlay, white felt slippers w/pink puffs.	120	85	98	55	35	45
1966	**JEEPERS CREEPERS** - Red/blue sun top w/blue polka-dots, red & blue striped capri pants, red plastic hat w/blue ties, red & blue beach ball, blue flats.	135	100	120	65	50	55
1969	**KNIT BIT** - Hot pink crochet-knit tunic top w/blue yarn tie belt, hot pink shorts, matching blue/hot pink crochet headband, hot pink knee socks, hot pink ankle boots.	120	90	100	55	40	48
1947	**LOLAPALOOZAS** - Pink w/lime polka-dotted short top w/lime ruffled sleeves, pink/lime dotted bell-bottom pants, sleeveless shirt w/pink/lime dots & stripes, lime skirt w/striped pleat & dotted belt w/brass buckle, pink floral print top w/lime ruffle, floral print shorts, pink flats.	165	115	140	85	70	78
1971	**PANTS 'N PINAFORE** - Orange split skirt dress w/yellow cummerbund & 2 gold buttons, white ruffled pinafore, orange sunbonnet, orange flats.	135	90	100	65	40	54
1950	**PATENT 'N PANTS** - Red vinyl jacket w/gold buttons, jumpsuit w/red/blue dots on white top, blue pants & red vinyl belt w/brass buckle, red flats.	150	100	125	65	50	58
1977	**PLAID CITY** - Lime/blue/white plaid jacket w/blue buttons & blue knit collar, blue knit turtleneck, lime top w/blue button & blue trim, lime pleated skirt, blue knit hat w/pompon, blue flats.	145	100	134	65	42	56
1943	**POPOVER** - White sheath dress w/white ruffled lace overlay, pink vinyl jumper w/yellow dots & lime cut-out dots, white lace hood & nylons, white flats.	225	150	170	90	70	80
1955	**POSY PARTY** - Blue/pink/yellow/white floral print dress w/white lace cuffs & hot pink ribbon accent, hot pink split short underslip w/floral print ruffled legs, white lace nylons, chocolate soda, silver spoon, hot pink flats.	185	125	160	90	65	76

SKIPPER 1900 SERIES FASHIONS (1966-70) - PART TWO CONTINUED

STOCK NO.	FASHION	NRFB HIGH	NRFB LOW	NRFB AVG	MINT & COMPLETE HIGH	MINT & COMPLETE LOW	MINT & COMPLETE AVG
1962	**QUICK CHANGES** - Lt. blue/orange/hot pink knit sweeter w/gold buttons, orange/blue pleated skirt, lt. blue shift, pink knit stockings w/orange tassels, pink or orange flats.	150	110	130	70	40	55
1961	**REAL SPORTY** - Yellow romper w/pink plastic chain link belt, yellow short jacket, hot pink lace nylons, hot pink ankle boots.	160	120	140	85	50	65
1942	**RIGHT IN STYLE** - Pink/green/yellow/blue floral print dress w/green waistband, matching floral print hat, green jumper w/white stitching, black glasses, white anklets, green flats.	235	140	180	110	70	88
1940	**ROLLA SCOOT** - Pink sleeveless sweater w/large flower applique, orange bell bottom pants, roller skates, orange flats.	195	150	175	95	65	80
1976	**SCHOOL'S COOL** - Multi-large floral print smock dress w/sheer white puffed sleeves & collar, hot pink fishnet nylons, hot pink ankle boots.	120	95	105	55	35	42
1956	**SKIMMY STRIPES** - Orange knit sweater dress w/hot pink/yellow/lime stripes, matching knee socks, orange felt cap, black book strap w/l red pencil, 1 tan pencil, Arithmetic book, English book, green glasses, orange flats or ankle boots.	220	150	195	150	70	100
1975	**SUNNY-SUITY** - Yellow lace romper w/hot pink waist band, matching granny hat w/white lace trim, hot pink vinyl bag w/3 yellow daisies, yellow vinyl sandals w/dot cut-outs.	115	90	98	40	32	38
1960	**TRIM TWOSOME** - Orange/pink/yellow/white striped sleeveless dress w/3 gold buttons, white crepe coat w/pink/white belt w/brass buckle, orange purse, orange flats.	100	80	88	65	38	50
1949	**VELVET 'N LACE** - Red velvet coat w/white faux fur collar & cuffs, red empire waist dress w/white lace bodice, short white gloves, white socks, black silver buckled shoes.	225	165	210	85	65	78
1959	**WARM 'N WONDERFUL** - Lime/blue color block plush coat w/lime vinyl trim, blue/lime striped knit mini dress, blue plastic cap, lime fishnet nylons, lime ankle boots or blue knee boots.	180	125	155	95	70	85

SKIPPER 1700 SERIES FASHIONS (1971-72)

STOCK NO.	FASHION	NRFB			MINT & COMPLETE		
		HIGH	LOW	AVG	HIGH	LOW	AVG
1731	**BUDDING BEAUTY** - Dark pink organdy mini-dress w/white/multi-floral bodice & lime ribbon waistband, dark pink or red flats.	75	55	65	45	30	36
1732	**DAISY CRAZY** - Hot pink mini-dress w/big daisy-print sleeves, collar & waist tie, yellow daisy-print knee socks, yellow flats.	68	55	60	40	28	35
1738	**FANCY PANTS** - Light blue w/pastel floral print ruffled capri-pants, matching ruffled top w/hot pink vinyl empire bodice, light blue shorts, hot pink vinyl bag w/3 yellow daisies, light blue flats.	135	80	110	55	38	42
1749	**LEMON FLUFF** - Yellow plush fur robe w/yellow satin ribbon & 2 daisies at the ends, yellow tricot 2-piece bell bottom pajamas w/white lace trim, yellow furry slippers.	100	75	84	50	40	45
1730	**LOTS OF LACE** - Mini-dress w/green velour bodice & white lace skirt w/lime velvet waistband & bow with lace pantyhose, lime green flats.	80	55	70	45	35	40
1747	**PINK PRINCESS** - Lime green short coat w/pink velvet ribbon trim & 4 gold buttons, pink mini-dress w/front pleat, lace trim & 3 gold buttons, light pink plush fur hat, pink sheer pantyhose, ice cream sundae, light pink flats.	95	75	85	50	32	42
1733	**RIK RAK RAH** - Blue cotton romper w/yellow & white rick-rack trim, mini-skirt w/white/blue stripes & yellow rick-rack, attached yellow vinyl suspenders w/2 yellow buttons, blue flats.	75	55	68	40	25	30
1736	**SUPER SLACKS** - Red w/white floral print pants w/red vinyl suspenders, matching hat w/red vinyl bill, white cotton blouse w/white lace trim, red flats.	75	50	60	40	25	30
1748	**TRIPLE TREAT** - Turquoise velour short jacket w/2 white buttons, turquoise velour pants w/turquoise/hot pink/green abstract print waistband, mini-dress w/matching abstract print embire bodice, turquoise velour skirt w/white lace hem, hot pink knit top, abstract print scarf, pink knee socks, blue flats.	120	85	100	65	40	52
1735	**TWICE AS NICE** - Pink/blue felt short coat, matching mini-dress, pink felt hat w/pompon, blue flats.	85	75	80	55	30	40
1737	**VELVET BLUSH** - Red velour mini-dress w/white organdy collar & cuffs w/white lace daisy trim, white organdy waistband & bow, white lace hose, white flats.	95	75	82	60	40	50
1746	**WOOLY WINNER** - Red bouclé wool short coat w/royal blue vinyl trim, matching red wool hat w/royal vinyl trim, mini-dress w/yellow bodice & royal/red/yellow plaid skirt, royal blue knee socks, red vinyl shoulder purse, royal blue ankle boots.	105	80	96	65	50	58

SKIPPER 3400 SERIES FASHIONS (1971-72)

STOCK NO.	FASHION	NRFB HIGH	NRFB LOW	NRFB AVG	MINT & COMPLETE HIGH	MINT & COMPLETE LOW	MINT & COMPLETE AVG
3476	**ALL OVER FELT** - Light blue felt jacket w/yellow trim & collar & light blue felt closure w/2 gold buttons, light blue/yellow felt sleeveless dress, light blue felt floppy hat, yellow felt shoulder purse w/yellow vinyl strap & gold button closure, light blue sheer hose, light blue flats.	150	90	115	75	50	60
3471	**BALLERINA** - Blue satin ballet costume w/pink tutu & cap sleeves, blue satin drawstring bag, pale pink ballet slippers.	80	60	70	42	30	35
3472	**DOUBLE DASHERS** - Navy short coat w/reddish orange large spots, collar & 2 placket closure w/4 gold buttons, reddish orange cotton mini-dress w/navy vinyl front trim & 2 gold buttons, reddish orange flats.	85	50	68	40	32	36
3477	**DRESSED IN VELVET** - Pink velvet swing coat w/large shawl-type collar & white plush fur trim, matching pink velvet hat w/white fur trim, mini-dress w/white bodice, pink velvet pleated skirt & green waistband w/white daisy lace trim, pink sheer hose, white flats.	150	85	115	60	50	55
3473	**GOIN' SLEDDIN'** - Yellow plush fur hooded jacket w/hot pink trim, hot pink pants, bright print blouse, yellow/pink sled, hot pink boots.	90	70	80	50	38	44
3470	**ICE-SKATIN'** - Orange velour skater dress w/3 white buttons & white plush fur hem, orange tights, white plush fur hat w/white ties, white ice skates w/silver blades.	75	60	68	48	35	42
3468	**LITTLE MISS MIDI** - Turquoise long-sleeve blouse w/3 gold orange buttons, gold-orange midi skirt w/pink/turquoise floral print, turquoise boots.	85	65	75	50	40	45
3478	**LONG 'N SHORT OF IT** - Red long coat w/5 gold buttons, red/blue/white abstract print sleeveless mini-dress, w/matching scarf w/white fringe, white hat w/2 red stripes & red pompon, red boots.	85	75	80	50	40	45
3473	**LULLABY LIME** - Lime green tricot sleeveless nightgown w/sheer lime overlay & ruffled hem, hot pink ribbon trim, hot pink felt slippers w/lime green puffs on each.	85	65	75	42	35	38
3465	**SWEET ORANGE** - Orange velour mini-dress w/ 3/4 sleeves & drop waist & white lace trim, white flats.	70	50	60	40	25	32
3467	**TEETER TIMERS** - Yellow sleeveless tunic top w/2 hot pink/floral print large patch pockets & collar, hot pink/floral pants, yellow teeter board.	60	50	55	35	20	26
3466	**TENNIS TIME** - White pleated V-neck tennis dress w/pink trim, white tennis socks, tennis racket, tennis ball, white tennis shoes.	70	60	65	30	20	26

SKIPPER FASHION ORIGINALS (1972)

STOCK NO.	FASHION	NRFB HIGH	LOW	AVG	MINT & COMPLETE HIGH	LOW	AVG
3293	**DREAM-INS** - Pastel floral & lattice print long nightgown w/pink ruffles & neck tie, pink slippers w/pink bows on each.	85	65	75	45	30	38
3291	**NIFTY KNICKERS** - Long sleeved yellow turtleneck, royal blue/tiny floral print knickers, red bib style vest w/yellow stitching & 2 yellow buttons, red boots.	95	75	82	50	35	44
3297	**PARTY PAIR** - Short dress w/white bodice w/pink collar & skirt w/floral "embroidery" band on skirt, white plush fur coat w/pink trim collar, cuffs & hem, pink flats.	95	75	85	52	40	46
3292	**PLAY PANTS** - Dark blue denim romper w/red vinyl suspenders, 2 gold buttons & red heart, red/white floral print blouse w/red turtleneck & sleeve trim, red knit knee socks, white tennis shoes.	85	65	74	50	40	45
3296	**RED, WHITE 'N BLUES** - Red/navy/white heart print peasant style dress w/red/navy ruffled bodice cuffs & hem, navy waist tie belt, red/navy V-neck top w/white trim, navy shorts w/white trim, red knee socks, navy flats.	90	70	82	60	40	50
3295	**TURN ABOUTS** - Red/yellow/navy abstract print knit pants, matching skirt, matching hat w/red pompon, yellow ribbed knit shorts, yellow ribbed knit long sleeved top w/red sleeves & yellow cuffs, sleeveless top of red/yellow/navy abstract print w/wide yellow ribbed knit waistband, red vinyl shoulder bag w/yellow trim, red flats.	90	75	84	60	45	52

❖❖❖❖❖❖❖❖❖❖❖❖❖❖❖

SKIPPER BEST BUY FASHION ORIGINALS (1972)

STOCK NO.	FASHION	NRFB HIGH	LOW	AVG	MINT & COMPLETE HIGH	LOW	AVG
3373	**FLOWER POWER** - White short sleeved blouse w/puffed, ruffled sleeves & front placket w/3 white buttons, dark pink/white floral print maxi skirt w/ruffled hem, lighter pink/white floral print mini skirt, belt w/black ribbon tie, pink flats.	55	45	48	36	25	30
3372	**FUN RUNNERS** - Dark denim jeans w/white stitching, yellow sleeveless shirt, red vinyl belt w/gold buckle, red/white print scarf, rose sunglasses, white tennis shoes.	52	35	40	32	20	26
3371	**SUPER SNOOZERS** - 2 piece pajamas w/tiny pink polka-dots & yellow/pink flower print w/white lace-trimmed short-sleeved top w/3 yellow buttons, matching pants, white comb brush mirror, 4 pink curlers.	60	50	55	40	25	32
3374	**WHITE, BRIGHT 'N SPARKLING** - Long white coat w/6 gold buttons & gold trim at waist, matching white shoulder purse w/gold chain handle & gold trim, white flats.	65	55	60	45	35	40

VINTAGE OUTFIT ACCESSORIES
SKIPPER 1900 SERIES FASHIONS

STOCK NO.	OUTFIT	MINT/COMPLETE		
		HIGH	LOW	AVG
1905 **BALLET CLASS**				
	Ballet Slippers	5	1	3
	Floral Headpiece	14	10	12
	Pink Ballet Bag	5	1	3
1923 **CAN YOU PLAY?**				
	Jump Rope	15	10	13
	Red Flats	8	6	7
	Scarf	12	8	10
	White Ball	10	6	8
1926 **CHILL CHASERS**				
	Red Flats	8	6	7
	Red Hat	24	15	20
	Socks	18	15	17
1912 **COOKIE TIME**				
	Cookie Mix	14	8	11
	Easy As Pie Cookbook	28	20	24
	Metal Bowl	24	10	17
	Red Flats	10	6	8
	Rolling Pin	3	1	2
	Spoon w/red handle	9	5	7
1933 **COUNTRY PICNIC**				
	Ball	50	35	43
	Blanket	15	12	14
	Blue Plate	18	10	14
	Butterfly	35	20	28
	Butterfly Net	24	15	20
	Hamburger	10	5	8
	Hot Dog on Fork	22	15	19
	Ice Cream Cone	24	15	20
	Napkin	18	13	16
	Pink Flats	12	8	10
	Strawberry Soda	15	12	14
	Thermos w/lid	30	20	25
	Tote	15	10	13
1911 **DAY AT THE FAIR**				
	Head Scarf	25	15	20
	Miniature Barbie	95	55	75
	Red Flats	8	3	6
1929 **DOG SHOW**				
	Dog Food Box	18	12	15
	Red Flats	8	6	7
	White Dog	145	125	135
1909 **DREAMTIME**				
	Alarm Clock	10	6	8
	Blue Kitty	12	8	10
	Blue Princess Phone	10	8	9

STOCK NO.	OUTFIT	MINT/COMPLETE HIGH	LOW	AVG
1909 DREAMTIME (continued)				
	Red Telephone Directory	15	12	14
	Slippers	8	3	6
1906 DRESS COAT				
	Hat	10	4	7
	Purse	10	6	8
	Short White Gloves	18	15	17
	Socks	18	15	17
	White Flats	12	8	10
1904 FLOWER GIRL				
	Bouquet	15	10	13
	Floral Headpiece	15	8	12
	Short White Gloves	18	15	17
	Socks	18	10	14
	White Flats	12	8	10
1920 FUN TIME				
	Ball	12	8	10
	Blue Flats	8	6	7
	Mallet	12	8	10
	Metal Wickets (2)	25	15	20
	Stake (2) ea.	15	10	13
1919 HAPPY BIRTHDAY				
	Cake	18	10	14
	Candles (6) ea.	20	15	18
	Doily	30	20	25
	Hat	25	10	18
	Invitation	25	18	22
	Present w/ribbon and tag	32	18	25
	Short White Gloves	18	15	17
	Snappers (2) ea.	25	18	22
	Socks	18	15	17
	White Flats	12	8	10
1934 JUNIOR BRIDESMAID				
	Flower Basket	65	45	55
	Hat	85	55	70
	Pink Flats	12	8	10
	Short White Gloves	18	15	17
1917 LAND & SEA				
	Hat	14	10	12
	Red Sunglasses	65	25	45
	White Flats	12	8	10
1935 LEARNING TO RIDE				
	Black Boots	20	15	18
	Black Crop	65	45	55
	Black Hat	20	15	18
	Short Black Gloves	75	48	62

VINTAGE OUTFIT ACCESSORIES
SKIPPER 1900 SERIES FASHIONS CONTINUED

STOCK NO.	OUTFIT	MINT/COMPLETE HIGH	LOW	AVG
1932 LET'S PLAY HOUSE				
	Baby	15	10	13
	Cradle	22	12	17
	Light Blue Flats	12	8	10
	Nursery Rhyme Book	22	12	17
	Yellow, Pink or Green Handkerchiefs ea.	15	8	12
1930 LOUNGIN' LOVELIES				
	Slippers	22	10	16
1903 MASQUERADE				
	Black Mask	20	12	16
	Black Shoes w/yellow poms	45	20	33
	Invitation	25	18	22
1913 ME 'N MY DOLL				
	Miniature Barbie	95	55	75
	Socks	18	15	17
	White Flats	12	8	10
1915 OUTDOOR CASUALS				
	Short White Gloves	18	15	17
	White Flats	12	8	10
	Yo-Yo	20	10	15
1914 PLATTER PARTY				
	Record Player	15	13	14
	Record w/Red or Blue Label ea.	20	10	15
	Red Flats	10	6	8
1916 RAIN OR SHINE				
	Cap	12	8	10
	Umbrella w/tassel	15	10	13
	White Rain Boots	10	5	8
1928 RAINY DAY CHECKERS				
	Black Flats	8	6	7
	Checkerboard	32	20	26
	Plastic Checkers	28	18	23
	Stockings	20	15	18
1901 RED SENSATION				
	Hat	20	15	18
	Short White Gloves	18	15	17
	Socks	18	10	14
1907 SCHOOL DAYS				
	Black Flats	8	3	6
	Bowl of Yarn	12	7	10
	Pink Knee High Socks	18	15	17
	White Knee High Socks	15	12	14
1921 SCHOOL GIRL				
	Apple	14	10	12
	Arithmetic Book	12	8	10
	Black Book Strap	5	3	4

VINTAGE OUTFIT ACCESSORIES
SKIPPER 1900 SERIES FASHIONS CONTINUED

STOCK NO.	OUTFIT	MINT/COMPLETE		
		HIGH	LOW	AVG
1921 **SCHOOL GIRL** (continued)				
	English Book	10	6	8
	Geography Book	13	10	12
	Glasses w/brown frames	55	35	45
	Red Flats	8	6	7
	Red Hat w/feather	15	8	12
	Red or Brown Pencil ea.	15	10	13
	Socks	18	15	17
1918 **SHIP AHOY**				
	Camera	35	15	25
	Mexico or Hawaii Brochure ea.	25	20	23
	Red Flats	10	6	8
	Sailboat	25	15	20
	Socks	18	15	17
1902 **SILK 'N FANCY**				
	Black Flats	10	6	8
	Gold Stretch Headband	18	12	15
	Socks	18	10	14
1908 **SKATING FUN**				
	Hat	10	5	8
	Muff	10	7	9
	Skates	15	10	13
1936 **SLEDDING FUN**				
	Boots	15	12	14
	Hat	10	7	9
	Mittens	25	18	22
	Sled	75	45	60
1910 **SUNNY PASTELS**				
	Pink Flats	12	8	10
	Tote	18	8	13
	Socks	18	10	14
1924 **TEA PARTY**				
	Placemats (2) ea.	12	8	10
	Spoon (2)	24	12	18
	Styrofoam Cake Slices	18	12	15
	Teapot	15	10	13
	Turquoise Cup	10	5	8
	Turquoise Plate	12	6	9
	Turquoise Saucer	10	5	8
	Yellow Flats	12	8	10
1922 **TOWN TOGS**				
	Black Flats	8	6	7
	Black/White Checked Hat	15	12	14
	Black/White Checked Stockings	15	12	14
1900 **UNDER-PRETTIES**				
	Pink Brush, Comb or Rollers ea.	3	1	2

RICKY FASHIONS (1965-67)

STOCK NO.	FASHION	NRFB HIGH	LOW	AVG	MINT & COMPLETE HIGH	LOW	AVG
1506	**LET'S EXPLORE** - Red/charcoal/white plaid long-sleeved shirt w/3 black buttons, grey, zippered slacks, red socks, black shoes.	150	100	120	65	50	58
1501	**LIGHTS OUT**- Yellow 2-piece cotton pajamas w/white collar & "R" initial on pocket, blue terry bathrobe, blue terry slippers.	98	75	90	55	40	50
1504	**LITTLE LEAGUER** - Red knit shirt w/large navy stripe, zippered blue jeans, red baseball cap w/a white "M", brown plastic catcher's mitt, baseball, red socks w/navy bands, white tennis shoes.	100	85	92	60	40	52
1502	**SATURDAY SHOW** - Long-sleeved shirt cotton shirt, red tie, khaki slacks, red socks, black shoes.	95	85	90	50	38	45
1505	**SKATEBOARD SET** - Red/grey pinstripe short-sleeved shirt w/4 red buttons, white zippered cotton shorts, tan skateboard w/painted red stripe, white socks, white tennis shoes.	125	90	100	50	40	46
1503	**SUNDAY SUIT** - Red/black/grey striped blazer w/3 buttons & black collar, white short-sleeved cotton dress shirt, black slacks, red socks, black shoes.	100	75	90	55	45	50

❖❖❖❖❖❖❖❖❖❖❖❖❖❖

TWIGGY FASHIONS (1968)

STOCK NO.	FASHION	NRFB HIGH	LOW	AVG	MINT & COMPLETE HIGH	LOW	AVG
1725	**TWIGGY-DOS** - Yellow ribbed knit mini-dress w/ green & white stripes, yellow vinyl purse w/gold chain, green/white beaded, 2-strand necklace, yellow kneesocks, yellow soft bow shoes.	285	195	250	150	100	128
1728	**TWIGGY GEAR** - Red/white/blue/pink knit tank top attached to white vinyl pants, blue vinyl belt w/gold buckle, rose hat w/blue band & ties, camera, royal blue soft buckle shoes.	260	185	235	130	85	110
1726	**TWIGGY TURNOUTS** - Mini tank dress w/silver lamé skirt & yellow/green/orange striped bodice, attached silver foil belt, yellow/orange/green striped nylon bra, matching striped panties, silver boots.	285	200	240	175	95	120
1727	**TWIGSTER** - Yellow/orange striped knit mini-dress w/checked top, matching checked scarf w/yellow fringe, orange cosmetic case, hot pink powder puff, eyelash brush, eyebrow pencil, hot pink comb & brush, hot pink hand mirror, orange, hard cut-out shoes.	275	180	230	150	90	115

VINTAGE OUTFIT ACCESSORIES
TWIGGY FASHIONS

STOCK NO.	OUTFIT	MINT/COMPLETE		
		HIGH	LOW	AVG
1725 **TWIGGY-DOS**				
	Green/White Double Strand Necklace	48	28	38
	Green/White Single Strand Necklace	40	24	32
	Yellow Cotton Knee Socks	30	18	24
	Yellow Vinyl Shoulder Bag	30	18	24
1728 **TWIGGY GEAR**				
	Black/Gray Camera	36	24	30
	Blue Plastic Belt	28	15	22
	Rose Color Floppy Hat	44	28	35
	Royal Blue Soft Buckle Flats	24	12	18
1726 **TWIGGY TURNOUTS**				
	Green Vinyl Bra	25	15	20
	Green Vinyl Bottoms	25	15	20
	Multicolored Stripe Bottoms	28	18	22
	Multicolored Stripe Nylon Bra	28	18	22
	Silver Boots	25	15	20
1727 **TWIGSTER**				
	Brown eyebrow Pencil	22	12	18
	Black Eyelash Brush	25	15	20
	Hot Pink Brush	8	2	5
	Hot Pink Comb	4	2	3
	Hot Pink/White Powder Puff w/orange strap	7	3	5
	Orange Hard Pointed Heels w/cutouts	20	12	15
	Orange Plastic Cosmetic Case	20	10	15
	Yellow/Orange Knit Scarf w/fringe	28	15	22

FRANCIE 1200 SERIES FASHIONS (1966-67) - PART ONE

STOCK NO. FASHION	NRFB			MINT & COMPLETE		
	HIGH	LOW	AVG	HIGH	LOW	AVG
1275 **BELLS** - Red/white/blue floral & diamond print sleeveless top, blue/white floral bell bottoms, matching cap, red vinyl shoulder bag or red vinyl oversized bag, royal blue soft buckle flats.	175	140	155	100	70	90
1287 **BORDER-LINE** - Yellow linen sleeveless pleated dress w/navy trim, matching jacket w/3 yellow buttons, yellow hat, yellow lace hose, black soft buckle flats.	198	150	180	120	75	98
1279 **BRIDGE BIT, THE** - White cable-knit sweater, royal blue/lime stitched accents, royal blue stretch pants w/elastic waist & gold buckle, throw pillow w/flower design, play book, deck of 26 cards, royal blue soft buckle flats.	350	250	300	175	125	150
1291 **CHECK THIS** - Black/white checked long sundress w/yellow ruffled chiffon trim & 6 yellow/white daisies, yellow chiffon scarf w/1 daisy, short white gloves, white hard heels w/cut-outs or white soft heels.	185	150	165	100	75	90
1259 **CHECKMATES** - Red/white/navy houndstooth plaid jacket w/self belt & gold buckle, matching pleated skirt, white embroidered shell, red vinyl shoulder bag, red soft heels or red hard heels.	175	140	158	90	70	80
1258 **CLAM DIGGERS** - Orange/yellow bold striped vinyl rain jacket w/6 gold buttons, matching hat, yellow knit shirt, orange cotton clam-digger shorts, orange glasses, yellow soft flats or soft heels.	250	175	205	115	75	92
1281 **CLEAR OUT!** - Red/white/blue bold striped knit dress, clear vinyl raincoat w/red trim & 5 blue closures, clear hood with face cut-out & red trim, red hat box w/red/white/blue decals, clear rainboots w/red trim.	325	285	300	195	150	185
1256 **CONCERT IN THE PARK** - Dress w/navy crepe skirt & white ruffled bodice w/red polka dots, navy vest w/matching dot lining, white hat w/red dots & navy ribbon, white purse w/red dots & red vinyl handles, red soft heels.	250	200	225	120	75	90
1280 **COOL WHITE** - White cotton sheath dress w/white organdy overlay & white appliqued flowers w/crystal bead centers, white cotton hair bow w/1 flower & hairpin underneath, white lace hose, white soft heels.	250	160	180	105	80	90
1257 **DANCE PARTY** - Pink crepe dress w/white crocheted collar & sleeves, white crocheted bonnet w/pink ties, half slip w/pink polka dots, white lace hose, record player, 2 records (1 red label, 1 blue), ice cream parfait, spoon, paper napkin, pink soft heels.	265	225	235	160	115	132
1290 **DENIMS ON!** - Jumpsuit w/yellow/blue/green bold striped tank shirt, yellow linen pants, & navy vinyl belt w/gold buckle, blue denim jacket w/6 gold buttons, matching denim hat w/vinyl bill, blue denim soft buckle flats.	175	125	150	95	60	80

FRANCIE 1200 SERIES FASHIONS (1966-67) - PART ONE CONTINUED

STOCK NO.	FASHION	NRFB HIGH	NRFB LOW	NRFB AVG	MINT & COMPLETE HIGH	MINT & COMPLETE LOW	MINT & COMPLETE AVG
1260	**FIRST FORMAL** - Gown w/periwinkle crepe bodice & white skirt w/organdy pastel floral eyelet overskirt, hot pink bow waist accent, hot pink ruffled organza cape, short white gloves, blue soft heels or hard heels w/cut-outs.	250	175	190	110	75	90
1252	**FIRST THINGS FIRST** - White lace full slip w/multi-bright floral hem panel, multi-floral pantaloons, tap pants, & garter belt w/4 pink garters, flesh-tone lace hose.	150	100	120	65	45	55
1254	**FRESH AS A DAISY** - Yellow sleeveless dress w/white or yellow lace w/green trimmed skirt, matching tote, white or yellow lace bonnet w/yellow ties, yellow soft heels.	175	100	150	80	50	70
1262	**FUR-OUT** - Black/brown/white fur coat w/red satin lining & black vinyl waist black vinyl tie belt, red stockings, red vinyl mittens, red knit hood, black vinyl spats, black soft buckle flats.	485	385	425	300	200	260
1296	**FURRY GO ROUND** (Sears) - Orange suede coat w/brown rows of fur, orange suede hood w/gold button closure, orange lace hose, orange vinyl boots.	550	475	520	325	250	286
1250	**GAD ABOUTS** - Lime/blue patterned knit sweater w/lime collar, matching stockings, lime knit skirt & hat, w/blue sunglasses (or rare blue or green striped version), lime flats or lime ankle boots.	225	165	195	115	90	100
1294	**GO GOLD** (Sears) - Gold lamé jacket w/pink lining & 6 gold buttons, gold belt w/gold buckle, gold lamé pants, gold/blue/hot pink lamé plaid shell, hot pink soft buckle flats.	500	475	486	285	225	276
1267	**GO, GRANNY, GO** - Green granny gown w/rose & daisy print & white lace trim, record player, record w/red or blue label, album cover, pink soft heels or pink hard heels w/cut-outs. Soft pink buckle flats or rare pink flats w/silver foil buckles also can be found.	165	120	148	95	70	82
1270	**GROOVY GET-UP** - Hot pink corduroy jacket w/4 black buttons & black plastic belt, hot pink corduroy pants & mini-skirt, pink/black striped knit shirt, matching hood & stockings, black soft ankle boots.	450	400	425	290	200	260
1272	**HI-TEEN** - Pink/yellow/red/green striped knit shirt, fuchsia wrap skirt w/yellow vinyl side belt, pink or red soft heels, red Skipper flats or red hard heels w/cut-outs.	135	100	120	70	50	60
1265	**HIP KNITS** - Turquoise knit shirt & stockings, turquoise/navy herringbone skirt w/yellow vinyl thin belt, yellow buckle flats or rare yellow flats w/gold buckles.	275	195	215	125	85	105

FRANCIE 1200 SERIES FASHIONS (1966-67) - PART ONE CONTINUED

STOCK NO.	FASHION	NRFB			MINT & COMPLETE		
		HIGH	LOW	AVG	HIGH	LOW	AVG
1274	**ICED BLUE** - Turquoise linen sleeveless dress w/white lace trim & lace neck bow, white lace hose, white soft heels.	150	90	115	60	35	45
1288	**IN-PRINT** - Pastel floral print dress w/ruffled hem, matching bonnet, green cotton sleeveless slip w/white trim, yellow soft heels or yellow hard heels w/cut-outs.	185	140	165	100	70	80
1251	**IT'S A DATE** - Empire waist cotton dress w/chartreuse/turquoise striped skirt & chartreuse dotted turquoise bodice w/white collar & French cuffs, attached chartreuse ribbon, pale aqua lace hose, blue soft heels.	175	120	140	80	50	62
1269	**LEATHER LIMELIGHT** - Fuchsia/lime/turquoise/white paisley print jersey shirt & skirt, white vinyl w/fuchsia trimmed skirt w/4 gold buttons, pants, & hood, white boots w/fuchsia trim, aqua soft buckle flats or rare royal blue soft buckle flats.	285	250	265	170	120	140
1284	**MISS TEENAGE BEAUTY** - Sleeveless 2 piece gown w/pink ruffled nylon skirt w/satin lining & white lace top w/pink/blue appliqued flowers, long white gloves, clear tiara w/silver glitter, silver loving cup w/ "F," 6 rose bouquet w/feathers, sash, light blue soft heels or light blue hard heels w/cut-outs.	1750	1025	1455	825	675	780
1289	**NOTE THE COAT!** - White textured crepe coat w/white lining & 8 gold buttons, optional soft white heels or white hard heels w/cut-outs.	100	70	82	50	38	44
1263	**ORANGE COZY** - Orange velvet dress w/black/grey yarn trim, matching hood, short black gloves, orange stockings, black soft ankle boots.	275	200	250	160	110	138
1293	**PARTNERS IN PRINT** (Sears) - Olive/multi-floral print jacket w/white lace collar & cuffs, olive/multi-floral pants & skirt, hot pink hat box w/*Francie* decal, pink soft heels or pink soft buckle flats.	500	425	475	300	260	280
1255	**POLKA DOTS 'N RAINDROPS** - Red vinyl raincoat w/white polka dots, zippered pockets & yellow lining, matching scarf w/yellow tie or rare matching hood, red plastic rainboots.	135	100	110	60	35	42
1295	**PROM PINKS** (Sears) - Sleeveless pink satin gown w/paler pink silk skirt & gold lamé trim, pink satin long coat w/gold lamé sleeve trim, gold foil belt w/gold buckle, headband w/gold lamé bow and ribbon, pink soft heels or pink hard heels w/cut-outs.	1500	1000	1360	650	460	565
1266	**QUICK SHIFT** - Olive knit turtleneck & stockings, hot pink felt jumper w/olive trim & waist tie, pink soft buckle flats or rare pink flats w/gold buckles.	225	165	186	125	90	105
1261	**SHOPPIN' SPREE** - White crepe sheath w/pink mini blocks, red/white herringbone coat w/8 white buttons, matching purse, short white gloves, pink soft heels.	175	135	150	90	70	82

FRANCIE 1200 SERIES FASHIONS (1966-67) - PART ONE CONTINUED

STOCK NO.	FASHION	NRFB HIGH	LOW	AVG	MINT & COMPLETE HIGH	LOW	AVG
1273	**SIDE-KICK** - Navy/white gingham dress w/white eyelet trim, 5 red buttons & red plastic or grosgrain bow, matching hat w/red band, red soft heels or red hard heels w/cut-outs.	100	85	90	60	40	50
1271	**SLUMBER NUMBER** - Yellow tricot peignoir w/pink/yellow/white lace overlay, yellow panty w/pink/white ruffle trim, sleeping mask w/pink ribbon ties, yellow felt slippers w/pink pompons.	100	75	90	55	35	40
1268	**STYLE SETTERS** - Multi-brights floral jersey dress & stockings, turquoise velvet cape & hood w/same floral jersey lining, blue soft heels.	295	225	265	155	100	140
1292	**SUMMER COOLERS** - Yellow cover up w/navy/red floral accents, navy/red floral 2-piece swimsuit w/red bows, yellow tote bag w/navy/red floral accent & red drawstring, umbrella, braided blonde or brunette hair piece w/red bow & gold barrette, granny glasses, cork sandals w/red ties.	495	395	455	325	250	298
1276	**SUMMER FROST** - White eyelet sheath w/pink lining & large pink back bow, blonde or brunette braid on a brass headband w/2 pink bows, pink soft heels or pink hard heels w/cut-outs.	200	150	174	120	80	92
1277	**SUN SPOTS** - Hot pink empire-waisted dress w/bright yellow sun spots, hot pink hat w/yellow hatband & 4 yellow flowers, pink vinyl purse w/daisy, hot pink soft heels or hot pink hard heels w/cut-outs.	175	125	145	100	75	86
1283	**SWEET 'N SWINGIN'** - Pale pink cotton gown w/embroidered nylon overskirt & pink/blue ribbon flowers w/green leaves at bodice, sheer pink nylon long coat w/flower-trimmed collar & cuffs, white clutch or white purse w/handle, pink soft heels or pink hard heels w/cut-outs or white soft or hard heels.	500	450	475	260	185	215
1264	**SWINGIN' SKIMMY** - Long-sleeve red knit dress w/navy braid trim & chartreuse knit cowl, chartreuse knit hood, red knit stockings, red soft ankle boots.	285	200	250	150	100	135
1253	**TUCKERED OUT** - White nightie w/blue/white gingham check ruffled hem, sleeves & bib, matching gingham bonnet w/3 flowers (red, white, blue), gingham booties, pink mirror, comb, brush & 4 or 6 pink curlers.	125	100	110	65	35	56
1286	**TWEED-SOMES** - Olive/hot pink/white tweed coat w/4 hot pink pocket flaps & 3 hot pink buttons, sleeveless dress w/hot pink bodice & matching tweed skirt, attached hot pink belt w/gold buckle, matching tweed cap, pale pink lace hose, hat box w/hot pink/green "Francie" decal, green/white plastic double or single strand of beads, hot pink soft heels.	375	275	300	190	150	180

FRANCIE 1200 SERIES FASHIONS (1968-71) - PART TWO

STOCK NO.	FASHION	NRFB			MINT & COMPLETE		
		HIGH	LOW	AVG	HIGH	LOW	AVG
1242	**ALTOGETHER ELEGANT** - Hot pink satin gown w/white brocade nylon overlay & silver braid trim, matching short jacket w/3 silver buttons, silver clutch, short white gloves, silver clutch, hot pink hard heels w/cut-outs, hot pink buckle flats, or silver-buckled flats.	250	175	195	160	100	140
1239	**BLOOM ZOOM** - Multi-brights floral nylon mini-dress, matching tights, orange felt vest w/2 buttons, aqua soft buckle flats.	100	85	95	65	40	50
1234	**COMBINATION, THE** - White plush coat w/ turquoise trim, multi-brights floral nylon shirt, turquoise suede skirt w/gold chain belt, green knit shell, matching stockings, white plush hat w/green trim, green ankle boots.	225	170	196	120	90	106
1215	**COMBO, THE** - Hot pink/blue checked knit coat, hot pink/blue striped knit skirt, matching shell w/ wide hot pink band, hot pink fringed scarf, hot pink lace or patterned hose, hot pink bow shoes or soft pointed heels.	250	175	210	130	90	115
1214	**CULOTTE-WOT?** - Fuchsia nylon sleeveless culotte dress w/white satin trim, white satin or taffeta hat w/elastic strap, white fishnet hose, green sunglasses w/white & pink dot trim, fuchsia or hot pink boots.	260	200	240	170	100	138
1217	**DREAMY WEDDING** - White satin sleeveless gown, daisy embroidered sheer white overdress, satin bow hairband veil, white 3 lily bouquet w/4 grosgrain streamers, white soft heels or white hard heels w/cut-outs.	385	295	350	220	160	195
1207	**FLOATING-IN** - White nylon underdress w/hot pink/multi-striped chiffon overdress & hot pink ruffled hem, hot pink short gloves, hot pink hard heels w/cut-outs.	250	185	205	135	90	122
1222	**GOLD RUSH** - Mini-dress w/gold lamé bodice/orange skirt & gold lamé fishnet overskirt, orange hard heels w/cut-outs.	100	75	85	55	40	48
1210	**HILL-RIDERS** - Lime cable knit sweater, lime/pink/purple striped cotton pants, lime soft ankle boots.	100	75	88	60	40	50

STOCK NO.	FASHION	NRFB			MINT & COMPLETE		
		HIGH	LOW	AVG	HIGH	LOW	AVG
1216	**LACE-PACE, THE** - Gold lamé mini-dress w/white lace overdress & pink satin trim, matching coat w/gold lamé top & pink satin bottom w/pink bow, white fishnet hose, hot pink soft bow heels.	265	175	225	130	100	120
1220	**LAND HO!** - Orange-red cotton sailor mini-dress w/turquoise trim & ties, matching hat w/turquoise button, orange necktie ring, aqua soft buckle or Skipper flats.	100	75	85	60	40	50
1227	**LONG ON LOOKS** - White ruffled blouse w/3 lime buttons, bright pink textured midi w/chartreuse ribbon waistband & bow, pink slip w/white string bow, pink fishnet hose, hot pink soft bow or soft pointed heels.	195	160	176	90	60	75
1230	**MERRY-GO-ROUNDERS** - Multi-pastel striped coat, w/3 gold buttons matching sleeveless dress w/lime bodice, matching hat, lime hose, lime soft bow heels.	325	200	250	150	105	126
1209	**MINI-CHEX** - Orange/yellow checked sleeveless knit dress w/orange sewn in cummerbund & 3 gold buttons, orange/yellow striped knee socks, orange purse, orange soft bow shoes.	130	100	115	65	45	55
1212	**NIGHT BLOOMS** - Pink/blue bold floral print nightgown w/white background & lace trim, pink sheer robe w/white lace trim, pink felt slippers w/white lace trim.	100	85	90	60	35	46
1213	**PAZAM!** - Transparent vinyl raincoat w/lime fuchsia/yellow abstract pattern, lime/fuchsia/yellow circle print culotte dress, lime 2-piece swimsuit, pink braid hairpiece w/gold barrette & lime bow, lime hard heels w/cut-outs.	235	185	210	150	100	125
1231	**PINK LIGHTNING** - Fuchsia knit culotte dress w/2 gold chains & 4 pink buttons, fuchsia vinyl coat w/orange trim, matching cap, fuchsia hose, rose round or green squared-off sunglasses, fuchsia ankle boots or soft buckle flats.	240	185	215	130	100	115
1240	**PONY COAT** - Dark brown/white pinto-patterned mini coat w/white vinyl trim & white belt w/silver buckle, white platforms or white low hard heels.	90	65	80	45	30	38
1237	**SATIN HAPPENIN'** - Fuchsia sleeveless satin jumpsuit, white or ivory lace overblouse w/fuchsia satin trim hot pink, low hard heels or soft buckle flats.	95	70	85	50	40	46

FRANCIE 1200 SERIES FASHIONS (1968-71) - PART TWO CONTINUED

STOCK NO.	FASHION	NRFB			MINT & COMPLETE		
		HIGH	LOW	AVG	HIGH	LOW	AVG
1208	**SILVER CAGE, THE** - Hot pink mini-dress w/silver lamé fishnet overdress, matching fishnet hose, silver clutch, hot pink soft bow shoes or hot pink soft heels.	150	100	120	80	60	70
1228	**SISSY SUITS** - Pink cotton suit jacket w/3 gold buttons, matching skirt w/2 gold buttons, white sleeveless lace-trimmed blouse w/3 pink buttons, pink/yellow striped vinyl belt w/gold buckle, hot pink shoulder bag, hot pink soft buckle flats.	280	200	240	125	90	115
1245	**SNAKE CHARMERS** - Faux snakeskin mini coat w/yellow fur trim & 2 gold buttons, dress w/snakeskin skirt, yellow bodice & orange vinyl belt w/gold buckle, snakeskin hat w/yellow fur trim, yellow pantyhose, yellow boots.	195	150	170	110	75	90
1238	**SNAPPY SNOOZERS** - Hot pink short nightie w/ruffle trim, matching ruffled short nylon robe, white felt slippers w/hot pink trim, optional hot pink or white comb & brush.	100	75	90	55	35	48
1225	**SNAZZ** - Pink/orange striped cotton mini-dress w/pink satin bowed waist & 3 daisy buttons, hot pink teddy w/orange lace trim, hot pink hard or soft pointed heels.	150	100	120	65	45	55
1226	**SNOOZE NEWS** - Orange ruffled peignoir w/orange ribbon & yellow daisy, matching sleeveless sheer robe w/ruffles & ribbon tie w/yellow daisy, hand mirror optional hot pink comb & brush, orange felt slippers w/poufs.	90	60	75	45	35	40
1219	**SOMETHIN' ELSE** - Yellow/pink floral cotton bodysuit w/1 yellow button, yellow cotton skirt w/6 pink buttons, yellow soft buckle flats.	75	50	62	40	28	32
1243	**STRIPED TYPES** - Navy/red knit sweater, navy/red striped knit pants, matching striped vest w/4 gold buttons, royal soft buckle flats.	80	60	76	50	35	44
1229	**SUGAR SHEERS** - White sheer smock dress w/multi-floral pattern, white cotton slip w/lace trim, hot pink record player, 1 record w/"Barbie" label pink fishnet hose, clear vinyl tote bag trimmed w/white or green lace, hot pink buckle flats or white soft heels.	250	200	225	140	100	120

FRANCIE 1200 SERIES FASHIONS (1968-71) - PART TWO CONTINUED

STOCK NO.	FASHION	NRFB			MINT & COMPLETE		
		HIGH	LOW	AVG	HIGH	LOW	AVG
1221	**TENNIS TUNIC** - White cotton tunic w/open weave trim, matching shorts w/lace trim, tennis racket, 1 ball, white tennis shoes.	80	60	70	45	28	38
1211	**TENTERRIFIC** - Lime/multi-floral mini-pleats swing dress, matching print scarf w/lime ribbon ties, lime lace tights, white purse w/green straps & pink flower, lime soft bow shoes.	195	170	180	115	88	98
1232	**TWO FOR THE BALL** - Sleeveless gown w/black velvet bodice, orangy satin waistband, & pink satin shorter skirt w/pink lace overlay, hot pink long chiffon coat w/3 buttons & black velvet tie waist w/rose, black velvet-covered headband, optional short black gloves, hot pink hard heels.	325	275	280	175	125	140
1224	**VESTED INTEREST** - Mini-dress w/yellow blouse bodice & yellow/hot pink/white check knit skirt, hot pink crocheted vest w/4 gold buttons, hot pink hard heels w/cut-outs or soft pointed heels or yellow hard heels w/cut-outs.	95	75	84	60	38	50
1233	**VICTORIAN WEDDING** - White satin gown w/3 tiered floral lace overlay tulle, veil w/satin open crown, bouquet w/5 white flowers & green tulle, white soft heels or hard heels w/cut-outs.	285	195	230	170	100	130
1244	**WEDDING WHIRL** - White satin gown w/dotted Swiss illusion overlay, bell sleeves & pink satin trim, pink ribbon covered crown veil, bouquet w/2 white flowers, white soft or hard heels w/cut-outs, or white low hard heels.	175	150	162	120	90	108
1218	**WILD 'N WOOLY** - Orange-trimmed vinyl coat w/orange/pink/white/yellow/blue stitched-in striped weave, matching skirt, bodysuit w/orange satin bodice & tap pants w/hot pink lace trim, orange vinyl clutch or shoulder bag, orange hard heels w/cut-outs.	160	115	130	85	60	75
1223	**YELLOW BIT, THE** - Yellow cotton mini-dress w/puffed sleeves, 8 light blue appliqued flowers & trim, light blue hose, light blue soft buckle flats.	135	100	120	85	55	70

FRANCIE 1700 SERIES FASHIONS (1970-71)

STOCK NO.	FASHION	NRFB HIGH	NRFB LOW	NRFB AVG	MINT & COMPLETE HIGH	MINT & COMPLETE LOW	MINT & COMPLETE AVG
1764	**CORDUROY CAPE** - Turquoise corduroy poncho cape w/yellow or white plush fur trim & 2 gold buttons w/loop closure, light blue boots w/faux tassels.	65	50	58	38	22	30
1763	**ENTERTAINER, THE** - Pink nylon jumpsuit w/bow at waist & white or ivory lace trim, pink low hard heels.	90	75	82	50	30	40
1769	**LONG ON LEATHER** - Red "leather" midi coat w/3 white buttons, red leather miniskirt w/attached white vinyl belt & silver buckle, fuchsia/blue/white abstract striped nylon shirt & matching tights, white fringed scarf, red leather boots.	175	125	150	90	75	80
1762	**PINK POWER!** - Bright pink nylon mini dress w/ruffled lace overdress & satin waist bow, bright pink sheer patterned hose, hot pink soft heels or hot pink hard heels.	125	90	110	60	48	56
1767	**PLAID PLANS** - Orange/red/yellow/white plaid vest, skirt, bell bottoms & matching tan w/green pompon, reddish orange knit sweater w/6 gold buttons, green fringed scarf, red low hard heels.	150	100	125	75	50	62
1761	**SUNNY SLACKS** - Yellow bell bottoms w/red/pink/blue abstract print, hot pink crepe bodysuit w/4 gold buttons, hot pink soft buckle flats or hot pink low hard heels.	75	60	65	40	25	35
1768	**WALTZ IN VELVET** - Red velvet gown w/white satin, lace covered bodice & satin waistband, red velvet bolero jacket w/white plush fur collar, white plush fur muff, optional white nylon half slip w/yellow flower & dark pink bow accent, white soft heels, white low hard heels or white hard heels w/cut-outs.	250	200	230	160	100	135
1766	**WILD BUNCH, THE** - Fuchsia/yellow/orange long plush fur coat w/orange vinyl trim, fuchsia/orange knit dress w/attached orange yarn belt, fuchsia knit hood w/orange vinyl bill & gold button closure, orange tights, gold chain necklace, camera, fuchsia short gloves, orange boots.	500	400	450	320	200	290

FRANCIE 3400 SERIES FASHIONS (1971-72)

STOCK NO.	FASHION	NRFB HIGH	LOW	AVG	MINT & COMPLETE HIGH	LOW	AVG
3288	**BRIDAL BEAUTY** - Peasant style wedding gown of textured cotton w/sheer puffed sleeves, satin collar, & ruffled bodice, white tulle face veil w/white satin bow, flower basket bouquet w/5 blue & 4 yellow flowers trimmed w/white lace & yellow ribbon, white low hard heels.	495	400	450	325	275	298
3449	**BUCKAROO BLUES** - Aqua suede skirt w/4 white buttons, white trim & gold chain at waist, matching short vest, matching suede boots w/white button on each, matching shoulder bag w/fringed trim & 1 white button, red/white/blue abstract print blouse.	175	100	150	80	55	65
3460	**CHANGE OFFS** - Multi-brights woven short jacket w/yellow vinyl collar & trim & 1 yellow button, matching pants, matching midi skirt, yellow knit shell, yellow lace-up style boots.	200	175	185	105	75	90
3278	**CHECKER CHUMS** - Mini dress w/red nylon bodice & navy/white checked skirt w/2 apple appliques, navy/white checked shoulder bag w/apple applique, red knee socks, black low heels or black Skipper flats.	175	150	160	90	70	80
3281	**COOL COVERALLS** - Blue denim bib overalls w/yellow moon & red star decals, white textured nylon sweater, blue denim backpack w/yellow vinyl straps & 2 gold buckles, yellow ankle boots.	130	100	115	75	55	65
3286	**DOUBLE UPS** - Navy suede blazer w/large lapel & red button closure, red full jumpsuit, red/white/navy abstract print skirt w/3 red buttons & navy suede trim, matching shorts w/2 red buttons, navy suede shoulder purse w/red vinyl trim, blue/red visor, navy suede boots w/red vinyl trim & gold ring on each.	350	275	300	175	145	160
3450	**DREAMY DUO** - Yellow nylon short nighty w/sheer yellow overlay & green/hot pink trim at empire waist, matching yellow long robe w/same green/hot pink trim.	120	80	90	55	35	45
3455	**FROSTY FUR** - White plush fur coat w/white vinyl sleeves & trim & 2 gold buttons, white hard heels.	100	75	88	50	35	46
3275	**LITTLE KNITS** - Hot pink/white abstract patterned knit sweater, hot pink nylon hot pants, matching hot pink knee socks, white vinyl belt w/gold buckle, white vinyl sandals.	145	100	120	70	50	60
3282	**LONG VIEW, THE** - Turquoise peasant style maxi dress w/blue/white floral embroidery, gold lamé trim at empire waist w/3 gold buttons, white low hard heels.	98	75	86	62	45	55

FRANCIE 3400 SERIES FASHIONS
(1971-72) CONTINUED

STOCK NO.	FASHION	NRFB HIGH	NRFB LOW	NRFB AVG	MINT & COMPLETE HIGH	MINT & COMPLETE LOW	MINT & COMPLETE AVG
3446	**MIDI BOUQUET** - Multi-brights floral print dress, matching scarf, hot pink vinyl belt w/silver buckle, rose sunglasses, hot pink low hard heels.	140	100	120	75	60	68
3451	**MIDI DUET** - White midi underdress w/pink & green sheer floral overdress & pink satin waistband w/bow, hot pink crepe vest w/long coattails, hot pink or pink low hard heels.	160	120	140	85	60	70
3444	**MIDI PLAID** - Dress w/red nylon bodice & red/white/navy large houndstooth plaid skirt w/attached white vinyl belt & gold buckle, red fringed scarf, red low hard heels.	90	65	78	40	30	35
3458	**OLDE LOOK** - Long peasant style dress w/multi-floral print & orange crochet trim at bodice & hem, orange felt vest w/yellow lacing, orange apron w/orange crochet trim & satin ties, orange crochet purse w/yellow cinched handle, orange low hard heels.	250	200	235	160	110	130
3461	**PEACH PLUSH** - Dark pink midi length flannel coat w/purple/pink/green/tan embroidered trim, matching dark pink skirt w/embroidered trim, dark pink satin shell, tan crocheted cap w/tan pompon, dark pink lace-up style boots.	295	200	270	195	155	178
3285	**PEACH TREATS** - Pink/orange/green/white floral print peasant dress w/orange sheer puffed long sleeves & orange cummerbund, white full slip w/eyelet trim, orange ruffled shawl, orange low hard heels.	295	200	275	200	150	188
3443	**SATIN SUPPER** - Sky blue satin sleeveless V-neck jumpsuit, green lace vest, aqua satin belt, green low hard heels.	90	70	82	60	38	45
3277	**SIMPLY SUPER** - Red peasant style dress w/cap sleeves & yellow/white floral pattern, white lace-up style boots.	95	85	90	50	32	42
3276	**SLACKS SUIT, THE** - Orange/yellow/white striped cotton short jacket w/orange suede trim w/yellow stitching & 3 gold buttons, matching pants w/suede trim & gold buckle, yellow vinyl shoulder purse w/orange suede trim & stitching & gold button closure, yellow low hard heels.	125	100	115	85	60	70

FRANCIE 3400 SERIES FASHIONS
(1971-72) CONTINUED

STOCK NO.	FASHION	NRFB			MINT & COMPLETE		
		HIGH	LOW	AVG	HIGH	LOW	AVG
3287	**SMASHIN' SATIN** - Aqua blue strapless long dress w/dark pink suede trim & 10 blue buttons, matching bolero style jacket w/suede collar & 4 blue buttons, matching hot pants, light blue sheer hose, aqua blue plush purse w/dark pink suede handle & 1 blue button, light blue low hard heels.	400	375	386	275	195	232
3453	**SNOOZE NEWS** - Hot pink peignoir w/sheer hot pink overlay w/white lace trim & hot pink bow, matching panties, optional cardboard mirror w/face, optional white or hot pink comb & brush, pink felt slippers w/silver beads on each.	90	70	80	55	40	46
3283	**SUITED FOR SHORTS** - Orange-red suede coat w/yellow stitching & zip front w/pull, orange-red/yellow/white abstract floral nylon print mock T, matching print hot pants, matching leg warmer style knee socks, yellow vinyl shoulder purse w/gold button & buckle closure, yellow low hard heels.	280	200	255	150	125	140
3454	**SUMMER NUMBER** - Fuchsia 2-piece halter style bikini w/yellow trim, wrap skirt of fuchsia/orange/yellow cotton w/yarn trim at waist, pink sunglasses.	80	60	70	50	35	44
3279	**TOTALLY TERRIFIC** - Royal blue/red/yellow/white plaid weave jacket w/royal blue vinyl trim, matching plaid cap w/royal vinyl bill, yellow pleated mini skirt w/navy stitching, red nylon bodysuit, yellow sheer hose, yellow vinyl shoulder purse w/gold button, royal blue soft Skipper flats w/ballet style ankle ties.	265	200	245	165	120	146
3459	**TWILIGHT TWINKLE** - Aqua sleeveless satin gown w/silver/aqua netting overdress & silver loop trim, long aqua plush vest w/matching silver trim & 2 silver buttons, silver foil clutch purse, silver foil tiara, aqua low hard heels.	275	215	250	150	130	142
3456	**WILD FLOWERS** - Multi brights abstract floral print peasant style dress, reddish orange low hard heels.	85	65	75	40	30	36
3448	**WITH-IT WHITES** - White sleeveless textured cotton vest top w/5 gold buttons & red stitching, matching pants w/2 gold buttons, matching bell bottoms w/2 gold buttons, red shell w/white stitching, red vinyl belt w/2 gold rings closure, red low hard heels.	165	100	130	75	50	60
3445	**ZIG-ZAG ZOOM** - Yellow/blue/orange/white abstract striped pants, matching patterned hat w/blue vinyl bill, yellow ribbed knit sleeveless shirt, blue vinyl belt w/gold buckle, optional transistor radio or pink or rose sunglasses, yellow ankle boots.	175	120	150	75	50	60

FRANCIE BEST BUY FASHIONS (1972)

STOCK NO.	FASHION	NRFB HIGH	LOW	AVG	MINT & COMPLETE HIGH	LOW	AVG
3369	**PINK 'N PRETTY** - Pink cotton mini dress w/short puffed sleeves, white eyelet front & white bow, pink rosebud print half slip & white laced trimmed panties, light pink low hard heels.	85	60	70	50	30	42
3366	**PRETTY FRILLY** - Yellow peasant style maxi w/blue/green/peach floral print, white lace trimmed cotton puffed sleeves & front w/2 black buttons & black trim, blue butterfly choker, black or yellow low hard heels.	80	55	68	48	30	40
3365	**READY! SET! GO!** - Aqua nylon sleeveless top, dark blue jeans w/white stitching, red scarf w/white polka dots & stars, brown vinyl belt w/gold buckle, rose sunglasses, white tennis shoes.	75	50	65	40	30	36
3368	**RED, WHITE & BRIGHT** - White textured cotton long fitted waist w/red suede collar, cuffs, pockets & 3 red buttons, red suede purse w/gold chain handle & gold button closure, white low hard heels.	75	55	65	42	30	36
3367	**RIGHT FOR STRIPES** - Aqua blue cotton apron style vest w/white stitching & 6 white buttons, aqua blue/white awning stripe peddle pushers & matching sleeveless short top, red/multi-floral print shoulder purse w/same print vinyl strap, aqua blue tennis shoes.	90	65	78	55	35	48
3364	**SLEEPY TIME GAL** - 2-piece cotton pajamas w/pink/yellow flower & light blue polka dot print, top has 3 blue buttons, turquoise comb, brush & mirror, blue felt slipper boots w/gold bead on each.	70	50	60	40	25	35

VINTAGE OUTFIT ACCESSORIES
FRANCIE 1200 SERIES FASHIONS

STOCK NO.	OUTFIT	MINT/COMPLETE HIGH	LOW	AVG
1242 ALTOGETHER ELEGANT				
	Hot Pink Flats w/silver foil buckle	95	45	70
	Hot Pink Hard Pointed Heels w/cutouts	32	15	22
	Short White Gloves	20	10	15
1275 BELLS				
	Hat	28	14	22
	Red Shiny Vinyl Shoulder Bag	28	14	22
	Red Vinyl Shoulder Bag (Checkmates)	32	15	24
1239 BLOOM ZOOM				
	Floral Tights	30	15	22
	Opaque Aqua Soft Buckle Flats	30	14	24
	Orange Felt Vest w/blue lining	30	14	24
1287 BORDER-LINE				
	Black Buckle Flats	30	20	25
	Bright Yellow Lacy Stockings	52	28	40
	Hat	50	20	35
1279 BRIDGE BIT, THE				
	Cards	85	45	65
	How to Play Bridge Book	32	18	25
	Pillow	30	18	24
	Royal Blue Buckle Flats	28	12	20
1291 CHECK THIS				
	Scarf	45	15	30
	Short White Glove	20	10	15
	White Hard Pointed Heels w/cutouts	28	15	22
	White Soft Pointed Heels	30	18	22
1259 CHECKMATES				
	HTF Red Vinyl Shoulder Bag	28	15	22
	Red Hard Pointed Heels w/cutouts	24	14	19
	Red Soft Pointed Heels	28	15	22
1258 CLAM DIGGERS				
	Rare White Sunglasses w/green stripe	65	38	50
	Rare White Sunglasses w/orange stripe	65	38	50
	VHTF Orange Sunglasses w/green stripe	55	35	45
	Yellow Soft Pointed Flats	24	18	21
	Yellow Soft Pointed Heels	24	18	21
1281 CLEAR OUT!				
	Boots	22	12	18
	Hatbox	95	35	65
	Hood	85	25	55
1234 COMBINATION, THE				
	Green Knit Stockings	25	15	20

VINTAGE OUTFIT ACCESSORIES
FRANCIE 1200 SERIES FASHIONS CONTINUED

STOCK NO.	OUTFIT	MINT/COMPLETE		
		HIGH	LOW	AVG
1234 **COMBINATION, THE** (continued)				
	White Curly Fur Hat w/green trim	60	25	42
1215 **COMBO, THE**				
	Hot Pink Fringed Scarf	35	20	28
	Hot Pink Lace Patterned Hose	40	28	34
	Hot Pink Soft Pointed Heels	25	15	20
1256 **CONCERT IN THE PARK**				
	Hat	30	18	24
	Purse	30	18	24
	Red Soft Pointed Heels	28	15	22
1280 **COOL WHITE**				
	Hair Bow w/pin	75	25	50
	Stockings	28	18	24
	White Soft Pointed Heels	28	18	24
1214 **CULOTTE-WOT?**				
	Green Plastic Sunglasses w/white & pink trim	95	75	80
	LONG White Fishnet Stockings	40	22	30
	White Satin OR Taffeta Floppy Hat	40	22	30
1257 **DANCE PARTY**				
	Black Record w/Blue OR Red Label ea.	15	10	13
	Blue/White Record Player	18	12	15
	Bonnet	24	15	19
	HTF Chocolate Sundae	18	12	15
	HTF Metal Spoon	24	15	19
	HTF Paper Napkin w/red & purple trim	24	15	19
	Pink Soft Pointed Heels	28	15	22
	White Textured Hose	28	20	24
1290 **DENIMS ON!**				
	Hat	30	15	22
	Navy Blue Belt	30	15	22
	Royal Blue Buckle Flats	24	12	18
1217 **DREAMY WEDDING**				
	Bouquet	62	35	48
	Veil	65	35	50
	White Hard Pointed w/cutouts	25	15	20
	White Soft Pointed Heels	30	14	24
1260 **FIRST FORMAL**				
	Light Blue Hard Pointed Heels w/cutouts	28	14	21
	Light Blue Soft Pointed Heels	24	12	18
1252 **FIRST THINGS FIRST**				
	HTF Beige Textured Hose	30	24	27

228

VINTAGE OUTFIT ACCESSORIES
FRANCIE 1200 SERIES FASHIONS CONTINUED

STOCK NO.	OUTFIT	MINT/COMPLETE		
		HIGH	LOW	AVG
1207 FLOATING-IN				
	Hot Pink Hard Pointed Heels w/cutouts	32	15	22
	Short Hot Pink Gloves	75	40	58
1254 FRESH AS A DAISY				
	Bonnet	28	20	24
	Tote	28	20	24
	Yellow Soft Pointed Heels	24	18	21
1262 FUR-OUT				
	Black Soft Buckle Flats	32	18	25
	Black Textured Vinyl Spats	95	55	75
	Black Vinyl Tie Belt	50	32	41
	Red Knit Hood	38	20	22
	Red Knit Stockings	38	20	22
	Red Vinyl Mittens	15	5	10
1296 FURRY GO ROUND				
	Orange Lacy Cotton Hose	55	25	40
	Orange Suede-like hood w/gold button	180	95	140
	Orange Vinyl Riding Boots	45	15	30
1250 GAD-ABOUTS				
	HTF Green Soft Pointed Flats	28	18	23
	RARE White Plastic Sunglasses w/blue stripe	95	60	78
	RARE White Plastic Sunglasses w/green stripe	95	60	78
	VHTF Blue Plastic Sunglasses w/green stripe	95	58	76
1294 GO GOLD				
	Gold Belt	50	35	43
	Hot Pink Soft Buckle Flats	28	15	22
1267 GO, GRANNY, GO				
	Hot Pink Soft Buckle Flats	25	15	20
	Hot Pink Soft Buckle Flats w/silver foil buckle	75	35	55
	Pink Hard Pointed Heels w/cutouts	24	15	19
	Pink Soft Pointed Heels	25	18	21
	Pink/White Paper Album Sleeve	75	25	50
	Record Player	18	10	14
	Record w/red or blue label	18	10	14
1222 GOLD RUSH				
	Opaque Orange Hard Heels w/cutouts	20	12	15
1270 GROOVY GET-UP				
	Hood	60	25	42
	Stockings	45	22	34
1272 HI-TEEN				
	Hot Pink Soft Pointed Heels	25	15	20
	Red Hard Pointed Heels w/cutouts	25	15	20

VINTAGE OUTFIT ACCESSORIES
FRANCIE 1200 SERIES FASHIONS CONTINUED

STOCK NO.	OUTFIT	MINT/COMPLETE HIGH	LOW	AVG
1272 HI-TEEN (continued)				
	Red Skipper Flat	10	3	6
	Red Soft Pointed Heels	24	12	18
1265 HIP KNITS				
	Belt	28	15	21
	Stockings	22	12	18
	Yellow Soft Pointed Flats	28	12	20
	Yellow Soft Pointed Flats w/gold foil buckles	75	35	55
1274 ICED BLUE				
	White Lacy Stockings	22	12	18
	White Soft Pointed Heels	30	14	24
1288 IN-PRINT				
	Bonnet	30	20	25
	Yellow Hard Pointed w/cutouts	30	18	24
	Yellow Soft Pointed Heels	28	15	22
1251 IT'S A DATE				
	Aqua Soft Pointed Heels	24	18	21
	HTF Pale Blue Textured Hose	48	38	43
1216 LACE-PACE, THE				
	White Fishnet Stockings	40	22	30
1220 LAND HO!				
	Aqua Skipper Flats	11	5	8
	Beanie w/aqua button on top	14	10	12
	Opaque Aqua Soft Buckle Flats	30	14	24
	Orange Plastic Neck Ring	35	20	28
1269 LEATHER LIMELIGHT				
	Aqua Soft Buckle Flats	38	22	30
	Boots	25	12	18
	Hood	25	12	18
	Royal Blue Soft Buckle Flats	30	15	22
1227 LONG ON LOOKS				
	Hot Pink Fishnet Hose	35	20	28
	Hot Pink Nylon Slip	22	12	18
	Hot Pink Soft Pointed Heels	25	15	20
1230 MERRY-GO-ROUNDERS				
	Green Floppy Hat w/stripe trim	48	24	36
	Lime Green Sheer Nylon Hose	40	22	30
1209 MINI-CHEX				
	Orange Vinyl Should Bag	30	18	24
	Orange/Yellow Stripe Knit Knee Socks	30	18	24

VINTAGE OUTFIT ACCESSORIES
FRANCIE 1200 SERIES FASHIONS CONTINUED

STOCK NO.	OUTFIT	MINT/COMPLETE		
		HIGH	LOW	AVG
1284 **MISS TEENAGE BEAUTY**				
	Bouquet	250	95	175
	Light Blue Hard Pointed Heels w/cutouts	30	12	22
	Long White Gloves	20	10	15
	Loving Cup	210	95	155
	Pale Blue Soft Pointed Heels	28	12	20
	Sash	110	35	75
	Tiara	150	55	100
1212 **NIGHT BLOOMS**				
	Pink Felt Slippers w/white lace trim	25	15	20
1289 **NOTE THE COAT!**				
	White Hard Pointed Heels w/cutouts	28	15	22
	White Soft Pointed Heels	30	18	24
1263 **ORANGE COZY**				
	Hood	38	18	28
	Short Black Gloves	68	44	56
	Stockings	46	22	34
1293 **PARTNERS IN PRINT**				
	Hatbox	95	35	65
	Pink Buckle Flats	28	15	22
	Pink Hard Pointed Heels w/cutouts	32	15	24
	Pink Soft Pointed Heels	28	15	22
1213 **PAZAM!**				
	Bright Pink OR Dark Pink Braid	25	15	20
	Green Hard Pointed Heels w/cutouts	30	18	24
	Green Vinyl Bottoms	25	15	20
	Green Vinyl Bra	25	15	20
1255 **POLKA DOTS 'N RAINDROPS**				
	Red Rainboots	15	10	13
	Red Vinyl Scarf	24	15	19
	Very Rare Hood w/gold bead closure	32	24	28
1295 **PROM PINKS**				
	Brass Headband w/gold bow and ribbon	58	28	45
	Gold Dimple Purse	8	2	5
	Gold Foil Belt w/gold buckle	55	25	40
	Pink Hard Pointed Heels w/cutouts	25	15	20
	Pink Soft Pointed Heels	28	15	22
1266 **QUICK SHIFT**				
	Hot Pink Soft Buckle Flats	25	15	20
	Hot Pink Soft Buckle Flats w/silver foil buckle	75	35	55
	Stockings	25	15	20

VINTAGE OUTFIT ACCESSORIES
FRANCIE 1200 SERIES FASHIONS CONTINUED

STOCK NO.	OUTFIT	MINT/COMPLETE		
		HIGH	LOW	AVG
1237 SATIN HAPPENIN'				
	Hot Pink Soft Buckle Flats	25	15	20
1261 SHOPPIN' SPREE				
	Pink Soft Pointed Heels	28	18	23
	Red Tweed Purse w/gold bead	24	14	19
	Short White Gloves	18	10	14
1273 SIDE-KICK				
	Hat	28	12	20
	Red Hard Pointed w/cutouts	25	15	20
	Red Soft Pointed Heels	24	12	18
1208 SILVER CAGE, THE				
	Clear Open Toe Heels w/silver glitter	45	22	35
	Hot Pink Fishnet Hose	30	18	24
	Silver Dimple Clutch	30	18	24
1228 SISSY SUITS				
	Hot Pink Knee Socks	30	18	24
	Hot Pink Shoulder Bag	28	15	22
	Hot Pink Soft Buckle Flats	25	15	20
	Pink Nylon Knee Socks	25	15	20
	Yellow/Pink Striped Belt	30	18	24
1271 SLUMBER NUMBER				
	Sleep Mask	15	5	10
	Slippers	22	5	14
1245 SNAKE CHARMERS				
	"Snakeskin" Hat w/yellow plush trim	40	22	32
	Yellow Boots (same as Twiggy's)	28	15	22
	Yellow Sheer Nylon Pantyhose	48	24	36
1238 SNAPPY SNOOZERS				
	White Felt Slippers with Hot Pink Accent	18	6	12
1225 SNAZZ				
	Hot Pink Hard Pointed Heels w/cutouts	30	15	22
	Hot Pink Nylon Teddy	30	15	22
	Hot Pink Soft Pointed Heels	25	15	20
1226 SNOOZE NEWS				
	Cardboard Portrait Mirror	15	10	13
	Orange Felt Slippers w/tangerine pouf	20	10	15
1219 SOMETHIN' ELSE				
	Yellow Soft Buckle Flats	24	15	20
1243 STRIPED TYPES				
	Royal Blue Soft Buckle Flats	24	12	18

VINTAGE OUTFIT ACCESSORIES
FRANCIE 1200 SERIES FASHIONS CONTINUED

STOCK NO.	OUTFIT	MINT/COMPLETE HIGH	LOW	AVG
1268 **STYLE SETTERS**				
	Hood	48	22	35
	Shoes	25	12	18
	Stockings	48	15	32
1229 **SUGAR SHEERS**				
	Black Record w/blue label	20	10	15
	Black Record w/red label	20	10	15
	Clear Vinyl Tote Bag w/green lace trim	52	28	40
	Clear Vinyl Tote Bag w/white lace trim	48	24	36
	Hot Pink/Blue/White Phonograph	20	10	15
	Hot Pink Buckle Flats	25	15	20
	Hot Pink Fishnet Hose	35	20	28
	White Soft Pointed Heels	30	14	24
1292 **SUMMER COOLERS**				
	Blonde OR Brunette Braid w/ribbon	28	12	20
	Granny Glasses	145	35	90
	Sandals	48	20	35
	Tote	15	10	13
	Umbrella	150	45	98
1276 **SUMMER FROST**				
	Blonde OR Brunette Braided Headband	32	15	22
	Pink Hard Pointed Heels w/cutouts	25	15	20
	Pink Soft Pointed Heels	32	15	22
1277 **SUN SPOTS**				
	Hat	35	22	28
	Hot Pink Hard Pointed Heels w/cutouts	32	15	22
	Hot Pink Soft Pointed Heels	25	15	20
	Tote	20	10	15
1283 **SWEET 'N SWINGIN'**				
	Envelope Purse	38	12	25
	Medium Pink Soft Heels	32	15	22
	Pink Hard Pointed w/cutouts	25	15	20
	Purse w/handle	45	15	30
	White Hard Pointed w/cutouts	25	15	20
	White Soft Pointed Heels	28	18	24
1264 **SWINGIN' SKIMMY**				
	Hood	65	35	50
	Stockings	45	28	36
1221 **TENNIS TUNIC**				
	Tennis Ball	9	3	6
	Tennis Racket	9	1	5
	White Sneakers	9	3	6

VINTAGE OUTFIT ACCESSORIES
FRANCIE 1200 SERIES FASHIONS CONTINUED

STOCK NO.	OUTFIT	MINT/COMPLETE		
		HIGH	LOW	AVG
1211 **TENTERRIFIC**				
	Lime Green Lacy Tights	30	18	24
	Multicolored Bonnet	35	20	28
	White Tote	18	8	12
1253 **TUCKERED OUT**				
	4 or 6 Pink Rollers ea.	5	2	4
	Booties	18	12	15
	Pink Brush	3	1	2
	Pink Comb	3	1	2
	Pink Mirror	3	1	2
1286 **TWEED-SOMES**				
	Hat	50	20	35
	Hatbox	95	35	65
	Hot Pink Soft Pointed Heels	32	15	22
	Necklace 1-Strand	45	20	32
	Necklace 2-Strand	48	22	35
	Pale Pink Lacy Stockings	48	24	36
1232 **TWO FOR THE BALL**				
	Brass Headband covered w/black velvet	52	28	40
	Hot Pink Hard Pointed Heels w/cutouts	30	15	22
	Short Black Gloves (optional)	70	45	58
1224 **VESTED INTEREST**				
	Hot Pink Hard Pointed Heels w/cutouts	30	15	22
	Hot Pink Soft Pointed Heels	25	15	20
	Yellow Hard Pointed Heels w/cutouts	30	18	24
1233 **VICTORIAN WEDDING**				
	Bouquet	75	48	60
	Veil w/headband covered w/white satin	52	28	40
	White Hard Pointed Heels w/cutouts	25	15	20
	White Soft Pointed Heels	30	14	24
1244 **WEDDING WHIRL**				
	3-Tired Veil	48	28	38
	Bouquet	48	24	36
	White Hard Pointed Heels w/cutouts	28	15	22
	White Soft Pointed Heels	30	14	24
1218 **WILD 'N WOOLY**				
	Orange Envelope Purse	11	5	8
	Orange Hard Pointed Heels w/cutouts	20	12	15
	Small Orange Vinyl Shoulder Bag	30	18	24
1223 **YELLOW BIT, THE**				
	Light Blue Soft Buckle Flats	30	15	22
	Sheer Pale Blue Nylon Stockings	40	22	30

VINTAGE OUTFIT ACCESSORIES
FRANCIE 1700 SERIES FASHIONS

STOCK NO.	OUTFIT	MINT/COMPLETE		
		HIGH	LOW	AVG
1764 **CORDUROY CAPE**				
	Light Blue Soft Majorette Boots	12	8	10
1769 **LONG ON LEATHER**				
	Hot Pink/White/Blue Zig Zag Nylon Tights	35	20	28
	Red Vinyl Boots	20	10	15
	White Nylon Scarf with Fringe	36	24	30
1762 **PINK POWER!**				
	Hot Pink Mesh Cotton Hose	48	28	38
	Hot Pink Soft Pointed Heels	25	15	20
1767 **PLAID PLANS**				
	Green Crepe-like Nylon Scarf	30	14	22
	Red/Orange Hat w/green pom	28	15	22
1768 **WALTZ IN VELVET**				
	White Fur Muff	28	15	22
	White Nylon Petticoat w/flower accent	95	35	65
	White Soft Pointed Heels	30	14	22
1766 **WILD BUNCH, THE**				
	Black/Gray Camera	36	24	30
	Fuschia Knit Hood w/orange vinyl bill	130	60	95
	Fuschia Short Gloves (rare)	100	50	75
	Gold Chain Necklace	130	60	95
	Orange Boots (same as Walking Jaime)	28	15	22
	Orange Knit Tights	60	25	42

VINTAGE OUTFIT ACCESSORIES FRANCIE 3400 SERIES FASHIONS

STOCK NO.	OUTFIT	MINT/COMPLETE		
		HIGH	LOW	AVG
3449 BUCKAROO BLUES				
	Aqua "suede" Boots	28	15	22
	Aqua "suede" Shoulder Bag	22	12	18
3460 CHANGE OFFS				
	Yellow Soft Lace Up Boots	18	10	14
3446 MIDI BOUQUET				
	Hot Pink Vinyl Belt w/silver buckle	30	18	24
	Rose Sunglasses	15	10	13
	Scarf	28	15	22
3444 MIDI PLAID				
	Red Nylon Scarf w/fringe	28	15	22
3458 OLDE LOOK				
	Orange Felt Vest	68	28	48
	Purse	60	30	45
3461 PEACH PLUSH				
	Beige Crocheted Cap	130	60	95
	Rose Soft Lace Up Boots	28	15	22
3443 SATIN SUPPER				
	Aqua Satin Belt	28	15	22
3453 SNOOZE NEWS				
	Hot Pink Felt Slippers w/silver bead	18	10	14
3459 TWILIGHT TWINKLE				
	Dimpled Flat Silver Purse	22	12	18
	Silver Foil Crown	130	60	95
3448 WITH-IT WHITES				
	Red Vinyl Belt	28	15	22
3445 ZIG-ZAG ZOOM				
	Multicolored Hat	26	14	20
	Pink OR Rose Sunglasses	15	10	13
	Textured Blue Vinyl Belt w/gold buckle	28	15	22
	Yellow Transistor Radio w/silver antenna	36	20	28

VINTAGE OUTFIT ACCESSORIES
FRANCIE 3200 SERIES FASHIONS

STOCK NO.	OUTFIT	MINT/COMPLETE		
		HIGH	LOW	AVG
3288 **BRIDAL BEAUTY**				
	Veil	148	95	120
	Flower Basket	130	60	95
	White Square Toe Heels	10	2	6
3278 **CHECKER CHUMS**				
	Navy/White Check Shoulder Bag	36	20	28
	Red Nylon Knee Socks	30	18	24
	Black Square Toe Heels	15	5	10
3281 **COOL COVERALLS**				
	White Nylon Sweater	48	28	38
	Blue Denim Backpack w/yellow straps	30	18	24
	Yellow Ankle Boots	18	10	14
3286 **DOUBLE UPS**				
	Navy Suede Purse w/red vinyl trim	48	24	36
	Navy Suede Boots w/red vinyl trim	60	30	45
	Navy Headband w/red vinyl visor	95	45	70
3275 **LITTLE KNITS**				
	Hot Pink Knee Socks	30	18	24
	White Vinyl Belt w/gold buckle	28	15	22
	White Vinyl Sandals	30	18	24
3285 **PEACH TREATS**				
	Orange cotton gauzy Shawl w/ruffle	95	45	70
	Orange Square Toe Heels	18	10	14
3276 **SLACKS SUIT, THE**				
	Yellow Vinyl Shoulder Bag w/suede trim	36	20	28
	Yellow Square Toe Heels	10	2	6
3287 **SMASHIN' SATIN**				
	Light Blue Sheer Nylon Stockings	36	24	30
	Light Blue Square Toe Heels	18	10	14
3283 **SUITED FOR SHORTS**				
	Multicolored Print Knee Socks	48	24	36
	Yellow Vinyl Shoulder Bag	36	24	30
	Yellow Square Toe Heels	10	2	6
3279 **TOTALLY TERRIFIC**				
	Multicolored Plaid Cap w/bill	36	24	30
	Yellow Sheer Nylon Stockings	48	24	36
	Yellow Vinyl Shoulder Bag	30	18	24
	Royal Blue Soft Skipper Flats w/ankle strap	95	45	65

VINTAGE OUTFIT ACCESSORIES
MISC. FRANCIE FASHIONS

STOCK NO.	OUTFIT	MINT/COMPLETE		
		HIGH	LOW	AVG
1042 **SWINGIN' SEPARATES GIFT SET**				
	Pale Pink OR White Eyelash Brush	18	12	15
	White Comb	3	1	2
	Yellow Soft Buckle Flats	24	15	20
	Yellow Soft Pointed Heels	24	15	20
1044 **SPORTIN' SET GIFT SET**				
	Pale Pink OR White Eyelash Brush	18	12	15
	RARE Blue Vinyl Mittens	120	50	85
	Tennis Ball	5	2	4
	Tennis Racket	8	2	5
	White Ice Skates	15	8	12
	White Cotton Socks	12	5	7
	White Sneakers	10	6	8
	White Comb	3	1	2
1548 **ORANGE ZIP**				
	Orange Soft Buckle Flats	30	18	24
3304 **CASEY GOES CASUAL GIFT SET**				
	Casey Earring	18	10	14
	Hot Pink Soft Buckle Flats	25	15	20
	Hot Pink Soft Pointed Heels	25	15	20

TUTTI FASHIONS (1966-69)

STOCK NO.	FASHION	NRFB HIGH	LOW	AVG	MINT & COMPLETE HIGH	LOW	AVG
3617	**BIRTHDAY BEAUTIES** - Light pink dress w/white daisies w/hot pink centers, white tights, invitation, white shoes.	175	125	150	75	50	65
3606	**CLOWNING AROUND** - Party dress w/black/white gingham skirt & yellow bodice w/white bow at collar & white cuffs, yellow panties, felt clown doll w/matching outfit, black shoes.	225	175	200	120	80	98
3607	**COME TO MY PARTY** - Aqua sleeveless party dress w/organdy overlay skirt & white lace overlay bodice w/light pink ribbon roses accents, aqua panties, white socks, white shoes.	155	100	140	60	50	55
3615	**FLOWER GIRL** - Full length sleeveless formal dress w/white organdy skirt over satin & light blue embroidery & blue satin band at hem & light blue satin bodice w/ribbon & flower, hat w/yellow netting & light blue ribbon, basket bouquet w/ribbon, white shoes.	325	280	300	150	110	128
3608	**LET'S PLAY BARBIE** - Short cotton dress w/red sleeveless bodice & blue/white grid pant skirt w/white lace & red braid hemline, matching white lace w/red tied headband, red panties, miniature Barbie, red miniature case w/American Girl face decal, white socks, white shoes.	325	275	298	185	150	165
3616	**PINK P.J.'s** - Light pink 2-piece sleeveless pajama set w/white lace trim & blue flower accent, miniature baby in pink/white lace bunting, light blue comb & brush, hot pink slippers.	175	125	150	95	75	85
3609	**PLANTIN' POSIES** - Orange/yellow sundress w/daisy accents, matching bonnet w/yellow ribbon ties, yellow panties, green plastic watering can, green plastic hand shovel, seed pocket, orange shoes.	160	115	136	80	60	70
3601	**PUDDLE JUMPERS** - Royal blue plastic raincoat w/3 clear buttons & white stitching, matching rainhat, white boots.	85	65	78	38	25	30
3603	**SAND CASTLES** - White sunsuit w/little orange polka-dots & orange ribbon accent, matching sunhat w/orange ribbon ties, red bucket w/sailboat decal, metal hand shovel, white socks, red strap shoes.	130	90	100	65	45	52
3614	**SEA-SHORE SHORTIES** - Lime green sundress w/blue daisy pattern & 3 white eyelet ruffles, matching 2-piece swimsuit w/white eyelet ruffles, lime/yellow/blue beach ball, blue sailboat w/white sail, white shoes.	160	135	146	80	55	70
3602	**SHIP SHAPE** - Turquoise sailor dress w/little white polka-dots, white sailor collar & red ribbon accent, matching aqua/white polka-dot panties, white tan w/red pompon, white socks, red strap shoes.	100	75	90	60	40	50
3604	**SKIPPIN' ROPE** - Multi-floral patterned smock dress w/rick-rack trim (2 color variations - 1 red background, 1 tan background), navy stretch-knit tights, red/white jump rope w/black handles, red shoes.	95	70	85	55	50	42

VINTAGE MISCELLANEOUS

DESCRIPTION	YEAR	NRFB
BARBIE CHILD-SIZE GIRL'S SLIP white w/Barbie name and pictures	1960s	200
BARBIE CHILD-SIZE LONG SLEEVED WHITE T-SHIRT w/PT on front	1960s	180
BARBIE CHILD-SIZE RED VELVET DRESS white lace on collar and sleeves	1960s	—
BARBIE CHILD-SIZE WOVEN SUN HAT blue striped or orange/yellow striped	1960s	350
BARBIE JACKET long sleeved with cuffs, red lining, gold buttons, red, blue and gold Barbie letters print	1960s	—
BARBIE JUMPER child size trimmed w/rick-rack	1960s	1000
BARBIE PILLOW trimmed, three edges with lace	1960s	—
BARBIE TOTE fabric, blue fabric handle and sides, front pocket	1960s	—
BARBIE DESIGNER TENNIS SHOES w/original box & hang tag	1961	250
SKETCH A FASHION pictures Austin Healy w/Barbie & Ken #225	1961	95
BARBIE & ME DRESS-UP SET (Standard Pyroxoloid)	1962	325
BARBIE CLOTH UMBRELLA w/clear horse handle, 21 inch	1962	225
BARBIE CUTLERY SET Woodlook Cardboard Box, gold colored plastic (Service for 6)	1962	—
BARBIE FAN CLUB KIT 6 issues Barbie Magazine, I.D. card, sew on emblem	1962	230
BARBIE HEIRLOOM SERVICE PLAYSET Irwin, Silver Service for 6, hostess set, butter knife, cake knife, salad fork/spoon, 2 candelabras	1962	180
BARBIE JUMBO TRADING CARDS (Dynamic Toy Co.)	1962	350 set
BARBIE/KEN JUMBO TRADING CARDS (Pak - 5 cards) Dynamic Toy Co.	1962	55 set
BARBIE/KEN JUMBO TRADING CARDS Dynamic Toy Co. #1702 & 1703	1962	350 set
BARBIE NURSE KIT (Pressman) #1195	1962	250
BARBIE NURSE OUTFIT child size	1962	—
BARBIE SHOPS BY PHONE (Irwin)	1962	200
BARBIE & KEN HANGERS various colors (SPP)	1963	55
BARBIE ELECTRIC DRAWING TABLE (Lakeside Toys Inc.)	1963	100
BARBIE FABRIC BY THE YARD mustard, brown, white, black and orange print	1963	75
BARBIE FAN CLUB APPLICATION	1963	15 .
BARBIE FESTIVE GIFT WRAP (Whitman)	1963	175
BARBIE HALLOWEEN COSTUME (Collegeville - 8 different changes)	1963	350
BARBIE HALLOWEEN COSTUME Queen of the Prom	1963	200
BARBIE, KEN & MIDGE ELECTRIC DRAWING TABLE (Lakeside Toys Inc.)	1963	140
BARBIE, KEN & MIDGE SCHOOL BOOK BAG	1963	385
BARBIE LETTER BOX (Montague)	1963	—
BARBIE LETTERS (Montague)	1963	—
BARBIE MIX AND MATCH SEPARATES 8 child size costumes	1963	—
BARBIE PETTIPANTS licensed, lace edge on legs, shows Ponytail Barbie in various outfits	1963	125
BARBIE SHELVES (Shore-Calnevar Inc. - Portable Home Display)	1963	97
BARBIE 'N SKIPPER GO TOGETHER DINING ROOM FURNITURE	1964	246
BARBIE 'N SKIPPER GO TOGETHER LIVING ROOM FURNITURE	1964	253
BARBIE FAN CLUB APPLICATION Canadian - Multi-language	1964	15
BARBIE MAGIC WINDOW (Watkins-Strathmore) #4929 Barbie, Midge and Barbie/Ken versions	1964	93

DESCRIPTION	YEAR	NRFB
BARBIE NOVELY TABLETOP DECORATION (American Greetings)	1964	118
BARBIE TENNIS SHOES white canvas w/blue, red & black print *Sears*	1964	—
BARBIE WIPE-AWAYS two vinyl coloring cloths w/8 wipe-away crayons (Twinco Products)	1964	85
SKIPPER BATH CLOSET Merry Mfg.	1964	153
SKIPPER PARTY CLOSET Merry Mfg. #2001	1964	148
SKIPPER ELECTRIC DRAWING TABLE (Lakeside Toys Inc.)	1964	110
SKIPPER HALLOWEEN COSTUME (Collegeville)	1964	214
SKIPPER LINEN CLOSET Merry Mfg. #2002	1964	126
BARBIE AROUND THE WORLD TRIP VIEW MASTERS (Sawyer - 1st edition) #B500	1965	100
BARBIE GOES TO A PARTY PAPER SET napkin, centerpiece and tablecloth (House of Paper)	1965	125
BARBIE GREETING CARD ASSORTMENT (American Greetings - each)	1965	165
BARBIE SHOE BAG Canvas - zippered w/handle and side pocket	1965	159
SKIPPER AND SKOOTER Retailor Display Box	1965	100
SKIPPER BILLFOLD cardboard	1965	N/A
SKIPPER SPELLING BOARD Bar Zim Mfg.	1965	N/A
SKIPPER WRAPPING PAPER "Skipper Says Happy Birthday" (Whitman)	1965	135
BARBIE AROUND THE WORLD TRIP VIEW MASTERS Gaf #B500	1966	—
FRANCIE ELECTRIC DRAWING TABLE (Lakeside Toys Inc.)	1966	125
TWIGGY, BALL PEN, Scripto Inc. #1159	1967	40
TWIGGY eye paint double duo by Yardley #7460	1967	65
TWIGGY Piccadilly adult pantyhose - varied colors	1967	25
BARBIE MATTEL-A-PHONE pink rotary dial, 5 doublesided discs	1968	130
BARBIE NEW FAN CLUB KIT Salute to Silver outfit, Portrait of Barbie, family and friends, membership certificate, issue of *Barbie Talk* Magazine	1969	125
JULIA - GAF Viewmaster reel w/16 page story booklet	1969	55
WORLD OF BARBIE STORE DISPLAY	1969	3000
SHEETS & PILLOW CASE Barbie, Mod Era, pictures full length Barbies and Kens	1970s	70
BARBIE FAN CLUB PAK includes all items from 1969 kit *Sears*	1970	70
BARBIE FAN CLUB PAK poster only, signatures reversed	1970	80
DRAWING SET New Living Barbie, Electric	1970	40
HANGERS #1065 World of Barbie	1970	30
BARBIE NEW FAN CLUB KIT Portrait of Barbie, family and friends, membership certificate, Barbie Talk Magazine, child size Barbie charm bracelet	1971	75
WALLPAPER "Every Pattern Under the Sun" Lot # 6Y2098 by Sunworthy (Canada)	1971	—
WISH YOU WERE HERE Postcard, 3D by Vari Vue, 4" x 6"	1971	15
BARBIE BEAUTY CENTER 17" #4027	1972	35
BARBIE FABRIC by the yard (Francie, Steffie, Busy Barbie and Talking Barbie)	1972	55
BARBIE GARDEN PATIO WITH REAL GROWIN' PLANTS #4284	1972	85
BEDSPREAD 84 x 99 W.T. Grant Co. NY, NY	—	—

VINTAGE VINYLS

DESCRIPTION	YEAR	NRFB
BARBIE AND SKIPPER BINDER pink, American Girl and Skipper (SPP)	1960s	200
BARBIE BINDER Made in Canada, blue with black edging, pictures full length American Girl in dress and coat	1960s	—
SKIPPER RED NURSE BAG #1760	1960s	300
BARBIE RECORD TOTE (SPP)	1961	135
BARBIE WALLET (Ponytail)	1961	185
BARBIE WALLET red, blue or black (SPP) #B208	1961	250
GIFT PILLOW Barbie & Ken vinyl 11 $^1/2$" diameter	1961	650
BARBIE AUTOGRAPH BOOK red, blue or black (Ponytail) #B22	1962	190
BARBIE CARRYALL WALLET red, blue or black (SPP) #B201	1962	200
BARBIE DIARY red, blue or black (SPP) #B33	1962	200
BARBIE PENCIL CASE red, blue or black (Ponytail) #B101	1962	240
BARBIE POCKET PHOTO ALBUM (SPP)	1962	270
BARBIE "SNIPS & SCRAPS" SCRAPBOOK (Ponytail)	1962	210
BARBIE VANITY FAIR RECORD PLAYER*	1962	1600
KNITTING FOR BARBIE purple vinyl (Miner Industries)	1962	155
BARBIE & MIDGE BRUNCH BAG/CAMERA BAG (SPP)	1963	350
BARBIE BINDER (Ponytail - w/Early Sketches on Front)	1963	300
BARBIE DICTIONARY red, blue or black #B440	1963	225
BARBIE NOTEBOOK black, Ponytail keychain attached with pencil case	1963	350
BARBIE TRANSISTOR RADIO CASE ONLY	1963	350
BARBIE BEACH BAG print w/pink base	1964	200
BARBIE BINDER WITH MIDGE & KEN blue, black, white or pink (SPP) #BB11	1964	300
BARBIE DESKETTE (SPP) black, Bubble Cut in Party Date	1964	185
BARBIE LOCKER VANITY (SPP - only one known to exist)	1964	155
BARBIE PERK UP CASE red, blue or black (SPP) #B501	1964	250
BARBIE WALLET masquerade, black or red (SPP)	1964	180
BARBIE ZIPPERED BINDER black or blue (Canada)	1964	250
SKIPPER BALLET BOX (black) Skipper wearing dress coat, Red Sensation and School Days	1964	200
SKIPPER WALLET red, blue, black or yellow (Ponytail)	1964	150
SKIPPER WALLET AND COIN PURSE	1964	300
SKIPPER - 3 RING BINDER blue, wearing Masquerade (SPP)	1965	225
SKIPPER - 3 RING BINDER yellow, wearing Masquerade (SPP)	1965	225

VINTAGE BEAUTY TOILETRIES

DESCRIPTION	YEAR	NRFB
BARBIE BEAUTY KIT (Roclar)	1961	195
BARBIE & ME DRESS UP SET (Standard Pyroxoloid Corp.) child-sized	1962	160
set brush, mirror, comb, stand up mirror & 3 pretend cosmetics		
BARBIE & ME VANITY SET (same as above plus extra brush, mirror & comb)	1962	185
BARBIE & ME DRESS UP SET (Standard Pyroxoloid Corp.)	1962	150
mirror, brush, comb, blue Friday Nite Date		
BARBIE & ME DRESS UP SET (Standard Pyroxoloid Corp.)	1962	150
square mirror, brush, Barbie wearing Orange Blossom		
BARBIE BUBBLE BATH (Roclar)	1963	98
BARBIE BUBBLING MILK BATH (Roclar)	1963	95
BARBIE COLOGNE (Roclar)	1963	95
BARBIE GLAMOUR COSMETICS 20 items (Merry Manufacturing)	1963	275
BARBIE LOTION (Roclar)	1963	95
BARBIE MAKE BELIEVE ROUGE AND POWDERS	1963	155
(Merry Manufacturing)		
BARBIE POWDER MITT (Roclar)	1963	130
BARBIE SHOWER MITT (Roclar)	1963	125
BARBIE GOOD MORNING MANICURE SET	1964	115
SKIPPER BATH CLOSET (Merry Manufacturing, Cincinnati, Ohio)	1964	150
BARBIE PRETTY-UP TIME mirror, brush and comb set, standard	1964	130
(Pyroxolid Corp.)		
BARBIE, SKIPPER & TUTTI PALMOLIVE SOAP (4/pkg) offer	1966	225
PALMOLIVE SOAP 4 bars w/Tutti doll offer	1996	N/A

VINTAGE BARBIE® & FAMILY WATCHES

DESCRIPTION	YEAR	MINT IN BOX		MINT	
		HIGH	LOW	HIGH	LOW
CURLY BANGS PONYTAIL					
Wristwatch	1963	450	300	190	95
Pendant	1963	550	400	350	250
SWIRL PONYTAIL					
Wristwatch	1964	400	275	195	150
Pendant	1964	500	400	350	225
BUBBLE CUT & KEN (Beating Heart)					
Wristwatch	1964	485	400	395	325
Pendant	1965	800	525	500	325
SKIPPER WRISTWATCH	1964	550	450	400	300
MIDGE WRISTWATCH	1964	550	450	400	300
COLOR MAGIC/LIVING BARBIE					
Wristwatch	1971	300	250	205	85
MOVING BARBIE ARMS					
Wristwatch w/extra bands	1974	195	125	75	45

❖❖❖❖❖❖❖❖❖❖❖❖❖❖❖

CLOCKS

DESCRIPTION	YEAR	MINT IN BOX		MINT	
		HIGH	LOW	HIGH	LOW
BRASS ALARM CLOCK blue ring w/numbers,					
Ponytail Barbie on face "Made in Germany"	1963	—	—	2000	1000
BRADLEY SWIRL STARLIGHT					
Boudoir Clock	1964	—	—	800	500
BRADLEY SWIRL PERSONAL					
Photo Clock	1964	—	—	790	500
BARBIE ELECTRIC WRISTWATCH					
Wall Clock (TNT) moving arms - electric	1974	450	200	250	175

VINTAGE TRANSPORTATION

DESCRIPTION *(By Irwin)*	YEAR OF ORGIN	NRFB HIGH	NRFB LOW	MINT & COMPLETE HIGH	MINT & COMPLETE LOW
BARBIE'S "AUSTIN HEALY" coral body with aqua seats.	1962	375	275	195	150
KEN'S "HOT ROD" blue with white interior, red roll bar.	1963	450	295	225	165
BARBIE'S "AUSTIN HEALY" lavender body with white seats. *Wards*	1964	3000	2800	2500	2300
BARBIE'S "AUSTIN HEALY" red & white	1964	3500	3300	2500	2300
BARBIE'S "AUSTIN HEALY" beige	1964	3500	3300	2500	2300
BARBIE'S "AUSTIN HEALY" turquoise	1964	1000	950	850	800
KEN'S "HOT ROD" red version, black engine and white seat. *Wards*	1964	1000	800	450	400
ALLAN'S "ROADSTER" turquoise with coral seats, white steering wheel. #5348 (Irwin)	1964	550	450	350	275
BARBIE, KEN, AND MIDGE "CONVERTIBLE" blue one piece body w/cut-out for legs. Silver sticker on trunk. Often called Skipper's car. (Irwin)	1964	200	175	150	100
BARBIE'S "SPEEDBOAT" blue-green with coral seats.	1964	1650	1100	800	650
BARBIE'S "SPEEDBOAT" ocean green with brown seats.	1964	2000	1500	1000	850
BARBIE'S "SPORT PLANE" blue body with cream seats, wings, & retractable landing gear. Red nose cone, silver turning blade & antenna.	1964	4000	3000	2000	1750
SKIPPER'S "SPEEDBOAT" same as Barbie's blue w/coral seats boat but different packaging.	1965	2000	1500	N/A	N/A
SKIPPER'S "SPORTS CAR" turquoise with brown seats, dark blue-green Mercedes Benz Conv. with dark brown seats. Silver steering wheel. *Wards*	1965	500	350	175	150
BARBIE BLUE-GREEN MERCEDES. Orange seats, white steering wheel. *Sears*	1968	500	450	300	250
BARBIE LIGHT BLUE-GREEN with light orange seats, white steering wheel. *Sears*	1969	500	450	300	250
BARBIE COUNTRY CAMPER #4994	1971	50	45	40	35
SUN 'N FUN BUGGY #1158	1971	200	150	100	75
BARBIE & KEN "OFFICIAL DUNE BUGGY" pink w/black roll bar, silver hubcaps and steering wheel. (Irwin)	1972	350	300	250	225
RED BOAT (Irwin) red w/white seats, engine partially shows, chrome trim, no windshield. *Ward's Exclusive*	1972	500	450	400	350

VINTAGE LUNCH BOXES

DESCRIPTION	YEAR OF ORGIN	MINT & COMPLETE HIGH	LOW
CANADIAN "BARBIE LUNCH KIT" Red vinyl 8¾ x 6 x 4. Ponytail 4 full figures in "Cotton Casual," "Resort Set," "Golden Girl," & "Winter Holiday" comes with Thermos.	1962	500	300
"BARBIE LUNCH KIT" Black vinyl 8¾ x 6 x 4. Ponytail 4 full figures in "Cotton Casual," "Resort Set," "Golden Girl" & "Winter Holiday" comes w/Thermos.	1962	175	90
"BARBIE LUNCH BOX" 8¾ x 8¾ x 3 Ponytail. Red vinyl, Thermos fits into separate bottom compartment w/side opening. Carried by a shoulder strap.	1962	350	250
"BARBIE AND MIDGE" BLACK VINYL. 8¾ x 6 x 4, Midge & Barbie heads in center, full length Barbie & Midge.	1962	165	85
"BARBIE AND MIDGE" BRUNCH BAG. Black vinyl. Oval cylinder w/zipper around the top. Pink Ponytail Barbie in "Winter Holiday" Blonde Bubble Cut head, pink-haired Midge head, Blonde Midge in a medium blue "Sorority Meeting." Carrying handle.	1963	350	200
"BARBIE AND MIDGE" Black vinyl. Ponytail in "Evening Splendor" w/pink fur trim & lining. Blonde Bubble Cut head. Pink-haired Midge head & a Midge in blue & black "After Five."	1964	150	95
"BARBIE AND FRANCIE" Black vinyl. 9¼ x 6¾ x 4. Blonde American Girl head. Barbie in pink "Music Center Matinee." Blonde Francie head. Francie in aqua "Gad-Abouts." Side of box has Barbie in a pink "Benefit Performance." Other side has Francie in yellow "Fresh as a Daisy."	1965	160	95
DOME TOP "BARBIE AND MIDGE" Black vinyl. 6 x 4½ x 8½. Top shows a Bubble Cut and a Midge head. Left side has Midge in "After Five." Right side has Ponytail in "Golden Elegance." Thermos is carried in the top rounded part of the box.	1965	375	300
"SKIPPER LUNCH BOX" Salmon vinyl. 9¼ x 6¾ x 4. Features Skipper on the front in "Country Picnic," right side in "Rainy Day Checkers," & the left side in "Lets Play Dolls."	1965	225	150
"SKIPPER LUNCH BOX" Pale pink vinyl. 9¼ x 6¾ x 4. Features Skipper on the front in "Silk 'N Fancy"	1965	125	120
CAMPUS QUEEN, metal, King Seeley w/Thermos.	1967	100	65
TODD, vinyl, Carson City Bank & Livery Stable (Ardee Mfg. Co.)	1967	N/A	N/A
JULIA, metal, King Seeley - Lime Green and Orange 1/2 pint Thermos - Bottle No. 2896 w/ blue lid.	1969	N/A	N/A
THE WORLD OF BARBIE, vinyl.	1971	75	50

246

VINTAGE THERMOS® BOTTLES

DESCRIPTION	YEAR OF ORGIN	MINT & COMPLETE HIGH	LOW
#2025 BLACK. Blonde Ponytail in pink & black stripe swimsuit, brunette Ponytail in blue & green casual dress, blonde Ponytail in green dress, blonde Ponytail in green & gold party dress, & a brunette Ponytail in red, yellow, & green sweater set and skirt.	1962	60	35
#145 CANADIAN BLACK. Barbie & Midge. Blonde Bubble Cut head & redhead Midge. Ponytail in "Evening Splendor" in yellow with red fur purse & lining. Redhead Midge in blue & black "After Five" with red cup.	1962	120	90
#2835 BLACK. Barbie, Midge & Skipper redhead Bubble Cut in "Friday Night Date," redhead Midge in "Party Date," and blonde Skipper in "Silk 'N Fancy" with beige cup.	1963	50	35
RED BUBBLE CUT HEAD & redhead Midge with red cup.	1963	75	44
CAMPUS QUEEN white	1967	45	35
#2825 THE WORLD OF BARBIE. Half pint, blue w/4 Barbies in mod dresses w/white cup.	1971	40	30

VINTAGE STRUCTURES

STOCK NO.	YEAR OF ORIGIN	DESCRIPTION	NRFB HIGH	NRFB LOW	NRFB AVG	MINT HIGH	MINT LOW	MINT AVG
816	1962	BARBIE'S DREAM HOUSE	350	225	300	195	100	160
817	1962	BARBIE'S FASHION SHOP	600	450	525	375	295	325
4090	1964	BARBIE & KEN LITTLE THEATRE	525	400	460	365	285	310
4092	1964	BARBIE'S NEW DREAM HOUSE	525	425	485	395	295	335
4093	1964	BARBIE GOES TO COLLEGE (Campus) Sears	695	485	575	375	325	355
4094	1965	SKIPPER'S DREAM ROOM	600	400	550	395	325	350
4095	1965	BARBIE'S DREAM KITCHEN - DINETTE	550	400	475	350	275	300
—	1965	BARBIE & SKIPPER'S DELUXE	285	150	225	175	120	138
		DREAM HOUSE Sears						
—	1965	SKIPPER'S SCHOOLROOM	600	500	550	475	350	420
3302	1966	FRANCIE HOUSE	160	130	150	135	100	115
3306	1966	TUTTI PLAYHOUSE with doll	175	120	145	95	70	86
—	1966	BARBIE & FRANCIE'S CAMPUS Sears	350	225	275	160	120	135
—	1966	BARBIE FAMILY DELUXE HOUSE	175	125	150	120	95	115
—	1966	SKIPPER'S DELUXE DREAM HOUSE Sears	600	500	575	475	300	400
—	1966	TUTTI & TODD PLAYHOUSE (w/out dolls) Sears	70	45	60	40	25	30
1005	1967	BARBIE FAMILY HOUSE	175	100	125	80	50	65
1026	1967	FRANCIE & CASEY STUDIO HOUSE	200	150	175	125	100	108
1066	1967	THE WORLD OF BARBIE FAMILY HOUSE	175	150	160	100	75	85
3300	1967	TUTTI'S PLAYHOUSE no doll included	95	75	85	75	50	56
3317	1967	TUTTI'S SUMMER HOUSE	110	85	90	60	40	50
3563	1967	TUTTI ICE CREAM STAND	300	200	250	165	100	145
5038	1967	TUTTI & CHRIS SLEEP & PLAY HOUSE	150	120	140	95	65	80
—	1967	3-HOUSE GROUP (Barbie/Francie/Tutti) Sears	200	125	150	175	95	150
1048	1968	THE WORLD OF BARBIE HOUSE	190	140	158	100	75	90
—	1968	TUTTI & CHRIS PATIO PICNIC HOUSE Sears	150	100	125	95	75	85
4961	1970	BARBIE LIVELY LIVIN' HOUSE	225	175	185	150	80	95
1148	1971	BARBIE FASHION STAGE	130	95	105	75	50	65
4983	1971	BARBIE CAFE TODAY	500	450	475	325	250	300
4984	1971	BARBIE'S TOWN & COUNTRY MARKET	150	115	135	85	60	75
—	1971	JAMIE'S PENTHOUSE Sears	525	400	455	400	300	375

BARBIE® PLACE-SETTINGS

STOCK NO.	YEAR OF ORIGIN	DESCRIPTION	NRFB HIGH	NRFB LOW	NRFB AVG	MINT HIGH	MINT LOW	MINT AVG
4985	1971	TEEN DREAM BEDROOM	100	75	85	55	40	50
4986	1971	LIVIN' ROOM	95	75	80	60	40	55
4987	1971	COOKIN' FUN KITCHEN	100	85	90	65	45	58
—	1971	BARBIE UNIQUE BOUTIQUE	185	160	175	145	100	115
4282	1972	BARBIE'S SURPRISE HOUSE	125	95	110	60	40	52
4283	1972	BARBIE'S MOUNTAIN SKI CABIN *Sears*	75	50	60	45	30	38
8662	1973	COUNTRY LIVING HOUSE	75	68	68	50	35	40
8665	1973	QUICK CURL BOUTIQUE	75	70	72	60	45	55
7825	1974	BARBIE TOWNHOUSE	70	60	65	50	35	40
7412	1975	BARBIE'S OLYMPIC SKI VILLAGE	70	55	62	45	30	40
9525	1976	FASHION PLAZA	85	75	78	50	30	42

❖❖❖❖❖❖❖❖❖❖❖❖❖❖❖

SUZY GOOSE FURNITURE

DESCRIPTION	NRFB HIGH	NRFB LOW	MINT HIGH	MINT LOW
CANOPY BED	—	—	120	100
Display Box	300	250	—	—
Cardboard Box	150	125	—	—
WARDROBE Cardboard Box	150	125	90	75
VANITY	—	—	60	50
Display Box	200	175	—	—
Cardboard Box	125	100	—	—
QUEEN SIZE BED Cardboard Box	250	225	90	60
CHIFFEROBE Cardboard Box	300	250	200	150
PINK VANITY	—	—	150	125
PINK WARDROBE	—	—	95	70
PINK CANOPY BED	—	—	215	165
PINK QUEEN SIZE BED	—	—	800	600
HOT PINK VANITY	—	—	100	75
HOT PINK WARDROBE	—	—	100	75
PIANO	—	—	575	450
Display Box	2500	2000	—	—
Cardboard Box	1000	750	—	—
FRANCIE A GO-GO BED Display Box	2500	2000	1350	1000
TUTTI and TODD "DUTCH" Display Box	1700	1500	800	700
KEN WARDROBE	—	—	90	60
Display Box	250	200	—	—
Cardboard Box	175	125	—	—
SKIPPER JEWEL BED Display Box	275	225	150	125
SKIPPER JEWEL VANITY Display Box	265	200	125	100
SKIPPER JEWEL WARDROBE Display Box	225	175	125	100
REGAL BED	—	—	2000	1600

MATTEL™ MODERN FURNITURE

STOCK NO.	DESCRIPTION	NRFB HIGH	NRFB LOW	MINT HIGH	MINT LOW
801	SOFA	75	55	30	20
802	EASY CHAIR	70	60	35	25
803	COFFEE TABLE	55	40	20	15
804	END TABLE & LAMP	60	50	—	—
	END TABLE	—	—	20	15
	LAMP	—	—	30	20
805	DINING TABLE & CHAIRS	120	100	—	—
	DINING TABLE	—	—	30	20
	CHAIR	—	—	20	12
806	BUFFET	100	75	35	25
807	QUEEN SIZE BED	100	75	—	—
	BED ONLY	—	—	35	25
	MATTRESS, BEDSPREAD, PILLOW	—	—	35	25
808	DRESSER & MIRROR	100	75	30	20
809	OPEN WARDROBE with cover	275	200	160	135
	NO HANGERS OR COVER	75	60	35	25
810	STUDIO SET	180	150	—	—
	SOFA BED	—	—	30	20
	CORNER TABLE	—	—	25	20
	LAMP	—	—	20	20
811	CONVERTIBLE SOFA	65	50	32	25
812	BEDROOM SET	450	385	—	—
813	LIVING ROOM SET	350	275	—	—
815	DINING ROOM SET	300	245	—	—

VINTAGE BOOKLETS/FLYERS

DESCRIPTION	YEAR	MINT
#1 (102nd St. L.A.)	1959	60
#2 (5150 Rosekrans Ave.)	1960	22
#3 (Hawthorne, CA)	1961	23
BARBIE GAME FLYER	1961	1
BARBIE SINGS FLYER	1961	3
DREAM HOUSE FLYER	1961	2
LT. BLUE - BARBIE/KEN	1961	3
PINK - BARBIE/KEN (dated)	1961	4
PINK - BARBIE/KEN (undated)	1961	5
"A MESSAGE TO PARENTS" BOOKLET	1962	25
BRIGHT BLUE - BARBIE/KEN/MIDGE (dated)	1962	4
DREAM HOUSE FLYER	1962	2
LT. BLUE - BARBIE/KEN (dated)	1962	4
WHITE - BARBIE/KEN/MIDGE (dated)	1962	5
YELLOW - BARBIE/KEN/MIDGE (dated)	1962	4
ALLAN, LITTLE THEATRE, TRAVEL COSTUMES FLYER	1963	2
BARBIE & FRANCIE COLOR MAGIC DESIGN SET #4040 INSTRUCTION BOOKLET	1963	6
CARNATION BARBIE & MIDGE BOOKLET (pink cover)	1963	100
CARNATION BARBIE & MIDGE BOOKLET (yellow cover)	1963	100
EXCLUSIVE FASHIONS BOOK 1	1963	6
EXCLUSIVE FASHIONS BOOK 2	1963	6
EXCLUSIVE FASHIONS BOOK 3	1963	6
EXCLUSIVE FASHIONS BOOK 4	1963	5
WHITE - SKIPPER	1963	7
BARBIE LA MODE DES ANNEES (French) all 1964 Fashions	1964	12
BRIO - Barbie, Ken & Skipper (Swedish)	1964	95
CUTE TIPS FOR SHOPPING TRIPS (SPP - Barbie Cases/Toys)	1964	60
EXCLUSIVE FASHIONS BOOK 1	1964	20
EXCLUSIVE FASHIONS BOOK 2	1964	15
EXCLUSIVE FASHIONS BOOK 3	1964	15
EXCLUSIVE FASHIONS BOOK 4	1964	15
SPP BOOKLET (cases, wallets, etc.)	1964	65
9 FACE WORLD OF BARBIE FASHIONS #1 (red)	1965	30
9 FACE WORLD OF BARBIE FASHIONS #2 (red)	1965	32

DESCRIPTION	YEAR	MINT
9 FACE WORLD OF BARBIE FASHIONS #3 (red)	1965	30
9 FACE WORLD OF BARBIE FASHIONS #4 (red)	1965	30
BARBIE ET SES AMIE Barbie & Her Friends (French)	1965	15
BARBIE ET SES AMIE Dolls & Fashions 1963-69 (French)	1965	—
BARBIES COLOR MAGIC WIGS	1965	25
BARBIES COLOR 'N CURL	1965	20
FASHION AND PLAY ACCESSORIES FOR SKIPPER, SKOOTER, ETC.	1965	15
SKIPPER, SKOOTER AND RICKY (yellow)	1965	5
TUTTI	1965	15
FRANCIE	1966	20
SKIPPER, SKOOTER, RICKY, TUTTI AND TODD FASHIONS AND PLAY ACCESSORIES	1966	20
THE WORLD OF BARBIE FASHIONS	1966	5
THE WORLD OF BARBIE FASHIONS (5 FACE) #1	1966	10
THE WORLD OF BARBIE FASHIONS #2	1966	10
THE WORLD OF BARBIE FASHIONS (5 FACE) #3	1966	5
THE WORLD OF BARBIE FASHIONS BOOK 1	1967	10
THE WORLD OF BARBIE FASHIONS BOOK 2	1967	8
THE WORLD OF BARBIE FASHIONS BOOK 3	1967	8
BARBIES WORLD: BRIGHT, SWINGING, NOW	1968	5
THE WORLD OF BARBIE FASHIONS BOOK 1	1968	6
THE WORLD OF BARBIE FASHIONS BOOK 2	1968	6
THE WORLD OF BARBIE FASHIONS BOOK 3	1968	6
THE WORLD OF BARBIE FASHIONS BOOK 4	1968	6
LIVING BARBIE - As Full of Life as You Are	1969	6
LIVE ACTION KEN ON STAGE - Instructions	1970	5
LIVE ACTION PJ ON STAGE - Instructions	1970	5
LIVING BARBIE AND LIVING SKIPPER	1970	2
THE LIVELY WORLD OF BARBIE	1971	25
THE BEAUTIFUL WORLD OF BARBIE	1972	25

VINTAGE BOOKS, COMIC BOOKS & COLORING BOOKS

DESCRIPTION	YEAR	MINT
BOOKS		
BARBIES FASHION SUCCESS (Random House)	1962	45
BARBIES NEW YORK SUMMER (Random House)	1962	45
HERE'S BARBIE (Random House)	1962	45
THE WORLD OF BARBIE (Random House)	1962	65
BARBIE AND KEN (Random House)	1963	43
BARBIES HAWAIIAN HOLIDAY (Random House)	1963	42
BARBIE SOLVES A MYSTERY (Random House)	1963	45
BARBIE GOES TO A PARTY (Wonderbook)	1964	20
BARBIE IN TELEVISION (Random House)	1964	45
BARBIE, MIDGE & KEN (Random House)	1964	45
BARBIE THE BABY-SITTER (Wonderbook)	1964	20
BARBIES ADVENTURES OF CAMP (Random House)	1964	62
BARBIES SECRET (Random House)	1964	45
EASY AS PIE COOKBOOK (Random House)	1964	123
FLINTSTONES COMIC BOOK July - Full page Carnation Barbie	1964	20
PORTRAIT OF SKIPPER (Wonderbook)	1964	20
BARBIE AND THE GHOST TOWN MYSTERY (Random House)	1965	45
BARBIE-GOR SUCCE Sweden (Random House)	1965	50
BARBIE-I NEW YORK Sweden (Random House)	1965	50
BARBIE LOSER ETT MYSTERIUM Barbie Loves a Mystery Sweden (Random House)	1965	50
BARBIE OCH KEN (Barbie & Ken) Sweden (Random House)	1965	50
BARBIE-PA HAWAII Sweden (Random House)	1965	50
BARBIES ADVENTURES TO READ ALOUD (Wonderbook)	1965	20
BARBIES CANDY STRIPED SUMMER (Random House)	1965	45
HAPPY GO-LUCKY SKIPPER (Random House)	1965	115
HAR KOMMER BARBIE (Here's Barbie) Sweden (Random House)	1965	50
SKIPPER, HAPPY-GO-LUCKY Carl Memlin (Random House)	1965	75
"BAKKEN EN BRADEN MET BARBIE" Dutch (Random House)	1966	80
"BARBIE EN HAAR TELEVISIE-BAAN" Dutch (Random House)	1966	80
BARBIE EN KEN Dutch (Random House)	1966	80
HIER IS BARBIE Dutch (Random House)	1966	90
BARBIE - HET MODEL MEISJE (German)	1968	20
COMIC BOOKS		
#1 DELL May-July 1962 (01-053-207)	1963	95
#2 DELL August-October 1962 (12-053-210)	1963	95
#3 DELL May-July 1963 (12-053-307)	1963	95
#4 DELL August-October 1963 (12-053-310)	1963	95
#5 DELL November-January 1964 (12-053-401)	1963	95
FLINTSTONES July (Carnation Barbie offer)	1964	25
COLORING BOOKS, STICKER BOOKS & SCRAPBOOKS		
BARBIE AND KEN 128 PAGE Coloring Book #1183 (Whitman)	1962	25
BARBIE COLOR BY NUMBER (Whitman)	1962	45
BARBIE AND KEN Coloring Book Authorized Edition #1183	1962	25
BARBIE AND KEN STICKER FUN	1963	60

VINTAGE BOOKS, COMIC BOOKS & COLORING BOOKS CONTINUED

DESCRIPTION	YEAR	MINT
COLORING BOOKS, STICKER BOOKS & SCRAPBOOKS (continued)		
BARBIE INTRODUCING MIDGE Coloring Book #1183	1963	25
MODERN MISS PLAY BOX Assorted Barbie & Ken Paper Dolls, Color Books, Sticker Books & Crafts *Sears Exclusive*	1963	160
BARBIE, KEN AND MIDGE 192 page Coloring Book #1146	1964	25
BARBIE, KEN AND MIDGE Coloring Book Authorized Edition #1640	1964	25
BARBIE, KEN AND MIDGE PLAY KIT - Suitcase containing 50 pieces color books, puzzle, sewing cards, stickers and more	1964	22
BARBIES SCRAPBOOK (Whitman)	1964	25
BARBIE and her little sister SKIPPER 192 page Authorized Edition #1640	1965	25
BARBIE AND SKIPPER #1015 (Whitman)	1965	23
SKIPPER Barbies Little Sister (Whitman)	1965	30
SKIPPER OFF TO CAMP STICKER FUN	1965	50
FRANCIE Coloring Book with doll and cut-out clothes #1094	1967	30
JULIA "A Coloring Book based on the NBC TV series" (Saalfield Publishing)	1968	25
1695 WORLD OF BARBIE	1971	35
NEW 'N GROOVY PJ Coloring Book #1662	1971	20
WORLD OF BARBIE Coloring Book #1651	1971	20
BARBIE MATCH 'N COLOR #1252	1972	20
PJ WITH HER FRIENDS STICKER BOOK (Whitman)	1972	25
BARBIE AND PJ - A Camping Adventure Coloring Book #1071	1973	20
BARBIE AND SKIPPER Coloring Book #1015 (1965)	1973	22
BUSY BARBIE FUN BOOK (Coloring Book) #1665	1973	22
ADVENTURES WITH BARBIE 1 - The Mysterious Dude of Ghost Ranch (PPS)	—	5
ADVENTURES WITH BARBIE 2 - Dancing the Night Away (PPS)	—	5
ADVENTURES WITH BARBIE 3 - Wildlife Rescue (PPS)	—	5
ADVENTURES WITH BARBIE 4 - Soda Shop Surprise (PPS)	—	5
ADVENTURES WITH BARBIE 5 - The Phantom of Shrieking Pond (PPS)	—	5
ADVENTURES WITH BARBIE 6 - Rollerblade Crusade (PPS)	—	5
ADVENTURES WITH BARBIE 7 - Ballet Debut (PPS)	—	5
ADVENTURES WITH BARBIE 8 - Holiday Magic (PPS)	—	5
ADVENTURES WITH BARBIE 9 - Star-Swept Adventure (PPS)	—	5
ADVENTURES WITH BARBIE 10 - Wild Horse Run (PPS)	—	5
ADVENTURES WITH BARBIE 11 - Animal Escapades (PPS)	—	5
ADVENTURES WITH BARBIE 12 - Mermaid Island (PPS)	—	5
BUSY BARBIE (Whitman)	—	15
COLOR FORMS, Barbie Deluxe Sewing Activity Set	—	12
COLOR FORMS, Barbie Make-up Kit	—	10
COLOR FORMS, Barbie Stencil Playset	—	10
COLOR FORMS, Magical Mansion	—	8
COLOR FORMS, Sparkle Art	—	8
MALIBU FRANCIE	—	5
SKIPPER SPORTS STAR	—	5
WESTERN BARBIE	—	5

VINTAGE CASES

DESCRIPTION	YEAR	MINT
BARBIE & STEFFIE SLEEP 'N KEEP CASE	1969	35
CARRYING		
FASHION QUEEN, BLACK, zippered	1964	141
MISS BARBIE, BLACK, zippered	1964	150
MISS BARBIE, RED, zippered	1964	140
MISS BARBIE, WHITE, zippered	1964	142
DOUBLE - TRUNKS		
BARBIE, BLACK, 4 Ponytails, 1 PT in zebra-striped swimsuit (Ponytail)	1961	25
BARBIE, BLACK, 4 Ponytails in zebra-striped swimsuit, variations of Knitting Pretty, Enchanted Evening & Swingin' Easy (Ponytail)	1961	35
BARBIE, BLUE, 4 Ponytails in zebra-striped swimsuit, variations of Knitting Pretty, Enchanted Evening & Swingin' Easy (Ponytail)	1961	30
BARBIE, BLACK, Barbie in Solo in the Spotlight, in the background wearing Enchanted Evening & Ballerina	1962	25
BARBIE, BLUE, Barbie in Solo in the Spotlight, in the background wearing Enchanted Evening & Ballerina	1962	25
BARBIE & KEN, BLACK, Party Date & Saturday Date	1963	30
BARBIE & KEN, BLUE, Barbie in Enchanted Evening, Ken in Tuxedo	1963	35
BARBIE & MIDGE DOLL CASE, BLUE, hard plastic, Barbie, Midge & 2 Kens	1963	25
BARBIE & MIDGE, RED	1963	25
BARBIE & MIDGE DOLL CASE, LIGHT PINK, hard plastic, Barbie, Midge & 2 Kens	1963	35
BARBIE & MIDGE DOLL CASE, RED, hard plastic, Barbie, Midge & 2 Kens	1963	25
BARBIE, BLACK	1963	15
BARBIE, BLUE, Stormy Weather & Winter Holiday	1963	25
BARBIE & HER FRIENDS (Barbie, Stacey, Francie & Skipper) hard plastic	1964	75
BARBIE & KEN COSTUME TRUNK Little Theatre Trunk (SPP)	1964	105
BARBIE & MIDGE, NAVY BLUE, w/Stormy Weather & Sorority Meeting	1964	60
BARBIE & SKIPPER, BEIGE	1964	30
BARBIE & SKIPPER, YELLOW	1964	30
BARBIE, BLUE, Country Fair & Suburban Shopper (SPP)	1964	30
BARBIE, BLUE, Trousseau Wedding Trunk (SPP)	1964	98
BARBIE, KEN & MIDGE, BLACK (SPP) blue & brown accessory drawers w/flowered walls	1964	45
BARBIE, YELLOW, Trousseau Wedding Trunk (SPP)	1964	103
BARBIE & FRANCIE, COLOR MAGIC, Barbie in Stripes Away & Francie in Bloom Bursts	1965	45
BARBIE & FRANCIE, WHITE	1965	30
BARBIE, FRANCIE & SKIPPER DOLL TRUNK, BLACK, Swiss Chalet in background (SPP)	1965	75
BARBIE & SKIPPER TRAVEL TRUNK, BLACK (SPP)	1965	75
BARBIE & SKIPPER VANITY TRUNK, LAVENDER, Barbie & Skipper looking in mirrors	1965	122
BARBIE & SKIPPER, BEIGE, double door, includes garment bag	1966	30
BARBIE & SKIPPER, BLUE, double door, horses in background	1966	75
BARBIE & SKIPPER, BLUE, double door, includes garment bag	1966	30

VINTAGE CASES CONTINUED

DESCRIPTION	YEAR	MINT
BARBIE & SKIPPER, GREY, double door, horses in background	1966	88
BARBIE, FRANCIE, CASEY & TUTTI hard plastic (SPP)	1966	95
FRANCIE & CASEY, Groovy Get Ups & Iced Blue	1966	35
BARBIE, FRANCIE & CASEY, GREEN, Bloom Bursts, In Print & Summer Frost	1967	90
BARBIE, World of Barbie, Barbie & Stacey in Mod outfits	1968	20
WORLD OF BARBIE, PINK, Ruffles, Swirls & Shirt Dressy	1968	15
WORLD OF BARBIE, WHITE, Ruffles, Swirls & Shirt Dressy	1968	15
BARBIE, BRIGHT PINK, World of Barbie	1969	20
BARBIE & MIDGE, LIGHT BLUE	—	20
BARBIE & STACEY, Barbie in Swirley Cue & Stacey in Mini Chex	—	40
FRANCIE		
LIGHT BLUE, 6 sided	1965	50
JAMIE		
PARTY PENTHOUSE (Mattel, Sears Exclusive)	1970	—
KEN		
GREEN	1961	20
LAVENDER, Ken with 3 Barbies (Ponytail)	1961	25
TEAL, Ken and 3 Barbies (Ponytail)	1961	22
YELLOW, Ken with 3 Barbies (Ponytail)	1961	25
GREEN, Ken in Rally Day, Barbie in Austin Healy	1962	20
LAVENDER, Ken in Casuals, Barbie in Austin Healy	1962	25
TEAL, Ken in Casuals, Barbie in Austin Healy	1962	20
VIOLET	1962	25
YELLOW, Ken in Casuals, Barbie in Austin Healy (Ponytail)	1962	25
YELLOW, Campus Hero	1963	20
MUSTARD, Ken with 3 Barbies (Ponytail)	—	—
MIDGE		
MIDGE, BLACK, Midge, Barbies Best Friend	1963	25
MIDGE, BLUE, Midge, Barbies Best Friend	1963	25
MIDGE, BLUE, Midge in Movie Date	1963	48
MIDGE, RED, Party Date	1963	22
ROUND HAT BOX		
BARBIE, BLACK, 3 Ponytails	1961	50
BARBIE, BLACK, Sketched Ponytail	1962	50
BARBIE & MIDGE TRAVEL PALS, BLACK, Bubble in Sorority Meeting, Midge in Movie Date	1963	75
BARBIE & MIDGE TRAVEL PALS, BLACK, Red Flare & Career Girl	1963	70
BARBIE & MIDGE TRAVEL PALS, WHITE, Red Flare & Career Girl	1963	88
BARBIE & FRANCIE, BLUE, Pretty Wild & Smart Switch	1965	55
BARBIE & FRANCIE, WHITE, Pretty Wild & Smart Switch	1965	65
BARBIE, FASHION QUEEN, BLACK, small round hat box case	1965	175
FRANCIE, WHITE, Mandarin	—	200

DESCRIPTION	YEAR	MINT
SINGLE		
BARBIE, BLACK, 4 Ponytails in non-Mattel clothes (several variations - Ponytail)	1961	21
BARBIE, BLUE, 4 Ponytails in non-Mattel clothes (variations - Ponytail)	1961	25
BARBIE, IVORY, 4 Ponytails in non-Mattel clothes (variations - Ponytail)	1961	30
BARBIE, BLACK, Enchanted Evening & Friday Night Date	1962	20
BARBIE, BLACK, Solo in the Spotlight	1962	25
BARBIE, BLUE, Enchanted Evening & Friday Night Date	1962	20
BARBIE, BLUE, Solo in the Spotlight	1962	22
BARBIE, RED, Bubble Cut wearing Enchanted Evening & Friday Night Date	1962	20
BARBIE & KEN, BLACK, Enchanted Evening & Tuxedo, smaller	1963	60
Barbie & Ken in background (Ponytail)		
BARBIE & KEN, BLUE, Enchanted Evening & Tuxedo, smaller	1963	50
Barbie & Ken in background (Ponytail)		
BARBIE & KEN, BLUE, Party Date & Saturday Date	1963	50
BARBIE & KEN, PINK, Enchanted Evening & Tuxedo, smaller	1963	60
Barbie & Ken in background (Ponytail)		
BARBIE & KEN, RED, Enchanted Evening & Tuxedo, smaller	1963	50
Barbie & Ken in background (Ponytail)		
BARBIE, BLACK, Barbie in green Sophisticated Lady	1963	25
BARBIE, BLACK, Bubble Cut in Red Flare (standing in front of blue luggage - SPP)	1963	20
BARBIE, BLACK, Bubble Cut in yellow version Red Flare (SPP)	1963	20
BARBIE, BLUE, Bubble Cut in Red Flare (standing in front of blue luggage - SPP)	1963	20
BARBIE, BLUE, Bubble Cut in yellow version of Red Flare	1963	20
BARBIE, RED, Bubble Cut in yellow version of Red Flare (standing in front	1963	20
of blue luggage - SPP)		
BARBIE, BLUE, Red Sophisticated Lady	1963	20
BARBIE, RED, Bubble Cut in Red Flare (standing in front		
of blue luggage - SPP)	1963	20
BARBIE, RED, green Sophisticated Lady	1963	25
BARBIE, WHITE, Bubble Cut in Red Flare	1963	18
BARBIE, WHITE, Bubble Cut in yellow version Red Flare (SPP)	1963	20
BARBIE & MIDGE, RED, (European) American Girl wearing Benefit Performance	1964	95
VANITY, Barbie & Skipper (SPP) Sears	1964	200
BARBIE & FRANCIE, RED, American Girl in Benefit Ball	1965	140
BARBIE & FRANCIE, WHITE, large, 2 pockets inside cover, 2 cupboard	1965	—
w/blue doors, holds 2 dolls, 2 hanger racks		
BARBIE, COLOR MAGIC, WHITE	1965	30
BARBIE, SIDE-PART, TITIAN (SPP) green, yellow, blue & white checked	1966	198
w/view window for doll (CASE ONLY)		
BARBIE, SIDE-PART, TITIAN (SPP) green, yellow, blue & white checked	1966	800
w/view window for doll (WITH BURNETTE SWIRL PT)		
BARBIE, WHITE, American Girl in Fashion Shiner	1967	25
BARBIE, BRIGHT BLUE, World of Barbie	1969	13

VINTAGE CASES CONTINUED

DESCRIPTION	YEAR	MINT
BARBIE, MISS BARBIE, RED	—	80
BARBIE, WHITE, red, black Fashion Queen	—	112
SKIPPER		
BEIGE, DOUBLE DOOR, Skipper in Dress Coat, Red Sensation & School Days	1964	15
BLUE DOUBLE DOOR, Skipper in Dress Coat, School Days & Red Sensation	1964	15
BLUE, SKIPPER wearing Red Sensation, doves on right side	1964	50
PURSE PAL (pink)	1964	150
PURSE PAL (blue)	1964	150
YELLOW, DOUBLE DOOR, Skipper in Dress Coat, School Days & Red Sensation	1964	15
BLUE, Airport Terminal Scene (SPP)	1965	118
BLUE, DOUBLE DOOR, Skipper in Land & Sea sailboat	1966	35
YELLOW, DOUBLE DOOR, Skipper in Land & Sea sailboat	1966	40
WHITE, #4966, Skipper wearing Budding Beauty	1969	10
ORANGE, #4966, Skipper wearing Budding Beauty	1970	30
SKIPPER AND FLUFF		
SKIPPER & FLUFF #4966 wearing Budding Beauty	1970	30
SKIPPER AND SKOOTER		
BLACK	1965	69
BLUE, Beach Scene	1965	45
YELLOW, Beach Scene	1965	45
BLUE, Skipper & Skooter in picture frames (SPP)	1966	30
BLUE, Skipper in School Girl (Mattel)	1966	30
PINK W/WHITE POLKA DOTS, viewing window, SPP (2 shades)	1966	150
PINK-SALMON, Skipper & Skooter in picture frames (SPP)	1966	30
YELLOW, Skipper in Funtime (Mattel)	1966	40
SKOOTER		
BLUE, double door, wearing Country Picnic	1965	67
BLUE, double door, Platter Party & Sunny Pastels (SPP)	1965	75
GREY, double door, wearing Country Picnic	1965	68
BLUE, Skipper & Skooter in picture frames (SPP)	1966	30
TRAIN		
BARBIE, BLACK, Ponytail silhouette w/4 full length views Barbie (Ponytail)	1961	60
BARBIE & MIDGE TRAVEL PALS, big Ponytail & Midge, smaller Bubble Cut in Sorority Meeting, Midge Movie Date	1963	76
BARBIE & MIDGE TRAVEL PALS, BLACK, Bubble Cut in Blue Knitting Pretty, Midge in Sheath Sensation & Barbie & Midge faces	1963	78

VINTAGE CASES CONTINUED

DESCRIPTION	YEAR	MINT
BARBIE & MIDGE TRAVEL PALS, RED, Bubble Cut in Blue Knitting	1963	70
Pretty, Midge in Sheath Sensation & Barbie & Midge faces		
BARBIE & MIDGE TRAVEL PALS, WHITE, Bubble Cut in Blue Knitting	1963	80
Pretty, Midge in Sheath Sensation & Barbie & Midge faces		
SKIPPER, BLUE, no illustration (SPP)	1965	125
SKIPPER, YELLOW, Airport Terminal Scene (SPP)	1965	175
SKIPPER & SKOOTER, BLUE (SPP)	1965	80
TRIPLE		
WORLD OF BARBIE, BLUE, Made for Each Other & Fancy Dancy	1969	20
TUTTI		
ORANGE, Flower Print background	1965	35
TUTTI SUMMER HOUSE (#3562)	1965	68
TUTTI ICE CREAM STAND (open view area)	1965	—
TUTTI PLAY CASE, pink, pale pink or blue w/view area	1966	—
TUTTI PLAYHOUSE	1966	45
BLUE w/window Walking My Dog & 3 other outfits	—	25
TUTTI AND CHRIS		
PATIO PICNIC CASE	1965	95
TUTTI & CHRIS HOUSE	1965	150
TUTTI & CHRIS, white w/peacock	1965	40
TUTTI & CHRIS, yellow w/view window	1965	45
TUTTI AND TODD		
TUTTI & TODD HOUSE	1965	45
TWIGGY		
FASHION TOTE, yellow vinyl, Mattel label, zipper	1967	90

VINTAGE GAMES

DESCRIPTION	YEAR	MINT
QUEEN OF THE PROM (1st issue)	1961	55
QUEEN OF THE PROM white box (2nd issue)	1963	55
BARBIES KEYS TO FAME	1964	65
SKIPPER GAME - BARBIE'S LITTLE SISTER	1964	52
THE BARBIE WORLD OF FASHION GAME (Mattel)	1967	65
TWIGGY (Milton Bradley) #4731	1967	55
MISS LIVELY LIVIN' GAME	1970	45

❖❖❖❖❖❖❖❖❖❖❖❖❖❖❖

VINTAGE JEWELRY

DESCRIPTION	YEAR	MINT
BARBIE AND MIDGE FASHION DOLL, Afternoon Wear Set, Aqua Marine Necklace/Earrings (Cleinman and Sons) #7300	1963	225
BARBIE AND MIDGE FASHION DOLL, Casual Wear Set, Ruby Necklace/Earrings (Cleinman and Sons) #7300	1963	225
BARBIE AND MIDGE FASHION DOLL, Evening Wear Set, Diamond Necklace/Earrings (Cleinman and Sons) #7300	1963	225
BARBIE PLAY JEWELRY, earrings and necklace set w/matching set for Barbie #7200 (Cleinman and Sons)	1963	200
BARBIE PLAY JEWELRY & JEWEL CHEST - three earring & necklace sets w/red vinyl case - red cardboard w/six compartments	1963	225
BARBIE PLAY JEWELRY SET - earring, necklace & tiara child & doll size	1963	200
BRACELET, Barbie Fan Club	1963	35
BRACELET, w/charm profile Ponytail	1963	35
RING, gold & rhinestone on blue bubble card #7000 The Official Barbie Play Ring	1963	100
RING, gold & rhinestone on yellow bubble card w/Ponytail logo #7000 The Official Barbie Play Ring	1963	125
BRACELET, gold tone chain w/gold ton w/charm w/'68 TNT	1968	35

VINTAGE MAGAZINES & CATALOGS

DESCRIPTION	YEAR	MINT
MAGAZINES		
BARBIE CLUB NEWS NEWSLETTER November	1960	75
BARBIE MAGAZINE FOR GIRLS September/October	1963	35
LIFE, August 1963 the *Most Popular Doll in Town* (Frank Sinatra)	1963	30
MCCALL'S MAGAZINE November	1963	10
BARBIE MAGAZINE FOR GIRLS January/February	1964	35
BARBIE MAGAZINE FOR GIRLS March/April	1964	65
BARBIE MAGAZINE FOR GIRLS May/June	1964	35
BARBIE MAGAZINE FOR GIRLS July/August	1964	65
BARBIE MAGAZINE FOR GIRLS September/October	1964	35
BARBIE MAGAZINE FOR GIRLS November/December	1964	65
ICE FOLLIES PROGRAM Shiptad and Johnson 9½" x 12¼"	1964	30
JACK AND JILL MAGAZINE (Skipper Ad) May	1964	—
JACK AND JILL MAGAZINE (Little Theatre Ad) July	1964	—
MCCALL'S MAGAZINE April	1964	10
MCCALL'S NEEDLEWORK & CRAFTS Fall/Winter	1964/65	10
WORLD OF BARBIE (Barbie Magazine Annual)	1964	100
BARBIE MAGAZINE FOR GIRLS January/February	1965	35
BARBIE MAGAZINE FOR GIRLS March/April	1965	35
BARBIE MAGAZINE FOR GIRLS May/June	1965	35
BARBIE MAGAZINE FOR GIRLS July/August	1965	35
BARBIE MAGAZINE FOR GIRLS September/October	1965	35
BARBIE MAGAZINE FOR GIRLS November/December	1965	35
JACK AND JILL MAGAZINE (Skipper and Skooter ad) April	1965	22
JACK AND JILL MAGAZINE (Color 'N Curl Ad)	1965	—
MATTEL CATALOG (32 pages of Barbie)	1965	95
MCCALL'S NEEDLEWORK & CRAFTS Spring/Summer	1965	10
MCCALL'S NEEDLEWORK & CRAFTS Fall/Winter	1965/66	10
BARBIE MAGAZINE FOR GIRLS January/February	1966	35
BARBIE MAGAZINE FOR GIRLS March/April	1966	35
BARBIE MAGAZINE FOR GIRLS May/June	1966	35
BARBIE MAGAZINE FOR GIRLS July/August	1966	35
BARBIE MAGAZINE FOR GIRLS September/October	1966	35

DESCRIPTION	YEAR	MINT
BARBIE MAGAZINE FOR GIRLS November/December	1966	35
JACK AND JILL MAGAZINE (Mattel ad including Tutti) August	1966	22
MCCALL'S NEEDLEWORK & CRAFTS Fall/Winter	1966/67	10
BARBIE MAGAZINE FOR GIRLS January/February	1967	30
BARBIE, THE MATTEL BARBIE MAGAZINE March/April	1967	12
BARBIE, THE MATTEL BARBIE MAGAZINE May/June	1967	12
BARBIE MAGAZINE FOR GIRLS July/August	1967	30
BARBIE MAGAZINE FOR GIRLS September/October	1967	30
BARBIE MAGAZINE FOR GIRLS November/December	1967	30
FAMILY CIRCLE MAGAZINE May	1967	10
FAMILY CIRCLE MAGAZINE "Negro Francie" December	1967	20
JACK AND JILL MAGAZINE (Contest with Barbie prizes) August	1967	22
MCCALL'S NEEDLEWORK & CRAFTS Winter	1967/68	10
BARBIE MAGAZINE FOR GIRLS January/February	1968	30
BARBIE MAGAZINE FOR GIRLS March/April	1968	30
BARBIE MAGAZINE FOR GIRLS May/June	1968	30
BARBIE MAGAZINE FOR GIRLS July/August	1968	30
BARBIE MAGAZINE FOR GIRLS September/October	1968	30
BARBIE MAGAZINE FOR GIRLS November/December	1968	30
TV GUIDE November 16	1968	5
BARBIE MAGAZINE FOR GIRLS January/February	1968	25
BARBIE MAGAZINE FOR GIRLS March/April	1969	25
BARBIE MAGAZINE FOR GIRLS May/June	1969	25
BARBIE MAGAZINE FOR GIRLS July/August	1969	25
BARBIE MAGAZINE FOR GIRLS September/October	1969	25
BARBIE MAGAZINE FOR GIRLS November/December	1969	25
MATTEL ANNUAL REPORT	1969	35
MATTEL CHRISTMAS TOY AND HOBBY ADVERTISING SUPPLEMENT	1969	20
BARBIE TALK MAGAZINE Premier Issue (January/February)	1970	40
BARBIE TALK MAGAZINE March/April	1970	30
BARBIE TALK MAGAZINE May/June	1970	30
BARBIE TALK MAGAZINE July/August	1970	70
(fan club certificate salute to silver outfit & booklet)		

DESCRIPTION	YEAR	MINT
BARBIE TALK MAGAZINE September/October	1970	35
BARBIE TALK MAGAZINE November/December	1970	35
MATTEL CHRISTMAS TOY AND HOBBY ADVERTISING SUPPLEMENT	1970	20
BARBIE TALK MAGAZINE January/February	1971	30
BARBIE TALK MAGAZINE March/April	1971	30
BARBIE TALK MAGAZINE May/June	1971	35
BARBIE TALK MAGAZINE July/August	1971	35
BARBIE TALK MAGAZINE Halloween/Thanksgiving	1971	35
BARBIE TALK MAGAZINE Christmas/New Year's	1971	35
MATTEL CHRISTMAS TOY AND HOBBY ADVERTISING SUPPLEMENT	1971	20
BARBIE TALK MAGAZINE Valentines	1972	40
BARBIE TALK MAGAZINE April	1972	40
BARBIE TALK MAGAZINE May	1972	40
BARBIE TALK MAGAZINE (last issue) June/July	1972	40
MCCALL'S NEEDLEWORK & CRAFTS Spring/Summer	1972	10
AMERICAN THREAD COMPANY (Star Book #192)	—	10
JACK & JILL w/Color 'N Curl Advertisement	—	15
JACK & JILL w/Little Theatre Advertisement	—	30
JACK & JILL w/Skipper & Skooter Advertisement	—	15
MCCALL'S CHRISTMAS MAKE-IT-IDEA'S Volume 14	—	10
MCCALL'S CREATIVE HANDRAFTS Volume 4	—	10
CATALOGS		
MATTEL CATALOG	1965	100
MATTEL DOLLS	1970	75

VINTAGE PATTERNS, SEWING & CRAFTS

DESCRIPTION	YEAR	MINT UNCUT & COMPLETE
DOLLY DARLING - Fashion Kit	1960s	10
GLAMOUR GIRL - Teen Doll Fashion Kit	1960s	10
BARBIE & KEN FASHION EMBROIDERY SET (Standard Toycraft Industries)	1962	225
BARBIE FASHION EMBROIDERY SET (Standard Toycraft Industries) #502	1962	250
BARBIE LUNCHEON EMBROIDERY SET (Standard Toycraft Industries)	1962	295
DELUXE KNITTING FOR BARBIE SETS (Miner Industries Inc.)	1962	225
KNITTING FOR BARBIE CANNISTER (#8013 - Miner Industries) 3 versions	1962	95
KNITTING FOR BARBIE CANNISTER store display (Miner Industries)	1962	2900
BARBIE, KEN & MIDGE FASHION EMBROIDERY SET	1963	295
(Standard Toycraft Industries)		
BARBIE WEAVING LOOM SET (Pressman Toy Corporation) #1147	1963	350
BARBIE & FRANCIE COLOR MAGIC DESIGNER SET	1965	475
JO'S HOBBY HOUSE - Doll Dressing Course (Bristol Tennessee)	1965	10
SKIPPER FASHION EMBROIDERY SET (Standard Toycraft Industries) #5301	1965	300
KNIT A WARDROBE OF SWEATERS FOR YOUR FAVORITE DOLL	1966	10
(from February 1966 *Woman's Day*)		
5940 GRIT PATTERN, KNIT OUTFIT	1971	10
BARBIE, FASHION KNITTER (HG Toys #554)	1971	85
50 DOLL PATTERNS, Book #650	—	10
NEEDLECRAFT SERVICE DESIGN 881 & 7023, DOLLS KNITTED WARDROBE	—	10
PARADE PATTERN P-199, CROCHETED WARDROBE	—	10
BARBIE WEAVING LOOM (Pressman)	—	10
ADVANCE PATTERNS		
GROUP A OR 9938 BARBIE	1961	35
GROUP B OR 9939 BARBIE	1961	35
GROUP C OR 2895 BARBIE	1962	35
GROUP D OR 2896 BARBIE	1962	35
GROUP E OR 2899 KEN	1962	25
3376 BARBIE (uses outfits from Groups C & D)	1964	40
3377 BARBIE (uses outfits from Groups C & D)	1964	40
3425 BARBIE	1964	40
3426 BARBIE	1964	40
3573 BARBIE	1965	40
AMERICAN THREAD BOOKLETS		
DOLL CLOTHES KNITTED & CROCHETED (Starbook No. 192)	—	10
DOLL DRESSES CROCHETED, KNITTED (Starbook No. 161)	—	10
ANNE ADAMS		
SKIPPER PATTERN 4808 & 4938	1965	15

VINTAGE PATTERNS, SEWING & CRAFTS CONTINUED

DESCRIPTION	YEAR	MINT UNCUT & COMPLETE
9993 BARBIE	1960	25
2519 BARBIE & KEN	1962	25
2892 BARBIE	1963	25
3316 BARBIE & KEN	1964	25
3317 BARBIE	1964	25
3350 SKIPPER	1964	25
3385 BARBIE	1964	25
3761 BARBIE	1965	25
COATS 'N CLARK		
DOLL WARDROBE, Book No. 151	1964	10
THE DOLL BOOK, Book No. 173	1966	10
SEW SIMPLE, TROUSSEAU WARDROBE	1968	10
BRIDE DOLL LEAFLET C.843	—	10
FASHIONS IN WOOL		
CLOTHES FOR FASHION MODEL DOLLS, Vol. 99	—	10
CROCHET & KNIT WARDROBE FOR FASHION MODEL DOLLS, Vol. 111	—	10
GARMENTS FOR FASHION MODEL DOLLS, Vol. 104	—	10
MCCALL'S		
6260 BARBIE	1961	25
6420 BARBIE & KEN	1962	25
6901 BARBIE & KEN	1963	35
6992 BARBIE & KEN	1963	25
7114 LITTLE GIRL & BARBIE	1963	45
7127 LITTLE GIRL & BARBIE	1963	45
7137 BARBIE	1963	25
7162 LITTLE GIRL & BARBIE	1963	45
7175 LITTLE GIRL & BARBIE	1963	45
7311 BARBIE	1964	25
7428 BARBIE & KEN	1964	25
7429 BARBIE	1964	25
7430 BARBIE & KEN	1964	25
7431 BARBIE	1964	25
7476 BARBIE-SCALE LUGGAGE, CLOSET & CAMPING ACCESSORIES	1964	50
7480 SKIPPER	1964	25
7531 LITTLE GIRL & BARBIE	1964	45
7545 LITTLE GIRL & BARBIE	1964	45
7716 SKIPPER	1965	25
7840 BARBIE	1965	25

VINTAGE PATTERNS, SEWING & CRAFTS CONTINUED

DESCRIPTION	YEAR	MINT UNCUT & COMPLETE
MCCALL'S (continued)		
7841 SKIPPER	1965	25
8357 SKIPPER	1966	25
8531 FRANCIE	1966	45
8532 BARBIE	1966	25
9099 BARBIE	1967	25
9605 BARBIE	1968	25
2123 BARBIE	1969	25
2580 BARBIE	1970	25
2970 TUTTI (DAWN, TOO!)	1971	25
3429 BARBIE	1972	25
SIMPLICITY		
4422 BARBIE & KEN	1961	25
4510 BARBIE	1961	25
4700 BARBIE	1962	25
5215 BARBIE	1963	25
5673 BARBIE	1964	25
5731 BARBIE (TRESSY, TOO!)	1964	25
5861 SKIPPER	1964	25
6208 BARBIE	1965	25
6275 SKIPPER	1965	25
8466 BARBIE	1969	25
9054 BARBIE & KEN	1970	25
9097 BARBIE	1970	25
9697 BARBIE	1971	25
9698 SUPERSIZE BARBIE (17 1/2")	1971	25
5330 BARBIE & KEN	1972	25
VIRGINIA LAKIN'S		
PETITE DOLL KNITTING BOOK, Book one	1962	10
TEEN DOLL KNITTING & CROCHETING BOOK, Book two	1963	10
TEEN DOLL KNITTING BOOK, Book two	1963	10
PETITE FASHION FESTIVAL, Book No. 4	1964	10
THE "LITTLE SISTERS" DOLL KNITTING BOOK, Book No. 5	1965	10
DOLL KNITTING & CROCHETING, Book No. 8	1967	10
DOLL KNITTING & CROCHETING MAGAZINE, Third Issue	1968	10
OLD FASHIONED DRESSES FOR TEEN & BRIDE DOLLS, Leaflet No. 3	1968	10
DOLL KNITTING & CROCHETING BOOK, Book 9	1969	10
PETITE DOLL KNITTING BOOK, Book one (revised)	1971	10
DOLL CROCHET, Book 12	1972	10
DOLL KNITTING & CROCHETING, Book 13	1972	10

VINTAGE PAPER DOLLS

STOCK NO.	YEAR OF ORIGIN	DESCRIPTION	MIP
WHITMAN-GOLDEN			
1963	1962	BARBIE & KEN CUT-OUTS	125
1971	1962	BARBIE & KEN CUT-OUTS (book)	125
4797	1962	BARBIE & KEN SUITCASE - Traveling Dolls (box)	120
1963	1962	BARBIE DOLL CUT-OUTS (book)	115
1957	1962	BARBIE DOLL CUT-OUTS (reprint #1963)	125
1966	1962	BARBIE DOLL CUT-OUTS (reprint #1963)	115
4601	1963	BARBIE #11001	115
4797	1963	BARBIE & KEN (box w/handle)	125
1976	1963	BARBIE & KEN CUT-OUTS (book)	95
1962	1963	BARBIE DOLL CUT-OUTS (book)	90
1976	1963	BARBIE, KEN & MIDGE PAPER DOLLS (book)	90
1962	1963	MIDGE, BARBIES BEST FRIEND CUT-OUTS	90
1944	1964	BARBIE & SKIPPER (book)	85
1957	1964	BARBIE & SKIPPER	85
1957	1964	BARBIE & SKIPPER (book)	80
1976	1964	BARBIE COSTUME DOLLS with Skipper, Ken, Midge & Allan (book)	110
4605	1964	BARBIE FASHION WINDOW WARDROBE (box)	160
4616	1964	BARBIES TRAVEL WARDROBE (box)	130
4605	1964	BARBIES WEDDING DRESS 'N FASHION CLOTHES (box)	150
4778	1964	SKIPPER & SKOOTERS FOUR (4) SEASON WARDROBE (box)	150
4607	1964	SKIPPER'S DAY-BY-DAY WARDROBE (box)	110
4785	1965	BARBIE & MIDGE TRAVEL WARDROBE (box)	150
4793	1965	BARBIE, MIDGE & SKIPPER (box)	150
1984	1965	SKIPPER - Barbies Little Sister	65
4607	1965	SKIPPER FASHION CALENDAR WARDROBE (box)	135
4639	1965	SKOOTER FASHION GO-ROUND (box)	145
1985	1965	SKOOTER PAPER DOLLS (book)	175
4793	1966	BARBIE & FRANCIE Barbies Mod'ern Cousin (box)	105
1976	1966	BARBIE, SKIPPER & SKOOTER PAPER DOLLS (book)	80
1980	1966	MEET FRANCIE Barbies Mod'ern Cousin Paper Dolls (book)	80
4701	1967	BARBIE (box)	65
4785	1967	BARBIE (box)	65
1976	1967	BARBIE HAS A NEW LOOK! PAPER DOLLS (book)	45
1996	1967	BARBIE HAS A NEW LOOK! PAPER DOLLS (reprint #1976)	65
1094	1967	FRANCIE (book)	40
1167	1967	FRANCIE (book)	40
1169	1967	FRANCIE (book)	40
1986	1967	FRANCIE, Barbies Mod'ern Cousin & Casey, Francie's New Friend (book)	75

STOCK NO.	YEAR OF ORIGIN	DESCRIPTION	MIP
WHITMAN-GOLDEN (continued)			
4622	1967	TUTTI (box)	85
—	1967	TWIGGY MAGIC PAPER DOLL	40
1999	1967	TWIGGY PAPER DOLL	45
1976	1968	BARBIE, CHRISTIE, STACEY PAPER DOLLS (book)	65
1978	1968	BARBIE, CHRISTIE, STACEY PAPER DOLLS (book, reprint #1976)	65
1995	1968	BUFFY PAPER DOLL	40
1991	1968	TUTTI PAPER DOLL, Barbie & Skipper's Tiny Sister	65
—	1968	TUTTI PAPER DOLL (box)	45
4763	1969	BARBIE, 2 Magic Dolls with stay on clothes (box)	40
1976	1969	BARBIE DOLLS AND CLOTHES (book)	65
1985	1969	BUFFY PAPER DOLL	40
1335	1969	JULIA (Saalfield Publishing)	45
4472	1969	JULIA ARTCRAFT (Saalfield Publishing)	40
5140	1969	JULIA ARTCRAFT (Julia, Marie, Corey & Earl)	55
1976	1970	BARBIE & KEN PAPER DOLLS	40
1985	1970	BARBIE & KEN PAPER DOLLS (reprint #1976)	40
1986	1970	BARBIE & KEN PAPER DOLLS (reprint #1976)	40
1973	1970	MRS. BEASLEY PAPER DOLL BOOK	40
1981	1970	NEW 'N GROOVY PJ PAPER DOLLS	40
4735	1971	BARBIE (box)	25
4331	1971	BARBIE MAGIC (box)	25
1976	1971	GROOVY WORLD OF BARBIE & HER FRIENDS PAPER DOLL (book)	50
1662	1971	NEW 'N GROOVY PJ (book)	25
4332	1971	NEW 'N GROOVY PJ (box)	25
1654	1971	PJ (book)	35
1981	1971	PJ COVER GIRL PAPER DOLL	50
1987	1971	WORLD OF BARBIE PAPER DOLLS (book)	45
1974	1972	GROOVY PJ PAPER DOLL FASHIONS	40
1996	1972	MALIBU BARBIE (box)	20
1994	1972	MALIBU BARBIE, The Sun Set (four pages)	25
1994	1972	MALIBU BARBIE, The Sun Set (six pages)	20
4718	1972	MALIBU PJ (box)	20
1986	1972	MRS. BEASLEY PAPER DOLL FASHIONS	40
1993	1972	MRS. BEASLEY PAPER DOLL FASHIONS	40
1875	1972	POS'N BARBIE (book)	40
1975	1972	POS'N BARBIE PAPER DOLL FASHIONS	40
4376-B	1972	WORLD OF BARBIE (box)	30
4343	1972	WORLD OF BARBIE PLAY FUN (box)	30

VINTAGE PUZZLES

DESCRIPTION	YEAR	MINT
BARBIE & KEN AT A DRIVE-IN Barbie & Ken (Whitman - 100 piece)	1963	50
BARBIE IN AFTER FIVE AT FASHION SHOP-Barbie & Ken (Whitman - 100 piece) 59¢	1963	50
BARBIE IN GUINEVERE AT LITTLE THEATRE Barbie & Ken (Whitman - 100 piece) 59¢	1963	50
MIDGE IN BUSY MORNING BY BIRD CAGE Midge (Whitman - 100 piece)	1963	65
BARBIE & KEN WISHING WELL (Whitman - 100 piece)	1963	50
BARBIE & SKIPPER ON A CAROUSEL HORSE (Whitman - 100 piece)	1964	50
SKIPPER & SKOOTER HAVING WATERSIDE PICNIC (Whitman) Frame Tray	1965	50
SKIPPER & SKOOTER UNDER UMBRELLA WITH SODA'S (Whitman - 100 piece)	1965	50
SKIPPER IN LAND & SEA Skipper (Whitman) Frame Tray	1965	45
SKIPPER IN SCHOOL GIRL Skipper (Whitman) Frame Tray	1965	45
TWIST 'N TURN & "MARLO FLIP" ON A BEACH WITH 2 KEN'S	1972	35

❖❖❖❖❖❖❖❖❖❖❖❖❖❖❖

VINTAGE RECORD & MUSIC RELATED

DESCRIPTION	YEAR	NFRB
BARBIE EMENEE RECORD PLAYER *Spiegel*	1961	850
"BARBIE SINGS" 6 Record Set #840	1961	65
"BARBIE SINGS" Demo 33 1/3 Record	1961	150
"BARBIE SINGS" Store Display	1961	1200
BARBIE VINYL RECORD TOTE* (black) Ponytail *Sears*	1961	125
BARBIE VINYL RECORD TOTE* (light blue) Ponytail *Spiegel*	1961	125
BARBIE TRANSISTOR RADIO bright orange - Vanity Fair - black vinyl carrying case and plug in earphone	1962	1300
BARBIE VANITY FAIR RECORD PLAYER*	1962	1600
BARBIE GE-TAR	1963	350
THE BARBIE LOOK The Musical World of Barbie Columbia Records	1964	175
THE BARBIE LOOK Columbia Records 33 1/3 Record (#0504)	1965	110
THE BIG GAME Columbia Records 33 1/3 Record (#0502)	1965	110
A HAPPY BARBIE BIRTHDAY The Musical World of Barbie Columbia Records 33 1/3 Record (#0506)	1965	110
"A PICNIC FOR SKIPPER" Columbia Records 33 1/3 Record (#0503) (Skipper, Skooter, Todd & Barbie on cover w/fireplace)	1965	110
SKIPPER, SKOOTER & RICKY (The Musical World of Barbie) Columbia Records 33 1/3 Record (#0505)	1965	110
THE WORLD OF BARBIE (The Musical World of Barbie) Columbia Records 33 1/3 Record (#0501)	1965	110
MATTEL-A-PHONE RECORDS	1968	8
"I'M HAPPY I'M BARBIE" 45 rpm	1970	10
PJ - "HEY LITTLE PJ GAL" & instrumental, 45rpm	1970	10

STANDS

DESCRIPTION	MINT
#1 2 PRONG PEDESTAL	1800
#2™ PEDESTAL	400
#3™ PEDESTAL	200
#4® PEDESTAL	125
BARBIE BLACK WIRE	15
BARBIE GOLD WIRE	15
FRANCIE GOLD WIRE	25
KEN BLACK WIRE	10
MIDGE (Japanese)	N/A
MOD CLEAR X	12
MOD CLEAR X (Barbie - w/talker box top seat - pink & purple)	25
MOD CLEAR X (Stacey - w/talker box top seat - green)	25
MOD CLEAR X (Christie - w/talker box top seat - yellow & orange)	25
MOD PINK X	4
MOD WHITE X	5
SKIPPER - RICKY GOLD WIRE	15

❖❖❖❖❖❖❖❖❖❖❖❖❖❖❖

VINTAGE TEA SETS

DESCRIPTION	YEAR	NFRB
Skipper Plastic Tea Set (service for 4) 43 piece	1965	—
Barbie Plastic Tea Set (service for 6) pink & white, 46 piece	1964	—
Barbie Plastic Tea Set (service for 4) 48 piece	1964	—
Barbie & Midge Plastic Tea Set (service for 4) blue & white, 44 piece	1965	—
Barbies Own Tea Set, full length picture of Barbie on each plate, portraits on saucers, set of 4, purple & white, 42 piece plastic	1962	—
SEARS		
Skipper Plastic Tea Set (service for 4) 44 piece *Sears*	1965	—
Barbie Plastic Tea Set (red & white) 62 piece *Sears*	1962	—
WARDS		
Barbie Plastic Tea Set (service for 6) 56 piece *Wards*	1962	—
Barbie Plastic Tea Set (service for 4) pink & white, 42 piece *Wards*	1962	—
Barbie Plastic Tea Set (service for 6) pink & white, 62 piece *Wards*	1963	—
IRWIN		
BARBIE HEIRLOOM SERVICE PLAY SET	1962	275
WORCHESTER INDUSTRIES		
BUBBLE CUT ON THE FRONT OF BOX, cups & saucers for party of 6 w/barbie on it, teapot, creamer, sugar, utensils and plates w/Barbie in 900 outfits, (Worchester Toy Co.) #946	1961	225

REGULAR & FOREIGN ISSUE
(1973 – PRESENT)

STOCK NO.	YEAR OF ORIGIN	DESCRIPTION	NRFB
12339	1994	3-LOOKS (Canada)	15
23061	1985	5th ANIVERSARIO (Spain)	120
—	1989	5th ANIVERSARIO (Portugal)	110
6747	1989	10th ANIVERSARIO (Spain) Pertegaz	110
—	1989	30th ANIVERSARIO (Venezuela - Rotoplast)	125
51-0452	1991	ACQUA MARINE (Venezuela)	45
—	1984	AERÓBICA (Mexico)	40
9423	1991	ALL AMERICAN Reebok	30
9099	1990	ALL STARS	25
9099	1991	ALL STARS Reebok (Canada)	24
—	1989	ALTA MODA (Brazil)	75
3137	1991	AMERICAN BEAUTY QUEEN (white)	30
3245	1991	AMERICAN BEAUTY QUEEN (black)	30
5640	1983	ANGEL FACE	40
15911	1997	ANGEL PRINCESS (white)	20
15912	1997	ANGEL PRINCESS (black)	20
1350	1989	ANIMAL LOVIN' (white)	25
4824	1989	ANIMAL LOVIN' (black)	25
1207	1986	ASTRONAUT (black)	50
2449	1986	ASTRONAUT (white)	60
—	1986	ASTRONAUT (Mexico)	60
10776	1994	BALI (Europe)	25
9093	1976	BALLERINA (1st version hair)	80
9093	1979	BALLERINA (2nd version hair)	50
—	1983	BALLERINA	50
26774	2000	BALLET LESSONS (white)	20
26775	2000	BALLET LESSONS (black)	20
18187	1998	BALLET RECITAL BARBIE & KELLY GIFT SET* (white) *Toys R Us, Target, K-Mart*	15
21388	1998	BALLET RECITAL BARBIE & KELLY GIFT SET* (black) *Toys R Us, Target, K-Mart*	15
7382	1977	BARBIE (Europe)	45
7382	1979	BARBIE (Europe)	35
7382	1980	BARBIE 2 versions (Canada)	35
5336	1983	BARBIE 3 outfit versions (Germany)	30
—	1987	BARBIE & BOB EM RITMO DE ROCK (Brazil)	65
2751	1990	BARBIE AND THE BEAT	25
7882	1974	BARBIE BABY SITS yellow	60
9146	1987	BARBIE CELEBRATION	50
1922	—	BARBIE DE FIESTA	—
B4320	1996	BARBIE DOLL Y SU RUESIÑOR (3 box versions)	—
—	1993	BARBIE IN INDIA Blonde or Brunette - various saris (India)	49
—	1996	BARBIE IN INDIA Burgundy Sari - Brunette (India)	55
3075	1987	BARBIE LOISIRS (France)	25
—	1989	BARBIE ROMANTICA (Spain)	—
6253	1984	BARBIE STAR SUPER DANSE (Europe)	40

REGULAR & FOREIGN ISSUE CONTINUED

STOCK NO.	YEAR OF ORIGIN	DESCRIPTION	NRFB
8588	1973	BARBIE WITH BENDABLE LEGS mod era head mold (Europe)	—
8586	1974	BARBIE WITH TWIST 'N TURN WAIST Steffie head mold (Europe)	—
3830	1993	BATH BLAST (black)	12
4159	1993	BATH BLAST (white)	15
22357	1999	BATH BOUTIQUE Blonde	15
22358	1999	BATH BOUTIQUE (black)	15
22359	1999	BATH BOUTIQUE Brunette	15
5274	1992	BATH MAGIC (white)	15
7951	1992	BATH MAGIC (black)	15
9601	1991	BATHTIME (white)	15
9603	1991	BATHTIME (black)	15
13199	1995	BAYWATCH (white)	15
13258	1995	BAYWATCH (black)	20
3237	1989	BEACH BLAST	10
—	1979	BEACH FUN (Europe & Canada)	30
1703	1980	BEACH PARTY Department Store Special	75
9102	1985	BEACH TIME (Europe & Canada)	27
18888	1998	BEAD BLAST Blonde	10
18889	1998	BEAD BLAST (black)	10
18891	1998	BEAD BLAST Brunette	10
18890	1998	BEAD BLAST Redhead	10
9599	1976	BEAUTIFUL	75
9599	1976	BEAUTIFUL BRIDE rooted eyelash Department Store Special	200
9907	1976	BEAUTIFUL BRIDE (Europe)	110
9907	1978	BEAUTIFUL BRIDE Superstar face Department Store Special	200
—	1987	BEAUTY AND DREAM (Japan)	75
1290	1980	BEAUTY SECRETS	55
11079	1993	BEDTIME white-soft body	15
11184	1993	BEDTIME black-soft body	15
9404	1991	BENETTON	35
—	1992	BENETTON (Europe)	50
4873	1991	BENETTON SHOPPING	25
20017	1998	BEYOND PINK	15
11689	1994	BICYCLIN' (white)	30
11817	1994	BICYCLIN' (black)	25
15998	1997	BIRTHDAY (white)	20
15999	1997	BIRTHDAY (black)	20
16000	1997	BIRTHDAY (Hispanic)	20
18224	1998	BIRTHDAY Blonde	20
18292	1998	BIRTHDAY Brunette	20
11333	1994	BIRTHDAY BARBIE (white)	25
11334	1994	BIRTHDAY BARBIE (black)	25
12954	1995	BIRTHDAY BARBIE (white)	20
12955	1995	BIRTHDAY BARBIE (black)	20
13253	1995	BIRTHDAY BARBIE (Hispanic)	20
3388	1993	BIRTHDAY PARTY (white)	30
7948	1993	BIRTHDAY PARTY (black)	25

REGULAR & FOREIGN ISSUE CONTINUED

STOCK NO.	YEAR OF ORIGIN	DESCRIPTION	NRFB
3679	1992	BIRTHDAY SURPRISE (white)	35
4051	1992	BIRTHDAY SURPRISE (black)	35
1293	1980	BLACK	80
17032	1997	BLOSSOM BEAUTY (white)	15
17033	1997	BLOSSOM BEAUTY (black)	15
—	1977	BRIDE BARBIE (Australia)	75
4799	1983	BRIDE BARBIE (Europe)	115
—	1987	BRILLANTES SECRETOS (Mexico)	50
12443	1995	BUBBLE ANGEL (white)	15
12444	1995	BUBBLE ANGEL (black)	15
12443	1996	BUBBLE FAIRY (Canada)	15
22087	1998	BUBBLE FAIRY	15
16131	1997	BUBBLING MERMAID (white)	10
16132	1997	BUBBLING MERMAID (black)	10
—	1987	BUNNY (Korea)	90
3311	1972	BUSY BARBIE w/holdin' hands	190
20359	1998	BUTTERFLY ART	10
13051	1995	BUTTERFLY PRINCESS (white)	20
13052	1995	BUTTERFLY PRINCESS (black)	20
3157	1993	CABOODLES	17
—	1988	CALIFORNIA (Italy)	—
4439	1988	CALIFORNIA	25
4439	1988	CALIFORNIA DREAM	25
11074	1994	CAMP (white)	25
11831	1994	CAMP (black)	25
5733	1992	CAPRI (Europe)	40
18218	1999	CHIC (Europe & Kaybee)	5
—	1980	CICLISTA (Mexico)	150
—	1988	CINDERELLA (Korea)	150
—	1983	CITY (Germany)	30
20122	1998	COOL BLUE	12
17487	1997	COOL SHOPPIN' (white)	15
17488	1997	COOL SHOPPIN' (black)	15
3022	1989	COOL TIMES	30
—	1984	CORAZON (Spain)	50
7123	1991	COSTUME BALL (white)	20
22904	1999	CELEBRATION CAKE (white) Brunette	20
22903	1999	CELEBRATION CAKE (black)	20
22902	2000	CELEBRATION CAKE (white) Blonde	20
24658	1999	CORDUROY COOL (white)	10
24659	1999	CORDUROY COOL Brunette	10
26107	1999	CORDUROY COOL (black)	16
26425	2000	COOL CLIPS (white)	15
25887	2000	COOL SKATING	20
7134	1991	COSTUME BALL (black)	20
4598	1984	CRYSTAL (white)	25
4859	1984	CRYSTAL (black)	25

273

STOCK NO.	YEAR OF ORIGIN	DESCRIPTION	NRFB
22069	1999	CRYSTAL GLITTER Blonde	15
22071	1999	CRYSTAL GLITTER Brunette	15
22070	1999	CRYSTAL GLITTER (black)	15
22072	1999	CRYSTAL GLITTER Redhead	15
—	1990	CRYSTAL PARTY (Japan)	95
12639	1995	CUT AND STYLE Blonde	20
12642	1995	CUT AND STYLE (black)	20
12643	1995	CUT AND STYLE Brunette	20
12644	1995	CUT AND STYLE Redhead	25
3509	1989	DANCE CLUB	35
4836	1990	DANCE MAGIC (white)	30
7080	1990	DANCE MAGIC (black)	30
13083	1995	DANCE MOVES (white)	15
13083	1995	DANCE MOVES (Europe)	20
13086	1995	DANCE MOVES (black)	15
11902	1994	DANCE 'N TWIRL (white)	40
12143	1994	DANCE 'N TWIRL (black)	40
7945	1985	DAY-TO-DAY (black)	40
7929	1985	DAY-TO-NIGHT (white)	45
7944	1985	DAY-TO-NIGHT (Hispanic)	50
20309	1987	DE MODA (Venezuela)	55
17255	1997	DENTIST Blonde	15
17707	1997	DENTIST Brunette	15
17478	1997	DENTIST (black)	15
3207	1981	DISCO (Europe)	30
3850	1988	DOCTOR	50
11160	· 1996	DOCTOR BARBIE	20
—	—	DOCTOR BARBIE (India)	38
25812	2000	DOROTHY	Retail
—	1988	DR. (Europe)	40
11814	1994	DR. BARBIE one baby	30
11160	1994	DR. BARBIE one baby	30 ·
14309	1995	DR. BARBIE white w/3 of 4 babies	20
—	1995	DR. BARBIE (Europe)	40
5466	1991	DREAM BRIDE (Europe)	132
1623	1992	DREAM BRIDE	55
3207	1992	DREAM BRIDE (France)	150
—	1994	DREAM BRIDE 2 versions (Philippines & Japan)	105
5868	1983	DREAM DATE	35
1647	1986	DREAM GLOW (Hispanic)	45
2242	1986	DREAM GLOW (black)	30
2248	1986	DREAM GLOW (white)	30
—	1986	DREAM GLOW - SUE NO DE ESTRELAS (Venezuela)	35
9180	1986	DREAM TIME 2 versions	25
10776	1994	DRESS 'N FUN (white)	10
11102	1994	DRESS 'N FUN (Hispanic)	10
12143	1994	DRESS 'N FUN (black)	10

STOCK NO.	YEAR OF ORIGIN	DESCRIPTION	NRFB
—	1985	DULCES SUEñOS (Spain)	65
2374	1993	EARRING MAGIC (black)	25
7014	1993	EARRING MAGIC Blonde	25
10255	1993	EARRING MAGIC Brunette	25
52-0509	1989	ES MERALDA (Venezuela)	125
18198	1997	EQUESTRIAN Blonde (Europe)	45
18198	1997	EQUESTRIAN dark hair (Europe)	45
9900	1977	EQUESTRIENNE (Europe)	165
—	1977	EQUESTRIENNE (Italy)	130
9900	1979	EQUESTRIENNE Superstar Face (Europe)	130
7093	1984	FABULOUS FUR Festival (Europe & Canada)	65
62692	1996	FASHION AVENUE Mackie Face (Japan)	40
5313	1982	FASHION JEANS (black)	40
5315	1982	FASHION JEANS (white)	30
2210	1978	FASHION PHOTO 2 versions	65
7193	1983	FASHION PLAY pink/white jumpsuit	25
—	1984	FASHION PLAY blue dress w/one sleeve (Europe & Canada)	25
—	1984	FASHION PLAY red dress (Europe & Canada)	25
—	1984	FASHION PLAY short yellow dress (Europe & Canada)	25
9429	1987	FASHION PLAY	30
4854	1987	FASHION PLAY white w/multi (Canada)	20
—	1987	FASHION PLAY (Europe & Canada)	15
—	1988	FASHION PLAY (Canada)	25
7231	1989	FASHION PLAY (England)	12
5766	1990	FASHION PLAY rose & pink dress	25
2713	1991	FASHION PLAY turquoise dress	23
5953	1991	FASHION PLAY (black)	15
5954	1991	FASHION PLAY (Hispanic)	15
9629	1991	FASHION PLAY (white)	15
—	1991	FASHION PLAY (Europe)	20
2730	1992	FASHION PLAY (white)	15
3842	1992	FASHION PLAY (black)	15
3860	1992	FASHION PLAY (Hispanic)	15
1380	1989	FASHION PLAY MODE (Canada)	20
2712	1989	FASHION PLAY MODE (Canada)	20
—	1999	FASHIONABLE BARBIE (Japan)	—
27788	2000	FASHION WARDROBE (white)	Retail
27789	2000	FASHION WARDROBE (black)	Retail
1189	1988	FEELIN' FUN (white) 1st issue	25
4808	1988	FEELIN' FUN (white) 2nd issue	20
4809	1989	FEELIN' FUN (black)	20
7373	1989	FEELIN' FUN (Hispanic)	20
—	1989	FELIZ ANNIVERSARY 3 versions (Brazil)	95
—	1981	FELIZ CUMPLEAÑOS (Spain)	55
—	1995	FLIGHT TIME (Europe)	58
—	1995	FLIGHT TIME (India)	60
18980	1998	FLIP 'N DIVE	15

REGULAR & FOREIGN ISSUE CONTINUED

STOCK NO.	YEAR OF ORIGIN	DESCRIPTION	NRFB
20535	1998	FLORIDA VACATION	10
—	1996	FLOWER DATE (Japan)	35
16063	1997	FLOWER FUN Blonde	6
16064	1997	FLOWER FUN (black)	6
16065	1997	FLOWER FUN Brunette	6
14030	1996	FLYING HERO (white)	24
14278	1996	FLYING HERO (black)	18
14457	1996	FOAM 'N COLOR pink	15
15098	1996	FOAM 'N COLOR yellow	15
15099	1996	FOAM 'N COLOR blue	15
10393	1993	FOUNTAIN MERMAID (white)	20
10522	1993	FOUNTAIN MERMAID (black)	20
7270	1975	FREE MOVING	150
2080	1992	FREURDSCHAFTS (Europe)	50
—	1996	FRIENDSHIP (Japan)	—
—	1985	FRUEHLINGSZAUBER Springtime Magic (Germany)	120
21386	1999	FRUIT FANTASY Blonde (Europe)	38
20319	1999	FRUIT FANTASY Brunette (Europe)	42
—	1984	FUN FASHION - STAR SAINT - TROP (Europe & Canada)	25
4558	1988	FUN TO DRESS pink bra/panties (white)	15
4558	1988	FUN TO DRESS bra/panties (Germany)	30
7668	1988	FUN TO DRESS pink bra/panties (black)	15
1372	1989	FUN TO DRESS pink teddy (white)	15
1373	1989	FUN TO DRESS pink teddy (black)	15
4808	1990	FUN TO DRESS pink camisole/panties (white)	15
4939	1990	FUN TO DRESS pink camisole/panties (black)	15
7373	1990	FUN TO DRESS pink camisole/panties (Hispanic)	15
4809	1992	FUN TO DRESS (Hispanic)	15
2570	1993	FUN TO DRESS blue terrycloth wrap (black)	15
2763	1993	FUN TO DRESS blue terrycloth wrap (Hispanic)	15
3240	1993	FUN TO DRESS blue terrycloth wrap (white)	15
—	1975	FUNTIME (Europe)	—
1739	1986	FUNTIME pink outfit (black)	28
1738	1987	FUNTIME lavender watch, blue outfit	25
3717	1987	FUNTIME blue watch	25
3718	1987	FUNTIME pink watch, pink outfit	30
—	1996	GARDALAND-BUONO SCONTO LIRE (Italy) LE 4000	45
1953	1989	GARDEN PARTY	28
19428	1999	GENERATION GIRL	15
25766	2000	GENERATION GIRL	15
1922	1986	GIFT GIVING	40
—	1986	GIFT GIVING - GEBURTSTAGS	35
1205	1989	GIFT GIVING	30
26251	2000	GLAM N GROOM	Retail
—	1989	GLAMOUR (Brazil)	125
25813	2000	GLINDA	Retail
3602	1993	GLITTER BEACH	10

STOCK NO.	YEAR OF ORIGIN	DESCRIPTION	NRFB
10965	1994	GLITTER HAIR Blonde	15
10966	1994	GLITTER HAIR Brunette	15
10968	1994	GLITTER HAIR Redhead (3 versions)	15
11332	1994	GLITTER HAIR black (2 versions)	15
7344	1990	GOLD COAST (Australia)	25
—	1976	GOLD MEDAL OLYMPIC (Australia)	50
7262	1975	GOLD MEDAL SKATER	85
7264	1975	GOLD MEDAL SKIER	85
7233	1975	GOLD MEDAL SWIMMER 2 box versions	85
1874	1981	GOLDEN DREAM 2 versions	50
—	1981	GOLDEN DREAM special	95
—	1981	GOLDEN DREAM straight arms	50
—	1981	GOLDEN DREAM w/coat	90
—	1990	GOLDSMITH INC. 6 foot	525
—	1983	GRAN GALA (Spain)	65
7025	1984	GREAT SHAPE (white) 1st version	25
7834	1984	GREAT SHAPE (black)	30
—	1984	GREAT SHAPE green outfit (England)	40
—	1986	GREAT SHAPE (white) 2nd version w/walkman	30
12126	1994	GYMNAST (white)	15
12153	1994	GYMNAST (black)	15
4043	1974	HAIR FAIR SET re-issue w/centered eyes	130
22882	1999	HAPPENIN' HAIR	15
1922	1981	HAPPY BIRTHDAY 1st version	50
1922	1984	HAPPY BIRTHDAY 2nd version	35
—	1989	HAPPY BIRTHDAY (Europe)	50
9561	1990	HAPPY BIRTHDAY (black)	35
7913	1991	HAPPY BIRTHDAY (black)	35
7914	1991	HAPPY BIRTHDAY (white)	35
14649	1996	HAPPY BIRTHDAY (white)	20
14662	1996	HAPPY BIRTHDAY (black)	20
14663	1996	HAPPY BIRTHDAY (Hispanic)	20
22902	1999	HAPPY BIRTHDAY (white)	20
22903	1999	HAPPY BIRTHDAY (black)	20
22904	1999	HAPPY BIRTHDAY Brunette	20
—	1990	HAPPY BRIDAL (Japan)	95
19661	1999	HAPPY WEDDING (Japan)	-
60472/ 73/74	1992	HAUTE COURTURE 4 versions (Taiwan & Japan)	100
—	1987	HAWAII (Argentina)	25
24614	2000	HAWAII	6
7470	1975	HAWAIIAN Department Store Special	45
7470	1982	HAWAIIAN 1 piece swimsuit	45
7470	1983	HAWAIIAN 2 piece swimsuit	35
5940	1991	HAWAIIAN FUN	15
2289	1978	HAWAIIAN SUPERSTAR (Canada & Europe)	160
1292	1980	HISPANIC RIO SENJORITA (Europe)	65

STOCK NO.	YEAR OF ORIGIN	DESCRIPTION	NRFB
2308	1993	HOLLYWOOD HAIR	25
24557	1999	HOLLYWOOD NAILS (black)	Retail
—	1999	HOLLYWOOD NAILS (white)	Retail
2249	1990	HOME PRETTY	25
1757	1983	HORSE LOVIN'	30
1757	1983	HORSE LOVIN' (Europe)	70
14879	1996	HORSE LOVIN'	22
15648	1997	HORSE LOVIN', SE	10
19268	1998	HORSE RIDIN' (white)	10
19269	1998	HORSE RIDIN' (black)	10
12456	1995	HORSE RIDING (Canada & Europe)	55
—	1987	HOSTESS (Canada)	20
13511	1995	HOT SKATIN' (white)	15
13512	1995	HOT SKATIN' (black)	15
17047	1997	HULA HAIR (white)	10
17048	1997	HULA HAIR (black)	10
20668	1999	I LOVE BARBIE	5
21156	1999	I LOVE BARBIE (Japan)	12
4218	1992	IBIZ (Europe)	30
7348	1990	ICE CAPADES (black) 50th Anniversary	35
7365	1990	ICE CAPADES (white) 50th Anniversary	40
9847	1991	ICE CAPADES (white)	35
15473	1996	IN LINE SKATING *JCPenney, FAO Schwarz* (Europe & Canada)	30
4061	1988	ISLAND FUN	15
—	1980	JAJIWADA ENS includes candle (Greek)	100
3901	1980	JEANS (Europe & Canada)	30
1189	1992	JEANS (Europe)	30
11185	1994	JEWEL & GLITTER (Canada & Mexico)	25
28066	2000	JEWEL GIRL	Retail
14586	1996	JEWEL HAIR MERMAID (white)	16
14587	1996	JEWEL HAIR MERMAID (black)	16
1737 4552/	1987	JEWEL SECRETS (white) 2 box versions	25
1756	1987	JEWEL SECRETS (black) 2 box versions	20
3986	1982	JOGGING (Europe & Canada)	30
—	1995	JOSE CARRERAS DOCTORA (Spain)	50
3197	1974	KELLOGG QUICK CURL	65
18975	1999	KISEKAE (Japan & Singapore)	Retail
2597	1979	KISSING 2 hair versions	40
—	1979	KISSING (Europe)	50
—	1985	LADY (Spain)	55
9725	1991	LIGHTS 'N LACE (white)	35
1116	1970	LIVING BARBIE	175
2249	1992	LIVING PRETTY (Canada)	40
—	1989	LLANERA (Venezuela)	95
10963	1994	LOCKET SURPRISE (white)	18
11224	1994	LOCKET SURPRISE (black)	18

STOCK NO.	YEAR OF ORIGIN	DESCRIPTION	NRFB
3075	1987	LOISIRS 3 versions (Canada & Europe)	20
7072	1984	LOVING YOU	62
—	1988	MA PREMIERE - MINICLUB (France)	—
3856	1982	MAGIC CURL (white)	50
3989	1982	MAGIC CURL (black)	45
11570	1994	MAGIC HAIR MERMAID (Europe)	50
2126	1986	MAGIC MOVES (white)	65
2127	1986	MAGIC MOVES (black)	35
1067	1976	MALIBU	—
—	1986	MARE (Italy)	55
—	1990	MELODY DREAM (Japan)	125
1434	1992	MERMAID 2 versions	19
61747	1996	MISS BARBIE Woolworth's, Coles Australia	35
—	—	MODA FESTA (Brazil)	—
—	1984	MODE FANTAISIE black dress (France)	40
—	1984	MODE FANTAISIE gold dress (France)	40
—	1984	MODE FANTAISIE tan/white pinstripe dress (France)	40
5766	—	MODE PASS (Canada)	50
25466	1999	MOVIE STAR	20
17714	1997	MOVIN' GROOVIN'	12
9988	1986	MUSIC LOVIN' (Europe & Canada)	42
—	1993	MY BEST FRIEND (India)	30
1875	1981	MY FIRST yellow & blue outfit, 2 versions	30
—	1981	MY FIRST yellow & blue outfit (Germany)	35
—	1981	MY FIRST yellow w/red halter dress (England)	50
—	1981	MY FIRST blue print dress w/white collar (England)	50
—	1981	MY FIRST (Europe)	50
1875	1983	MY FIRST (white) pink check outfit	40
1875	1984	MY FIRST (white) pinafore w/pink bow	35
9858	1984	MY FIRST (black) white pinafore w/pink bow	35
1801	1987	MY FIRST (black) knee length ballerina pink	20
5979	1987	MY FIRST (Hispanic) knee length ballerina pink	25
1788	1987	MY FIRST (white) knee length ballerina pink	20
1281	1988	MY FIRST (black) white gown	20
1282	1988	MY FIRST (Hispanic) white gown	20
1280	1988	MY FIRST (white) white gown	20
9942	1990	MY FIRST (white)	20
9943	1990	MY FIRST (black)	20
9944	1990	MY FIRST (Hispanic)	20
3861	1992	MY FIRST (black) light blue dress	20
3864	1992	MY FIRST (Hispanic) light blue dress	20
3839	1992	MY FIRST (white) light blue dress	20
2767	1993	MY FIRST (black) blue ribbon on box	18
2770	1993	MY FIRST (Hispanic) blue ribbon on box	18
2516	1993	MY FIRST (white) blue ribbon on box	18
11342	1994	MY FIRST (Asian) pale pink dress	17
11340	1994	MY FIRST (black) pale pink dress	15

REGULAR & FOREIGN ISSUE CONTINUED

STOCK NO.	YEAR OF ORIGIN	DESCRIPTION	NRFB
11341	1994	MY FIRST (Hispanic) pale pink dress	15
11294	1994	MY FIRST (white) pale pink dress	15
16005	1997	MY FIRST JEWELRY FUN Blonde	10
16006	1997	MY FIRST JEWELRY FUN (black)	10
16007	1997	MY FIRST JEWELRY FUN (Hispanic)	10
16008	1997	MY FIRST JEWELRY FUN (Asian)	10
13064	1995	MY FIRST PRINCESS (white) blue dress	15
13065	1995	MY FIRST PRINCESS (black) blue dress	15
13066	1995	MY FIRST PRINCESS (Hispanic) blue dress	15
13067	1995	MY FIRST PRINCESS (Asian) blue dress	15
14592	1997	MY FIRST TEA PARTY (white) without tea set	10
14593	1997	MY FIRST TEA PARTY (black) without tea set	10
14875	1997	MY FIRST TEA PARTY (Hispanic)	10
14876	1997	MY FIRST TEA PARTY (Asian)	10
2517	1993	MY SIZE (white)	110
11212	1993	MY SIZE (black)	115
15649	1996	MY SIZE* Redhead QVC	140
20493	1998	MY SIZE ANGEL (white)	100
20494	1998	MY SIZE ANGEL (black)	100
12052	1994	MY SIZE BRIDE (white)	95
12053	1994	MY SIZE BRIDE (black)	95
25863	2000	MY SIZE BUTTERFLY (white)	135
25864	2000	MY SIZE BUTTERFLY (black)	135
15909	1996	MY SIZE DANCING (white)	100
15910	1996	MY SIZE DANCING (black)	100
13767	1995	MY SIZE PRINCESS Blonde	90
13768	1995	MY SIZE PRINCESS (black)	90
17801	1997	MY SIZE RAPUNZEL (white)	100
17802	1997	MY SIZE RAPUNZEL (black)	100
10997	1993	NAF NAF (Europe)	45
—	1988	NEW WAVE (Brazil)	125
7807	1973	NEWPORT THE SPORT'S SET	165
15428	1996	OCEAN FRIENDS (white)	25
15429	1996	OCEAN FRIENDS (black)	25
15123	1996	OLYMPIC GYMNAST Blonde, 2 earring versions	20
15124	1996	OLYMPIC GYMNAST (black) 2 earring versions	20
18501	1997	OLYMPIC SKATER (white)	10
18503	1997	OLYMPIC SKATER (black)	10
7378	1976	OLYMPICA (Italy)	140
—	1996	OTOMODACHI (Mattel Japan Barbie)	35
10039	1993	PAINT 'N DAZZLE Blonde	15
10057	1993	PAINT 'N DAZZLE Redhead, 2 versions	15
10058	1993	PAINT 'N DAZZLE (black)	15
10059	1993	PAINT 'N DAZZLE Brunette	15
2545	1993	PARTY CHANGES (Europe)	45
—	1987	PARTY CRUISE (Canada)	20
—	1986	PARTY PINK (Mexico)	35

italic indicates cross reference

STOCK NO.	YEAR OF ORIGIN	DESCRIPTION	NRFB
4629	1988	PARTY PINK (Europe)	30
9925	1977	PARTYTIME 3 versions (Europe & Canada)	135
—	1978	PARTYTIME 3 versions (Europe)	75
4798	1983	PARTYTIME	25
—	1983	PARTYTIME (Europe & Canada)	25
—	1989	PASSEIO 2 versions (Brazil)	150
7926	1985	PEACHES 'N CREAM (white)	40
9516	1985	PEACHES 'N CREAM (black)	35
18576	1997	PEARL BEACH	10
4551	1988	PERFUME PRETTY (white)	35
4552	1988	PERFUME PRETTY 2 versions (black)	45
14603	1996	PET DR. (white)	20
15302	1996	PET DR. (black)	20
23007	1999	PET LOVIN' Blonde	15
23008	1999	PET LOVIN' (black)	15
2290	1978	PICTURE PRETTY (Europe)	110
3554	1982	PINK & PRETTY	40
3554	1982	PINK & PRETTY (England)	90
5239	1982	PINK & PRETTY (special)	80
—	2000	PILOT 2 hair versions	15
—	1981	PLAYTIME (Germany)	25
5336	1984	PLAYTIME	20
—	1987	POOL SIDE (Canada)	20
1067	1978	PORTOFINO (Europe)	80
2598	1979	PRETTY CHANGES 1st version w/perfume (Japan)	95
2598	1979	PRETTY CHANGES 2nd version w/out perfume	75
13611	1995	PRETTY DREAM (white) 18 inch soft body	25
13630	1995	PRETTY DREAM (black) 18 inch soft body	22
2901	1992	PRETTY HEARTS	20
14473	1996	PRETTY HEARTS (white)	10
14474	1996	PRETTY HEARTS (black)	10
14475	1996	PRETTY HEARTS (Hispanic)	10
14473	1997	PRETTY HEARTS (foreign)	10
24652	2000	PRETTY FLOWERS (white)	6
24653	2000	PRETTY FLOWERS (black)	6
24654	2000	PRETTY FLOWERS Brunette	6
24655	2000	PRETTY FLOWERS Redhead	6
20666	1998	PRETTY IN PLAID Blonde	5
20667	1998	PRETTY IN PLAID Redhead	5
20668	1998	PRETTY IN PLAID Brunette	5
21570	1998	PRETTY IN PLAID (black)	5
—	1984	PRETTY PARTY (England)	38
9823	1992	PRETTY SURPRISE	20
18407	1998	PRINCESS (Asian)	12
22894	1999	PRINCESS (Asian)	15
23477	2000	PRINCESS (Asian)	15
18405	1998	PRINCESS (black)	12

STOCK NO.	YEAR OF ORIGIN	DESCRIPTION	NRFB
18406	1998	PRINCESS (Hispanic)	12
18404	1998	PRINCESS (white)	12
22891	1999	PRINCESS (white)	15
23474	2000	PRINCESS (white)	15
22892	1999	PRINCESS (black)	15
23475	2000	PRINCESS (black)	15
22893	1999	PRINCESS Brunette	15
23476	2000	PRINCESS Brunette	15
28521	2000	PRINCESS BRIDE (white)	Retail
28552	2000	PRINCESS BRIDE (black)	Retail
9217	1976	QUICK CURL DELUXE Jergens	105
—	1976	QUICK CURL DELUXE (Europe)	110
—	1996	RAJASTHANI BRIDE, 6 sided box (India)	69
3248	1992	RAPPIN' ROCKIN'	40
17646	1997	RAPUNZEL (white)	15
18164	1997	RAPUNZEL (black)	15
—	1999	RAPUNZEL (2nd version) pink crown white or black	Retail
23474	1999	RAINBOW PRINCESS (white)	11
26357	2000	RAINBOW PRINCESS (white)	Retail
23475	1999	RAINBOW PRINCESS (black)	11
26358	2000	RAINBOW PRINCESS (black)	Retail
23476	1999	RAINBOW PRINCESS (brunette)	11
—	1999	RIVERIA - International	10
—	1986	REGALOS (Spain)	55
—	1984	RITMIC (Spain)	45
7344	1990	RIVIERA (Europe)	25
—	1982	RIZOS (Spain)	55
—	1986	ROCK STAR (Europe)	45
1140	1986	ROCKER	45
3055	1987	ROCKER 2nd Edition	50
—	1987	ROCKER BARBIE (Venezuela - Rotoplast)	95
1880	1980	ROLLER SKATING	60
2214	1992	ROLLERBLADE	35
1861	1993	ROMANTIC BRIDE (white)	35
11054	1993	ROMANTIC BRIDE (black)	35
—	1996	ROOPVATI RAJASTHANI S.E. (India)	—
—	1987	ROQUEIROS (Brazil)	150
12345	1991	ROVER BARBIE (Mars Special Edition)	62
12433	1995	RUFFLE FUN (white) 2 versions	15
12434	1995	RUFFLE FUN (black) 2 versions	15
12435	1995	RUFFLE FUN (Hispanic) 2 versions	15
—	1981	SAFARI (Denmark & Australia)	40
5471	1993	SEA HOLIDAY (*Toys R Us* & Europe)	30
9109	1984	SEA LOVIN' (Europe)	35
—	1985	SEA LOVIN' (Europe & Canada)	40
3836	1993	SECRET HEARTS (black)	25
7902	1993	SECRET HEARTS (white)	30

STOCK NO.	YEAR OF ORIGIN	DESCRIPTION	NRFB
26422	2000	SECRET MESSAGES	Retail
4931	1988	SENSATIONS	60
14457	1996	SHAMPOO MAGIC pink	15
15098	1996	SHAMPOO MAGIC yellow	15
23421	2000	SIT IN STYLE	12
4547	1988	SKATING STAR 1988 Winter Olympics (Sears & Canada)	75
7511	1991	SKI FUN	25
20489	1999	SLEEPING BEAUTY (white)	19
20490	1999	SLEEPING BEAUTY (black)	19
12696	1995	SLUMBER PARTY soft body (white)	20
12697	1995	SLUMBER PARTY soft body (black)	20
3550	1992	SNAP 'N PLAY (white)	20
3556	1992	SNAP 'N PLAY (black)	20
—	1980	SNOW PRINCESS (Sweden & Finland)	—
20151	1999	SOCCER	12
14320	1996	SONGBIRD (white) 2 versions	17
14486	1996	SONGBIRD (black)	17
—	1996	SONGBIRD (Japan)	65
—	1991	SONHO DE FERIAS (Brazil)	50
—	1988	SONHO DE PERFUME (Brazil)	95
13132	1996	SPARKLE BEACH 2 hair versions	10
2482	1992	SPARKLE EYES (white)	28
5950	1992	SPARKLE EYES (black)	28
—	1978	SPIEL MIT (Europe)	65
16169	1997	SPLASH 'N COLOR	6
—	1986	SPORT MUSIC (Mexico)	45
9949	1977	SPORTING (Europe)	155
—	1980	SPORTS STAR (Germany & Canada)	30
—	1991	SPRING BRIDE (Europe)	65
—	1982	SPRINGTIME MAGIC (Europe)	45
2096	1989	ST. TROPEZ	45
—	1990	STAR PRINCESS (Japan)	95
1112	1984	STAR SAINT TROP' (Europe & Canada)	25
—	1984	STAR SUPER DANSE 2 (France)	45
19224	1998	STICKER CRAZE Blonde	10
19914	1998	STICKER CRAZE Brunette	10
19913	1998	STICKER CRAZE (black)	10
18219	1998	STYLE (Canada)	8
12291	1995	STYLE (Europe & Canada)	25
20766	1999	STYLE (Europe & Kaybee)	8
20767	1999	STYLE (Europe & Kaybee)	8
1283	1989	STYLE MAGIC	35
—	1991	SUMMER BRIDE (Europe)	65
4218	1993	SUN COAST (Australia)	40
1067	1984	SUN GOLD MALIBU (white)	25
4970	1985	SUN GOLD MALIBU (Hispanic)	25
7745	1985	SUN GOLD MALIBU (black)	18

STOCK NO.	YEAR OF ORIGIN	DESCRIPTION	NRFB
10953	1994	SUN JEWEL	12
1067	1979	SUN LOVIN' MALIBU	45
1390	1992	SUN SENSATION 2 versions	25
1067	1975	SUNSET MALIBU white box	—
7806	1973	SUN VALLEY - THE SPORT'S SET	85
1067	1982	SUNSATIONAL (white)	27
4970	1982	SUNSATIONAL MALIBU (Hispanic)	40
5838	1983	SUPER DANCE	38
—	1983	SUPER DANCE 2 versions (Europe & Canada)	25
—	1983	SUPER DANCE (Spain)	40
7025	1984	SUPER DANCE (Europe)	30
9805	1976	SUPER FASHION FIREWORKS 3 variations	125
15821	1996	SUPER GYMNAST pink/turquoise (Europe, Canada, Kaybee)	20
23105	1999	SUPER GYMNAST (white)	15
23106	1999	SUPER GYMNAST (black)	15
3101	1987	SUPER HAIR (white)	25
3296	1987	SUPER HAIR (black)	19
9828	1977	SUPER SIZE 18 inch	230
9975	1977	SUPER SIZE BRIDE 18 inch	275
2844	1979	SUPER SIZE W/SUPER HAIR 18 inch	250
9720	1977	SUPERSTAR w/comb	60
9720	1977	SUPERSTAR w/necklace	60
—	1977	SUPERSTAR (Germany)	80
2207	1978	SUPERSTAR In the Spotlight	71
A2001	1978	SUPERSTAR Sutekina - folk roman (Japan)	97
A2405	1978	SUPERSTAR Sutekina - leather look (Japan)	98
A2201	1978	SUPERSTAR Sutekina - light blue ruffled dress/hat (Japan)	93
A2403	1978	SUPERSTAR Sutekina - long white dress w/lace show, Evening white (Japan)	91
A2401	1978	SUPERSTAR Sutekina - long yellow dress w/flower & leaf print, Evening yellow (Japan)	92
A2402	1978	SUPERSTAR Sutekina - metallic green, purple & rose long dress w/boa, Color Cocktail (Japan)	90
A1801	1978	SUPERSTAR Sutekina - pink dress (Japan)	90
A2404	1978	SUPERSTAR Sutekina - pink roses (Japan)	90
A2601	1978	SUPERSTAR Sutekina - wedding (Japan)	100
9720	1978	SUPERSTAR Promotional	90
—	1978	SUPERSTAR (Spain)	100
A2407	1979	SUPERSTAR Ballerina Confello Fairy (Japan)	80
A1502	1979	SUPERSTAR Casual (Japan)	80
A1601	1979	SUPERSTAR light pink dress w/ribbon belt - yellow flower (Japan)	80
A1501	1979	SUPERSTAR one piece pink (Japan)	80
A1601	1979	SUPERSTAR one piece yellow (Japan)	80
A1802	1979	SUPERSTAR Wild Flower (Japan)	80
2762	1987	SUPERSTAR Glamorous U.S.	45
7965	1987	SUPERSTAR Glamorous U.S.	45
9258	1987	SUPERSTAR Glamorous U.S.	45
9259	1987	SUPERSTAR Glamorous U.S.	45

STOCK NO.	YEAR OF ORIGIN	DESCRIPTION	NRFB
9261	1987	SUPERSTAR Glamorous U.S.	45
1604	1989	SUPERSTAR (white)	45
1605	1989	SUPERSTAR (black)	30
12379	1994	SUPER TALK (black)	35
12290	1994	SUPER TALK (white)	35
—	1994	SUPER TALK Dutch (Europe)	75
12372	1994	SUPER TALK French (Europe)	75
—	1994	SUPER TALK German (Europe)	75
—	1994	SUPER TALK Italian (Europe)	75
—	1991	SWEET DREAMS (Europe)	55
13611	1995	SWEET DREAMS (white)	20
13630	1995	SWEET DREAMS (black)	20
7796	1974	SWEET SIXTEEN	75
—	1974	SWEET SIXTEEN (Germany)	100
20780	1998	SWEET TREATS (white)	10
20955	1998	SWEET TREATS (black)	10
18608	1998	SWEETHEART Blonde	5
18609	1998	SWEETHEART (black)	5
18610	1998	SWEETHEART Brunette	5
18700	1998	SWEETHEART Redhead	5
11505	1994	SWIM 'N DIVE (white)	25
11734	1994	SWIM 'N DIVE (black)	25
24590	2000	SWIMMING CHAMPION (white)	14
25644	2000	SYDNEY 2000 (white)	37
26302	2000	SYDNEY 2000 (black)	37
—	1987	SYNCHRO TEMPO LIBERO Funtime (France)	45
2093	1993	TAHITI (Europe)	24
17350	1997	TALK WITH ME* (white) includes software	30
17370	1997	TALK WITH ME* (black) includes software	30
9912	1991	TEACHER (India)	85
13195	1995	TEACHER (black) no panties	55
13914	1995	TEACHER (white) no panties	55
13914	1996	TEACHER (white) painted panties	25
13915	1996	TEACHER (black) painted panties	25
16210	1996	TEACHER (Hispanic) painted panties	25
18975	1998	TEDDY BEAR (Japan)	—
1612	1992	TEEN TALK (black) 2 hair versions	30
—	1992	TEEN TALK Blonde (England)	55
4709	1992	TEEN TALK Blonde (France)	55
—	1992	TEEN TALK Blonde (Germany)	55
—	1992	TEEN TALK Blonde (Italy)	55
—	1992	TEEN TALK Blonde (Netherlands)	55
—	1992	TEEN TALK Blonde (Spain)	55
5745	1992	TEEN TALK Blonde, Brunette, Redhead (2 box versions)	30
5745	1992	TEEN TALK - "MATH CLASS IS TOUGH"	70
1760	1987	TENNIS (Europe & Canada)	19
20504	1998	TIE DYE	10

STOCK NO.	YEAR OF ORIGIN	DESCRIPTION	NRFB
1112	1992	TOTALLY HAIR Blonde	25
1117	1992	TOTALLY HAIR Brunette	30
5948	1992	TOTALLY HAIR (black)	25
—	1991	TRENDY STYLE (Europe)	40
—	1982	TRINIDAD (Italy)	—
10257	1993	TROLL	20
1022	1986	TROPICAL (black)	20
1646	1986	TROPICAL (Hispanic)	25
1017	1986	TROPICAL (white)	20
—	1986	TROPICAL (Europe)	20
—	1986	TROPICAL (Spain)	30
—	1986	TROPICAL (Venezuela)	25
12446	1995	TROPICAL SPLASH 2 versions	8
—	1987	TUDO QUE VOCE QUER SER (Brazil)	150
10390	1993	TWINKLE LIGHTS (white)	45
10521	1993	TWINKLE LIGHTS (black)	40
15086	1996	TWIRLING BALLERINA (white)	20
15087	1996	TWIRLING BALLERINA (black)	20
18421	1998	TWIRLING MAKEUP Blonde	8
5723	1983	TWIRLY CURLS (black)	40
5724	1983	TWIRLY CURLS (Hispanic)	40
5579	1983	TWIRLY CURLS (white)	45
—	1987	UPTOWN (Canada)	20
20528	1998	VERY VELVET	15
22249	1999	VERY VELVET Brunette (Taiwan) Mackie face	30
3677	1992	VRIEND SCHAP (Europe)	50
9608	1991	WEDDING DAY 2 box versions	35
2125	1989	WEDDING FANTASY (Venezuela)	100
2125	1990	WEDDING FANTASY (white)	50
7011	1990	WEDDING FANTASY (black)	45
—	1991	WEEKEND Adidas (Europe)	45
1757	1981	WESTERN 3 hair styles	55
1757	1981	WESTERN (Europe)	70
—	1983	WESTERN (Spain)	65
2930	1990	WESTERN FUN (black)	35
9932	1990	WESTERN FUN (white)	35
10293	1993	WESTERN STAMPIN' (white)	27
10539	1993	WESTERN STAMPIN' (black)	30
4103	1990	WET 'N WILD	22
—	1991	WINTERTIME BRIDE (Europe)	65
17317	1997	WORKIN' OUT	10
—	1999	WORKING WOMAN (white)	20
—	1999	WORKING WOMAN (black)	20
8352	1991	YACHT CLUB (Europe)	31
8354	1991	YACHT CLUB (Europe)	30
8357	1991	YACHT CLUB (Europe)	30
8376	1991	YACHT CLUB (Europe)	30

NEWER FAMILY DOLLS

STOCK NO.	YEAR OF ORIGIN	DESCRIPTION	NRFB

Alan (90's version only has one "L" in the name)
9607	1991	WEDDING DAY (2 box versions)	35

Alexia (Kayla)
11209	1994	ALEXIA TRESOR - LOCKET SURPRISE KAYLA (Europe)	40

Ana
20972	1999	GENERATION GIRL (3 versions)	15

Asha
1752	1991	ASHA* Toys R Us	28
5777	1992	BEACH DAZZLE* Toys R Us	12
3457	1993	BEACH STREAK* Toys R Us	12
10291	1993	SOUL TRAIN* Toys R Us	20
12676	1994	ASHA I* 1st A.A. Collection Toys R Us	22
13532	1995	ASHA II* 2nd A.A. Collection Toys R Us	20
15139	1996	ASHA III* 3rd A.A. Collection Toys R Us	20

Becky (11½ inch)
4967	1988	BIBOPS (Europe)	40
4977	1988	SENSATIONS	30
15761	1997	SHARE A SMILE* Toys R Us	20
20202	1998	I'M THE SCHOOL PHOTOGRAPHER	15
24662	1999	PARALYMPIC	20

Becky (4 inch)
14853	1993	LI'L FRIEND OF KELLY	10

Belinda
4976	1988	SENSATIONS	35

Belinda (4 inch)
24602	1999	BIKER BABY	6

Bibi
4977	1988	BIBOP'S Sensations (Europe)	55

Bobby
4960	1988	BIBOP'S (Europe)	105

Bobsy
4967	1988	SENSATIONS	35

indicates cross reference

NEWER FAMILY DOLLS CONTINUED

Blaine

STOCK NO.	YEAR OF ORIGIN	DESCRIPTION	NRFB
26111	2000	GENERATION GIRL - Blaine	20

Carla

7377	1974	CARLA green box, re-issue (Europe)	95
7377	1977	CARLA pink box, re-issue (Europe)	95

Chelsie (11½ inch)

3698	1989	HIGH SCHOOL	25
20967	1999	GENERATION GIRL	15
26848	2000	GENERATION GIRL	20

Chelsie (4 inch)

14852	1996	LI'L FRIEND OF KELLY	10
16004	1997	CHELSIE	8
17054	1997	POOL FUN	10
20854	1998	ARTIST	6
18911	1998	BUTTERFLY CATCHER	6
20856	1998	COW GIRL	6
18034	1998	WINTER COAT	6
24594	1999	BAKER	6

Chris

8130	1975	CHRIS red/white/blue dress (Europe)	250
8130	1976	CHRIS floral yellow dress (Europe)	150
8130	1977	CHRIS blue/white dress (Europe)	90

Christie

9839	1977	SUPER SIZE (18 inch)	230
2324	1978	FASHION PHOTO	63
9950	1978	SUPERSTAR	62
—	1979	KISSING (Europe)	58
1295	1979	PRETTY REFLECTIONS	72
1295	1980	BEAUTY SECRETS	55
1293	1980	EBONY (Europe)	60
2955	1980	KISSING	72
7745	1979	SUN LOVIN' MALIBU	40
3249	1981	GOLDEN DREAM	50
—	1981	GOLDEN DREAM (Europe)	45
3555	1982	PINK & PRETTY	55
7745	1982	SUNSATIONAL MALIBU (2 head molds)	30
—	1984	MILLE LUCI (Crystal - Italy)	60
7745	1984	SUNSATIONAL (New Face)	35
4443	1988	CALIFORNIA	35

indicates cross reference

NEWER FAMILY DOLLS CONTINUED

Christie (CONTINUED)

STOCK NO.	YEAR OF ORIGIN	DESCRIPTION	NRFB
4443	1988	CALIFORNIA DREAM	30
4443	1988	CLUB CALIFORNIA	30
4092	1988	ISLAND FUN	20
3253	1989	BEACH BLAST	15
3217	1989	COOL TIMES	25
1288	1989	STYLE MAGIC	30
9352	1990	ALL STARS	20
2754	1990	BARBIE AND THE BEAT (Christie)	15
4121	1990	WET 'N WILD	15
9425	1991	ALL AMERICAN	30
9407	1991	BENETTON	28
5944	1991	HAWAIIAN FUN	15
9728	1991	LIGHTS & LACE	30
4887	1992	BENETTON SHOPPING (Europe)	40
3265	1992	RAPPIN ROCKIN'	40
2217	1992	*ROLLERBLADE*	35
1393	1992	SUN SENSATION	15
4907	1993	GLITTER BEACH	15
12451	1995	TROPICAL SPLASH	10
14355	1996	SPARKLE BEACH 3 hair versions	8
17715	1997	MOVIN' GROOVIN'	12
18578	1997	PEARL BEACH	5
17372	1997	SHARE A SMILE* *Toys R Us*	20
16174	1997	SPLASH 'N COLOR	8
17319	1997	WORKIN' OUT	10
20019	1998	BEYOND PINK	15
20360	1998	BUTTERFLY ART	10
18981	1998	FLIP 'N DIVE	10
20536	1998	FLORIDA VACATION	10
19667	1998	PURPLE PANIC	10
20505	1998	TIE DYE	8
18422	1998	TWIRLING MAKEUP	8
20529	1998	VERY VELVET	10
20206	1998	WNBA*	15
22088	1999	BUBBLE FAIRY	10
22883	1999	HAPPENIN' HAIR	10
26428	1999	MOVIE STAR	20
20351	1999	SOCCER	10
26426	2000	COOL CLIPS	15
26230	2000	COOL BLADING	Retail

indicates cross reference

NEWER FAMILY DOLLS CONTINUED

Christie (CONTINUED)

STOCK NO.	YEAR OF ORIGIN	DESCRIPTION	NRFB
26230	2000	COOL SKATING	15
26252	2000	GLAM N GROOM	Retail
24615	2000	HAWAII	6
—	2000	HOLLYWOOD NAILS	Retail
26423	2000	SECRET MESSAGES	Retail
23422	2000	SIT IN STYLE	10
25488	2000	SWIMMING CHAMPION	15
26252	2000	GLAM 'N GROOM	15

Christie (10 inch)

STOCK NO.	YEAR OF ORIGIN	DESCRIPTION	NRFB
1952	1989	TEEN TIME	30
7079	1990	COOL TOPS	25
9434	1991	BABYSITTER	25
1433	1991	TOTALLY HAIR* Toys R Us	20
2710	1992	PET PALS	20
3933	1993	CHEERLEADING	20
11548	1994	COOL CRIMP	15
12943	1995	PIZZA PARTY	15
14314	1996	PHONE FUN	12

Courtney (11½ inch)

STOCK NO.	YEAR OF ORIGIN	DESCRIPTION	NRFB
17354	1997	TEEN	20
19668	1998	COOL TEEN	10
22230	1999	TOTALLY YO YO	12
24992	2000	PAJAMA FUN	10

Dana

STOCK NO.	YEAR OF ORIGIN	DESCRIPTION	NRFB
1196	1986	ROCKER	45
3158	1987	BARBIE AND THE ROCKERS (Dana)	40

Danbie

STOCK NO.	YEAR OF ORIGIN	DESCRIPTION	NRFB
—	1984	DANBIE (Korea)	250

Dee Dee

STOCK NO.	YEAR OF ORIGIN	DESCRIPTION	NRFB
—	1986	ROCK STAR (Europe)	50
1141	1986	ROCKER	45
3160	1987	BARBIE AND THE ROCKER'S (Dee Dee)	40

Deidre

STOCK NO.	YEAR OF ORIGIN	DESCRIPTION	NRFB
18655	1998	AFRICAN DRESS	6
18914	1998	BALLERINA	6

indicates cross reference

STOCK NO.	YEAR OF ORIGIN	DESCRIPTION	NRFB
Deidre (CONTINUED)			
18318	1998	COAT	6
20861	1998	COWGIRL	6
21641	1998	DRESS-UP	6
Deidre (4 inch)			
16466	1997	DEIDRE pink gingham dress	6
17323	1997	DEIDRE peach party dress	6
17323	1998	BIRTHDAY	6
16466	1998	PICNIC	6
18319	1998	SAILOR	6
24607	1999	TENNIS	6
Delphine			
26929	2000	DELPHINE - Fashion Model Collector*	Retail
Derek			
2428	1986	ROCKER	65
3137/ 3173	1987	BARBIE AND THE ROCKER'S (Derek) 2 versions	60
Devon			
3513	1989	DANCE CLUB	60
Diva			
—	1986	ROCK STAR (Europe)	50
2427	1986	ROCKER	60
3159	1987	BARBIE AND THE ROCKER'S (Diva)	55
—	1987	ROCK STAR (Brazil - Rotoplast)	95
—	—	GLAMOUR* (Estrela)	150
Dude			
3637	1989	DUDE (Jazzie)	40
Ellie			
—	1985	BARBIES FRIEND (Takara) Japan	80
Fashion Friends			
7026	1991	PARTY DRESS* K-Mart	25
7010	1991	PRETTY TEEN* K-Mart	22
7019	1991	SWIM SUIT* K-Mart	20

*indicates cross reference

291

NEWER FAMILY DOLLS CONTINUED

Flora

—	1985	BARBIES FRIEND (Takara) Japan	80

Francie

14608	1996	30th ANNIVERSARY* (Gad-About)	60
17607	1997	WILD BUNCH*	46

Ginger

—	1988	ANIMAL LOVIN'	40

Jamal

7795	1992	JAMAL* *Toys R Us*	30
3802	1993	BEACH STREAK* *Toys R Us*	15
10288	1993	SOUL TRAIN* *Toys R Us*	22

Janet

11477	1994	HAPPY MEAL	20
12984	1995	*POLLY POCKET*	15
14611	1996	GYMNAST	15
16735	1997	BICYCLIN'	15
19670	1998	FLASHLIGHT FUN (Tigger)	10
22014	1999	BOWLING PARTY	12
24991	2000	AWESOME SKATEBOARD	12

Jazzie

3635	1989	HIGH SCHOOL	30
3634	1989	TEEN DANCE	35
3631	1989	TEEN LOOKS – CHEERLEADER	25
3632	1989	TEEN LOOKS – SWIMSUIT	25
3633	1989	TEEN LOOKS – WORKOUT	25
4088	1990	SUN LOVIN'	30
9294	1991	HAWAIIAN FUN	25
5507	1991	TEEN SCENE (2 box versions)	30
5473	1992	SUN SENSATION	25
4935	1993	GLITTER BEACH	15

Jenny (4 inch)

16467	1997	JENNY (Li'l Friend)	6
18653	1998	GARDENER	6
20858	1998	HAWAIIAN	6
18913	1998	SUNFLOWER	6
24598	1999	JESTER	6

indicates cross reference

STOCK NO.	YEAR OF ORIGIN	DESCRIPTION	NRFB

Kayla

STOCK NO.	YEAR OF ORIGIN	DESCRIPTION	NRFB
3512	1989	DANCE CLUB	70
11209	1994	LOCKET SURPRISE	20
20855	1998	BACK TO SCHOOL	8
20859	1998	DRESS-UP	8
24606	2000	KWANZA	6

Keeya (4 inch)

STOCK NO.	YEAR OF ORIGIN	DESCRIPTION	NRFB
18917	1998	KWANZA	6
21642	1998	BACK TO SCHOOL	6

Kelly

STOCK NO.	YEAR OF ORIGIN	DESCRIPTION	NRFB
12489	1995	BABY SISTER (white)	12
13256	1995	BABY SISTER (black)	12
14552	1996	BATH TIME FUN (white)	10
14553	1996	BATH TIME FUN (black)	10
18582	1997	EATIN' FUN (white)	8
18596	1997	EATIN' FUN (black)	8
17052	1997	POOL FUN (white)	10
17589	1997	POOL FUN (white)	10
16066	1997	POTTY TRAINING (white)	10
16067	1997	POTTY TRAINING (black)	10
18187	1998	BALLET RECITAL BARBIE & KELLY GIFT SET* (white)	15
21388	1998	BALLET RECITAL BARBIE & KELLY GIFT SET* (black)	15
19810	1998	KELLY & GINGER GIFT SET*	25
18717	1998	KELLY & TOMMY POWER WHEELS GIFT SET* (white) pink	20
18718	1998	KELLY & TOMMY POWER WHEELS GIFT SET* (black) pink	20
19809	1998	HOLIDAY SISTERS GIFT SET* Barbie, Stacie & Kelly	25
19625	1998	LI'L PALS GIFT SET*	25
20346	1998	PONY & KELLY GIFT SET*	20
23966	1999	CUDDLY SOFT (white)	50
—	1999	CUDDLY SOFT (black)	50
20333	1999	GIGGLES AND SWING BARBIE AND KELLY GIFT SET* (white)	15
20534	1999	GIGGLES AND SWING BARBIE AND KELLY GIFT SET* (black)	15
22226	1999	TINY STEPS (white)	8
22227	1999	TINY STEPS (black)	8
24596	1999	PRINCESS (white)	6
—	1999	PRINCESS (black)	6
25599	2000	PRINCESS	6
25818	2000	MUNCHKIN - LULLABYE LEAGUE	7
24645	2000	SUPER SLIDE (white)	17
24749	2000	SUPER SLIDE (black)	17

indicates cross reference

NEWER FAMILY DOLLS CONTINUED

Ken

STOCK NO.	YEAR OF ORIGIN	DESCRIPTION	NRFB
1088	1976	MALIBU (pink box)	—
2683	1978	BEACH FUN – Strandspa	30
9927	1978	PARTYTIME (Europe & Canada)	54
1088	1978	PORTOFINO (Europe)	65
2168	1978	SPIEL MIT (Europe)	62
—	1978	SUPERSTAR (German)	50
2211	1978	SUPERSTAR w/ring (1st version)	42
2211	1978	SUPERSTAR w/out ring (2nd version)	40
—	1979	BEACH FUN (Europe & Canada)	30
2960	1979	HAWAIIAN	46
—	1979	SPORTS STAR (Canada)	45
—	1980	GOLDEN NIGHT	42
—	1980	JEANS (Germany)	30
1294	1980	SPORT 'N SHAVE	44
1336	1980	SPORTS STAR (Germany)	40
1088	1980	SUN LOVIN' MALIBU	43
3208	1981	DISCO (Germany & Canada)	46
2960	1981	HAWAIIAN	50
1881	1981	ROLLERSKATING	40
3600	1981	WESTERN	27
3553	1982	ALL STAR	45
5316	1982	FASHION JEANS	38
3988	1982	JOGGING (Europe & Canada)	25
1088	1982	SUNSATIONAL MALIBU white – painted hair	29
3849	1982	SUNSATIONAL black – painted hair	28
3849	1982	SUNSATIONAL black – rooted hair	52
5839	1982	SUPER SPORT	24
4077	1983	DREAM DATE	28
7495	1983	HAWAIIAN	28
3600	1983	HORSE LOVIN'	30
3903	1983	JEANS (France)	30
4974	1983	SAFARI (Australia)	50
4971	1983	SUNSATIONAL (Hispanic)	40
—	1983	SUPER DANCE (Europe & Canada)	25
693	1984	CEREMONIE (France)	65
4898	1984	CRYSTAL (white)	31
9036	1984	CRYSTAL (black)	40
7318	1984	GREAT SHAPE	20
—	1984	GREAT SHAPE green outfit (England)	45
7495	1984	HAWAIIAN	38
1088	1984	SUN GOLD MALIBU (white)	24

NEWER FAMILY DOLLS CONTINUED

STOCK NO.	YEAR OF ORIGIN	DESCRIPTION	NRFB

Ken (CONTINUED)

STOCK NO.	YEAR OF ORIGIN	DESCRIPTION	NRFB
4971	1984	SUN GOLD MALIBU (Hispanic)	34
3849	1984	SUN GOLD MALIBU (black)	32
—	1984	TAKARA salmon sweats w/"Ken" towel, shoes	95
—	1984	TAKARA SCHOOLBOY blue blazer w/school crest, blue shirt, loafers, glasses	125
9103	1985	BEACH TIME (Europe & Canada)	25
9018	1985	DAY TO NIGHT (black)	27
9019	1985	DAY TO NIGHT (white)	30
—	1985	POUPEE – SUPER REGATE (France)	45
9110	1985	SEA LOVIN' (Europe & Canada)	35
3849	1985	SUN GOLD (black)	25
4971	1985	SUN GOLD (Hispanic)	30
2250	1986	DREAM GLOW (white)	20
2421	1986	DREAM GLOW (black)	25
—	1986	GREAT SHAPE	35
2388	1986	MUSIC LOVIN' (Europe & Canada)	30
1020	1986	TROPICAL (white)	16
1023	1986	TROPICAL (black)	21
1023	1986	TROPICAL (Europe)	12
—	1987	CREPE SHOP (Ma Ba – Japan)	85
—	1987	FANTASY (Ma Ba – Japan)	85
1719	1987	JEWEL SECRETS (white) 2 box versions	35
3232	1987	JEWEL SECRETS (black) 2 box versions	25
3131	1987	ROCKER (2 editions)	40
1761	1987	TENNIS (Europe)	18
4441	1988	CALIFORNIA	25
4441	1988	CALIFORNIA DREAM	20
4441	1988	CLUB CALIFORNIA (Canada)	24
4118	1988	DOCTOR	30
—	1988	DR. (Europe)	35
4060	1988	ISLAND FUN	15
—	1988	NEW WAVE (Brazil)	125
—	1988	OLYMPICO (Venezuela)	95
4554	1988	PERFUME GIVING (white)	28
4555	1988	PERFUME GIVING (black)	32
4554	1988	PERFUME PRETTY (Europe)	35
1351	1989	ANIMAL LOVIN'	30
3238	1989	BEACH BLAST	14
3215	1989	COOL TIMES	18
3511	1989	DANCE CLUB	26
51-0297	1989	LLANERA (Venezuela)	95

indicates cross reference

STOCK NO.	YEAR OF ORIGIN	DESCRIPTION	NRFB
Ken (CONTINUED)			
1389	1989	MY FIRST (white)	20
1535	1989	SUPER STAR 1st Edition (white)	30
—	1989	SUPER STAR 2nd Edition (white)	30
1550	1989	SUPER STAR (black)	27
9361	1990	ALL STAR	25
7081	1990	DANCE MAGIC (white)	25
7082	1990	DANCE MAGIC (black)	18
—	1990	GOLDSMITH INC. (6 foot)	525
7375	1990	ICE CAPADES 50th Anniversary	24
9940	1990	MY FIRST (Prince)	14
9934	1990	SUNCHARM (Europe)	30
9934	1990	WESTERN FUN	25
4104	1990	WET 'N WILD	17
9424	1991	ALL AMERICAN Reebok	20
9406	1991	BENETTON Pink Stamp Club (Canada & Europe)	38
7154	1991	COSTUME BALL (white)	22
7160	1991	COSTUME BALL (black)	20
5941	1991	HAWAIIAN FUN	15
9940	1991	MY FIRST	25
1110	1991	PORCELAIN*	130
7512	1991	SKI FUN	30
9609	1991	WEDDING DAY 2 box versions	32
4876	1992	BENETTON SHOPPING (Europe)	43
5352	1992	MARINE* (black) stars & stripes	42
7574	1992	MARINE* (white) stars & stripes	45
3841	1992	MY FIRST (white)	17
1807	1992	MY FIRST (black)	15
4903	1992	RAPPIN ROCKIN' (2 hair versions)	25
2215	1992	ROLLERBLADE (2 hair versions)	35
5476	1992	SEA HOLIDAY (Europe)	33
3149	1992	SPARKLE SURPRISE (2 hair versions)	28
1392	1992	SUN SENSATION	15
1115	1992	TOTALLY HAIR (2 mold versions)	25
1237	1993	ARMY* (white) Desert Storm	45
5619	1993	ARMY* (black) Desert Storm	42
2290	1993	EARRING MAGIC	46
4904	1993	GLITTER BEACH	10
4829	1993	HOLLYWOOD HAIR	22
1503	1993	MY FIRST (white)	12
3876	1993	MY FIRST (black)	12
10998	1993	NAF NAF (Europe)	40

indicates cross reference

NEWER FAMILY DOLLS CONTINUED

Ken (CONTINUED)

STOCK NO.	YEAR OF ORIGIN	DESCRIPTION	NRFB
7988	1993	SECRET HEARTS	25
10294	1993	WESTERN STAMPIN'	38
11554	1994	AIRFORCE* (white)	29
11555	1994	AIRFORCE* (black)	18
11075	1994	CAMP	30
10964	1994	LOCKET SURPRISE	14
19054	1994	SUN JEWEL	10
13200	1995	BAYWATCH (white)	19
13259	1995	BAYWATCH (black)	17
13237	1995	BUTTERFLY PRINCE KEN (Canada & Europe)	43
13513	1995	HOT SKATIN' (white)	16
12741	1995	RHETT BUTLER* Gone With The Wind	58
12956	1995	SHAVING FUN	24
12447	1995	TROPICAL SPLASH (2 versions)	20
13515	1995	WINTER SPORT Canada, Europe & JCPenney, FAO, Toys R Us	25
15469	1996	COOL SHAVIN'	16
14837	1996	GREAT DATE	14
15474	1996	IN LINE SKATING Canada, Europe, JCPenney, FAO	25
—	1996	MY FIRST (India)	40
15430	1996	OCEAN FRIENDS (2 editions)	14
15499	1996	PROFESSOR HENRY HIGGINS* My Fair Lady	59
16497	1996	SCARECROW* Wizard of Oz	104
14837	1996	SONGBIRD (Europe)	28
14350	1996	SPARKLE BEACH	8
14902	1996	TIN MAN* Wizard of Oz	78
17588	1997	BIG BROTHER KEN & BABY BROTHER TOMMY (black)	14
17055	1997	BIG BROTHER KEN & BABY BROTHER TOMMY (white)	14
16573	1997	COWARDLY LION* Wizard of Oz	160
14837	1997	GREAT DATE	12
—	1997	MY FIRST KEN – Leo – India	65
18502	1997	OLYMPIC SKATER (white)	12
18504	1997	OLYMPIC SKATER (black)	12
18577	1997	PEARL BEACH	7
18080	1997	PRINCE	26
16170	1997	SPLASH 'N COLOR	12
—	1997	MA BA* (Japan - white sleeveless sweater, white polo shirt, shorts, loagers, watch, glasses)	125
20778	1998	COOL LOOKIN'	10
18898	1998	DR. KEN & LITTLE PATIENT TOMMY* (white)	15
18899	1998	DR. KEN & LITTLE PATIENT TOMMY* (black)	15
20491	1998	PRINCE Sleeping Beauty	25

indicates cross reference

NEWER FAMILY DOLLS CONTINUED

Ken (CONTINUED)

STOCK NO.	YEAR OF ORIGIN	DESCRIPTION	NRFB
19209	1998	TOTALLY COOL (Casual)	11
19387	1998	TOTALLY COOL (Formal)	11
22995	1999	BUTTERFLY ART	15
20496	1999	FLORIDA VACATION	8
22235	1999	HARLEY KEN #1* – Toys R Us	111
23788	1999	SHAVE 'N STYLE (white)	12
23937	1999	SHAVE 'N STYLE (black)	12
20491	1999	PRINCE	27
23941	2000	COOL SCHOOL	12
—	2000	HARLEY KEN #2* – Toys R Us	86
26359	2000	RAINBOW PRINCE	15
25814	2000	COWARDLY LION	Retail
25815	2000	TIN MAN	Retail
25816	2000	SCARECROW	Retail
24616	2000	HAWAII	6
25678	2000	SWEETHEART*	60

Kenny

STOCK NO.	YEAR OF ORIGIN	DESCRIPTION	NRFB
—	1986	ROCK STAR (Argentina)	100

Kevin

STOCK NO.	YEAR OF ORIGIN	DESCRIPTION	NRFB
9351	1990	COOL TOPS	25
9325	1991	KEVIN	25
2711	1992	PET PALS	20
4713	1993	BASKETBALL	20
11549	1994	COOL CRIMP	15
12944	1995	PIZZA PARTY	15

Kira (ALSO SEE MARINA)

STOCK NO.	YEAR OF ORIGIN	DESCRIPTION	NRFB
9409	1990	BENETTON	35
4120	1990	WET 'N WILD	15
9427	1991	ALL AMERICAN Reebok	28
5943	1991	HAWAIIAN FUN	20
2218	1992	ROLLERBLADE	35
1447	1992	SUN SENSATION	20
4924	1993	GLITTER BEACH	19
19056	1994	SUN JEWEL	10
12449	1995	TROPICAL SPLASH	10
14032	1996	FLYING HERO	16
15431	1996	OCEAN FRIENDS	25
14351	1996	SPARKLE BEACH (2 hair versions)	10

*indicates cross reference

NEWER FAMILY DOLLS CONTINUED

STOCK NO.	YEAR OF ORIGIN	DESCRIPTION	NRFB

Kira (ALSO SEE MARINA) (CONTINUED)

17717	1997	MOVIN' GROOVIN'	12
18580	1997	PEARL BEACH	10
16173	1997	SPLASH 'N COLOR	8
20362	1998	BUTTERFLY ART	12
20531	1998	VERY VELVET	15
20349	1998	WNBA*	15
20352	1999	SOCCER	11
23424	2000	SIT IN STYLE	10

Kotbie

—	1984	KOTBIE (Korea)	250

Lara

20968	1999	GENERATION GIRL	15
25769	2000	GENERATION GIRL	20

Laura

3179	1987	PRINCESSE LAURA – JEWEL SECRETS (Europe)	55
—	1988	NURSE SCHWESTER PRINCESSE	45
4557	1988	PARFUM DE REVE – PREFUME PRETTY (Europe)	45
—	1989	FRAGANSI* (Estrela – Brazil)	85

Lia

—	1988	PERFUME (Estrela – Brazil)	90
—	1988	ROCK STAR (Estrela – Brazil)	115
—	1989	MODE JEANS (Estrela – Brazil)	90

Liana (4 inch)

24601	1999	GOLFER	6

Li'l Friends

3536	1992	LI'L FRIENDS yellow border window (Europe)	40
3537	1992	LI'L FRIENDS blue border window (Europe)	40
3538	1992	LI'L FRIENDS purple border window (Europe)	40
3539	1992	LI'L FRIENDS green border window (Europe)	40
2202	1993	LI'L FRIENDS purple denim	38
2203	1993	LI'L FRIENDS Brunette (Europe)	38
2204	1993	LI'L FRIENDS green hair bow/shirt (Europe)	38
2205	1993	LI'L FRIENDS b/w dress (Europe)	38
2206	1993	LI'L FRIENDS pink, green, white dress (Europe)	38
11855	1994	LI'L FRIENDS yellow hat (Europe)	36

indicates cross reference

NEWER FAMILY DOLLS CONTINUED

| STOCK NO. | YEAR OF ORIGIN | DESCRIPTION | NRFB |

Li'l Friends (CONTINUED)

STOCK NO.	YEAR OF ORIGIN	DESCRIPTION	NRFB
11854	1994	LI'L FRIENDS pink hat (Europe)	36
11853	1994	LI'L FRIENDS red hat (Europe)	36
11856	1994	LI'L FRIENDS blue hat (Europe)	36

Lorena (4 inch)

24603	1999	TENNIS	6

Mari

26112	2000	GENERATION GIRL	20

Maria (4 inch)

24593	1999	LEMONADE STAND	6

Marina (ALSO SEE KIRA)

2056	1986	TROPICAL (Europe)	25
3244	1989	SUN MAGIC (Europe)	25
9409	1991	BENETTON (Europe)	45
4898	1992	BENETTON SHOPPING (Europe)	72
7740	1992	WEEKEND Adidas (Europe)	40
15431	1996	OCEAN FRIENDS (Europe & U.S.)	25

Marisa (4 inch)

17053	1997	POOL FUN	6
16002	1997	LI'L FRIEND	6
18992	1998	GYM	6
18036	1998	PARTY DRESS	6
24600	1999	LITTLE SWIMMER	6

Melody (4 inch)

14854	1993	LI'L FRIENDS OF KELLY	10
16003	1997	MELODY	8
18654	1998	BALLERINA	6
18912	1998	BUNNY	6
22206	1998	GARDENING	6
18035	1998	SAILOR	6
24599	1999	WIZARD	6

Midge

4442	1988	CALIFORNIA	30
4442	1988	CALIFORNIA DREAM	30
4442	1988	CLUB CALIFORNIA (Canada)	30

*indicates cross reference

NEWER FAMILY DOLLS CONTINUED

Midge (CONTINUED)

STOCK NO.	YEAR OF ORIGIN	DESCRIPTION	NRFB
3216	1989	COOL TIMES	28
9360	1990	ALL STAR	30
2752	1990	BARBIE AND THE BEAT (Midge)	40
7513	1991	SKI FUN* (Canada & *Toys R Us*)	30
9606	1991	WEDDING DAY (2 box versions)	40
5476	1992	HOLIDAY AT SEA (Europe)	35
10256	1993	EARRING MAGIC	25
7018	1993	EARRING MAGIC (Europe)	35
10999	1993	NAF NAF (Europe)	40
7957	1993	PORCELAIN – 30th ANNIVERSARY*	131
11077	1994	CAMP	15
13085	1995	DANCE MOVES (Canada, Europe & U.S.)	30
13393	1995	HOT SKATIN'	16
13236	1995	SLUMBER PARTY (soft body)	15
13514	1995	WINTER SPORT (Canada, Europe & *Toys R Us*)	35
15475	1996	IN-LINE SKATING (Europe, Canada & FAO Schwarz)	17
14589	1996	JEWEL HAIR MERMAID	20
18976	1998	35TH ANNIVERSARY* (Senior Prom) *Toys R Us*	48
18982	1998	DIVING	11
20538	1998	FLORIDA VACATION	8
24617	2000	HAWAII	6

Miko

STOCK NO.	YEAR OF ORIGIN	DESCRIPTION	NRFB
2056	1986	TROPICAL	25
—	1986	TROPICAL (Europe)	25
4065	1988	ISLAND FUN	15
3244	1989	BEACH BLAST	15

Monica (Whitney)

STOCK NO.	YEAR OF ORIGIN	DESCRIPTION	NRFB
24605	1991	MONICA (India)	—

Nia

STOCK NO.	YEAR OF ORIGIN	DESCRIPTION	NRFB
9933	1990	WESTERN FUN	60

Nia (4 inch)

STOCK NO.	YEAR OF ORIGIN	DESCRIPTION	NRFB
20860	1998	PLAYTIME	6
24605	1999	BAKER	6

Nichelle

STOCK NO.	YEAR OF ORIGIN	DESCRIPTION	NRFB
1751	1991	NICHELLE* *Toys R Us*	25
5775	1992	BEACH DAZZLE* *Toys R Us*	15

indicates cross reference

NEWER FAMILY DOLLS CONTINUED

Nichelle (CONTINUED)

STOCK NO.	YEAR OF ORIGIN	DESCRIPTION	NRFB
3456	1993	BEACH STREAK* *Toys R Us*	15
10290	1993	SOUL TRAIN* *Toys R Us*	20
20966	1999	GENERATION GIRL	14
25767	2000	GENERATION GIRL	20

Nikki

STOCK NO.	YEAR OF ORIGIN	DESCRIPTION	NRFB
1352	1989	ANIMAL LOVIN'	30
17353	1997	TEEN	15
19667	1998	COOL TEEN	15
22229	1999	TOTALLY YO YO	12
24993	2000	PAJAMA FUN	10

Noel

STOCK NO.	YEAR OF ORIGIN	DESCRIPTION	NRFB
—	1986	BARBIES FRIEND* (Ma Ba) High School Series	100

PJ

STOCK NO.	YEAR OF ORIGIN	DESCRIPTION	NRFB
1187	1979	SUN LOVIN' MALIBU	—
1187	1982	SUNSATIONAL	40
5869	1983	DREAM DATE	45
1187	1984	SUN GOLD	35
7455	1984	SWEET ROSES	30

Reina

STOCK NO.	YEAR OF ORIGIN	DESCRIPTION	NRFB
—	2000	SCHOOL GIRL (Japanese Exclusive)	—

Scott

STOCK NO.	YEAR OF ORIGIN	DESCRIPTION	NRFB
1019	1980	SCOTT	100

Shani

STOCK NO.	YEAR OF ORIGIN	DESCRIPTION	NRFB
1750	1991	SHANI* *Toys R Us*	30
5774	1992	BEACH DAZZLE* *Toys R Us*	15
—	1992	BEACH DAZZLE PLUS 2 FASHIONS* *Sears*	42
3428	1993	BEACH STREAK* Toys R Us	15
11215	1993	JEWEL & GLITTER (Foreign)	30
10289	1993	SOUL TRAIN* *Toys R Us*	25
19058	1994	SUN JEWEL* *Toys R Us*	15

Shelly

STOCK NO.	YEAR OF ORIGIN	DESCRIPTION	NRFB
—	1995	BABY SISTER (Europe)	25
14552	1996	BATHTIME FUN (Europe)	15

NEWER FAMILY DOLLS CONTINUED

Shelly (CONTINUED)

STOCK NO.	YEAR OF ORIGIN	DESCRIPTION	NRFB
12489	1996	BEDTIME FUN (Europe)	15
14906	1996	LI'L FRIENDS OF SHELLY Chelsie, Becky & Melody (Europe)	10

Sidney

STOCK NO.	YEAR OF ORIGIN	DESCRIPTION	NRFB
20969	1999	TEEN SCENE	15

Skip-Chan

STOCK NO.	YEAR OF ORIGIN	DESCRIPTION	NRFB
S1301	1979	SALMON SATIN DRESS	175
S1201	1979	HOT PINK SATIN DRESS	175
S1302	1979	SKIP-CHAN	175
S1202	1979	SKIP-CHAN	175

Skipper (10 inch)

STOCK NO.	YEAR OF ORIGIN	DESCRIPTION	NRFB
7379	1976	GOLD MEDAL	85
1069	1975	SUNSET MALIBU	75
9428	1976	DELUXE QUICK CURL	75
7193	1976	IN VACANZA (Italy)	—
1069	1976	MALIBU	50
9226	1976	PARTYTIME (Europe)	50
7379	1977	SIMPATIA (Italy)	80
1069	1978	MALIBU	50
9926	1978	PARTYTIME (Europe)	100
1069	1978	PORTOFINO (Europe)	65
2167	1978	SPIEL MIT (Europe)	60
—	1979	BEACH FUN (Europe & Canada)	40
1069	1979	SUN LOVIN' MALIBU	25
3902	1980	JEANS (Germany)	40
—	1980	SPORTS STAR (Germany)	35
2756	1980	SUPER TEEN	45
—	1981	DISCO (Germany)	35
—	1981	SAFARI (Denmark & Australia)	40
3987	1982	JOGGING (Europe)	35
1069	1982	SUNSATIONAL	35
5029	1982	WESTERN	35
5029	1983	HORSE LOVIN'	30
—	1983	SUPER DANCE (Europe)	35
7417	1984	GREAT SHAPE	32
—	1984	GREAT SHAPE green outfit (England)	45
—	1984	RITMIC (Spain)	45
1069	1984	SUN GOLD	30
1069	1984	SUNSATIONAL MALIBU	—

indicates cross reference

STOCK NO.	YEAR OF ORIGIN	DESCRIPTION	NRFB
Skipper (10 inch) (CONTINUED)			
—	1985	BEACHTIME (Europe)	35
7927	1985	HOT STUFF	30
—	1985	NAUTIC (Spain)	50
—	1985	POUPEE - STAR REGATE (France)	45
9111	1985	SEA LOVIN' (Europe)	40
—	1985	SUPER STYLE - SUPER	—
2854	1986	MUSIC LOVIN' (Europe & Canada)	40
1021	1986	TROPICAL	22
1021	1986	TROPICAL (Europe)	20
—	1987	FAIRY FANTASY (India)	40
3133	1987	JEWEL SECRETS (white) 2 box versions	60
—	1987	MY FIRST (India)	30
1762	1987	TENNIS (Europe & Canada)	25
4440	1988	CALIFORNIA (Europe)	35
4064	1988	ISLAND FUN	15
5899	1988	TEEN FUN (Workout Teen)	20
5893	1988	TEEN FUN (Cheerleader)	20
5899	1988	TEEN FUN (Party Teen)	20
4855	1988	TEEN SWEETHEART	25
3242	1989	BEACH BLAST	15
1950	1989	HOMECOMING QUEEN (white)	30
2390	1989	HOMECOMING QUEEN (black)	30
4867	1989	PEPSI SPIRIT* *Toys R Us*	55
1915	1989	STYLE MAGIC (Canada)	30
1951	1989	TEEN TIME	30
4989	1990	COOL TOPS (white)	20
5441	1990	COOL TOPS (black)	20
1075	1990	DREAM DATE* *Toys R Us*	35
4817	1990	DREAM DATE (white)	25
4849	1990	DREAM DATE (black)	25
4138	1990	WET 'N WILD	15
1599	1991	BABY SITTER (black)	20
9433	1991	BABY SITTER (white)	21
9324	1991	BEAUTY PAGEANT* *Toys R Us*	30
5942	1991	HAWAIIAN FUN	15
—	1991	SCHOOL-GOING (India)	40
1430	1991	TOTALLY HAIR SKIPPER* *Toys R Us*	35
7970	1992	BATHTIME FUN* *Target*	25
2709	1992	PET PALS (white)	20
4049	1992	PET PALS (black)	20
1446	1992	SUN SENSATION	15
3931	1993	BATON TWIRLING (white)	15

*indicates cross reference

NEWER FAMILY DOLLS CONTINUED

Skipper (10 inch) (CONTINUED)

STOCK NO.	YEAR OF ORIGIN	DESCRIPTION	NRFB
7498	1993	BATON TWIRLING (black)	15
4920	1993	GLITTER BEACH	10
2309	1993	HOLLYWOOD HAIR	20
10506	1993	MERMAID AND THE MERTWINS	22
12071	1994	BABYSITTER (white)	12
12072	1994	BABYSITTER (black)	12
11076	1994	CAMP	16
11179	1994	COOL CRIMP (white)	15
11547	1994	COOL CRIMP (black)	15
11396	1994	PORCELAIN - 30th ANNIVERSARY* LE 7000	161
19055	1994	SUN JEWEL	10
—	1995	FAIRY FANTASY (India)	—
12920	1995	PIZZA PARTY (white)	15
12942	1995	PIZZA PARTY (black)	15
12448	1995	TROPICAL SPLASH	12
14312	1996	PHONE FUN (white)	15
14313	1996	PHONE FUN (black)	15
14352	1996	SPARKLE BEACH 2 hair versions	10
16171	1997	SPLASH 'N COLOR	10
22228	1999	TOTALLY YO YO	12
24619	2000	HAWAII	6

Skipper (11½ inch)

STOCK NO.	YEAR OF ORIGIN	DESCRIPTION	NRFB
19223	1997	PEARL BEACH TEEN (white)	10
17351	1997	TEEN (white)	10
17602	1997	TEEN (black)	10
20334	1998	COOL SITTER TEEN w/4 babies (white)	15
20335	1998	COOL SITTER TEEN w/4 babies (black)	15
19666	1998	EXTREME GREEN TEEN	15
20495	1998	FLORIDA VACATION	10
24592	2000	PAJAMA FUN	10

Skooter

STOCK NO.	YEAR OF ORIGIN	DESCRIPTION	NRFB
7381	1976	FUNTIME (Europe)	—

Stacie (11½ inch)

STOCK NO.	YEAR OF ORIGIN	DESCRIPTION	NRFB
3636	1989	HIGH SCHOOL	30
19809	1998	HOLIDAY SISTERS GIFT SET* (Barbie, Stacie, Kelly)	25

Stacie (4 inch)

STOCK NO.	YEAR OF ORIGIN	DESCRIPTION	NRFB
4240	1992	STACIE	25
4115	1993	PARTY 'N PLAY (black)	15
5411	1993	PARTY 'N PLAY (white)	15
10227	1993	STACIE BUTTERFLY PONY GIFT SET*	20

indicates cross reference

STOCK NO.	YEAR OF ORIGIN	DESCRIPTION	NRFB
Stacie (4 inch) (CONTINUED)			
11587	1993	TOON TOWN* *Disney*	30
11474	1994	HAPPY MEAL	20
12982	1995	POLLY POCKET	20
14609	1996	GYMNAST	15
16568	1996	GYMNAST* *JCPenney*	25
16734	1997	BICYCLIN'	12
19669	1998	FLASHLIGHT FUN (Pooh Bear)	10
19625	1998	LI'L PALS GIFT SET*	25
22013	1999	BOWLING PARTY	12
24644	2000	AWESOME SKATEBOARD	13
Stephanie			
—	1986	TEACHER (Ma Ba) High School Series	130
Steven			
4093	1988	ISLAND FUN	15
3251	1989	BEACH BLAST	15
4137	1990	WET 'N WILD	15
5945	1991	HAWAIIAN FUN	15
1396	1992	SUN SENSATION	15
4918	1993	GLITTER BEACH	15
19059	1994	SUN JEWEL	12
12452	1995	TROPICAL SPLASH	12
14353	1996	SPARKLE BEACH	10
18581	1997	PEARL BEACH	10
16175	1997	SPLASH 'N COLOR	9
22996	1999	BUTTERFLY ART	12
20497	1999	FLORIDA VACATION	6
24620	2000	HAWAII	6
Susie (MELODY) (4 inch)			
—	1996	LI'L FRIEND OF SHELLY (Germany)	12
Tamika (4 inch)			
18916	1998	PICNICER	6
24604	2000	LEMONADE STAND	6
Tara Lynn			
10295	1993	WESTERN STAMPIN'	70
Teresa			
5503	1988	CALIFORNIA	25
5503	1988	CALIFORNIA DREAM	25

indicates cross reference

STOCK NO.	YEAR OF ORIGIN	DESCRIPTION	NRFB

Teresa (CONTINUED)

STOCK NO.	YEAR OF ORIGIN	DESCRIPTION	NRFB
—	1988	CLUB CALIFORNIA (Canada)	35
4117	1988	ISLAND FUN	15
3249	1989	BEACH BLAST	15
3218	1989	COOL TIMES	25
9353	1990	ALL STAR	30
4136	1990	WET 'N WILD	15
9426	1991	ALL AMERICAN	25
9408	1991	BENETTON (Europe)	60
9727	1991	LIGHTS 'N LACE	35
4880	1992	BENETTON SHOPPING (Europe)	85
3270	1992	RAPPIN' ROCKIN'	45
2216	1992	*ROLLERBLADE*	35
4921	1993	GLITTER BEACH	10
2316	1993	HOLLYWOOD HAIR	25
10885	1993	SPOTS AND DOTS* *Toys R Us*	40
11078	1994	CAMP	25
11214	1994	JEWEL & GLITTER (Canada & Mexico)	28
12244	1994	PARTYTIME* *Toys R Us*	25
11928	1994	QUINCEANERA* *Toys R Us*	30
19057	1994	SUN JEWEL	12
13489	1994	SUNFLOWER* *Toys R Us*	25
13201	1995	BAYWATCH (Europe)	50
13238	1995	BUTTERFLY PRINCESS	25
13084	1995	DANCE MOVES	15
13235	1995	SLUMBER PARTY soft body	15
12450	1995	TROPICAL SPLASH	10
14031	1996	FLYING HERO	20
14588	1996	JEWEL HAIR MERMAID	15
14484	1996	SONGBIRD (1st version)	25
14354	1996	SPARKLE BEACH 3 hair versions	10
15299	1996	TWIRLING BALLERINA	25
17602	1997	101 DALMATIANS* *Toys R Us*	20
17617	1997	35th ANNIVERSARY* *Wal-Mart*	30
17035	1997	BLOSSOM BEAUTY	20
17239	1997	GRAN GALA* *Toys R Us*	22
17049	1997	HULA HAIR	15
17716	1997	MOVIN' GROOVIN'	15
—	1997	PALMERS* Bikini w/black net cover-up, LE 2500	120
18579	1997	PEARL BEACH	8
18232	1997	SHOPPING TIME* *Wal-Mart*	20
14484	1997	SONGBIRD (2nd version)	18
16172	1997	SPLASH 'N COLOR	10

indicates cross reference

STOCK NO.	YEAR OF ORIGIN	DESCRIPTION	NRFB
Teresa (CONTINUED)			
17318	1997	WORKIN' OUT	6
20018	1998	BEYOND PINK	12
20361	1998	BUTTERFLY ART	8
18983	1998	FLIP 'N DIVE	
20537	1998	FLORIDA VACATION	6
19668	1998	PERFECT PINK	10
20166	1998	PUZZLE CRAZE* *Wal-Mart*	12
20506	1998	TIE DYE	10
18423	1998	TWIRLING MAKEUP	10
20530	1998	VERY VELVET	15
19263	1998	WILD STYLE * *Toys R Us*	20
20350	1998	WNBA*	17
22089	1999	BUBBLE FAIRY	15
22884	1999	HAPPENIN' HAIR	15
26429	1999	MOVIE STAR (Foreign)	20
25504	1999	MILENNIUM*	45
20207	1999	SOCCER	12
26231	2000	COOL BLADING	Retail
26427	2000	COOL CLIPS	15
26424	2000	COOL SKATING	20
26253	2000	GLAM N GROOM	Retail
24618	2000	HAWAII	6
—	2000	HOLLYWOOD NAILS	Retail
—	2000	MOVIE STAR	15
26424	2000	SECRET MESSAGES	Retail
23423	2000	SIT IN STYLE	10
25489	2000	SWIMMING CHAMPION	14
Todd (12 inch)			
4253	1983	GROOM	50
Todd (4 inch)			
8129	1975	TODD plaid shorts (England)	75
8129	1975	TODD striped shorts (England)	80
8129	1976	TODD red shorts (England)	—
8129	1977	TODD blue shorts (England)	65
7903	1993	PARTY 'N PLAY	15
11475	1994	HAPPY MEAL	15
Tommy (4 inch)			
18898	1998	DR. KEN & LITTLE PATIENT TOMMY* (white)	15
18899	1998	DR. KEN & LITTLE PATIENT TOMMY* (black)	15
20852	1998	FIREMAN	8

indicates cross reference

NEWER FAMILY DOLLS CONTINUED

Tommy (4 inch) (CONTINUED)

STOCK NO.	YEAR OF ORIGIN	DESCRIPTION	NRFB
18717	1998	KELLY & TOMMY POWER WHEELS GIFT SET* (white)	20
18718	1998	KELLY & TOMMY POWER WHEELS GIFT SET* (black)	20
18037	1998	SAILOR	8
20853	1998	WINTER FUN	8
22012	1999	HAIRCUT (white)	8
22017	1999	HAIRCUT (black)	8
24595	1999	PILOT	6
25817	2000	MUNCHKIN - Mayor	7
25819	2000	MUNCHKIN - Lollipop Guild	7
24597	1999	PRINCE	6

Tori

STOCK NO.	YEAR OF ORIGIN	DESCRIPTION	NRFB
20969	1999	GENERATION GIRL	14
25768	2000	GENERATION GIRL	20

Tracy

STOCK NO.	YEAR OF ORIGIN	DESCRIPTION	NRFB
4103	1983	BRIDE	39

Tutti

STOCK NO.	YEAR OF ORIGIN	DESCRIPTION	NRFB
8128	1975	TUTTI (Europe)	150
8128	1976	TUTTI (Europe)	75
8128	1977	TUTTI (Europe)	65

Valerie

STOCK NO.	YEAR OF ORIGIN	DESCRIPTION	NRFB
—	1978	VALERIE (Mexico)	210

Viky

STOCK NO.	YEAR OF ORIGIN	DESCRIPTION	NRFB
—	1988	ANIMAL LOVIN'* (Estrela - Brazil)	90
—	1988	ROCK STAR* (Estrela - Brazil)	115
—	1989	PASSEIO* (Estrela - Brazil)	103

Whitney (11½ inch)

STOCK NO.	YEAR OF ORIGIN	DESCRIPTION	NRFB
3179	1987	JEWEL SECRETS (2 box versions)	60
4405	1988	NURSE	80
4557	1988	PERFUME PRETTY	45
1290	1989	STYLE MAGIC	40
7735	1992	ULTRA HAIR (Europe)	80

Whitney (4 inch)

STOCK NO.	YEAR OF ORIGIN	DESCRIPTION	NRFB
11476	1994	HAPPY MEAL	20
12983	1995	POLLY POCKET	20
14610	1996	GYMNAST	15
16736	1997	BICYCLIN'	10
19671	1998	FLASHLIGHT FUN (Piglet)	10
22015	1999	BOWLING PARTY	10
24990	2000	AWESOME SKATEBOARD	12

indicates cross reference

BARBIE® MILLICENT ROBERTS FASHIONS

STOCK NO.	YEAR	DESCRIPTION	HIGH	LOW	AVG
16076	1996	HOMECOMING	40	15	27
16077	1996	PICNIC IN THE PARK	40	15	27
17568	1997	ALL DECKED OUT Nautical	35	10	17
17570	1997	CITY SLICKER Raincoat	35	10	17
17569	1997	COURT FAVORITE Tennis	35	10	17
17571	1997	JET SET LUGGAGE ENSEMBLE	35	10	17
17676	1997	LIME TIME ACCESSORY	30	10	20
17567	1997	PERFECTLY SUITED	30	10	20
17678	1997	RED HOT ACCESSORY	30	10	20
17675	1997	SIGNATURE SERIES ACCESSORY	30	10	20
17677	1997	SPECTACULAR SPECTATORS ACCESSORY	30	20	25
		1st *Official Barbie Collectors Club*			
—	1998	GALLERY OPENING 2nd *Official Barbie Collectors Club* LE	40	30	35
19433	1998	GREEN THUMB	40	20	30
19772	1998	SNOW CHIC, SO CHIC	40	20	30
22306	1999	EXECUTIVE LUNCHEON 3rd *Official Barbie Collectors Club*	—	—	—

❖❖❖❖❖❖❖❖❖❖❖❖❖❖❖

OSCAR DE LA RENTA FASHIONS

STOCK NO.	YEAR	DESCRIPTION	HIGH	LOW	AVG
9258	1982	HEAVENLY HOLIDAYS I	75	60	68
7092	1983	SPRINGTIME MAGIC II	55	50	103
7438	1983	SILVER SENSATION III 25th Anniversary	45	40	42
9258	1984	COLLECTOR SERIES IV red/gold gown	40	30	35
9259	1984	COLLECTOR SERIES V blue/green gown	40	30	35
9260	1984	COLLECTOR SERIES VI gold/hot pink gown	40	30	35
9261	1984	COLLECTOR SERIES VII gold/black w/boa	40	30	35
—	1985	COLLECTOR SERIES VIII blue w/boa	38	30	33
2763	1985	COLLECTOR SERIES IX red gown/jacket	38	30	34
—	1985	COLLECTOR SERIES X pink,wine & gold gown/jacket	38	30	34
—	1985	COLLECTOR SERIES XI pink/gold gown & short dress	38	30	34
—	1985	COLLECTOR SERIES XII blue/gold gown	46	30	38

CLASSIQUE FASHIONS

NO.	YEAR	DESCRIPTION	HIGH	LOW	AVG
1646	1992	FIFTH AVENUE STYLE - 1st Collection	45	35	40
1618	1992	HOLLYWOOD PREMIERE - 1st Collection	45	35	40
—	1993	FLOWER SHOWER - 2nd Collection	50	35	43
10151	1993	SATIN DREAMS - 2nd Collection	50	35	43

❖❖❖❖❖❖❖❖❖❖❖❖❖❖❖

HAUTE COUTURE (HIGH FASHION) FASHIONS

STOCK

NO.	YEAR	DESCRIPTION	HIGH	LOW	AVG
5841	1983	BLACK DOTTED NET/SATIN DRESS, black jumpsuit, black shoes	50	40	45
5842	1983	ORANGE/BROWN JACKET, gaucho pants, brown shoes, beige blouse, brown skirt	50	40	45
5843	1983	BLUE SWEATER, pants, skirt cowl neck piece, blue shoes	50	40	45
5844	1983	GRAY PIN-STRIPED COAT, pants, gray blouse, red belt, hat tote, shoes	49	42	45
5845	1983	BROWN TWEED JACKET, scarf, hat, beige blouse, brown belt, purse, boots, jodhpurs	50	35	43
5846	1983	ONE-SLEEVED GOWN, gold lamé skirt, royal blue/gold top, blue velvet one sleeved jacket, blue/gold belt, purse, blue shoes	50	35	42
4873	1984	RED & BLACK VELVET JACKET, gaucho pants, white lace blouse, black skirt, boots, shoes (same as 5842)	45	35	40
4874	1984	WHITE KNIT SWEATER, skirt, pants, cowl neck piece, pink scarf, panty hose, belt, white shoes (same as 5843)	45	45	40
7201	1984	BLUE-GRAY TWEED PANT, skirt, shawl, mohair sweater, tam, blue shoes	45	40	43
7202	1984	GREEN/WHITE LACE GOWN, jacket, white purse, shoes	48	36	42
7204	1984	PINK/WHITE OVER DRESS, straw hat, purse, belt, white slip, shoes	45	39	42
9148	1985	GRAY-ROSE FUR TRIMMED JACKET, gray skirt, purse, shoes, shell, pants	42	40	41
9149	1985	BRONZE/GOLD/COPPER/PLUM 2 PIECE GOWN, taupe shoes	50	40	45
9150	1985	BLACK/GRAY FUR TRIMMED COAT, hat, dress, red/black blouse black skirt, black panty hose, purse, shoes	48	40	44
9151	1985	BLACK/BROWN/RUST VELVET JACKET, black skirt, rust blouse/ pants, belt, purse, hat, shoes	45	40	43
12167	1994	RED VELVET GOWN, plaid shawl, gold blazer, pumps, purse (Europe)	60	55	50
12168	1994	RAINBOW SILK GOWN, stripped blazer, black velvet purse (Europe)	60	55	50
12166	1994	METALLIC GREEN/LAVENDER BODICE, lavender skirt gown gold purse (Europe)	45	40	43
12165	1994	BLACK/WHITE SPOTTED GOWN, black velour gab, charm	45	40	43

BEST BUY FASHIONS

STOCK NO.	YEAR	DESCRIPTION	HIGH	LOW	AVG
		BARBIE			
7200	1975	BEST BUY	15	8	12
7203	1975	BEST BUY	15	8	12
7204	1975	BEST BUY	15	8	12
7205	1975	BEST BUY	15	8	12
7206	1975	BEST BUY	15	8	12
7208	1975	BEST BUY	15	8	12
7209	1975	BEST BUY	15	8	12
7210	1975	BEST BUY	15	8	12
7211	1975	BEST BUY	15	8	12
7271	1975	BEST BUY *Gold Medal*	15	8	12
7272	1975	BEST BUY *Gold Medal*	15	8	12
7413	1975	BEST BUY *Gold Medal*	15	8	12
7414	1975	BEST BUY	15	8	12
7415	1975	BEST BUY	15	8	12
7417	1975	BEST BUY	15	8	12
7418	1975	BEST BUY	15	8	12
7419	1975	BEST BUY *Gold Medal*	15	8	12
7420	1975	BEST BUY	15	8	12
7421	1975	BEST BUY	15	8	12
7422	1975	BEST BUY	15	8	12
7423	1975	BEST BUY	15	8	12
7424	1975	BEST BUY	15	8	12
9046	1975	BEST BUY *Sears*	15	10	13
9153	1976	BEST BUY	15	8	12
9154	1976	BEST BUY	15	8	12
9155	1976	BEST BUY	15	8	12
9156	1976	BEST BUY	15	8	12
9157	1976	BEST BUY	15	8	12
9158	1976	BEST BUY *Bicentennial*	25	15	20
9160	1976	BEST BUY	15	8	12
9161	1976	BEST BUY *Bicentennial Blouse/Jeans*	25	15	20
9162	1976	BEST BUY	15	8	12
9163	1976	BEST BUY	15	8	12
9164	1976	BEST BUY *Bicentennial Gown*	25	20	23
9424	1976	FASHION ORIGINAL *DSS*	25	15	20
9571	1976	BEST BUY	15	8	12
9572	1976	BEST BUY	15	8	12
9573	1976	BEST BUY	15	5	10

BEST BUY FASHIONS CONTINUED

STOCK NO.	YEAR	DESCRIPTION	HIGH	LOW	AVG
9574	1976	BEST BUY	15	5	10
9575	1976	BEST BUY	15	5	10
9576	1976	BEST BUY	15	5	10
9577	1976	BEST BUY	15	5	10
9578	1976	BEST BUY	15	5	10
9579	1976	BEST BUY	15	5	10
9580	1976	BEST BUY	15	5	10
9581	1976	BEST BUY	15	5	10
9582	1976	BEST BUY	15	5	10
9682	1976	BEST BUY *Sears*	15	10	13
2230	1978	BEST BUY	15	5	10
9684	—	BEST BUY	15	5	10
		FRANCIE			
7273	1975	BEST BUY *Gold Medal*	15	5	10
		KEN			
7225	1975	BEST BUY	15	5	10
7245	1975	BEST BUY *Gold Medal*	15	5	10
9130	1975	BEST BUY	15	5	10
9128	1976	BEST BUY	15	5	10
9129	1976	BEST BUY	15	5	10
9132	1976	BEST BUY	15	5	10
9167	1976	BEST BUY *Get Up 'N Go*	15	5	10
9696	1976	BEST BUY *Sears*	15	10	13
		SKIPPER			
7223	1975	BEST BUY	15	10	13
7226	1975	BEST BUY	15	10	13
7274	1975	BEST BUY *Gold Medal*	15	10	13
9124	1976	BEST BUY	15	10	13
9165	1976	BEST BUY *Get Up 'N Go*	15	10	13
9166	1976	BEST BUY	15	10	13
		SWEET 16			
9553	1975	BEST BUY	18	15	17
9558	1975	BEST BUY	18	15	17

MISCELLANEOUS FASHIONS

STOCK NO.	YEAR	DESCRIPTION	HIGH	LOW	AVG
		ALL STARS			
—	1989	ALL STARS	6	4	5
		ASTRONAUT			
—	1986	DAZZLING DANCER shiny blue dress, tights, blue boots, arm coverings	40	20	30
—	1986	GALAXY A GOGO silver/white short outfit, long cape, tights, boots	40	20	30
—	1986	SPACE RACER silver skirt/jacket, boots, red tights, top, hat, belt	40	20	30
—	1986	STARLIGHT SLUMBERS white & silver pengoir set	40	20	30
—	1986	WELCOME TO VENUS	40	20	30
		"B" ACTIVE FASHIONS			
—	1984	B ACTIVE FASHION	5	5	5
		BALLERINA			
9650	1975	BALLERINA	7	5	6
		BANDAI (Japan)			
—	—	VARIETY DRESS PACKS, pink formal ball gowns, earrings shoes	31	23	27
—	—	VARIETY DRESS PACKS, pink cotton sundress w/lace, hat, purse	31	23	27
—	—	DRESS MAKE-UP KITS, pink formal ball gowns w/appliques to create own design	31	23	27
—	—	ANNA DOLL EXCLUSIVE, *Baskin Robbin*, pink uniform w/apron, cap, shoes socks, shakes & ice cream cones	40	30	35
		BARGAIN FASHIONS			
1024	1978	BARGAIN FASHIONS	5	5	5
1026	1978	BARGAIN FASHIONS	5	5	5
1028	1978	BARGAIN FASHIONS	5	5	5
1029	1978	BARGAIN FASHIONS	5	5	5
3441	1978	BARGAIN FASHIONS	5	5	5
5195	1978	BARGAIN FASHIONS	5	5	5
5198	—	BARGAIN FASHIONS			
		BEGINNERS FASHIONS			
1368	1979	WRAP 'N TIE FRONT OR BACK	5	5	5
1369	1979	WRAP 'N TIE ROBE OR GOWN	5	5	5
		BRIDAL COLLECTION (FOREIGN)			
—	1992	BRIDAL COLLECTION	35	35	35
		CALIFORNIA			
4468	1987	CALIFORNIA	7	5	6
		CAROL SPENCER			
—	1992	FIFTH AVENUE STYLE	25	25	25
—	1992	HOLLYWOOD PREMIERE	25	25	25
		COLLECTOR SERIES			
—	1983	COLLECTOR SERIES II - Springtime Magic	50	40	45
—	1983	COLLECTOR SERIES III - Silver Sensation	55	50	53

MISCELLANEOUS FASHIONS CONTINUED

STOCK NO.	YEAR	DESCRIPTION	HIGH	LOW	AVG
		DESIGNER COLLECTION			
5654	1982	DATE NIGHT	12	—	12
5835	1982	AFTERNOON PARTY	18	12	15
1079	1983	SKI PARTY	18	—	18
7080	1983	HORSE BACK RIDING	22	18	20
7082	1983	IN THE SPOTLIGHT	22	17	20
7081	1983	BEDTIME BEAUTY	18	12	15
7083	1983	CAN	18	12	15
		DESIGNER ORIGINALS			
1446	1976	DESIGNER ORIGINALS	20	16	18
2668	1978	ROYAL BALL	20	14	17
3800	1981	FUN 'N FANCY	15	13	14
		DISNEY			
17990	1998	DISNEY FUN FASHIONS (Theme Park catalogue exclusive)	25	20	22
		DREAM GLOW			
2191	1985	BALLET DRESS	20	18	19
2193	1985	DREAM GLOW Ken (white suit)	15	8	12
2192	1985	PURPLE DRESS	20	12	16
2188	1985	WHITE DRESS	22	17	20
2189	1985	YELLOW DRESS	20	8	19
		FASHION AVENUE			
—	1998	CHICAGO CUBS LE 10,000 (8-23-98 game giveaway)	76	55	66
		FASHION CLASSICS			
5703	1982	FASHION CLASSIC	5	3	4
		FASHION COLLECTIBLES			
1008	1978	FASHION COLLECTIBLES	5	5	5
1362	1979	FASHION COLLECTIBLES	5	5	5
1903	1980	FASHION COLLECTIBLES	5	5	5
1905	1980	FASHION COLLECTIBLES	5	5	5
3679	1981	FASHION COLLECTIBLES	3	3	3
3688	1981	FASHION COLLECTIBLES	5	5	5
		FASHION FANTASY			
—	1982	FASHION FANTASY	5	5	5
—	1983	FASHION FANTASY - Letter Perfect	5	5	5
—	1983	FASHION FANTASY - Romantic Valentine	5	5	5
—	1983	FASHION FANTASY - Sportin' Occasion	5	5	5
—	1983	FASHION FANTASY - Star Struck	7	7	7
—	1982	GREEN	10	8	9
4283	1982	SILVER	15	10	12
5540	1982	CAN	10	8	9
5547	1982	DREAM TIME	10	8	9
4810	1983	A LITTLE LUXURY	8	8	8
4811	1983	CURTAINS UP	10	8	9
4814	1983		10	8	9
4815	1983	LETTER PERFECT	7	7	7

MISCELLANEOUS FASHIONS CONTINUED

STOCK NO.	YEAR	DESCRIPTION	HIGH	LOW	AVG
		FASHION FAVORITES			
—	1978	TOWN 'N TRAVEL	15	12	14
2788	1978	RAIN OR SHINE	15	12	14
1939	1979	BEACH DAZZLER	8	5	6
3792	1979	FASHION FAVORITES	8	5	6
1400	1979	PLEASANT DREAMS	12	12	12
3446	1979	FASHION FAVORITES	18	18	18
5205	1979	FASHION FAVORITES	5	5	5
		FASHION FUN			
5713	1982	FASHION FUN	5	5	5
5716	1982	FASHION FUN	5	5	5
4801	1983	FASHION FUN - Fun in the Sun	5	5	5
4803	1983	FASHION FUN - Holiday Hostess	5	5	5
4804	1983	FASHION FUN - Everyday Outing	5	5	5
4805	1983	FASHION FUN - Perfectly Pink	5	5	5
4808	1983	FASHION FUN - Right in Step	5	5	5
7904	1983	FASHION FUN	5	5	5
7908	1983	FASHION FUN	5	5	5
7909	1983	FASHION FUN	5	5	5
		FASHION ORIGINAL			
9422	1974	RED VELVET CAPE w/white trim	35	30	33
		FASHION PLAYSET			
—	1984	FASHION PLAYSET - Bath Fun	20	20	20
—	1984	FASHION PLAYSET - Travel	20	20	20
—	1984	FASHION PLAYSET - Vet Fun	20	20	20
—	1984	FASHION PLAYSET - Water Sport	20	20	20
		FINISHING TOUCHES			
2460	1984	HATS, etc.	12	8	10
2458	1984	SHOES, etc.	17	15	16
		GENERATION GIRL			
24325	2000	MARI - Patchwork		Retail	
24336	2000	MARI - Paisley		Retail	
24327	2000	BARBIE - Pink Bouffant		Retail	
24340	2000	BARBIE - Casual		Retail	
24328	2000	BLAINE - Americana		Retail	
24332	2000	BLAINE - Hawaiian		Retail	
24329	2000	NICHELLE - Pink Terry		Retail	
24230	2000	NICHELLE - Aqua Sparkle		Retail	
24331	2000	TORI - Warm-Up		Retail	
24333	2000	TORI - Purple Dress		Retail	
24337	2000	LARA - Zip Hood		Retail	
24339	2000	LARA - Princess		Retail	
		GET UP 'N GO			
7242	1974	YELLOW JACKET/SKIRT, striped scarf	25	20	22
9739	1974	RED SHINE FUN RAIN TIME	25	20	22
		JAZZIE			
3777	1989	TEEN SCENE	10	10	10
3773	1989	TEEN SCENE	10	8	9

STOCK NO.	YEAR	DESCRIPTION	HIGH	LOW	AVG
		JEWEL SECRETS			
—	1986	KEN - silver & white tuxedo	25	20	22
1863	1986	SKIPPER - lavender lace/lame gown	18	15	17
1862	1986	WHITNEY - silver & blue lame gown	21	14	18
1861	1986	YELLOW TOP w/long satin skirt	15	10	13
		LINGERIE (Europe)			
—	1994	LAVENDER & BABY BLUE FLORAL HALTER/PANTIES, chiffon robe, pumps, grooming set	30	20	25
—	1994	MINT GREEN SILK BODYSUIT, thigh highs, chiffon robe, pumps, grooming set	30	20	25
—	1994	PINK TERRY CLOTH ROBE & TOWEL, slippers & grooming set	30	20	25
—	1994	PINK & RED FLORAL HALTER/PANTIES, chiffon robe, pumps, grooming set	30	20	25
		LOCKET SURPRISE			
11559	1993	PEACH DRESS W/GLITTER SHOES, lip gloss	6	5	6
11558	1993	GOLD & LAVENDER W/GLITTER & FLORAL PRINT ON SKIRT, shoes & blush	6	5	6
		MISC FASHIONS			
—	1980	CLASSIC COWGIRL	16	15	16
1958	1979	GOLD SPUN	18	18	18
2061	1975	FASHION	25	25	25
2579	1975	FASHION	15	15	15
2580	1975	FASHION	25	25	25
3807	1975	FASHION	25	25	25
9662	1975	FASHION	25	25	25
9664	1975	FASHION	15	15	15
9664	1975	FASHION	25	25	25
2062	1977	FASHION	25	25	25
		MY FIRST			
3677	1981	MY FIRST	5	5	5
4870	1983	MY FIRST	8	6	7
7918	1984	SWEATER SKIRT	8	6	7
7920	1984	RECITAL	7	5	6
7921	1984	YELLOW NIGHTGOWN	6	5	5
1368	1980	WRAP 'N TIE FRONT OR BACK	3	3	3
1372	1980	SLIP ON 'N TIE SLINKEROO	2	2	2
7921	1984	MY FIRST	6	6	6
1864	1988	MT FIRST	6	6	6
9265	1989	MY FIRST	3	3	3
5610	1982	MY FIRST	5	5	5
4868	1983	MY FIRST	5	5	5
7918	1984	MY FIRST	6	6	6
7920	1984	MY FIRST	6	6	6
7921	1984	MY FIRST	6	6	6
		PARIS FASHIONS			
1911	1988	RED/WHITE & GREEN LONG SKIRT W/HEART	20	15	18
1908	1988	BLACK/WHITE MINI SKIRT, maroon jacket, top, hat, shoes, bag	20	15	18

MISCELLANEOUS FASHIONS CONTINUED

STOCK NO.	YEAR	DESCRIPTION	HIGH	LOW	AVG
		PARIS FASHIONS continued			
1907	1988	RED PRINT DRESS W/POLKA-DOT TRIM, jacket, hat, shoes	20	15	18
1909	1988	FLOWERED PRINT MINI-DRESS, yellow slip	20	15	18
		PARIS PRETTY			
6558	1989	FLOWER PRINT SWEATER, pleated skirt	12	10	11
6558	1989	BLUE FLOWER PRINT JACKET, satin skirt	12	10	11
		PARTY NIGHTS			
5848	1982	3 GOWNS	12	10	11
		PERFUME PRETTY			
4623	1987	PERFUME PRETTY			
		PRET A PORTER			
—	1994	HORIZONTAL BRIGHT JACKET, black pants, fuchsia hat and scarf	45	38	41
—	1994	GREY FUR SKI JACKET, turquoise jumpsuit, gloves & hat	42	39	40
—	1994	RED LEATHER RAINCOAT, velour tam, boots, umbrella	40	40	40
—	1994	FUSCHIA, BLUE & GREEN COAT, blue hat w/feather, black boots	44	40	42
		PRIVATE COLLECTION			
1943	1988	GOWN W/RED & GREEN FLOWERS, SHOES	20	10	15
1940	1988	GOWN W/BLUE LACE OVER ROSE, fur hat, purse, boa, shoes	20	10	15
1944	1988	BURGUNDY SEQUIN SKIRT	20	15	18
1941	1988	PASTEL COLORED SKIRT, peplum, pink bodice	20	15	18
4507	—	BRIDE	20	20	20
7097	—				
4962	—	PRIVATE COLLECTION floral gown	15	10	13
7096-					
4962	—	PRIVATE COLLECTION fuschia/teal outfit w/fuchsia boa	15	10	13
7113-					
4962	—	PRIVATE COLLECTION fuchsia/purple gown, jacket, gold purse	15	10	13
4509	—	WHITE FUR COAT w/gold accessories	20	20	20
		RIDING SET ENSEMBLE (England)			
—	1987	15 PIECES	60	50	55
		ROMANTIC WEDDING			
3102	1986	BRIDE	20	20	20
3105	1986	BRIDEMAID	20	20	20
—	1986	FLOWER GIRL	20	20	20
3104	1986	GROOM	20	20	20
		SHOPPING SPREE			
3807	1975	SHOPPING SPREE	12	10	11
		SPECTACULAR FASHIONS			
7216	1983	BLUE MAGIC	22	15	18
7218	1983	DANCE SENSATION	16	15	16
7219	1983	IN THE PINK	16	15	16
7217	1983	RED SIZZLE	27	20	24

STOCK NO.	YEAR	DESCRIPTION	HIGH	LOW	AVG
		SPRINGTIME MAGIC			
7092	1984		45	35	40
—	1998	STARLIGHT SPLENDOR FASHION SET (2 versions) *Sam's Club*	25	20	23
		STORYBOOK FASHIONS			
26434	2000	EGYPTIAN	10	10	10
26435	2000	GENIE	10	10	10
26436	2000	MERMAID	10	10	10
26437	2000	PINK PRINCESS	10	10	10
		SUPERSTAR			
2252	1977	SUPERSTAR FASHION	65	50	58
2480	1977	SUPERSTAR FASHION	65	50	58
2481	1977	SUPERSTAR FASHION	65	50	58
—	1979	SUPERSTAR ALTA MODA	30	30	30
		SWEATER SOFT FASHION			
4478	1987		22	20	21
4487	1987		20	16	18
		TAKARA			
—	1981	COLLECTORS DRESS French maid costume, wine bottle, glasses	55	45	50
—	1981	DRESS COLLECTION ski set red ski jumpsuit	55	45	50
—	1981	COLLECTORS DRESS JBL Airline Stewardess	55	50	53
—	1981	COORDINATE DRESS COLLECTION plaid blouse, yellow pants, bag, jacket, dress, boom box	92	58	75
—	1981	FASHION SENSE UP GOODS guitar, diary, books, pillow, teddy bear	89	52	71
		THE JEANS LOOK FASHION			
—	1987	THE JEANS LOOK FASHION	6	6	6
		TWICE AS NICE			
4824	1983	DOUBLE DAZZLE	8	5	7
4828	1983	PARTY PAIR	8	6	7
7951	1984		8	6	7
7952	1984		8	6	7
7953	1984		8	6	7
		WEDDING OF THE YEAR			
5743	1982	BRIDE	15	14	15
5745	1982	BRIDESMAID	12	10	11
3788	1989	BRIDE	12	10	11
5746	1989	BRIDESMAID	8	8	8
3790	1989	PINK	10	8	9
		WEDDING PARTY			
1416	1979	BRIDE	20	20	20
1417	1979	BRIDESMAID	16	15	16
7965	1984	BRIDE	17	15	15
7967	1984	BRIDESMAID	15	15	15

STOCK NO.	YEAR	DESCRIPTION	HIGH	LOW	AVG
		WESTERN FASHIONS			
3577	1981		10	6	8
3578	1981		13	10	12
		KEN			
1375	—	FASHION COLLECTIBLES	6	4	5
1377	—	FASHION COLLECTIBLES	6	4	5
1379	—	FASHION COLLECTIBLES	6	4	5
2791	—	FASHION COLLECTIBLES	6	4	5
2794	—	FASHION COLLECTIBLES	6	4	5
2064	1977	FASHION	18	16	17
3794	1981	FASHION FAVORITES	14	13	14
—	1988	JEANS FASHION	8	7	8
		MIDGE			
9632	1990	MIDGE WEDDING DAY FASHION	13	10	12
9635	1990	MIDGE WEDDING DAY FASHION	13	10	12
		SKIPPER			
9124	1975	BEST BUY FASHIONS	15	10	13
1942	1978	FASHION COLLECTIBLES	9	9	9
2803	1978	FASHION COLLECTIBLES	9	9	9
2806	1978	FASHION COLLECTIBLES	9	9	9
3778	1978	FASHION COLLECTIBLES	6	4	5
2811	1978	FASHION FAVORITES	22	20	21
1384	1979	FASHION COLLECTIBLES	12	10	11
1419	1979	WEDDING PARTY FASHIONS FLOWER GIRL	12	9	10
1943	1980	FASHION COLLECTIBLES	7	7	7
1945	1980	FASHION COLLECTIBLES	7	7	7
—	1980	FASHION FAVORITES CLAN-TASTIC	10	8	9
4275	1982	FASHION FANTASY	18	16	17
5811	1982	FASHION FANTASY	5	5	5
4876	1983	FASHION FANTASY	6	5	6
4878	1983	FASHION FANTASY	6	5	5
4882	1983	FASHION FANTASY FIRST DANCE	6	5	6
—	1983	FASHION FANTASY SHORT 'N SWEET	6	5	6
7983	1984	SO ACTIVE FASHIONS	5	4	4
7979	1984	SO ACTIVE FASHIONS	6	4	5
1968	1984	WEDDING PARTY FLOWER GIRL	12	10	11
1863	1986	JEWEL SECRETS	15	12	14
—	1988	LOOKIN' LIVELY	4	4	4
3791	1989	WEDDING OF THE YEAR	10	10	10
3371	—	BEST BUY	15	10	14

NEWER MISCELLANEOUS – SPECIAL EDITIONS

STOCK NO.	YEAR	DESCRIPTION	HIGH	LOW	AVG
10610	1993	ANGEL LIGHTS LE	125	50	88
14479	1995	MATTEL 50TH ANNIVERSARY	324	165	244
15780	1996	ANDALUCIA — FLEMENCO	75	30	53
15846	1996	EMPRESS SISSY LE	154	68	111
15948	1996	ESCADA	135	70	103
—	1997	PRINCESS SISSY (Europe)	131	61	96
—	1998	LIFE BALL (Austria) LE 1000 - Aids Life (Vivienne Westwood)	500	500	500
—	1999	BIEDERMEIER (Elfie Stelzer)	75	50	68
—	2000	BURBERRY	500	173	336
24994	2000	HANAE MORI - International exclusive	99	82	90
24636	2000	MANNS CHINESE THEATRE (white)	65	60	63
24998	2000	MANNS CHINESE THEATRE (black)	65	60	63
25792	2000	YUMING - STYLE	75	75	75

❖❖❖❖❖❖❖❖❖❖❖❖❖❖

PORCELAIN COLLECTION

STOCK NO.	YEAR	DESCRIPTION	NRFB HIGH	LOW	AVG
—	1980	BARBIE DOLL '59 Blonde - LE 12, 17" Marschang/Wilson	—	—	—
—	1980	BARBIE DOLL '59 Brunette - LE 12, 17" Marschang/Wilson	—	—	—
1708	1986	BLUE RHAPSODY, LE 6000	590	378	484
3415	1987	ENCHANTED EVENING, LE 10,000	485	129	252
5475	1988	BENEFIT PERFORMANCE, LE 10,000	446	133	230
2641	1989	WEDDING PARTY, LE 10,000	625	262	444
7613	1990	SOLO IN THE SPOTLIGHT	240	120	180
5313	1990	SOPHISTICATED LADY	225	100	168
9973-9993	1991	GAY PARISIENNE 1st Brunette *Porcelain Treasures Collection*	264	156	180
9973-9997	1991	GAY PARISIENNE* 1st Blonde (Disney) LE 300 *Porcelain Treasures Collection*	667	375	521
9973-9999	1991	GAY PARISIENNE* 1st Redhead (Disney) LE 300 *Porcelain Treasures Collection*	702	444	573
1110	1991	KEN - 30th ANNIVERSARY*	160	100	130
1553	1992	CRYSTAL RHAPSODY* Brunette (Disney)	695	400	548
5351	1992	PLANTATION BELLE* 2nd Blonde (Disney) LE 300 *Porcelain Treasures Collection*	605	425	515
7526	1992	PLANTATION BELLE 2nd Redhead *Porcelain Treasures Collection*	195	141	168
7957	1993	MIDGE - 30th ANNIVERSARY*	165	97	131
1249	1993	SILKEN FLAME 3rd Brunette *Porcelain Treasures Collection*	231	107	167
11099	1993	SILKEN FLAME Blonde* (Disney) LE 400	500	500	500
11396	1994	SKIPPER - 30th ANNIVERSARY* LE 7000	200	121	161
19364	2000	WIZARD OF OZ - Dorothy with Toto*		Retail	
23880	2000	WIZARD OF OZ - Wicked Witch*		Retail	

indicates cross reference

321

BOB MACKIE SERIES

STOCK NO.	YEAR	DESCRIPTION	NRFB HIGH	LOW	AVG
5405	1990	GOLD 1st	580	375	478
2704	1991	STARLIGHT SPLENDOR 2nd	625	580	603
2703	1991	PLATINUM 3rd	680	490	585
4248	1992	NEPTUNE'S FANTASY 4th	700	525	613
4247	1992	EMPRESS BRIDE 5th	757	465	611
10803	1993	MASQUERADE BALL 6th	484	295	389
12046	1994	QUEEN OF HEARTS 7th	360	195	271
14056	1995	GODDESS OF THE SUN 8th	195	135	165
14105	1996	MOON GODDESS 9th	190	120	155
17934	1997	MADAME DU BARBIE 10th	282	275	278
CELEBRATION OF DANCE SERIES (Porcelain)					
23451	1999	TANGO	299	217	258
CUSTOMIZED LIMITED EDITION					
23276	1999	LE PAPILLON* *FAO Exclusive*	300	135	219
	2000	Lady Liberty * *FAO Exclusive*, LE 15,000	300	160	230
INTERNATIONAL BEAUTY COLLECTION					
20648	1998	FANTASY GODDESS OF ASIA	240	138	188
22044	1999	FANTASY GODDESS OF AFRICA	240	130	185
25859	2000	FANTASY GODDESS OF THE AMERICAS		Retail	
JEWEL ESSENCE COLLECTION					
15522	1997	AMETHYST AURA*	165	92	129
15519	1997	DIAMOND DAZZLE*	174	96	135
15521	1997	EMERALD EMBERS*	142	88	115
15520	1997	RUBY RADIANCE*	142	87	114
15523	1997	SAPPHIRE SPLENDOR*	139	94	117

NOSTALGIC SERIES/ VINTAGE REPRODUCTIONS

STOCK NO.	YEAR	DESCRIPTION	NRFB HIGH	LOW	AVG
11590	1994	35th ANNIVERSARY Blonde (1st Edition Curved Eyebrow)	55	22	38
11782	1994	35th ANNIVERSARY Brunette (2nd Edition Arched Eyebrow)	60	25	36
11590	1994	35th ANNIVERSARY Blonde (2nd Edition Arched Eyebrow)	55	20	39
11591	1994	35th ANNIVERSARY GIFT SET* Blonde	125	75	110
11591	1994	35th ANNIVERSARY Brunette (Mattel Festival)	575	400	518
11782	1994	35th ANNIVERSARY Brunette (1st Edition Curved Eyebrow)	75	40	68
13675	1995	BUSY GAL	75	40	60
13534	1995	SOLO IN THE SPOTLIGHT Blonde	40	20	27
13820	1995	SOLO IN THE SPOTLIGHT Brunette	45	22	31
14608	1996	30th ANNIVERSARY* (Francie Gad-About)	90	30	59
14992	1996	ENCHANTED EVENING Blonde	45	20	30
15407	1996	ENCHANTED EVENING Brunette	50	20	33
15280	1996	POODLE PARADE	70	30	45
17382	1997	FASHION LUNCHEON	75	35	48
18448	1997	SILKEN FLAME Brunette	45	20	32
18449	1997	SILKEN FLAME Blonde	45	20	32
17119	1997	WEDDING DAY Blonde	40	15	25
17120	1997	WEDDING DAY Redhead	40	15	25
17607	1997	WILD BUNCH* (Francie)	62	30	45
18976	1998	MIDGE 35th ANNIVERSARY GIFT SET* Senior Prom Toys R Us	56	40	40
18941	1998	TWIST 'N TURN (SMASHEROO)* Brunette	70	30	45
		Collector's Request Limited Edition			
23258	1998	TWIST 'N TURN (SMASHEROO)* Redhead	70	30	45
		Collector's Request Limited Edition			
21510	1999	COMMUTER SET* Collector's Request Limited Edition	70	50	49

HAPPY HOLIDAYS SERIES

STOCK NO.	YEAR	DESCRIPTION	NRFB HIGH	LOW	AVG
1703	1988	HOLIDAY (red gown)	800	450	625
1703	1988	INTERNATIONAL HOLIDAY (red gown)	700	400	550
3523	1989	HOLIDAY (white gown)	270	175	222
4098	1990	HOLIDAY (white) fuchsia gown	160	120	140
4543	1990	HOLIDAY (black) fuchsia gown	145	85	115
1871	1991	HOLIDAY (white) green gown	200	110	155
2696	1991	HOLIDAY (black) green gown	160	80	120
1429	1992	HOLIDAY (white) silver gown	150	120	135
2396	1992	HOLIDAY (black) silver gown	130	95	107
10824	1993	HOLIDAY (white) red/gold gown	118	90	144
10911	1993	HOLIDAY (black) red/gold gown	112	80	70
12155	1994	HOLIDAY (white) gold gown	150	80	115
12155	1994	HOLIDAY* Brunette (gold gown) Festival, LE 540	1100	500	800
12156	1994	HOLIDAY (black) gold gown	110	59	85
14123	1995	HOLIDAY (white) 2 dress versions, green metallic gown	85	50	68
14124	1995	HOLIDAY (black) 2 dress versions, green metallic gown	93	55	74
14123	1995	HOLIDAY w/ornament* (green metallic gown) *JCPenney*	105	75	90
15646	1996	HOLIDAY (white) burgundy, gold, white fur	75	40	58
15647	1996	HOLIDAY (black) burgundy, gold, white fur	65	40	53
17832	1997	HOLIDAY (white) 2 box versions, red/white ribbon gown	55	15	35
17833	1997	HOLIDAY (black) 2 box versions, red/white ribbon gown	50	15	33
17832/ 20416	1997	HOLIDAY* Blonde (Mattel Official Barbie Collectors Club)	125	75	100
20200	1998	HOLIDAY (white) black gown	50	20	35
20201	1998	HOLIDAY (black) black gown	45	20	32

❖❖❖❖❖❖❖❖❖❖❖❖❖❖

HAPPY HOLIDAYS INDIA

STOCK NO.	YEAR	DESCRIPTION	NRFB HIGH	LOW	AVG
—	1996	HAPPY HOLIDAYS SE	150	125	135
—	1997	HAPPY HOLIDAYS SE	140	125	130
—	1998	HAPPY HOLIDAYS BARBIE & KEN GIFT SET*	130	80	105

❖❖❖❖❖❖❖❖❖❖❖❖❖❖

HAPPY HOLIDAYS INTERNATIONAL

STOCK NO.	YEAR	DESCRIPTION	NRFB HIGH	LOW	AVG
12432	1994	INTERNATIONAL HOLIDAY 1994	150	80	115
13545	1995	INTERNATIONAL HOLIDAY 1995	130	65	83
15816	1996	INTERNATIONAL HOLIDAY 1996	78	65	72

DOLLS OF THE WORLD/INTERNATIONALS

STOCK NO.	YEAR	DESCRIPTION	NRFB HIGH	LOW	AVG
1602	1980	ITALIAN	250	175	213
1600	1980	PARISIAN	225	125	175
1601	1980	ROYAL	210	150	180
3262	1981	ORIENTAL	150	125	138
3263	1981	SCOTTISH	170	120	145
3898	1982	ESKIMO	120	100	110
3897	1982	INDIA	160	125	143
4031	1983	SPANISH	110	95	103
4032	1983	SWEDISH	170	95	133
7517	1984	IRISH	145	125	135
7541	1984	SWISS	110	85	98
9481	1985	JAPANESE	180	95	137
2997	1986	GREEK	85	70	78
9841	1986/87	JAPANESE	185	90	135
2995	1986	PERUVIAN	85	70	78
3188	1987	GERMAN	110	65	88
3189	1987	ICELANDIC	110	95	103
4928	1988	CANADIAN (2 hair versions)	125	70	75
4929	1988	KOREAN	90	55	73
1917	1989	MEXICAN	50	35	43
1916	1989	RUSSIAN	75	60	68
9094	1990	BRAZILIAN	75	50	63
7376	1990	NIGERIAN	65	45	55
7330	1991	CZECHOSLOVAKIAN	130	99	115
9844	1991	ESKIMO (re-issue)	70	50	60
7329	1991	MALAYSIAN	70	45	58
9843	1991	PARISIAN (re-issue)	60	50	55
9845	1991	SCOTTISH (re-issue)	120	95	105
4973	1992	ENGLISH	75	65	70
4647	1992	JAMAICAN (blue earrings)	55	35	50
4647	1992	JAMAICAN (silver earrings)	80	40	60
4963	1992	SPANISH (re-issue)	55	45	50
3626	1993	AUSTRALIAN (2 box versions)	60	25	43
2256	1993	ITALIAN (re-issue - 2 box versions)	65	35	50
1753	1993	NATIVE AMERICAN I (2 box versions)	80	40	60
11180	1994	CHINESE	39	25	33

STOCK NO.	YEAR	DESCRIPTION	NRFB HIGH	LOW	AVG
12043	1994	DOLLS OF THE WORLD GIFT SET* (Dutch, Kenyan, Chinese)	85	75	80
11104	1994	DUTCH	40	37	39
11181	1994	KENYAN	40	25	33
11609	1994	NATIVE AMERICAN II	75	40	58
13939	1995	DOLLS OF THE WORLD GIFT SET* (German, Irish, Polynesian)	65	50	60
12698	1995	GERMAN (re-issue)	30	15	23
12998	1995	IRISH (re-issue)	55	37	46
14449	1995	MEXICAN (re-issue)	25	20	23
12699	1995	NATIVE AMERICAN III	40	25	33
12700	1995	POLYNESIAN	40	20	30
15283	1996	DOLLS OF THE WORLD GIFT SET* (Japanese, Norwegian, Indian)	85	75	80
15303	1996	GHANAIAN	35	10	23
14451	1996	INDIAN (re-issue)	32	10	21
14163	1996	JAPANESE (re-issue)	40	20	30
15304	1996	NATIVE AMERICAN IV* Toys R Us	40	25	33
14450	1996	NORWEGIAN (pink flowers) LE 3000	95	40	68
14450	1996	NORWEGIAN (red flowers)	40	30	35
16495	1997	ARCTIC	25	15	20
16499	1997	FRENCH	32	25	29
18558	1997	NATIVE AMERICAN V (mislabled as IV)	50	25	37
18560	1997	POLISH	25	25	25
16754	1997	PUERTO RICAN	30	25	27
16500	1997	RUSSIAN (re-issue)	30	25	27
18561	1997	THAI	25	25	25
18559	1998	CHILEAN	25	20	23
18560	1998	POLISH	25	20	23
21553	1999	AUSTRIAN	25	20	22
21507	1999	MOROCCAN	25	20	22
21506	1999	PERUVIAN	25	20	22
24672	2000	SWEDISH	30	20	25
24670	2000	SPANISH	30	20	25
24671	2000	NORTHWEST NATIVE AMERICAN	30	20	25

*indicates cross reference

STORE EXCLUSIVES & SPECIAL EDITIONS

STOCK NO.	YEAR	DESCRIPTION	NRFB HIGH	LOW	AVG
		40th ANNIVERSARY			
21384	1999	ANNIVERSARY BATHING SUIT (white)	40	30	35
22336	1999	ANNIVERSARY BATHING SUIT (black)	40	30	35
21923	1999	40th ANNIVERSARY CRYSTAL JUBILEE*	300	139	220
23041	1999	40th ANNIVERSARY GALA* Toy Fair Bumble Bee, LE 20,000	140	80	110
23276	1999	40th ANNIVERSARY Bob Mackie Le Papillion* *FAO Schwarz*	300	135	219
	2000	40th ANNIVERSARY - STEIFF BEAR LE 1500*	275	155	215
		A GARDEN OF FLOWERS			
22337	1999	ROSE	55	35	45
		AMERICAN BEAUTY SERIES			
4930	1988	MARDI GRAS	75	40	58
3966	1989	ARMY	40	30	35
		AMERICAN CLASSICS			
22831	1999	COCA-COLA DRIVE-IN WAITRESS	80	45	63
		AMERICAN STORIES			
12578	1995	COLONIAL	30	18	24
12577	1995	PILGRIM	32	20	26
12680	1995	PIONEER	30	20	25
14715	1996	AMERICAN INDIAN #1	40	20	30
14612	1996	CIVIL WAR NURSE	25	20	22
14756	1996	PIONEER SHOPKEEPER	25	20	23
17313	1997	AMERICAN INDIAN #2	30	25	27
17312	1997	PATRIOT	30	20	25
		AMES			
2909	1991	PARTY IN PINK	45	24	35
2452	1992	DENIM 'N LACE	35	25	30
5756	1992	HOT LOOKS	35	29	32
5654	1993	COUNTRY LOOKS	35	25	30
17695	1997	LADYBUG FUN*	25	15	20
19280	1998	ICE CREAM	20	20	20
22895	1999	STRAWBERRY PARTY	20	15	20
	2000	EXTREME 360	20	20	20
		APPLAUSE			
5315	1990	BARBIE STYLE	35	20	27
3406	1991	HOLIDAY	35	20	27
		ARTIST SERIES			
17783	1997	WATER LILY (Monet) 1st	132	87	110
19366	1998	SUNFLOWER (Van Gogh) 2nd	108	70	89
23884	1999	REFLECTIONS OF LIGHT (Renoir) 3rd	90	59	75

indicates cross reference

STORE EXCLUSIVES & SPECIAL EDITIONS
CONTINUED

STOCK NO.	YEAR	DESCRIPTION	NRFB HIGH	LOW	AVG
		AVON			
15201	1996	SPRING BLOSSOM (white)	32	20	26
15202	1996	SPRING BLOSSOM (black)	30	20	25
15571	1996	WINTER VELVET 1st (white) *Winter Theme*	35	20	27
15587	1996	WINTER VELVET 1st (black) *Winter Theme*	30	20	25
10746	1997	SPRING PETALS Blonde	39	22	31
16872	1997	SPRING PETALS Brunette	39	22	31
16871	1997	SPRING PETALS (black)	37	22	31
16353	1997	WINTER RHAPSODY 2nd Blonde *Winter Theme*	45	20	32
16873	1997	WINTER RHAPSODY 2nd Brunette *Winter Theme*	45	25	35
16354	1997	WINTER RHAPSODY 2nd (black) *Winter Theme*	40	20	30
17690	1997	MRS. P.F.E. ALBEE *Representative Exclusive* LE	65	40	53
20330	1998	MRS. P.F.E. ALBEE II	80	45	63
18658	1998	SPRING TEA PARTY (white)	30	20	25
—	1998	SPRING TEA PARTY (black)	30	20	25
19357	1998	WINTER SPLENDOR 3rd (white) *Winter Theme*	35	35	35
19358	1998	WINTER SPLENDOR 3rd (black) *Winter Theme*	35	35	35
20317	1999	STRAWBERRY SORBET (white)	45	25	35
20318	1999	LEMON LIME SORBET (black)	45	25	35
22202	1999	REPRESENTATIVE (white)	50	40	45
22203	1999	REPRESENTATIVE (black)	40	40	40
—	1999	REPRESENTATIVE Hispanic	35	30	32
—	2000	BLUSHING BRIDE (white) Representative	35	30	32
—	2000	BLUSHING BRIDE (black) Representative	35	30	32
		B. BOUTIQUE			
19020	1999	BOUTIQUE (England)	50	30	40
		BAKERY (McGlynn's and Others)			
1511	1991	DECO-PAC (white)	102	45	73
1534	1991	DECO-PAC (black)	95	40	68
		BALLERINA DREAMS (Singapore)			
—	1999	BALLERINA DREAMS SE	35	25	30
		BALLROOM BEAUTIES			
14070	1995	STARLIGHT WALTZ	90	40	65
14954	1995	STARLIGHT WALTZ* Brunette, LE 1500 (Disney)	450	225	338
15685	1996	MIDNIGHT WALTZ	75	40	58
16705	1996	MIDNIGHT WALTZ* Brunette, LE 10,000 *Barbie Shoppe Internet*	125	80	103
17763	1997	MOONLIGHT WALTZ	80	45	63
		BANDAI (JAPAN)			
—	1989	STAR PRINCESS (30th Anniversary)	250	225	235
—	1990	I LOVE BARBIE (Crystal Party - pink or blue)	80	40	60
—	1990	HAPPY BRIDAL (white dress or pink dress)	110	40	75
—	1990	I LOVE BARBIE (Afternoon Tea - blue or green)	75	60	68

* indicates cross reference

STORE EXCLUSIVES & SPECIAL EDITIONS
CONTINUED

STOCK NO.	YEAR	DESCRIPTION	NRFB HIGH	LOW	AVG
		BANDAI (JAPAN) (continued)			
—	—	ANNA (red/white gingham dress jacket, earrings, makeup, perfume)	60	50	55
—	—	ANNA (pink satin dress w/white lace makeup, hair bow, shoes)	65	55	60
—	—	BARBIE KITCHEN RESTAURANT (pink waitress outfit, food items, plates, cutlery)	165	140	153
—	—	CHRISTIE LAIN (lavender dotted dress w/pink tie, sweater/jacket)	65	60	63
—	—	MELODY DREAM (pink or green ball gowns)	95	85	90
—	—	NOZOMI (Pink sweater, blue shorts, boots, hair brush)	60	60	60
—	—	TALKING BARBIE (magenta satin dress - talks in Japanese)	125	115	120
		BARBIE MILLICENT ROBERTS COLLECTION			
16079	1996	BMR MATINEE TODAY*	60	40	50
17567	1997	BMR PERFECTLY SUITED*	75	30	52
19791	1998	PINSTRIPE POWER*	50	25	37
		BILL BLASS			
17040	1997	BILL BLASS BARBIE	90	40	65
		BARBIE 2000			
27409	2000	BARBIE (white)		Retail	
27410	2000	BARBIE (black)		Retail	
		BILLY BOY			
3421	1986	BILLY BOY - FEELING GROOVY "Glamour-a-go-go"	278	92	185
6279	1986	BILLY BOY* (French - 2 versions) Le Nouveau Theatre de la Mode	334	115	225
		BIRDS OF BEAUTY COLLECTION (Mystery of Nature)			
19365	1998	PEACOCK 1st	100	60	80
22957	1999	FLAMINGO 2nd	100	60	80
27682	2000	SWAN		Retail	
		BIRTHDAY WISHES COLLECTION			
21228	1999	BIRTHDAY WISHES (white)	40	24	32
21509	1999	BIRTHDAY WISHES (black)	40	24	32
24667	2000	BIRTHDAY WISHES (white)	50	35	43
24668	2000	BIRTHDAY WISHES (black)	50	35	43
		BLOKKER			
15611	1996	100th ANNIVERSARY(Belgium/Netherlands)	65	40	53
		BLOOMINGDALE'S			
12152	1994	SAVVY SHOPPER - Nicole Miller	60	40	50
14452	1995	DONNA KARAN - DKNY Brunette	90	50	70
14545	1995	DONNA KARAN - DKNY Blonde	80	45	63
16290	1996	BARBIE AT BLOOMINGDALE'S* (Souvenir Shopper) SE	30	15	23
16211	1996	CALVIN KLEIN	60	35	48
15950	1997	RALPH LAUREN	75	43	59

indicates cross reference

STORE EXCLUSIVES & SPECIAL EDITIONS
CONTINUED

STOCK NO.	YEAR	DESCRIPTION	NRFB HIGH	LOW	AVG
		BLOOMINGDALE'S (continued)			
20376	1998	OSCAR DE LA RENTA*	61	36	49
		BRIDAL COLLECTION			
27674	2000	MILLENNIUM WEDDING (white)		Retail	
27764	2000	MILLENNIUM WEDDING (black)		Retail	
27765	2000	MILLENNIUM WEDDING (Hispanic)		Retail	
		CELESTIAL COLLECTION			
27690	2000	EVENING - STAR PRINCESS		Retail	
27688	2000	MORNING - SUN PRINCESS		Retail	
27689	2000	MIDNIGHT - MOON PRINCESS		Retail	
		CHILDREN'S COLLECTOR SERIES			
13016	1995	RAPUNZEL 1st	64	41	52
14960	1996	LITTLE BO PEEP 2nd	149	101	125
16900	1997	CINDERELLA 3rd	42	24	33
18586	1998	SLEEPING BEAUTY 4th	38	19	29
21130	1999	SNOW WHITE 5th	40	30	35
24673	2000	BEAUTY 6th - Final	40	40	40
		CHILDREN'S DAY (Germany)			
18350	1998	CHILDREN'S DAY	35	20	27
		CHILDREN'S PALACE/CHILD WORLD			
4217	1989	DANCE CLUB GIFT SET*	65	40	53
4385	1990	DISNEY (white)	60	29	44
9385	1990	DISNEY (black)	52	27	39
		CHRISTIAN DIOR			
13168	1995	CHRISTIAN DIOR	110	46	78
16013	1996	CHRISTIAN DIOR II (50th Anniversary House of Dior)	98	40	69
		CHUCK E. CHEESE			
14615	1996	CHUCK E. CHEESE	40	20	30
		CITY SEASONS COLLECTION			
19367	1998	AUTUMN IN PARIS 1st	65	30	47
19430	1998	SPRING IN TOKYO 4th	55	30	43
19363	1998	SUMMER IN SAN FRANCISCO* 3rd Blonde *FAO Schwarz*	80	55	67
—	1998	SUMMER IN SAN FRANCISCO* Redhead, LE 50 *FAO Schwarz*	150	135	140
19429	1998	WINTER IN NEW YORK 2nd	45	30	40
22257	1999	AUTUMN IN LONDON 6th	50	30	40
23499	1999	SPRING IN TOKYO VINTAGE* (*Barbie Collectibles, Internet & Japan Exclusive*)	50	20	35
19431	1999	SUMMER IN ROME 5th	40	30	35
22258	1999	WINTER IN MONTREAL 7th	40	30	35

indicates cross reference

STORE EXCLUSIVES & SPECIAL EDITIONS
CONTINUED

STOCK NO.	YEAR	DESCRIPTION	NRFB HIGH	LOW	AVG
		CLASSIC BALLET SERIES			
17056	1997	SUGAR PLUM FAIRY(Nut Cracker) 1st	40	30	35
18509	1998	SWAN QUEEN IN SWAN LAKE (white) 2nd	35	30	32
18510	1998	SWAN QUEEN IN SWAN LAKE (black) 2rd	30	30	30
20851	1999	MARZIPAN (Nutcracker) 3rd	32	30	31
25642	2000	SNOW FLAKE 4th	40	20	35
		CLASSIQUE SERIES			
1521	1992	BENEFIT BALL Carol Spencer	106	75	90
10149	1993	CITY STYLE Janet Goldblatt	90	45	67
10148	1993	OPENING NIGHT Janet Goldblatt	95	54	67
11622	1994	EVENING EXTRAVAGANZA (white) Kitty Black Perkins	92	48	70
11638	1994	EVENING EXTRAVAGANZA (black) Kitty Black Perkins	85	54	70
11623	1994	UPTOWN CHIC Kitty Black Perkins	125	72	96
12999	1995	MIDNIGHT GALA Abbe Littleton	82	40	61
15461	1996	STARLIGHT DANCE (white) Cynthia Young	55	30	43
15819	1996	STARLIGHT DANCE (black) Cynthia Young	55	30	43
17136	1997	ROMANTIC INTERLUDE (white) Ann Driskill	45	30	37
17137	1997	ROMANTIC INTERLUDE (black) Ann Driskill	40	30	35
19361	1998	EVENING SOPHISTICATE	50	30	40
		CLOTHES MINDED COLLECTION			
22833	1999	TREND FORECASTER	50	30	40
		COLLECTOR'S REQUEST LIMITED EDITION			
21510	1999	COMMUTER SET 2nd*	70	50	60
18941	1999	TWIST 'N TURN (SMASHEROO)* 1st Brunette	70	30	50
23258	1999	TWIST 'N TURN (SMASHEROO)* 1st Redhead	70	40	45
24930	2000	SOPHISTICATED LADY 3rd	60	60	60
		COCA-COLA SERIES			
22831	1999	COCA-COLA #1 (car hop)	75	40	57
—	1999	COCO-COLA #1 Brunette - *Walt Disney World*, LE 1500	100	75	88
24637	2000	COCA-COLA #2	60	45	53
25678	2000	SWEETHEART KEN*	60	60	60
		COOL COLLECTING			
25525	2000	NOSTALGIC TOYS	60	35	48
		DIRECT MAIL (BARBIE COLLECTIBLES/TIMELESS CREATIONS)			
		Angels of Music Collection			
18894	1998	HARPIST ANGEL (white)	75	35	55
20551	1998	HARPIST ANGEL (black)	75	35	55
21414	1999	HEARTSTRING ANGEL (white)	80	40	60
21915	1999	HEARTSTRING ANGEL (black)	79	40	59

indicates cross reference

STORE EXCLUSIVES & SPECIAL EDITIONS
CONTINUED

STOCK NO.	YEAR	DESCRIPTION	NRFB HIGH	LOW	AVG
B.M. Jewel Essence Collection					
15522	1997	AMETHYST AURA*	165	92	129
15519	1997	DIAMOND DAZZLE*	174	96	135
15521	1997	EMERALD EMBERS*	142	88	115
15520	1997	RUBY RADIANCE*	142	87	114
15523	1997	SAPPHIRE SPLENDOR*	139	94	117
Barbie Shoppe Internet					
16705	1996	MIDNIGHT WALTZ* Brunette, LE 10,000	125	80	103
23499	1999	VINTAGE SPRING IN TOKYO *	50	20	35
Celebrating 40 Years of Dreams					
23041	1999	40th ANNIVERSARY GALA - 40 BARBIE - LE 20,000, Bumble Bee*	95	80	87
Coca-Cola Fashion Classic Series					
15762	1996	SODA FOUNTAIN SWEETHEART 1st	130	60	95
17341	1997	AFTER THE WALK* 2nd	70	30	50
19739	1998	SUMMER DAYDREAMS 3rd	72	35	52
Enchanted Seasons Collection					
11875	1994	SNOW PRINCESS 1st	110	80	95
12905	1994	SNOW PRINCESS* Brunette (Mattel Festival) LE 285	840	500	660
12989	1995	SPRING BOUQUET 2nd	105	70	87
15204	1996	AUTUMN GLORY 3rd	100	70	85
15683	1997	SUMMER SPLENDOR 4th	100	70	85
Fabergé Porcelain Collection					
19816	1998	IMPERIAL ELEGANCE	400	168	284
27028	2000	IMPERIAL SPLENDOR	400	400	400
(The) Gold and Silver Porcelain Barbie Set					
10246	1993	GOLD SENSATION ("1st in a set") LE 15,000	225	141	183
11305	1994	SILVER STARLIGHT ("2nd in a set") LE 8500	230	120	175
Grand Ole Opry					
17782	1997	COUNTRY ROSE* C.E.	75	35	55
17864	1998	RISING STAR	70	30	50
23498	1999	COUNTRY DUET	70	30	50
Haute Couture Collection (Robert Best)					
15528	1996	PORTRAIT IN TAFFETA 1st	135	47	91
17572	1997	SERENADE IN SATIN 2nd	160	135	148
20186	1998	SYMPHONY IN CHIFFON 3rd (white)	85	61	73
21295	1998	SYMPHONY IN CHIFFON 3rd (black)	80	58	69
21923	1999	CRYSTAL JUBILEE 4th* 40th Anniversary LE	300	139	220

indicates cross reference

STORE EXCLUSIVES & SPECIAL EDITIONS
CONTINUED

STOCK NO.	YEAR	DESCRIPTION	NRFB HIGH	LOW	AVG
Holiday Porcelain Collection					
14311	1995	HOLIDAY JEWEL 1st	190	110	150
15760	1996	HOLIDAY CAROLER 2nd	162	70	116
18326	1997	HOLIDAY BALL 3rd	105	60	83
20128	1998	HOLIDAY GIFT 4th	122	81	101
Hong Kong Commemorative Edition					
16708	1997	CHINESE EMPRESS* LE	150	90	120
20649	1998	GOLDEN QI-PAO* (Asia) LE 8888	76	42	59
Inspirational Series					
27286	2000	Goddess of Beauty and Love	Retail		
28112	2000	Goddess of Spring	Retail		
Lifestyles of the West Collection					
23205	1999	WESTERN PLAINS	80	70	75
Masquerade Gala Collection					
18867	1998	ILLUSION BARBIE	132	72	102
20647	1998	RENDEZVOUS	89	73	60
24501	2000	VENETION OPULENCE	89	89	89
Oscar de La Renta					
20376	1999	OSCAR DE LA RENTA*	61	36	49
Presidential Porcelain Collection					
1553	1992	CRYSTAL RHAPSODY 1st, Blonde, LE 15,000	174	128	151
1553	1992	CRYSTAL RHAPSODY* Brunette (Disney) LE 250	600	385	492
10950	1993	ROYAL SPLENDOR 2nd, LE 10,000	130	91	111
12825	1996	EVENING PEARL 3rd	135	117	151
Royal Jewel Collection					
25680	2000	EMPRESS OF EMERALDS* *QVC*	100	100	100
26926	2000	QUEEN OF SAPPHIRES	100	100	100
Runway Collection					
17031	1997	IN THE LIMELIGHT 1st Byron Lars, LE	228	151	190
19848	1998	CINNABAR SENSATION (black)	95	36	65
23420	1999	CINNABAR SENSATION (white)	71	49	60
23478	1999	PLUM ROYALE	151	67	109
26935	2000	INDIGO OBSESSION	Retail		
Ultimate Collection					
24505	2000	MILLENNIUM BRIDE	Retail		
Vera Wang – Designers Salute to Hollywood					
19788	1998	VERA WANG 1st*	143	79	111
23027	1999	VERA WANG 2nd	103	54	78

* indicates cross reference

STORE EXCLUSIVES & SPECIAL EDITIONS
CONTINUED

STOCK NO.	YEAR	DESCRIPTION	NRFB HIGH	LOW	AVG
Victorian Tea Porcelain Collection					
20983	1999	MINT MEMORIES	225	101	163
25507	2000	ORANGE PEKOE	248	150	198
Wedding Flower Collection					
12953	1995	STAR LILY BRIDE 1st	180	149	164
14541	1996	ROMANTIC ROSE BRIDE 2nd	180	135	157
16962	1997	BLUSHING ORCHID BRIDE 3rd	140	78	109
		DISNEY			
10722	1992	EURO DISNEY - DISNEY WEEKEND	80	20	60
10247	1993	DISNEY FUN	75	30	52
10723	1993	DISNEY WEEKEND BARBIE GIFT SET*	60	50	55
10724	1993	DISNEY WEEKEND BARBIE AND KEN GIFT SET*	70	65	68
11587	1993	TOON TOWN* (Stacie)	35	25	30
11650	1994	DISNEY FUN II	55	35	45
13533	1995	DISNEY FUN III	45	30	38
12957	1995	DISNEY FUN (Europe)	75	50	62
16525	1996	DISNEY 25th ANNIVERSARY DISNEYWORLD	45	15	30
17058	1997	DISNEY FUN IV	40	30	35
20363	1998	ANIMAL KINGDOM (white)	30	15	17
20989	1998	ANIMAL KINGDOM (black)	30	15	17
20315	1998	DISNEY WEEKEND FUN - BARBIE, KEN, KELLY & TOMMY DISNEYLAND GIFT SET*	70	26	48
20221	1998	DISNEY WEEKEND FUN - BARBIE, KEN, KELLY & TOMMY WALT DISNEY WORLD GIFT SET*	70	26	48
18970	1998	SAFARI	35	25	30
24105	1999	TOYSTORY - Tour Guide	40	20	30
—	2000	WALT DISNEY WORLD	40	20	30
		ELLESSE (ski) Asian Market LE			
—	1996	ELLESSE SNOW WEAR COLLECTION (5 versions)	60	56	61
		ENCHANTED WORLD OF FAIRIES COLLECTION			
25639	2000	FAIRY OF THE FOREST	60	50	55
		ESSENCE OF NATURE COLLECTION			
19847	1998	WATER RHAPSODY 1st	85	67	76
22834	1999	WHISPERING WIND 2nd	80	80	80
26327	2000	DANCING FIRE 3rd	80	80	80
		ESTRELA			
—	1979	SUPER STAR BARBIE (Brazil)	200	125	163
—	1986	BARBIE & BOB (Em Rit Mo De Rock) Brazil	400	300	350
—	1988	ANIMAL LOVIN'* (Viky - Brazil)	100	80	90
105038	1988	CHARME EM LINGERIE	95	75	85
—	1988	ROCK STAR* (Viky - Brazil)	130	100	115

*indicates cross reference

STORE EXCLUSIVES & SPECIAL EDITIONS
CONTINUED

STOCK NO.	YEAR	DESCRIPTION	NRFB HIGH	LOW	AVG
		ESTRELA continued			
—	1989	PASSEIO* (Viky - Brazil)	120	86	103
—	1989	FRAGANSI* (Laura - Brazil)	90	80	85
—	1989	ROCK STAR (Brazil)	150	100	125
105020	—	BRIDE BARBIE (Brazil)	150	95	123
—	—	GLAMOUR* (Diva)	200	100	150
—	—	MODA FACIL (Brazil)	40	25	33
		EXPO (World's Fair)			
18616	1998	EXPO '98 (Lisbon Portugal)	100	75	88
		EXPRESSIONS OF INDIA SERIES (Premium Collector Dolls)			
—	1997	MYSTICAL MANIPURI	85	55	70
—	1997	RAJASTHANI BARBIE AND KELLY	125	85	105
—	1997	PUNJABI	85	41	63
—	1997	SUNDARI	85	50	68
—	1998	BARBIE AND KEN BRIDAL SET (Rajasthani)	130	80	45
—	1997	RAJASTHANI BARBIE	85	41	63
		F.A. HOFFMAN, IDEE & SPIEL			
—	1996	100th ANNIVERSARY - STEPPIN' OUT	50	40	45
		FAIRWEATHERS CLOTHING STORE (Canada)			
18984	1997	DANIEL HECHTER, LE	48	25	35
		FAO SCHWARZ			
7734	1989	GOLDEN GREETINGS	101	76	89
5946	1990	WINTER FANTASY	100	50	75
5946	1990	WINTER FANTASY (w/extra head)	110	55	83
2921	1991	NIGHT SENSATION	61	26	44
1539	1992	MADISON AVENUE	61	24	43
2017	1993	ROCKETTE, LE	115	60	88
12749	1994	SHOPPING SPREE	40	20	30
11652	1994	SILVER SCREEN	101	46	74
13257	1995	CIRCUS STAR	69	40	55
14061	1995	JEWELED SPLENDOR (125th Anniversary)	91	63	49
13516	1995	WINTER SPORTS* *FAO, JCPenney, Toys R Us*	35	25	30
17298	1997	BARBIE DOLL AT FAO	35	10	23
20377	1998	PHANTOM OF THE OPERA GIFT SET* (also at select theaters)	153	125	139
19850	1998	WINTER RIDE GIFT SET*	86	31	59
		American Beauty Collection			
14664	1996	STATUE OF LIBERTY 1st	105	51	76
17557	1997	GEORGE WASHINGTON 2nd	55	28	42
		City Seasons Collection			
19363	1998	SUMMER IN SAN FRANCISCO* Blonde	168	93	131
—	1998	SUMMER IN SAN FRANCISCO* Redhead, LE 50	250	135	193

indicates cross reference

STORE EXCLUSIVES & SPECIAL EDITIONS
CONTINUED

STOCK NO.	YEAR	DESCRIPTION	NRFB HIGH	LOW	AVG
Customized Limited Edition					
23276	1999	LE PAPILLON* Bob Mackie	300	135	219
—	2000	LADY LIBERTY	300	160	230
Floral Signature Collection					
15814	1996	ANTIQUE ROSE, LE 10,000	192	152	172
17556	1997	LILY, LE 10,000	138	95	117
		FASHION MODEL COLLECTION			
26930	2000	LINGERIE Blonde		Retail	
26931	2000	LINGERIE Brunette		Retail	
26929	2000	DELPHINE*		Retail	
		FASHION SAVVY			
17860	1997	TANGERINE TWIST (black)	30	21	26
19632	1998	UPTOWN CHIC	36	16	26
		FRED MEYER			
17695	1997	LADYBUG FUN*	25	15	20
19280	1998	ICE CREAM*	20	20	20
		FRIENDSHIP (German Reunification - Berlin Wall)			
5506	1990	FRIENDSHIP 1st (pale pink dress)	50	25	38
2080	1991	FRIENDSHIP 2nd (pink skirt)	40	15	28
3677	1992	FRIENDSHIP 3rd (red hearts)	30	12	21
		GAP			
16449	1996	GAP (white)	60	30	45
16450	1996	GAP (black)	50	35	43
18547	1997	GAP GIFT SET* (white)	50	37	49
18548	1997	GAP GIFT SET* (black)	50	35	43
		GIVENCHY			
24635	2000	GIVENCHY - Fashion Design Series	80	80	80
		GREAT ERAS			
3702	1993	GIBSON GIRL 1st	75	41	58
4063	1993	FLAPPER 2nd	102	68	85
11397	1994	EGYPTIAN QUEEN 3rd	85	46	66
11478	1994	SOUTHERN BELLE 4th	68	56	62
12791	1995	MEDIEVAL LADY 5th	55	36	46
12792	1995	ELIZABETHAN QUEEN 6th	60	36	48
15005	1996	GRECIAN GODDESS 7th	87	21	29
14900	1996	VICTORIAN LADY 8th	46	20	33
16707	1997	FRENCH LADY 9th	36	23	30
16708	1997	CHINESE EMPRESS 10th	62	30	46
—	1997	CHINESE EMPRESS* (Hong Kong Commemorative Edition)	150	90	120

* indicates cross reference

STORE EXCLUSIVES & SPECIAL EDITIONS
CONTINUED

STOCK NO.	YEAR	DESCRIPTION	NRFB HIGH	LOW	AVG
		GREAT FASHIONS OF THE 20th CENTURY			
18630	1998	PROMENADE IN THE PARK 1st	41	25	33
19631	1998	1920's DANCE 'TIL DAWN 2nd	45	22	34
21531	1998	1930's STEPPIN' OUT 3rd	36	26	31
22162	1999	FABULOUS FORTIES 4th	59	59	59
		GREAT PORCELAIN AND CRYSTAL HOUSES			
25641	2000	WEDGWOOD	92	70	81
		HALLMARK GOLD CROWN EXCLUSIVES			
12579	1994	VICTORIAN ELEGANCE 1st	36	12	24
14106	1995	HOLIDAY MEMORIES 2nd	31	16	22
15621	1996	YULETIDE ROMANCE 3rd/last	31	16	21
		Be My Valentine Collector Series			
14880	1996	SWEET VALENTINE 1st	35	16	26
16536	1997	SENTIMENTAL VALENTINE 2nd	33	11	22
18091	1998	FAIR VALENTINE 3rd	31	16	24
		Holiday Homecoming Collector Series			
17094	1997	HOLIDAY TRADITIONS 1st	47	15	31
18651	1998	HOLIDAY VOYAGE 2nd	45	21	33
19792	1999	HOLIDAY SENSATION 3rd/final	38	27	33
		HARRODS/HAMLEYS/SELFRIDGES (England)			
17590	1996	EASY CHIC, LE 250 (also Harrods - England)	800	400	600
15513	1996	WEST END, LE 20,000 (England)	40	10	25
		HILLS			
4843	1989	PARTY LACE	45	35	40
3274	1990	EVENING SPARKLE	45	30	37
3549	1991	MOONLIGHT ROSE, LE	62	29	46
1879	1992	BLUE ELEGANCE	60	45	53
12412	1994	*POLLY POCKET*	30	20	25
13940	1995	SEA PEARL MERMAID	25	20	22
15684	1996	TEDDY FUN	23	15	19
19784	1998	SIDEWALK CHALK*	22	15	18
		HOLIDAY ANGELS			
28080	2000	HOLIDAY ANGEL (white)	Retail		
28081	2000	HOLIDAY ANGEL (black)	Retail		
		HOLLYWOOD LEGENDS			
12701	1994	DOROTHY Wizard of Oz 1st version (cardboard lid)	150	86	118
12045	1994	SCARLETT O'HARA (green)	94	50	72
12815	1994	SCARLETT O'HARA (red)	106	50	78
12997	1994	SCARLETT O'HARA (green/white) picnic	90	40	65

indicates cross reference

STOCK NO.	YEAR	DESCRIPTION	NRFB HIGH	LOW	AVG
		HOLLYWOOD LEGENDS continued			
13254	1994	SCARLETT O'HARA (black/white) New Orleans	90	40	65
12701	1995	DOROTHY Wizard of Oz 2nd version (plastic lid)	125	53	88
14901	1995	GLINDA THE GOOD WITCH (Wizard of Oz)	110	85	98
13676	1995	MARIA	50	30	40
12741	1995	KEN AS RHETT BUTLER*	78	38	58
16497	1996	KEN AS SCARECROW* (Wizard of Oz)	138	70	104
14902	1996	KEN AS TIN MAN* (Wizard of Oz)	100	50	78
15497	1996	MY FAIR LADY #2 (Ascot)	89	20	55
15498	1996	MY FAIR LADY #3 (flowers)	75	25	50
15500	1996	MY FAIR LADY #4 (Embassy Ball)	99	40	69
15501	1996	MY FAIR LADY #1 (pink)	75	25	50
15499	1996	PROFESSOR HENRY HIGGINS - KEN* (My Fair Lady)	78	40	,59
16573	1997	KEN AS COWARDLY LION* (Wizard of Oz)	180	140	160
17452	1997	MARILYN MONROE (red) Gentlemen Prefer Blondes	70	38	54
17451	1997	MARILYN MONROE (pink) Gentlemen Prefer Blondes	65	42	54
17455	1997	MARILYN MONROE (white) Seven Year Itch	65	40	53
		HOLLYWOOD MOVIE STAR COLLECTION			
26914	2000	HOLLYWOOD PREMIERE, 1st	50	50	50
26925	2000	BY THE POOL, 2nd		Retail	
		HOME SHOPPING CLUB			
1865	1991	EVENING FLAME	165	142	154
19788	1999	VERA WANG, 1st*	143	79	111
—	1999	GOLDEN ALLURE LE 30,000	25	20	22
—	1999	PREMIERE NIGHT	37	20	28
		HUDSON BAY			
—	1995	CITY STYLE (325th Anniversary) LE 3000	115	105	110
—	1995	GOVERNOR'S BALL	115	80	97
—	1996	ARCADIAN COURT	120	75	97
63987	1996	SWEET MOMENTS GIFT SET*	50	40	45
—	1997	BARBIE ON BAY	40	20	30
63569	1997	SCHOOL SPIRIT	40	35	38
—	1997	TOYLAND JOU JOU	40	35	38
		JAPAN AIR LINES			
64347	1997	JAL, LE 30,000, domestic flights	165	165	165
		JCPENNEY			
2820	1991	WEDDING DAY KELLY & TODD GIFT SET*	40	25	33
11285	1993	CABOODLES BARBIE & CABOODLES CASE	35	25	30
12665	1994	HAPPY MEAL STACIE & WHITNEY GIFT SET*	35	25	30
14123	1995	HAPPY HOLIDAY w/ornament*	105	75	90
14406	1995	*POLLY POCKET* GIFT SET*	40	20	30
14073	1995	TRAVELIN' SISTERS PLAYSET*	60	35	47

indicates cross reference

STORE EXCLUSIVES & SPECIAL EDITIONS
CONTINUED

STOCK NO.	YEAR	DESCRIPTION	NRFB HIGH	LOW	AVG
		JCPENNEY (continued)			
13516	1995	WINTER SPORTS* *FAO, JCPenney, Toys R Us*	35	25	30
15441	1996	ARIZONA JEANS #1	32	18	25
16567	1996	FOAM 'N COLOR GIFT SET*	40	20	30
16568	1996	GYMNAST STACIE*	30	20	25
18020	1997	ARIZONA JEAN CO #2	30	20	25
19873	1998	ARIZONA JEAN CO #3	20	15	17
		Evening Elegance Series			
7057	1990	EVENING ELEGANCE (2 dress variations)	100	60	80
2702	1991	ENCHANTED EVENING	108	60	84
1278	1992	EVENING SENSATION	70	50	60
10684	1993	GOLDEN WINTER	68	45	56
12191	1994	NIGHT DAZZLE Blonde	70	40	55
14010	1995	ROYAL ENCHANTMENT	60	40	50
15570	1996	WINTER RENAISSANCE	45	40	43
17235	1997	EVENING MAJESTY	45	35	40
19783	1998	EVENING ENCHANTMENT	40	25	33
		JUBILEE			
3756	1989	PINK JUBILEE (Convention Doll) LE 1200	1100	610	855
12009	1994	GOLD JUBILEE, LE 5000	490	312	406
12009	1994	GOLD JUBILEE (International) LE 2000	450	300	375
		K-MART			
4870	1989	PEACH PRETTY	40	25	32
7026	1991	PARTY DRESS FASHION FRIENDS*	35	20	27
7010	1991	PRETTY TEEN FASHION FRIENDS*	28	20	24
7019	1991	SWIM SUIT FASHION FRIENDS*	24	20	22
3117	1992	PRETTY IN PURPLE (white)	40	20	30
3121	1992	PRETTY IN PURPLE (black)	35	20	27
18506	1998	MARCH OF DIMES - WALKAMERICA (white)	20	20	20
18507	1998	MARCH OF DIMES - WALKAMERICA (black)	20	20	20
20843	1999	WALK AMERICA - March of Dimes Gift Set* (white)	25	12	19
20844	1999	WALK AMERICA - March of Dimes Gift Set* (black)	25	12	19
—	2000	BBQ BASH	18	15	17
		KASTNER & OEHLER			
—	1999	KASTNER & OEHLER LE 100	—	—	—
		KAY BEE			
18594	1997	FANTASY BALL	35	20	27
19708	1998	STARLIGHT CAROUSEL	24	15	20
20782	1998	FASHION AVENUE	19	15	17
10924	1993	WEDDING FANTASY GIFT SET	75	50	63

STORE EXCLUSIVES & SPECIAL EDITIONS
CONTINUED

STOCK NO.	YEAR	DESCRIPTION	NRFB HIGH	LOW	AVG
		KEBAYA (Malaysia) (Special Series)			
—	1998	PINK	40	20	30
—	1998	GREEN	40	20	30
—	1998	WHITE	40	20	30
		KEEPSAKE TREASURES			
19360	1998	THE TALE OF PETER RABBIT	42	30	36
		KRESGE			
9805	1977	BARBIE & HER SUPER FASHION FIREWORKS (3 styles)	125	95	118
		LAZARUS			
—	1995	BLACK DIAMOND, LE 1000	495	325	410
—	1995	FUR COAT (assorted colors)	125	80	103
—	1995	FUR COAT (dark green mink)	200	125	163
—	1995	FUR COAT (pink mink)	299	125	213
		MA BA (JAPAN)			
—	1986	BARBIES FRIEND* (Noel) High School Series	105	95	100
—	1986	BEAUTIFUL BARBIE - PRINCESS FANTASY	150	85	95
—	1986	DIAMOND DREAM BARBIE	150	90	110
—	1986	PB BRIDE Brunette Ponytail (Red Kimono)	200	150	170
—	1986	PET ON PET (Barbie-Mouse)	185	100	130
—	1986	PET ON PET (Barbie-Bear)	100	70	85
—	1986	PET ON PET (Barbie-Rabbit - white satin dress, rabbit ear head piece, socks, shoes)	85	75	80
—	1987	CAMPUS COLLECTION	120	85	95
—	1987	CAMPUS COLLECTION SCHOOL GIRL	95	85	90
—	1987	CITY BARBIE COLLECTION (red/white plaid dress)	100	80	90
—	1987	CREPE SHOP (pink waitress uniform, pumps, pink bow tie)	100	75	85
—	1987	PART OF THE CAMPUS COLLECTION (Bandai)	80	50	65
—	1987	PB BARBIE (red gown)	400	300	365
—	1987	PB BARBIE Brunette Bubble Cut	400	300	365
—	1987	PB BARBIE Blonde Ponytail	400	300	365
—	1987	PB BARBIE (black/white checked dress)	400	300	365
—	1988	PB PINK GOWN/WHITE JACKET (Brunette Ponytail)	200	125	170
—	1988	SUPER DRESS	80	50	65
—	1997	KEN* (Japan - white sleeveless sweater, white polo shirt, shorts, loafers, watch, glasses)	150	100	125
—	—	BARBIE IN LA (blue & white lace up front short dress, white blouse, pumps, hair bow)	85	75	80
—	—	BEAUTY & DREAM (crimped hair, pink satin dress w/white overskirt)	85	75	80
—	—	FANTASY	95	90	92
—	—	PET ON PET (red skirt w/black cats)	95	90	92
—	—	PRINCESS (pale yellow satin dress w/white lace & pearls, red bow, earrings)	85	75	80

indicates cross reference

STORE EXCLUSIVES & SPECIAL EDITIONS
CONTINUED

STOCK NO.	YEAR	DESCRIPTION	NRFB HIGH	LOW	AVG
		MA BA (JAPAN) (continued)			
—	—	RESORT (calico skirt, brown & white gingham jacket, hat, shoes)	85	80	82
—	—	SCHOOL GIRL (black school blazer, blue dress, red tie, black beret, socks, loafers)	95	85	90
—	—	SCHOOL GIRL - TENNIS (pale yellow outfit, white sweater, racket, ball, pink head band, shoes, socks)	95	85	92
		MACY'S			
16289	1996	CITY SHOPPER - NICOLE MILLER	46	24	35
17603	1997	ANNE KLEIN	39	23	31
		MAGIC AND MYSTERY			
27287	2000	MERLIN AND MORGAN LEFAY		Retail	
		MAJOR LEAGUE BASEBALL			
23881	1999	YANKEES (white)	50	40	35
24471	1999	YANKEES (black)	50	40	35
23882	1999	DODGERS (white)	50	40	35
24472	1999	DODGERS (black)	50	40	35
23883	1999	CUBS (white)	50	40	35
24473	1999	CUBS (black)	50	40	35
		MATTEL OFFICIAL BARBIE COLLECTORS CLUB			
16498	1997	GRAND PREMIERE MEMBERS CHOICE - 1st edition	120	66	93
17832	1997	HAPPY HOLIDAYS* Blonde	125	75	100
18892	1998	CAFE SOCIETY (Carol Spencer) 2nd	99	52	75
23041	1999	40TH ANNIVERSARY GALA - 40 Barbie - Celebrating 40 years of Dreams, LE 20,000 Bumble Bee*	140	80	110
22836	1999	EMBASSY WALTZ - 3rd	59	59	59
26068	2000	CLUB COUTURE - 4th	59	59	59
		MATTEL BARBIE SHOPPE INTERNET			
16705	1996	MIDNIGHT WALTZ* Brunette, LE 10,000 *Ballroom Beauties*	195	85	140
		MATTEL FESTIVAL			
—	1994	35th ANNIVERSARY FESTIVAL (pink) LE 3500	300	110	205
11591	1994	35th ANNIVERSARY GIFT SET* Brunette, LE 975	400	210	305
11160	1994	DOCTOR (Brunette) LE 1500	125	50	87
—	1994	FESTIVAL BANQUET Blonde	160	100	130
—	1994	FESTIVAL BANQUET Redhead	170	105	137
—	1994	FESTIVAL BANQUET MATTEL EMPLOYEE'S Brunette	225	225	225
11921	1994	GYMNAST Brunette, LE 1500	70	40	55
12155	1994	HAPPY HOLIDAYS* Brunette, LE 540	1100	500	800
—	1994	HAUTE COUTURE (rainbow) LE 500	300	320	250
—	1994	HAUTE COUTURE (red velvet) LE 480	190	190	190
12191	1994	NIGHT DAZZLE Brunette, LE 420	242	210	226
12905	1994	SNOW PRINCESS* Brunette, LE 285	840	500	660

italic indicates cross reference

STORE EXCLUSIVES & SPECIAL EDITIONS
CONTINUED

STOCK NO.	YEAR	DESCRIPTION	NRFB HIGH	LOW	AVG
		MEIJERS			
0863	1992	SOMETHING EXTRA	45	22	34
10051	1993	SHOPPING FUN	35	22	29
17695	1997	LADYBUG FUN*	25	15	20
18167	1997	HULA HOOP	20	20	20
19280	1998	ICE CREAM*	20	15	17
		MERCANTILE STORES COMPANY INC.			
15831	1996	SPECIAL OCCASION	70	30	50
18216	1997	SPECIAL OCCASION II	54	20	37
		MERVYN'S			
4983	1983	BALLERINA (white)	80	65	73
4984	1983	BALLERINA (black)	80	65	73
7093	1986	FABULOUS FUR	70	65	68
		MILITARY (AAFES)			
15133	1996	SWEET DAISY	40	25	33
18141	1997	PONYTAILS	30	15	23
19592	1998	MAKING FRIENDS (white)	30	15	22
19593	1998	MAKING FRIENDS (black)	30	15	22
—	1999	YOUR PEN PAL (white)	20	10	15
—	1999	YOUR PEN PAL (black)	20	10	15
		MONTGOMERY WARD			
3210	1972	#1 REPLICA (shipping box)	800	590	710
—	1972	#1 REPLICA (pink box)	890	790	840
—	1978	MALIBU BARBIE & HER 10-SPEEDER GIFT SET*	95	85	90
		NATIONAL BASKETBALL ASSOCIATION			
20735	1998	ATLANTA HAWKS (black)	21	8	15
20734	1998	ATLANTA HAWKS (white)	21	8	15
20717	1998	BOSTON CELTICS (black)	21	8	15
20716	1998	BOSTON CELTICS (white)	21	8	15
20699	1998	CHARLOTTE HORNETS (black)	21	8	15
20698	1998	CHARLOTTE HORNETS (white)	21	8	15
20693	1998	CHICAGO BULLS (black)	21	8	15
20692	1998	CHICAGO BULLS (white)	21	8	15
20737	1998	CLEVELAND CAVALIERS (black)	21	8	15
20736	1998	CLEVELAND CAVALIERS (white)	21	8	15
20729	1998	DALLAS MAVERICKS (black)	21	8	15
20728	1998	DALLAS MAVERICKS (white)	21	8	15
20731	1998	DENVER NUGGETS (black)	21	8	15
20730	1998	DENVER NUGGETS (white)	21	8	15
20707	1998	DETROIT PISTONS (black)	21	8	15
20706	1998	DETROIT PISTONS (white)	21	8	15
20743	1998	GOLDEN STATE WARRIORS (black)	21	8	15

italic indicates cross reference

STORE EXCLUSIVES & SPECIAL EDITIONS
CONTINUED

STOCK NO.	YEAR	DESCRIPTION	NRFB HIGH	LOW	AVG
		NATIONAL BASKETBALL ASSOCIATION (continued)			
20742	1998	GOLDEN STATE WARRIORS (white)	21	8	15
20701	1998	HOUSTON ROCKETS (black)	21	8	15
20700	1998	HOUSTON ROCKETS (white)	21	8	15
20713	1998	INDIANA PACERS (black)	21	8	15
20712	1998	INDIANA PACERS (white)	21	8	15
20745	1998	L.A. CLIPPERS (black)	21	8	15
20744	1998	L.A. CLIPPERS (white)	21	8	15
20705	1998	L.A. LAKERS (black)	21	8	15
20704	1998	L.A. LAKERS (white)	21	8	15
20695	1998	MIAMI HEAT (black)	21	8	15
20694	1998	MIAMI HEAT (white)	21	8	15
20739	1998	MILWAUKEE BUCKS (black)	21	8	15
20738	1998	MILWAUKEE BUCKS (white)	21	8	15
20703	1998	MINNESOTA TIMBERWOLVES (black)	21	8	15
20702	1998	MINNESOTA TIMBERWOLVES (white)	21	8	15
20715	1998	N.Y. KNICKS (black)	21	8	15
20714	1998	N.Y. KNICKS (white)	21	8	15
20727	1998	NEW JERSEY NETS (black)	21	8	15
20726	1998	NEW JERSEY NETS (white)	21	8	15
20749	1998	ORLANDO MAGIC (black)	21	8	15
20748	1998	ORLANDO MAGIC (white)	21	8	15
20725	1998	PHILADELPHIA 76ERS (black)	21	8	15
20724	1998	PHILADELPHIA 76ERS (white)	21	8	15
20711	1998	PHOENIX SUNS (black)	21	8	15
20710	1998	PHOENIX SUNS (white)	21	8	15
20721	1998	PORTLAND TRAILBLAZERS (black)	21	8	15
20720	1998	PORTLAND TRAILBLAZERS (white)	21	8	15
20747	1998	SACRAMENTO KINGS (black)	21	8	15
20746	1998	SACRAMENTO KINGS (white)	21	8	15
20723	1998	SAN ANTONIO SPURS (black)	21	8	15
20722	1998	SAN ANTONIO SPURS (white)	21	8	15
20719	1998	SEATTLE SUPERSONICS (black)	21	8	15
20718	1998	SEATTLE SUPERSONICS (white)	21	8	15
20741	1998	TORONTO RAPTORS (black)	21	8	15
20740	1998	TORONTO RAPTORS (white)	21	8	15
20709	1998	UTAH JAZZ (black)	21	8	15
20708	1998	UTAH JAZZ (white)	21	8	15
20733	1998	VANCOUVER GRIZZLIES (black)	21	8	15
20732	1998	VANCOUVER GRIZZLIES (white)	21	8	15
20697	1998	WASHINGTON WIZARDS (black)	21	8	15
20696	1998	WASHINGTON WIZARDS (white)	21	8	15
		NOLAN MILLER COUTURE COLLECTION			
20662	1998	NOLAN MILLER (2 lace versions) Sheer Illusion	86	57	72
		NURSERY RHYMES COLLECTION			
21740	1999	BARBIE HAD A LITTLE LAMB	40	16	28

indicates cross reference **343**

STORE EXCLUSIVES & SPECIAL EDITIONS
CONTINUED

STOCK NO.	YEAR	DESCRIPTION	NRFB HIGH	LOW	AVG
		OLYMPIC 2000 SERIES			
25644	2000	SYDNEY OLYMPIC PIN COLLECTOR (white)		Retail	
26302	2000	SYDNEY OLYMPIC PIN COLLECTOR (black)		Retail	
—	2000	OLYMPIC ATHLETE - Australia	17	17	17
—	2000	OLYMPIC ATHLETE - Canada	17	17	17
—	2000	OLYMPIC ATHLETE - Brazil	17	17	17
—	2000	OLYMPIC ATHLETE - France	17	17	17
—	2000	OLYMPIC ATHLETE -Germany	17	17	17
—	2000	OLYMPIC ATHLETE - Greece	17	17	17
—	2000	OLYMPIC ATHLETE - Italy	17	17	17
—	2000	OLYMPIC ATHLETE - Mexico	17	17	17
—	2000	OLYMPIC ATHLETE - Puerto Rico	17	17	17
		OSCO			
3808	1993	PICNIC PRETTY	45	30	36
		OSHOGATSU			
14024	1995	OSHOGATSU I	80	42	61
—	1995	OSHOGATSU I (Japanese version)	90	45	67
16093	1996	OSHOGATSU II	60	23	42
		PALLENDORF			
—	1997	DAS SPEILZEUG (5 dress versions) Austria, LE 100	325	195	260
		PALMERS (Austria)			
—	1996	PALMERS (green employee uniform - 1st) LE 1500	253	250	252
—	1996	PALMERS (employee apprentice uniform , white garter and green hair ribbon - 2nd) LE 1300	230	200	215
—	1997	PALMERS* (aqua bikini with black piping, black net coverup and towel - 3rd) LE 2500 Teresa	130	110	120
—	1997	PALMERS ANGEL (Nightgown and robe - Die Weihnachts)	40	40	40
—	1998	PALMERS COACH DRIVER (green uniform, green hat, black boots, green coin & shopping bag)	100	75	88
—	2000	MILLENNIUM 2000 (silver top and short skirt)	100	75	88
		PHILIPPINE			
Abaca Collection					
—	2000	FIESTA BARBIE 2 versions		Retail	
Ethnic					
61369-9906					
	1994	TAGAKAOLO	125	80	103
61369-9907					
	1994	B' LAAN	125	80	103
61369-9908					
	1994	ILONGOT	125	80	103
61369-9909					
	1994	GA 'CLANG	125	80	103

* indicates cross reference

STOCK NO.	YEAR	DESCRIPTION	NRFB HIGH	LOW	AVG
Fantasy Ethnic					
9903	1994	IBALOI	150	125	135
9905	1994	MANGYAN	175	130	140
Filipina Collection (1st edition)					
9899	1991		165	120	135
9907	1991		150	115	130
Filipina Collection					
9902	1993	BARO at SAYA	150	100	125
Flores de Laz					
—	—	PURPLE	55	45	50
60652	—	RED	55	45	50
Flores de Maya-Santa Cruzan Festival Collection					
9990	1998	REYNA BANDERADA (The Flag Bearer)	125	100	115
9991	1998	REYNA EMPERIATRIX (The Empress)	125	100	118
9992	1998	REYNA CARIDAD (Queen of Charity)	125	100	115
9993	1998	REYNA ELENA (Queen Helena)	125	100	118
9994	1998	REYNA ESPERANZA (Queen of Hope)	125	110	120
9995	1998	REYNA ESTHER (Queen of the Aetas)	125	100	115
9996	1998	REYNA FE (Queen of Faith)	135	115	125
9997	1998	REYNA DE LAS FLORES (Queen of May Blossoms)	130	120	126
9998	1998	REYNA JUSTICIA (Queen of Justice)	130	115	122
9999	1998	REYNA MORA (Muslim Queen)	130	115	125
Misc. Philippine - Richwell Trading Corporation					
4688	1988	DAZZLING PRETTY	25	20	22
4788	1988	DAZZLING PRETTY	25	20	22
4788	1988	DAZZLING PRETTY	25	20	22
6446	1989	PARTY FUN	18	15	17
6452	1989	PARTY FUN	18	15	17
6458	1989	PARTY FUN	18	15	17
6467	1989	PARTY FUN	18	15	17
8898	1990	PRETTY IN PINK	24	20	22
8900	1990	PRETTY IN PINK	24	20	22
8902	1990	PRETTY IN PINK	24	24	24
8902	1990	SUMMER SPLASH	18	18	18
7363	1991	LUV 'N LACEY	25	25	25
7362	1991	DREAM GIRL	75	75	75
7367	1991	LUV 'N LACEY	25	25	25
7369	1991	LUV 'N LACEY	25	25	25
7370	1991	LUV 'N LACEY	25	25	25
8436	1991	TRENDY STYLE	25	25	25
8444	1991	TRENDY STYLE	25	25	25
8446	1991	TRENDY STYLE	25	25	25

* indicates cross reference

STOCK NO.	YEAR	DESCRIPTION	NRFB HIGH	LOW	AVG
Misc. Philippine - Richwell Trading Corporation (continued)					
8447	1991	TRENDY STYLE	25	25	25
0144	1992	FASHION FUN	20	20	20
6856	1992	GARDEN PRETTY	25	25	25
6867	1992	GARDEN PRETTY	25	25	25
6869	1992	GARDEN PRETTY	25	25	25
6871	1992	GARDEN PRETTY	25	25	25
—	1993	GLAMOUR GIRL	75	75	75
61175	1994	ULTRA GLAMOUR	85	85	85
61176	1994	ULTRA GLAMOUR	85	85	85
62016	1995	SIMPLY PRETTY	24	24	24
62330	1995	STYLISH BARBIE	45	45	45
62331	1995	STYLISH BARBIE	45	45	45
62332	1995	STYLISH BARBIE	45	45	45
15121	1996	SPECIAL EDITION	30	30	30
15122	1996	SPECIAL EDITION	30	30	30
15124	1996	SPECIAL EDITION	30	30	30
15131	1996	WATCH BARBIE	32	32	32
15135	1997	JEWEL ME BARBIE	30	30	30
15138	1997	SPARKLE BARBIE	32	32	32
63810	1997	SPRINGTIME	25	25	25
63810	1997	SPRINGTIME	25	25	25
63810	1997	SPRINGTIME	25	25	25
63810	1997	SPRINGTIME	25	25	25
63822	1998	CAMPUS GIRL - CHEERLEADER	35	35	35
63822	1998	CAMPUS GIRL - STUDENT	35	35	35
63822	1998	CAMPUS GIRL - STUDENT	35	35	35
63822	1998	CAMPUS GIRL - STUDENT	35	35	35
63823	1998	TRENDY STYLE	32	32	32
63823	1998	TROPICAL FUN	30	30	30
63823	1998	TRENDY STYLE	28	28	28
64515	1998	DAISY	35	35	35
Nostalgic					
15142	1996	NOSTALGIC-SOLO IN SPOTLIGHT	55	50	53
62327	1996	NOSTALGIC-SOLO IN SPOTLIGHT	55	50	53
—	1996	NOSTALGIC-SOLO IN SPOTLIGHT	55	50	53
Philippine Centennial Collection (1st edition) Large Box					
9983	1998	CENTENNIAL	45	45	45
9986A	1998	CENTENNIAL	45	45	45
9987	1998	CENTENNIAL	45	45	45
9987	1998	CENTENNIAL	45	45	45
9989	1998	CENTENNIAL	45	45	45
9989A	1998	CENTENNIAL	45	45	45
9990	1998	CENTENNIAL	45	45	45
9991	1998	CENTENNIAL	45	45	45

* indicates cross reference

STORE EXCLUSIVES & SPECIAL EDITIONS
CONTINUED

STOCK NO.	YEAR	DESCRIPTION	NRFB HIGH	LOW	AVG
Philippine Centennial Collection (1st edition) Small Box					
9983	1998	CENTENNIAL - LE	45	45	45
9986	1998	CENTENNIAL - LE	45	45	45
9987	1998	CENTENNIAL - LE	45	45	45
9989	1998	CENTENNIAL - LE	45	45	45
9990	1998	CENTENNIAL - LE	45	45	45
9991	1998	CENTENNIAL - LE	45	45	45
Philippine Centennial Collection (2nd edition)					
9984	1998	CENTENNIAL	45	45	45
9985	1998	CENTENNIAL	45	45	45
9988	1998	CENTENNIAL	45	45	45
9992	1998	CENTENNIAL	45	45	45
9993	1998	CENTENNIAL	45	45	45
Philippine Islands Collection with Caretelas					
15128	1996	PHILIPPINE ISLANDS	60	40	50
15128	1996	PHILIPPINE ISLANDS	60	40	50
15128	1996	PHILIPPINE ISLANDS	60	40	50
15128	1996	PHILIPPINE ISLANDS	60	40	50
15142	1996	PHILIPPINE ISLANDS	60	40	50
Philippine Islands Collection					
63819	1997	PHILIPPINE ISLANDS	40	15	28
63819	1997	PHILIPPINE ISLANDS	40	15	28
63819	1997	PHILIPPINE ISLANDS	40	15	28
63819	1997	PHILIPPINE ISLANDS	40	15	28
63819	1997	PHILIPPINE ISLANDS	40	15	28
64525	1998	PHILIPPINE ISLANDS	40	15	28
64525	1998	PHILIPPINE ISLANDS	40	15	28
64525	1998	PHILIPPINE ISLANDS	40	15	28
Philippine Masterpiece Lacey Splendour Collection (hand glued)					
9988	1998	SAVIOR FAIRE	60	50	55
9989	1998	SAVIOR FAIRE	60	50	55
9990	1998	SAVIOR FAIRE	60	50	55
9991	1998	SAVIOR FAIRE	60	50	55
9992	1998	SAVIOR FAIRE	60	50	55
9993	1998	SAVIOR FAIRE	60	50	55
Richwell Dress 'N Play					
8889	1990		35	30	33
8891	1990		35	30	33
8892	1990		35	30	33
8893	1990		35	30	33

indicates cross reference

STORE EXCLUSIVES & SPECIAL EDITIONS
CONTINUED

STOCK NO.	YEAR	DESCRIPTION	NRFB HIGH	LOW	AVG
Richwell Sweat Dreams					
8449	1991	BLUE	40	35	38
8458	1991	ROSE	40	35	38
8459	1991	WHITE W/ PINK TRIM	40	35	38
8463	1991	YELLOW	40	35	38
Santa Cruzan Festival					
9901	1997	REYNA de las AETAS	125	125	125
9904	1997	REYNA JUSTICIA	125	125	125
9907	1997	REYNA CARIDAD	125	125	125
9910	1997	REYNA EMPERIATRIX	125	125	125
Store Exclusive - Uniwide Warehouse Club					
15140	1996	US BARBIE	45	40	43
15140	1996	US BARBIE	45	40	43
		POP CULTURE SERIES			
15006	1996	STAR TREK* (30th Anniversary Gift Set)	39	21	30
17450	1997	BARBIE LOVES ELVIS* Gift Set	70	38	54
19630	1998	X-FILES Mulder & Scully Gift Set* 1st version long hair	110	50	80
19630	1998	X-FILES Mulder & Scully Gift Set* 2nd version short hair	65	31	48
22953	1999	BARBIE LOVES FRANKIE Gift Set*	100	65	83
24638	2000	WONDER WOMAN*	40	30	35
27276	2000	THE ADDAMS FAMILY Gift Set*	75	50	63
		PREMIUMS			
3269	1972	FORGET-ME-NOT'S (*Kellogg* Company)	—	—	—
3553- 960	1989	STARLIGHT BLUE (Mail-in Lady Lovely Locks)	70	40	55
11546	1994	KRAFT-TREASURES	75	38	57
18456	1997	GENERAL MILLS - WINTER DAZZLE (white)	35	35	35
18457	1997	GENERAL MILLS - WINTER DAZZLE (black)	35	35	35
Kool-Aid					
10309	1993	WACKY WAREHOUSE #1	50	20	35
11763	1994	WACKY WAREHOUSE #2	48	30	39
15620	1996	WACKY WAREHOUSE #3	45	20	32
Little Debbie					
10123	1993	LITTLE DEBBIE #1	50	30	40
14616	1996	LITTLE DEBBIE #2	40	22	35
16352	1998	LITTLE DEBBIE#3	30	12	21
24977	1999	LITTLE DEBBIE #4 40th Anniversary	35	20	27
		PRIMA BALLERINA SERIES			
1648	1991	SWAN LAKE-MUSIC BOX	154	120	137
5472	1992	NUTCRACKER-MUSIC BOX	169	130	150

indicates cross reference

STORE EXCLUSIVES & SPECIAL EDITIONS
CONTINUED

STOCK NO.	YEAR	DESCRIPTION	NRFB HIGH	LOW	AVG
		PRO SPORTS			
20442	1998	NASCAR 50TH ANNIVERSARY	38	10	24
22954	1999	NASCAR #2	30	10	20
25636	2000	NASCAR #3 - Scuderia Ferrari	40	20	30
		QVC			
15649	1996	MY SIZE Redhead	120	80	100
21632	1999	TWEETY LOVES BARBIE*	45	27	36
25680	2000	EMPRESS OF EMERALDS - Royal Jewels Collection*	100	100	100
—	2000	SLEEP OVER PARTY	46	30	38
		RADIO SHACK			
25-1992	1991	EARRING MAGIC W/SOFTWARE PAK	30	12	21
		RUSSELL STOVER			
14617	1996	RUSSELL STOVER EASTER w/Easter Basket (checkered)	35	20	28
14956	1996	RUSSELL STOVER EASTER w/Easter Basket (print)	35	20	28
17091	1997	RUSSELL STOVER EASTER	30	20	25
		SEARS			
9044	1975	BARBIE & HER US OLYMPIC WARDROBE GIFT SET*	120	110	115
9042	1975	GOLD MEDAL GIFT SET* (Winter Sports)	90	85	80
9044	1975	GOLD MEDAL GIFT SET* (Olympic Wardrobe)	95	92	93
2998	1986	CELEBRATION (100th Anniversary)	80	65	73
4550	1987	STAR DREAM	70	45	58
7669	1988	LILAC & LOVELY	60	30	45
3596	1989	EVENING ENCHANTMENT	55	29	42
5588	1990	LAVENDER SURPRISE (black)	50	40	45
9049	1990	LAVENDER SURPRISE (white)	50	35	43
2586	1991	SOUTHERN BELLE	55	35	45
—	1992	BEACH DAZZLE plus 2 fashion, Gift Set Shani*	52	40	46
3817	1992	BLOSSOM BEAUTIFUL	240	117	174
2306	1992	DREAM PRINCESS	53	27	40
10292	1994	ENCHANTED PRINCESS (Canada only)	54	30	42
12410	1994	SILVER SWEETHEART	50	32	41
13911	1995	RIBBONS & ROSES	50	30	40
15533	1996	EVENING FLAME	45	25	35
17125	1997	BLUE STARLIGHT, SE	40	20	30
19130	1998	PINK REFLECTIONS	25	20	22
		SERVICE MERCHANDISE			
1364	1991	BLUE RHAPSODY	142	75	108
1886	1992	SATIN NIGHTS (2 earring versions)	70	30	50
10994	1993	SPARKLING SPLENDOR	68	40	54
12005	1994	CITY SOPHISTICATE	60	21	41
13612	1995	RUBY ROMANCE	58	30	44
15531	1996	SEA PRINCESS	50	35	42

italic indicates cross reference

STOCK NO.	YEAR	DESCRIPTION	NRFB HIGH	LOW	AVG
		SERVICE MERCHANDISE (continued)			
17153	1997	DREAM BRIDE (white)	55	20	38
17933	1997	DREAM BRIDE (black)	20	20	20
19777	1998	EVENING SYMPONY	30	15	23
		Jewelry Collection Series			
20204	1998	DEFINITELY DIAMONDS	64	48	56
		SHOPKO/VENTURE			
3142	1991	BLOSSOM BEAUTY	43	27	35
1876	1992	PARTY PERFECT	40	25	32
19784	1998	SIDEWALK CHALK*	22	15	18
		SINGAPORE AIRLINES			
—	1991	SINGAPORE GIRL I (brown box)	116	54	85
—	1994	SINGAPORE GIRL II (pink box)	75	26	50
		SPIEGEL			
3347	1991	STERLING WISHES	84	26	55
4116	1992	REGAL REFLECTIONS	210	51	130
10969	1993	ROYAL INVITATION	116	43	78
12077	1994	THEATRE ELEGANCE	150	76	113
14009	1995	SHOPPING CHIC (white)	75	15	45
15801	1996	SHOPPING CHIC (black)	75	15	45
15591	1996	SUMMER SOPHISTICATE	115	20	65
17441	1997	WINNER'S CIRCLE, LE	72	20	46
20866	1998	GOLDEN QI-PAO*	76	42	59
		STARS & STRIPES (Military)			
3360	1990	AIR FORCE	50	31	41
9693	1991	NAVY (white)	42	30	36
9694	1991	NAVY (black)	43	28	36
7549	1992	MARINE (white)	45	22	34
7594	1992	MARINE (black)	30	24	27
2810	1992	MARINE GIFT SET* (black)	70	62	66
4704	1992	MARINE GIFT SET* (white)	61	40	51
5352	1992	MARINE KEN* (black)	40	38	42
7574	1992	MARINE KEN* (white)	50	40	45
1234	1993	ARMY (Desert Storm - white)	35	20	28
5618	1993	ARMY (Desert Storm - black)	30	25	27
5626	1993	ARMY GIFT SET* (white)	70	56	63
5627	1993	ARMY GIFT SET* (black)	70	60	65
5619	1993	ARMY KEN* (black)	44	40	42
1237	1993	ARMY KEN* (white)	50	40	45
11552	1994	AIR FORCE (Thunderbirds - white)	31	25	28
11553	1994	AIR FORCE (Thunderbirds - black)	30	20	25
11581	1994	AIR FORCE GIFT SET* (Thunderbirds - white)	70	50	60

indicates cross reference

STOCK NO.	YEAR	DESCRIPTION	NRFB HIGH	LOW	AVG
		STARS & STRIPES (Military) (continued)			
11582	1994	AIR FORCE GIFT SET* (Thunderbirds - black)	60	40	50
11555	1994	AIR FORCE KEN* (black)	40	20	30
11554	1994	AIR FORCE KEN* (white)	39	20	29
		STEIFF			
—	2000	40th ANNIVERSARY - Steiff Bear LE 1,500*	275	155	215
		STORYBOOK FAVORITES COLLECTION			
24639	2000	RAGGEDY ANN AND ANDY	20	20	20
		SUMMIT			
7027	1990	SUMMIT (white)	35	20	26
7028	1990	SUMMIT (black)	35	12	24
7029	1990	SUMMIT (Asian)	37	15	26
7030	1990	SUMMIT (Hispanic)	36	18	27
		SUPERMARKET/DRUG STORE			
2783	1991	TRAIL BLAZIN'	35	20	28
2001	1992	PARTY PREMIERE	35	21	28
2901	1992	PRETTY HEARTS	34	29	32
3208	1992	SWEET SPRING	33	20	27
10217	1993	BACK TO SCHOOL	30	22	26
10280	1993	HOLIDAY HOSTESS, LE	42	27	35
3161	1993	RED ROMANCE	35	20	28
3477	1993	SPRING BOUQUET	25	20	23
11182	1994	B MINE	35	16	26
11276	1994	EASTER FUN	25	20	23
12192	1994	HOLIDAY DREAMS	31	25	28
13966	1995	CAROLING FUN	30	10	20
12793	1995	EASTER PARTY	36	10	23
13741	1995	SCHOOLTIME FUN	20	10	15
12675	1995	VALENTINE BARBIE	32	16	24
15578	1996	EASTER BASKET	20	10	15
15003	1996	GRADUATION - CLASS OF '96	20	20	20
15581	1996	HOLIDAY SEASON (white) SE	20	12	16
15583	1996	HOLIDAY SEASON (black)	15	10	13
15579	1996	SCHOOL SPIRIT	15	10	13
14644	1996	VALENTINE	25	10	18
17099	1997	BACK TO SCHOOL, SE (white)	15	10	13
17100	1997	BACK TO SCHOOL, SE (black)	10	10	10
16491	1997	BIRTHDAY SURPRISE (white) SE	15	10	13
17320	1997	BIRTHDAY SURPRISE (black) SE	12	10	11
16315	1997	EASTER	15	10	13
16487	1997	GRADUATION (white) SE	15	10	12
16489	1997	GRADUATION (black) SE	15	10	12
17618	1997	HOLIDAY TREATS (black)	10	10	10

indicates cross reference

STOCK NO.	YEAR	DESCRIPTION	NRFB HIGH	LOW	AVG
		SUPERMARKET/DRUG STORE (continued)			
17236	1997	HOLIDAY TREATS Blonde	10	10	10
18012	1997	HOLIDAY TREATS Brunette	10	10	10
16311	1997	VALENTINE FUN (white)	15	8	11
16313	1997	VALENTINE FUN (black)	15	8	11
19626	1998	COCA-COLA PICNIC (white) SE	22	10	16
19627	1998	COCA-COLA PICNIC (black) SE	25	10	17
19047	1998	COLOR WITH ME	16	8	12
17651	1998	EASTER	15	10	12
18909	1998	FESTIVE SEASON Blonde	15	10	13
18910	1998	FESTIVE SEASON (black)	15	10	12
17830	1998	GRADUATION 1998* (white)	10	10	10
17831	1998	GRADUATION 1998* (black)	10	10	10
18487	1998	SCHOOLTIME FUN (white)	10	8	9
18488	1998	SCHOOLTIME FUN (black)	10	5	7
17649	1998	VALENTINE, SE	10	8	9
20542	1999	EASTER SURPRISE (white)	19	10	15
20339	1999	MAKE A VALENTINE (white)	13	10	11
20340	1999	MAKE A VALENTINE (black)	13	10	11
22967	1999	TREE TRIMMING (white)	11	11	11
22968	1999	TREE TRIMMING (black)	11	11	11
—	2000	CAMPBELL ALPHABET SOUP	15	10	12
—	2000	COCA-COLA FLASH	15	10	12
		TAKARA (JAPAN)			
—	1981	CRYSTAL BARBIE	110	50	80
—	1981	DREAM BARBIE (several versions)	112	60	86
—	1981	ROMANTIC BRIDE BARBIE	275	117	147
—	1981	WHITE FANTASY BARBIE	123	85	104
—	1981	CASUAL CITY (long Blonde hair & long granny dress)	55	40	47
—	1981	CASUAL CITY (short Blonde hair & plaid pants)	55	40	47
—	1981	CASUAL CITY (short Blonde hair & plaid skirt)	55	40	47
—	1982	CITY COLOUR SERIES (blue)	55	45	50
—	1982	CITY COLOUR SERIES (pink)	55	45	50
—	1982	CITY COLOUR SERIES (purple)	55	45	50
—	1982	CITY COLOUR SERIES (red)	55	45	50
—	1982	CITY COLOUR SERIES (white)	55	45	50
—	1982	CITY COLOUR SERIES (yellow)	55	45	50
—	1982	EXCELINA BARBIE (fur jacket)	120	90	105
—	1982	EXCELINA BARBIE (white dress)	118	90	99
—	1982	EXCELINA BARBIE (print dress)	122	92	107
—	1982	FLORA LYCEANNE (Barbies friend)	120	80	100
—	1982	FRUIT KISS BARBIE	125	85	105
—	1982	SWEET COUNTRY BARBIE	141	75	108
—	1982	WEDDING	175	140	160
—	1983	CASUAL (red felt jacket w/floral appliques, white polkadot dress)	65	60	63
—	1983	SUN SHOWER (suntan)	60	50	55

italic *indicates cross reference*

STORE EXCLUSIVES & SPECIAL EDITIONS
CONTINUED

STOCK NO.	YEAR	DESCRIPTION	NRFB HIGH	LOW	AVG
		TAKARA (JAPAN) (continued)			
—	1984	BARBIE MINK	800	550	675
—	1984	CASUAL (dark blue sweater)	85	65	75
—	1984	CASUAL (pink coulotte dress, anchor earrings)	75	73	74
—	1984	CASUAL SCHOOLGIRL (red jacket w/ school crest gray flannel skirt)	95	75	85
—	1984	EXCELINA (pink ball gown w/white satin top)	95	80	88
—	1984	EXCELINA (black dress w/black and white gingham top w/lace)	95	82	89
—	1984	EXCELINA (black shear dress w/peach overlay)	75	70	73
—	1984	TWINKLE NIGHT BARBIE	175	100	138
635151	1985	AMERICAN DOLL	430	300	365
—	1985	CANDY POP (long yellow fur coat over pink knit dress)	60	40	50
—	1985	CANDY POP (Scotty dog overall w/red top)	70	50	60
—	1985	CITY COLOR WHITE (white sailor suit over blue/white striped top)	80	60	70
—	1985	EXCELINA (white fur trim dress)	140	110	75
—	1985	KANSAI (5 versions)	200	180	190
—	1985	KIMONO (pink or lavender)	108	81	95
—	1985	PARTY COLLECTION DREAM	70	35	54
—	1985	SWEET POP (denim jacket over yellow print dress)	85	70	77
		TARGET			
7476	1989	GOLD 'N LACE	46	22	34
5955	1990	PARTY PRETTY	43	16	30
2954	1991	CUTE 'N COOL	41	18	30
2587	1991	GOLDEN EVENING	54	24	39
7970	1992	BATHTIME FUN SKIPPER*	30	20	25
3203	1992	DAZZLIN' DATE	40	15	28
5413	1992	PRETTY IN PLAID	38	15	27
0411	1992	WILD STYLE	35	18	27
4583	1993	BASEBALL	32	15	24
10202	1993	GOLF DATE	40	20	30
14110	1995	STEPPIN' OUT	29	14	22
15612	1996	CITY STYLE (1st version)	30	15	20
16458	1996	PET DOCTOR Brunette	32	30	31

indicates cross reference

STORE EXCLUSIVES & SPECIAL EDITIONS
CONTINUED

STOCK NO.	YEAR	DESCRIPTION	NRFB HIGH	LOW	AVG
		TARGET (continued)			
16210	1996	TEACHER Brunette	35	25	30
15172	1996	VALENTINE	35	15	25
16485	1997	35th ANNIVERSARY (white)	34	14	24
17608	1997	35th ANNIVERSARY (black)	31	12	22
17237	1997	CITY STYLE (2nd version)	20	10	15
17238	1997	HAPPY HALLOWEEN BARBIE & KELLY GIFT SET*	42	18	30
16059	1997	VALENTINE ROMANCE	25	20	22
18952	1998	CITY STYLE (3rd version)	15	10	12
19717	1998	CLUB WEDD Blonde	21	9	15
19718	1998	CLUB WEDD Brunette	21	9	15
20423	1998	CLUB WEDD (black)	21	9	15
19014	1998	EASTER EGG HUNT SE GIFT SET*	50	27	39
23796	1999	HALLOWEEN LI'L FRIENDS OF KELLY GIFT SET*	35	20	28
23460	1999	HALLOWEEN FUN BARBIE AND KELLY GIFT SET*	30	20	25
—	1999	TOMMY AND KELLY SOCCER SET	20	15	17
17830	1998	GRADUATION 1998*	10	5	8
19874	1998	HALLOWEEN PARTY BARBIE & KEN GIFT SET*	40	13	26
18306	1998	VALENTINE DATE, SE	19	10	15
22360	1999	CLUB WEDD Blonde	19	19	19
22362	1999	CLUB WEDD Brunette	19	19	19
22361	1999	CLUB WEDD (black)	19	19	19
21720	1999	EASTER BUNNY FUN BARBIE & KELLY GIFT SET*	28	8	18
20465	1999	VALENTINE STYLE (white)	18	12	15
22150	1999	VALENTINE STYLE (black)	16	12	14
—	1999	XHILRATION (white)	20	10	15
—	1999	XHILRATION (black)	20	10	15
		TIMELESS SENTIMENTS			
19633	1998	ANGEL OF JOY (white)	54	25	40
20929	1998	ANGEL OF JOY (black)	50	25	38
24240	1999	ANGEL OF PEACE (white)	50	30	40
24241	1999	ANGEL OF PEACE (black)	50	30	40

*indicates cross reference

STORE EXCLUSIVES & SPECIAL EDITIONS
CONTINUED

STOCK NO.	YEAR	DESCRIPTION	NRFB HIGH	LOW	AVG
		TIMELESS TREASURES			
26834	2000	WIZARD OF OZ - Dorothy with Toto - Porcelain*	Retail		
26835	2000	WIZARD OF OZ - Wicked Witch - Porcelain*	Retail		
		TOGETHER FOREVER COLLECTION			
19364	1998	ROMEO AND JULIET GIFT SET* 1st	100	61	80
23880	1999	KING ARTHUR AND QUEEN GUINEVERE* 2nd	95	70	83
		TOYS R US			
9058	1985	DANCE SENSATION	65	40	52
1675	1986	VACATION SENSATION (blue)	52	30	41
7799	1988	SHOW 'N RIDE GIFT SET*	45	35	40
7801	1988	TENNIS STAR BARBIE & KEN GIFT SET*	60	56	58
4893	1989	DENIM FUN - COOL CITY BLUES GIFT SET*	65	60	63
9180	1989	DREAM TIME	40	35	38
4885	1989	PARTY TREATS	35	20	28
4869	1989	*PEPSI* SPIRIT	80	31	55
4867	1989	*PEPSI* SPIRIT SKIPPER*	56	34	55
7635	1989	SWEET ROSES	55	30	43
1675	1989	VACATION SENSATION (pink)	85	75	80
5947	1990	COOL LOOKS	35	25	30
1075	1990	DREAM DATE SKIPPER*	40	30	35
5408	1990	WESTERN FUN GIFT SET*	65	45	55
5949	1990	WINTER FUN	60	45	53
1752	1991	ASHA*	38	18	28
3177	1991	BARBIE & FRIENDS DISNEY DELUXE GIFT SET*	74	60	67
9324	1991	BEAUTY PAGEANT SKIPPER*	32	28	30
1751	1991	NICHELLE*	30	20	25
2721	1991	SCHOOL FUN (white - 2 versions)	35	18	27
4111	1991	SCHOOL FUN (black - 2 versions)	35	18	27
1750	1991	SHANI*	32	28	30
7513	1991	SKI FUN MIDGE*	38	22	30
2917	1991	SWEET ROMANCE	30	27	29

italic *indicates cross reference*

STORE EXCLUSIVES & SPECIAL EDITIONS
CONTINUED

STOCK NO.	YEAR	DESCRIPTION	NRFB HIGH	LOW	AVG
		TOYS R US (continued)			
1433	1991	TOTALLY HAIR COURTNEY*	25	15	20
1430	1991	TOTALLY HAIR SKIPPER*	40	30	35
2820	1991	WEDDING DAY KELLY & TODD GIFT SET*	40	22	31
3722	1992	BARBIE FOR PRESIDENT (white - Presidential Seal)	91	40	66
3940	1992	BARBIE FOR PRESIDENT (black - Presidential Seal)	63	31	47
3722	1992	BARBIE FOR PRESIDENT (white - star)	45	31	38
5777	1992	BEACH DAZZLE ASHA*	15	9	12
5775	1992	BEACH DAZZLE NICHELLE*	17	13	15
5774	1992	BEACH DAZZLE SHANI*	20	10	15
1490	1992	COOL & SASSY (white)	28	16	22
4110	1992	COOL & SASSY (black)	28	14	21
1882	1992	FASHION BRIGHTS (white)	25	20	23
4112	1992	FASHION BRIGHTS (black)	25	20	23
7795	1992	JAMAL*	33	27	30
1276	1992	RADIANT IN RED (white)	48	12	30
4113	1992	RADIANT IN RED (black)	46	15	30
2257	1992	SPRING PARADE (black)	40	25	33
7008	1992	SPRING PARADE (white)	45	33	39
10527	1993	BARBIE LOVES TO READ DELUXE GIFT SET*	48	32	40
3457	1993	BEACH STREAK ASHA*	13	11	12
3802	1993	BEACH STREAK JAMAL*	18	12	15
3456	1993	BEACH STREAK NICHELLE*	16	14	15
3428	1993	BEACH STREAK SHANI*	16	14	15
10713	1993	DREAM WEDDING GIFT SET* (black)	48	40	44
10712	1993	DREAM WEDDING GIFT SET* (white)	57	49	53
4581	1993	MALT SHOP	40	20	30
10608	1993	MOONLIGHT MAGIC (white)	110	70	90
10609	1993	MOONLIGHT MAGIC (black)	100	45	73
10688	1993	POLICE OFFICER (white)	75	22	49
10689	1993	POLICE OFFICER (black)	75	25	50
10682	1993	SCHOOL SPIRIT (white)	30	28	29
10683	1993	SCHOOL SPIRIT (black)	30	28	29

indicates cross reference

STORE EXCLUSIVES & SPECIAL EDITIONS
CONTINUED

STOCK NO.	YEAR	DESCRIPTION	NRFB HIGH	LOW	AVG
		TOYS R US (continued)			
10291	1993	SOUL TRAIN ASHA*	22	18	20
10288	1993	SOUL TRAIN JAMAL*	25	20	22
10290	1993	SOUL TRAIN NICHELLE*	22	18	20
10289	1993	SOUL TRAIN SHANI*	28	22	25
10491	1993	SPOTS 'N DOTS	50	35	43
10885	1993	SPOTS 'N DOTS TERESA*	48	32	40
11020	1993	WESTERN STAMPIN' - Western Star Horse Gift Set* (blue)	60	30	45
13478	1993	WESTERN STAMPIN' - Western Star Horse Gift Set* (red)	50	30	40
12676	1994	ASHA I* 1st *A.A. Collection*	30	30	30
14108	1994	MY SIZE BRIDE Brunette	125	70	98
12243	1994	PARTYTIME (white)	25	24	25
12244	1994	PARTYTIME TERESA*	26	24	25
11928	1994	QUINCEANERA TERESA*	40	20	30
10958	1994	SUN JEWEL SHANI*	16	14	15
13488	1994	SUNFLOWER	20	16	18
13489	1994	SUNFLOWER TERESA*	28	22	25
13556	1994	WEDDING PARTY GIFT SET* (black)	44	20	32
13557	1994	WEDDING PARTY GIFT SET* (white)	45	35	40
11020	1994	WESTERN STAMPIN'	35	30	33
13532	1995	ASHA II* 2nd *A.A. Collection*	24	18	22
14274	1995	PARTYTIME (black)	25	20	23
13558	1995	PEN FRIEND	25	20	23
13239	1995	POG FUN	25	20	23
13555	1995	PURPLE PASSION (white) LE	45	30	38
13554	1995	PURPLE PASSION (black) LE	40	30	35
14073	1995	TRAVELIN' SISTERS PLAYSET*	75	55	65
13516	1995	WINTER SPORTS* *FAO Schwarz, JCPenney, Toys R Us*	35	25	30
15139	1996	ASHA III* 3rd *A.A. Collection*	22	18	20
15610	1996	BIRTHDAY FUN KELLY* (Barbie, Kelly & Chelsie)	35	35	35
15136	1996	CRYSTAL SPLENDOR (white)	36	18	27
15137	1996	CRYSTAL SPLENDOR (black)	32	17	25
15121	1996	GOT MILK (white)	25	12	19

indicates cross reference

STORE EXCLUSIVES & SPECIAL EDITIONS
CONTINUED

STOCK NO.	YEAR	DESCRIPTION	NRFB HIGH	LOW	AVG
		TOYS R US (continued)			
15122	1996	GOT MILK (black)	25	12	19
15649	1996	MY SIZE BRIDE Redhead	100	65	82
15304	1996	NATIVE AMERICAN IV* *Dolls of the World*	40	25	33
15125	1996	OLYMPIC GYMNAST (Redhead)	40	20	30
15141	1996	PINK ICE "First in a series"	115	68	92
17248	1997	101 DALMATIANS (white) SE	23	17	20
17601	1997	101 DALMATIANS (black) SE	24	10	17
17602	1997	101 DALMATIANS (Teresa) SE*	23	17	20
17242	1997	GARDENING FUN BARBIE & KELLY GIFT SET*	22	20	21
17239	1997	GRAN GALA TERESA*	24	20	22
17692	1997	*HARLEY-DAVIDSON*, LE	560	385	473
18511	1997	*OREO* FUN (75th Anniversary)	18	8	13
16692	1997	SAPPHIRE SOPHISTICATE Brunette, SE	40	22	31
17247	1997	SHARE A SMILE BARBIE	30	14	22
15761	1997	SHARE A SMILE BECKY*	30	10	20
17372	1997	SHARE A SMILE CHRISTIE*	26	14	20
15060	1997	SHOW PARADE W/STAR STAMPIN' HORSE GIFT SET* (black)	35	25	30
15059	1997	SHOW PARADE W/STAR STAMPIN' HORSE GIFT SET* (white)	35	25	30
17243	1997	WEDDING FANTASY GIFT SET* (Barbie & Ken)	40	20	30
20038	1998	GOLDEN ANNIVERSARY 50TH	95	50	73
18979	1998	CHARITY BALL (white - COTA)	40	20	30
19132	1998	CHARITY BALL (black - COTA)	40	20	30
19809	1998	CHRISTMAS SISTER'S GIFT SET*	35	15	25
20441	1998	*HARLEY-DAVIDSON* #2	162	123	143
18895	1998	I'M A TOYS R US KID* (white) - 50th Anniversary Gift Set	30	10	20
21040	1998	I'M A TOYS R US KID* (black) - 50th Anniversary Gift Set	30	10	20
18976	1998	MIDGE - 35TH ANNIVERSARY* (Senior Prom) SE	56	40	48
20376	1998	OSCAR DE LA RENTA*	61	36	49
19262	1998	WILD STYLE SE	22	10	16
19263	1998	WILD STYLE TERESA SE*	21	20	20
19850	1998	WINTER RIDE GIFT SET* (FAO, Toys R Us)	55	43	49
21377	1999	101 DALMATIANS (Brunette)	20	12	16

indicates cross reference

STORE EXCLUSIVES & SPECIAL EDITIONS
CONTINUED

STOCK NO.	YEAR	DESCRIPTION	NRFB HIGH	LOW	AVG
		TOYS R US (continued)			
21375	1999	101 DALMATIANS (Blonde)	20	12	16
—	1999	101 DALMATIANS (black)	20	12	16
22435	1999	SPACE CAMP* (white)	30	25	27
22426	1999	SPACE CAMP* (black)	30	25	27
22256	1999	HARLEY-DAVIDSON #3	90	70	80
22255	1999	HARLEY-DAVIDSON KEN #1*	120	102	111
25637	2000	HARLEY-DAVIDSON #4	153	70	112
—	2000	HARLEY-DAVIDSON KEN #2*	92	80	86
—	2000	LET'S DRIVE - BARBIE/SKIPPER GIFT SET*	40	40	40
—	2000	SIGN LANGUAGE	25	20	23
Career Collection					
12149	1994	ASTRONAUT (white)	50	35	42
12150	1994	ASTRONAUT (black)	50	40	45
13472	1995	FIREFIGHTER (black)	40	35	38
13553	1995	FIREFIGHTER (white)	55	50	53
15803	1996	DR. BARBIE (white)	30	25	28
15804	1996	DR. BARBIE (black)	30	25	28
17240	1997	PALEONTOLOGIST* (white)	25	11	18
17241	1997	PALEONTOLOGIST* (black)	27	9	18
18368	1998	PILOT (white)	25	16	21
19384	1998	PILOT (black)	22	16	19
—	1999	MARINE BIOLOGIST (white)	20	20	20
—	1999	MARINE BIOLOGIST (black)	20	20	20
26288	2000	BARBIE FOR PRESIDENT (white)	Retail		
26284	2000	BARBIE FOR PRESIDENT (black)	Retail		
—	2000	BARBIE FOR PRESIDENT - Hispanic - Online exclusive	Retail		
Society Style Collection					
12322	1994	EMERALD ELEGANCE (white)	65	30	48
12323	1994	EMERALD ELEGANCE (black)	45	30	38

indicates cross reference

STORE EXCLUSIVES & SPECIAL EDITIONS
CONTINUED

STOCK NO.	YEAR	DESCRIPTION	NRFB HIGH	LOW	AVG
Society Style Collection **(continued)**					
13255	1995	SAPPHIRE DREAM #1	49	23	36
15061	1996	RADIANT ROSE #2 (black)	52	18	35
15140	1996	RADIANT ROSE #2 (white)	54	20	37
17443	1997	EMERALD ENCHANTMENT #3	60	40	50
		TWIST 'N TURN COLLECTION			
21911	1999	FAR OUT	55	30	42
		U.S. SPACE CAMP			
22425	1999	SPACE CAMP* (white)	25	20	22
22426	1999	SPACE CAMP* (black)	25	20	22
		ULTRA LIMITED EDITION			
16091	1996	PINK SPLENDOR, LE 10,000	400	305	352
17641	1997	BILLIONS OF DREAMS, LE	300	166	233
		UNICEF			
1920	1989	UNICEF (white)	35	15	25
4770	1989	UNICEF (black)	30	15	23
4774	1989	UNICEF (Asian)	40	18	29
4782	1989	UNICEF (Hispanic)	40	17	29
		UNIVERSITY			
17699	1997	AUBURN (white)	15	5	10
18346	1997	AUBURN (black)	15	5	10
17753	1997	CLEMSON (white)	15	5	10
18349	1997	CLEMSON (black)	15	5	10
17750	1997	DUKE (white)	15	5	10
19665	1997	DUKE (black)	15	5	10
17749	1997	GEORGETOWN (white)	15	5	10
18341	1997	GEORGETOWN (black)	15	5	10
17194	1997	NORTH CAROLINA STATE (white)	15	5	10

italic *indicates cross reference*

STORE EXCLUSIVES & SPECIAL EDITIONS
CONTINUED

STOCK NO.	YEAR	DESCRIPTION	NRFB HIGH	LOW	AVG
		UNIVERSITY (continued)			
20127	1997	NORTH CAROLINA STATE (black)	15	5	10
17752	1997	OKLAHOMA STATE	15	5	10
17698	1997	PENN STATE (white)	15	5	10
18344	1997	PENN STATE (black)	15	5	10
17191	1997	UNIVERSITY OF ARKANSAS	15	5	10
17700	1997	UNIVERSITY OF FLORIDA (white)	15	5	10
18343	1997	UNIVERSITY OF FLORIDA (black)	15	5	10
17192	1997	UNIVERSITY OF GEORGIA (white)	15	5	10
18345	1997	UNIVERSITY OF GEORGIA (black)	15	5	10
17755	1997	UNIVERSITY OF ILLINOIS	15	5	10
17794	1997	UNIVERSITY OF MIAMI (white)	15	5	10
18348	1997	UNIVERSITY OF MIAMI (black)	15	5	10
17398	1997	UNIVERSITY OF MICHIGAN (white)	15	5	10
18342	1997	UNIVERSITY OF MICHIGAN (black)	15	5	10
17193	1997	UNIVERSITY OF NEBRASKA	15	5	10
17554	1997	UNIVERSITY OF TENNESSEE (white)	15	5	10
18347	1997	UNIVERSITY OF TENNESSEE (black)	15	5	10
17792	1997	UNIVERSITY OF TEXAS	15	5	10
17754	1997	UNIVERSITY OF VIRGINIA	15	5	10
17195	1997	UNIVERSITY OF WISCONSIN	15	5	10
19170	1998	ALABAMA (white)	19	5	12
19422	1998	ALABAMA (black)	19	5	12
19162	1998	ARIZONA STATE	19	5	12
19152	1998	BRIGHAM YOUNG (white)	19	5	12
19155	1998	EAST CAROLINA (white)	19	5	12
19426	1998	EAST CAROLINA (black)	19	5	12
19159	1998	GEORGIA TECH (white)	19	5	12
19427	1998	GEORGIA TECH (black)	19	5	12
20044	1998	INDIANA	19	5	12
20367	1998	IOWA	19	5	12
19156	1998	KANSAS STATE (white)	19	5	12
19167	1998	NORTHWESTERN (white)	19	5	12

*indicates cross reference

STORE EXCLUSIVES & SPECIAL EDITIONS
CONTINUED

STOCK NO.	YEAR	DESCRIPTION	NRFB HIGH	LOW	AVG
		UNIVERSITY (continued)			
19425	1998	NORTHWESTERN (black)	19	5	12
20125	1998	OKLAHOMA	19	5	12
19868	1998	PURDUE	19	5	12
19870	1998	STANFORD (white)	19	5	12
20124	1998	STANFORD (black)	19	5	12
19163	1998	SYRACUSE (white)	19	5	12
19419	1998	SYRACUSE (black)	19	5	12
17191	1998	UNIVERSITY OF ARKANSAS (white)	19	5	12
17751	1998	UNIVERSITY OF ARIZONA	19	5	12
19169	1998	UNIVERSITY OF COLORADO (white)	19	5	12
19866	1998	UNIVERSITY OF CONNECTICUT	19	5	12
19153	1998	UNIVERSITY OF KENTUCKY (white)	19	5	12
19867	1998	UNIVERSITY OF MARYLAND (white)	19	5	12
20123	1998	UNIVERSITY OF MARYLAND (black)	19	5	12
20126	1998	UNIVERSITY OF TEXAS (black)	19	5	12
19171	1998	VIRGINIA TECH UNIVERSITY (white)	19	5	12
19420	1998	VIRGINIA TECH UNIVERSITY (black)	19	5	12
19869	1998	WASHINGTON STATE	19	5	12
21166	1999	AIR FORCE ACADEMY	20	10	15
21159	1999	ARMY	20	10	15
21189	1999	BOSTON COLLEGE	20	15	17
21226	1999	BOSTON UNIVERSITY	20	15	17
21231	1999	CINCINNATI	20	15	17
21219	1999	LSU (white)	20	15	17
21220	1999	LSU (black)	20	15	17
21245	1999	MARSHALL	20	15	17
21192	1999	MASSACHUSETTS	20	15	17
21193	1999	MINNESOTA	20	15	17
21190	1999	MISSISSIPPI STATE (white)	20	15	17
21191	1999	MISSISSIPPI STATE (black)	20	15	17
21194	1999	MONTANA	20	15	17
21167	1999	NORTH CAROLINA A & T (white)	20	15	17

italic *indicates cross reference*

STORE EXCLUSIVES & SPECIAL EDITIONS
CONTINUED

STOCK NO.	YEAR	DESCRIPTION	NRFB HIGH	LOW	AVG
		UNIVERSITY (continued)			
21168	1999	NORTH CAROLINA A & T (black)	20	15	17
21169	1999	PITTSBURGH	20	15	17
21227	1999	SAN DIEGO STATE (white)	20	15	17
21228	1999	SAN DIEGO STATE (black)	20	15	17
21195	1999	SOUTH CAROLINA (white)	20	15	17
21196	1999	SOUTH CAROLINA (black)	20	15	17
21229	1999	TEXAS TECH (white)	20	15	17
21230	1999	TEXAS TECH (black)	20	15	17
21232	1999	UNIVERSITY OF MISSISSIPPI (white)	20	15	17
21233	1999	UNIVERSITY OF MISSISSIPPI (black)	20	15	17
21216	1999	UNIVERSITY OF VIRGINIA	20	15	17
21234	1999	UNLV	20	15	17
21197	1999	UTAH	20	15	17l
21160	1999	VANDERBILT	20	15	17
21172	1999	VILLANOVA	20	15	17
21246	1999	WYOMING	20	15	17
21173	1999	XAVIER	20	15	17
		VEDES			
11843	1993	VEDES STAR *Vedes Department Store* (Germany)	85	69	77
		VICTORIAN HOLIDAY			
28395	2000	VICTORIAN HOLIDAY BARBIE AND KELLY*	Retail		
		VICTORIAN SERIES			
25526	2000	VICTORIAN BARBIE WITH CEDRIC BEAR	60	35	43
		WAL-MART			
4589	1987	PINK JUBILEE (25th Anniversary)	47	15	31
1374	1988	FRILLS & FANTASY	45	15	30
3963	1989	LAVENDER LOOKS	40	20	30
7335	1990	DREAM FANTASY	45	40	42

indicates cross reference

STORE EXCLUSIVES & SPECIAL EDITIONS
CONTINUED

STOCK NO.	YEAR	DESCRIPTION	HIGH	LOW	AVG
		WAL-MART (continued)			
3678	1991	BALLROOM BEAUTY	40	29	35
2282	1992	ANNIVERSARY STAR (30th Anniversary)	40	29	35
10592	1993	SUPER STAR (white)	40	30	35
10711	1993	SUPER STAR (black)	45	20	33
11645	1993	TOOTH FAIRY (pink lavender 1st edition)	25	20	23
12096	1994	COUNTRY WESTERN STAR (Hispanic)	35	20	28
12097	1994	COUNTRY WESTERN STAR (white)	29	19	24
12096	1994	COUNTRY WESTERN STAR (black)	28	20	24
13614	1995	COUNTRY BRIDE (white)	30	20	25
13615	1995	COUNTRY BRIDE (black)	25	18	22
13516	1995	COUNTRY BRIDE (Hispanic)	45	10	28
11645	1995	TOOTH FAIRY (blue/pink - 2nd edition)	20	15	18
15510	1996	SKATING STAR (white)	20	15	18
15511	1996	SKATING STAR (Hispanic)	25	20	22
16691	1996	SKATING STAR (black)	20	15	18
15652	1996	SWEET MAGNOLIA (white)	20	20	20
15653	1996	SWEET MAGNOLIA (black)	20	6	20
15654	1996	SWEET MAGNOLIA (Hispanic)	20	20	20
17245	1997	35TH ANNIVERSARY(Blonde)	30	25	28
17616	1997	35TH ANNIVERSARY(black)	30	25	28
17617	1997	35TH ANNIVERSARY TERESA*	35	25	30
18018	1997	PRETTY CHOICES (black)	25	20	23
17971	1997	PRETTY CHOICES (Blonde)	25	20	23
18019	1997	PRETTY CHOICES (Brunette)	25	20	23
18230	1997	SHOPPING TIME (Blonde)	20	15	18
18231	1997	SHOPPING TIME (black)	20	15	18
18232	1997	SHOPPING TIME TERESA*	25	15	20
20022	1998	BRONZE SENSATION*	65	28	47
19355	1998	PORTRAIT IN BLUE (white)	15	10	12
19356	1998	PORTRAIT IN BLUE (black)	15	10	12
20164	1998	PUZZLE CRAZE (white)	16	12	14
20165	1998	PUZZLE CRAZE (black)	16	12	14

indicates cross reference

STORE EXCLUSIVES & SPECIAL EDITIONS
CONTINUED

STOCK NO.	YEAR	DESCRIPTION	NRFB HIGH	LOW	AVG
		WAL-MART (continued)			
20166	1998	PUZZLE CRAZE TERESA*	14	10	12
21524	1998	TOMMY & KELLY POWERWHEELS GIFT SET*	25	15	20
17246	1998	TOOTH FAIRY	17	12	15
23239	1999	JEWEL SKATING	15	11	13
		WALGREENS			
9025	1990	PARTY SENSATION	75	50	63
		WARNER BROTHERS			
21632	1999	TWEETY LOVES BARBIE*	45	20	33
24638	2000	WONDER WOMAN*		Retail	
		WESSCO			
—	1995	INTERNATIONAL TRAVELER #1 (In flight)	75	40	58
13912	1995	INTERNATIONAL TRAVELER #1 (Duty Free Shop)	70	33	51
16158	1996	INTERNATIONAL TRAVELER #2 (In flight)	50	30	40
15184	1996	INTERNATIONAL TRAVELER #2 (Duty Free Shop)	50	30	40
15186	1997	CARNIVAL CRUISE	50	35	43
		WHOLESALE CLUB			
9025	1990	PARTY SENSATION	42	19	31
5408	1990	WESTERN STAMPIN' STAR HORSE GIFT SET*	45	40	43
3712	1991	ALL AMERICAN STAR STEPPER GIFT SET*	50	40	45
9601	1991	BATHTIME	25	15	20
2366	1991	JEWEL JUBILEE	68	40	54
7151	1992	100 PIECE - VERSION #1 GIFT SET*	35	30	32
7151	1992	100 PIECE - VERSION #2 GIFT SET*	35	30	32
3196	1992	FANTASTICA	70	40	55
7009	1992	PEACH BLOSSOM *Sam's Club*	60	30	45
7142	1992	*ROLLERBLADE* GIFT SET*	52	40	46
1858	1992	ROYAL ROMANCE *Price Club*	102	50	76
7131	1992	SPARKLE EYES GIFT SET* *Sam's Club*	62	50	60

indicates cross reference

STOCK NO.	YEAR	DESCRIPTION	NRFB HIGH	LOW	AVG
		WHOLESALE CLUB (continued)			
7149	1992	SUN SENSATION GIFT SET — SPRAY & PLAY*	60	45	52
1859	1992	VERY VIOLET *Pace*	78	30	54
—	1993	DRESSING FUN - LOTS OF FASHIONS GIFT SET* (pink dress)	55	55	55
—	1993	DRESSING FUN - LOTS OF FASHIONS GIFT SET* (purple dress)	55	55	55
10339	1993	FESTIVA (2 scarf versions)	75	50	63
10928	1993	HOLLYWOOD HAIR GIFT SET*	42	19	31
10379	1993	ISLAND FUN GIFT SET*	35	25	30
10926	1993	PAINT 'N DAZZLE GIFT SET*	35	18	27
10929	1993	SECRET HEARTS GIFT SET *	50	40	45
10924	1993	WEDDING FANTASY GIFT SET*	84	43	63
11020	1993	WESTERN STAMPIN' GIFT SET*	69	55	62
10927	1993	WESTERN STAMPIN' DELUXE PLAYSET*	30	30	30
11481	1994	BEACH FUN GIFT SET* *Wholesale*	35	30	32
12184	1994	BEDTIME GIFT SET* *Wholesale*	45	35	40
12384	1994	SEASON'S GREETINGS	62	44	53
10658	1994	WINTER ROYALE	125	48	72
13181	1995	BARBIE & CHAMPION HORSE RIDING GIFT SET*	79	65	72
12371 13511/	1995	DENIM & RUFFLES GIFT SET* *BJ's*	75	55	65
11929	1995	HOT SKATIN' BARBIE & MUSTANG DELUXE GIFT SET*	47	22	35
13744	1995	ME & MY MUSTANG *Sam's Club*	30	16	23
13613	1995	WINTER'S EVE	42	21	32
15820	1996	1950's *Sam's Club*	50	20	35
16290 14879/	1996	BARBIE AT BLOOMINGDALE'S* (Souvenir Shopper) SE	30	15	23
15648	1996	HORSE LOVIN' BARBIE & NIBBLES GIFT SET*	40	20	30
—	1996	OLYMPIC GIFT SET*	45	25	35
15952	1996	SILVER ROYALE, SE	125	69	97
15334	1996	WINTER FANTASY Blonde	50	19	35
15530	1996	WINTER FANTASY Brunette	55	19	37
17252	1997	60's FUN Blonde *Sam's Club*	35	24	30
17693	1997	60's FUN Redhead *Sam's Club*	35	22	29

indicates cross reference

STORE EXCLUSIVES & SPECIAL EDITIONS
CONTINUED

STOCK NO.	YEAR	DESCRIPTION	NRFB HIGH	LOW	AVG
		WHOLESALE CLUB (continued)			
17341	1997	AFTER THE WALK* 2nd *Coca-Cola Fashion Classic Series* *Sam's Club*	70	30	50
17864	1997	COUNTRY ROSE* C.E. *1st Grand Ole Opry - Sam's Club*	75	35	55
15987	1997	ROSE BRIDE	45	18	31
17251	1997	SPARKLE BEAUTY *BJ's*	35	15	25
17642	1997	SWEET MOMENTS	35	25	30
17666	1997	WINTER FANTASY #2 Brunette	45	30	38
17249	1997	WINTER FANTASY #2 Blonde	40	30	35
19928	1998	70's FUN Blonde *Sam's Club*	26	18	22
19929	1998	70's FUN Brunette *Sam's Club*	26	18	22
20022	1998	BRONZE SENSATION* *Sam's Club*	65	28	47
19016	1998	DINNER DATE Blonde	18	15	16
19037	1998	DINNER DATE Redhead	18	15	16
19218	1998	WINTER EVENING Blonde	29	18	24
19220	1998	WINTER EVENING Brunette	30	18	24
—	1998	WORKIN' OUT* (outfits vary)	15	10	12
—	2000	SISTERS CELEBRATION KRISSY AND BARBIE - *Sam's Club*		Retail	
		WINN-DIXIE			
7637	1989	PARTY PINK	30	20	25
5410	1990	PINK SENSATION	30	15	23
3284	1991	SOUTHERN BEAUTY	35	15	25
		WINTER PRINCESS (THEME) COLLECTION			
10655	1993	WINTER PRINCESS 1st	275	128	201
12123	1994	EVERGREEN PRINCESS 2nd Blonde	110	50	80
13173	1994	EVERGREEN PRINCESS* Redhead *Disney* LE 1500	203	108	156
13598	1995	PEPPERMINT PRINCESS 3rd	60	31	45
15826	1996	JEWEL PRINCESS 4th	57	16	37
—	1999	JEWEL PRINCESS* Brunette *Disney* LE 1500	140	90	115
17780	1997	MIDNIGHT PRINCESS 5th	52	25	39
18486	1997	MIDNIGHT PRINCESS* Brunette *Disney* LE	127	74	98

indicates cross reference

STORE EXCLUSIVES & SPECIAL EDITIONS
CONTINUED

STOCK NO.	YEAR	DESCRIPTION	NRFB HIGH	LOW	AVG
		WNBA			
20205	1998	WNBA BARBIE	25	9	17
20206	1998	WNBA CHRISTIE*	20	10	15
20350	1998	WNBA TERESA*	20	10	15
20349	1998	WNBA KIRA*	20	10	15
		WOOLWORTHS			
4842	1989	SPECIAL EXPRESSIONS (white) white dress	30	18	24
7346	1989	SPECIAL EXPRESSIONS (black) white dress	25	12	19
5504	1990	SPECIAL EXPRESSIONS (white) pink dress	18	14	16
5505	1990	SPECIAL EXPRESSIONS (black) pink dress	19	10	15
2582	1991	SPECIAL EXPRESSIONS (white) blue dress	17	10	14
2583	1991	SPECIAL EXPRESSIONS (black) blue dress	19	10	15
3197	1992	SPECIAL EXPRESSIONS (white) salmon dress	20	14	17
3198	1992	SPECIAL EXPRESSIONS (black) salmon dress	28	13	21
3200	1992	SPECIAL EXPRESSIONS (Hispanic) salmon dress	28	15	22
2522	1992	SWEET LAVENDER (white)	29	17	23
2523	1992	SWEET LAVENDER (black)	30	19	25
10048	1993	SPECIAL EXPRESSIONS (white) pastel print	20	12	16
10049	1993	SPECIAL EXPRESSIONS (black) pastel print	22	16	19
10050	1993	SPECIAL EXPRESSIONS (Hispanic) pastel print	22	16	19
		ZELLERS (CANADA)			
—	1994	ROLLERSKATING BARBIE & HER ROLL ALONG PUPPY GIFT SET*	72	30	51
15833	1996	FASHION AVENUE	30	25	28
—	1996	TEDDY BEAR	40	25	33
—	1997	LE CHIC	25	25	25
19020	1998	BARBIE LOVES ZELLERS	30	20	25

NEWER GIFT SETS

STOCK NO.	YEAR	DESCRIPTION	NRFB
7796	1974	SWEET SIXTEEN	78
9044	1975	BARBIE & HER US OLYMPIC WARDROBE* *Sears*	115
9042	1975	GOLD MEDAL BARBIE* *Sears*	85
9044	1975	GOLD MEDAL BARBIE* *Sears*	93
9045	1975	OLYMPIC GYMNAST (PJ)	92
9613	1976	BALLERINA ON TOUR (1st hair version)	145
—	1976	BARBIE AND HER HORSE DANCER (Canada)	70
—	1976	BARBIE PLUS 3	75
9953	1977	BARBIE PLUS 3 FASHIONS	95
2422	1977	SUPERSTARS (Barbie & Ken)	137
—	1978	MALIBU BARBIE & HER 10-SPEEDER* *Ward's*	90
2753	1978	MALIBU BARBIE FASHION COMBO (DSS)	75
2583	1978	SUPERSTAR-FASHION CHANGE ABOUTS	125
2207	1978	SUPERSTAR - IN THE SPOTLIGHT	75
9613	1979	BALLERINA ON TOUR (2nd hair version)	95
2977	1979	KISSING BARBIE EXTRA VALUE SET	95
1702	1980	BEAUTY SECRETS PRETTY REFLECTIONS	92
1703	1980	MALIBU BARBIE - THE BEACH PARTY with case (DSS)	65
—	1981	4 ESTACIONES (Mexico)	95
3533	1981	GOLDEN DREAM GLAMOROUS NIGHTS	74
—	1982	ET SON CHIEN PRINCE (France)	160
5939	1982	PINK & PRETTY (Modeling Set)	75
4431	1983	BARBIE & FRIENDS (PJ, Ken & Barbie)	77
4984	1983	CAMPIN' OUT (Barbie & Ken)	75
7583	1983	LOVING YOU	55
4079	1983	TWIRLY CURLS *Department Store special*	70
—	1984	GREAT SHAPE (Skipper, Barbie & Ken) England	45
7563	1984	LOVING YOU *Department Store special*	65
—	1985	DANCE SENSATION	50
9514	1985	HAPPY BIRTHDAY *Department Store special*	65
9678	1985	HAPPY BIRTHDAY BARBIE PARTY GIFT SET	85
6279	1985	LE NOUVEAU THEATER DE LA MODE* (Billy Boy) France	225
—	1985	MY FIRST (Haar eerste Haar Liefste) Holland	80
—	1985	SENSACION (Mexico)	90
2996	1986	TROPICAL - DELUXE	45

indicates cross reference

NEWER GIFT SETS CONTINUED

STOCK NO.	YEAR	DESCRIPTION	NRFB
—	1987	BARBIE & KEN WEDDING (Bandai) Japan	119
—	1987	CUTIE GIFT SET (Maba) Japan, LE 500	150
—	1987	KOREA GIFT SET	125
8790	1987	MEINE ERSTE BARBIE LET (Europe)	75
7799	1988	SHOW 'N RIDE* *Toys R Us*	40
7801	1988	TENNIS STAR BARBIE & KEN* *Toys R Us*	58
4217	1989	DANCE CLUB* (Children's Palace)	53
4893	1989	DENIM FUN* (Barbie, Ken & Skipper - Cool City Blues) *Toys R Us*	63
—	1989	DRESS ME 1+2 (Europe)	24
7272	1990	BARBIE & SNOWBALL HER PET DOG	20
5409	1990	DANCE MAGIC (Barbie & Ken)	43
9600	1990	FLIGHT TIME KEN	35
9916	1990	FLIGHT TIME BARBIE (black)	35
2066	1990	FLIGHT TIME BARBIE (Hispanic)	62
9584	1990	FLIGHT TIME BARBIE (white)	40
—	1990	HAPPY BRIDAL (Barbie & Ken - several versions) Japan	200
4841	1990	HOT DANCIN' SET	70
—	1990	ON THE GO (Europe)	60
5408	1990	WESTERN FUN* *Toys R Us*	55
5408	1990	WESTERN STAMPIN' STAR HORSE* *Wholesale Club*	43
3712	1991	ALL AMERICAN STAR STEPPER* *Wholesale Club*	45
3177	1991	BARBIE AND FRIENDS DISNEY DELUXE* *Toys R Us*	67
2483	1991	MY 1st BARBIE FASHION DELUXE FASHION	35
9852	1991	WEDDING PARTY MIDGE	104
2820	1991	WEDDING DAY KELLY/TODD* *Toys R Us, JCPenney*	33
7151	1992	100 PIECE - VERSION #1* *Wholesale Club*	47
7151	1992	100 PIECE - VERSION #2* *Wholesale Club*	47
—	1992	BEACH DAZZLE PLUS 2 FASHIONS SHANI* *Sears*	42
3331	1992	DREAM WARDROBE	35
2810	1992	MARINE* (black) Barbie & Ken	71
4704	1992	MARINE* (white) Barbie & Ken	50
7142	1992	*ROLLERBLADE* BARBIE* *Wholesale Club*	55
5716	1992	SHARIN' SISTER'S #1 (Barbie, Skipper & Stacie)	45
2262	1992	SNAP 'N PLAY DELUXE	30
7131	1992	SPARKLE EYES* *Sam's Club*	60

indicates cross reference

370

STOCK NO.	YEAR	DESCRIPTION	NRFB
7149	1992	SUN SENSATION - SPRAY & PLAY* *Wholesale Club*	52
5627	1993	ARMY* (black) Barbie & Ken	63
5626	1993	ARMY* (white) Barbie & Ken	65
11285	1993	CABOODLES BARBIE & CABOODLES CASE* *JCPenney*	29
10723	1993	DISNEY WEEKEND BARBIE*	55
10724	1993	DISNEY WEEKEND BARBIE & KEN*	68
10713	1993	DREAM WEDDING* (black) Barbie Stacie & Todd *Toys R Us*	44
10712	1993	DREAM WEDDING* (white) Barbie Stacie & Todd *Toys R Us*	53
—	1993	DRESSING FUN-LOTS OF FASHIONS* (purple dress) *Wholesale Club*	55
—	1993	DRESSING FUN-LOTS OF FASHIONS* (pink dress) *Wholesale Club*	55
10527	1993	BARBIE LOVES TO READ DELUXE* *Toys R Us*	40
3826	1993	FUN TO DRESS FASHION	20
10928	1993	HOLLYWOOD HAIR* *Wholesale Club*	31
10379	1993	ISLAND FUN* (Barbie & Ken) *Wholesale Club*	30
—	1993	LI'L FRIEND & ROCKING HORSE (Italy)	100
—	1993	LI'L FRIEND & WALKER (Italy)	100
10926	1993	PAINT 'N DAZZLE* *Wholesale Club*	27
10929	1993	SECRET HEARTS* (Barbie & Ken) *Wholesale Club*	45
10143	1993	SHARIN' SISTER'S #2 (Barbie, Skipper & Stacie)	39
10227	1993	STACIE BUTTERFLY PONY*	20
10924	1993	WEDDING FANTASY* *Wholesale Club, Kay Bee*	78
11020	1993	WESTERN STAMPIN'* (blue outfit) *Toys R Us*	45
10927	1993	WESTERN STAMPIN' DELUXE PLAYSET* *Wholesale Club*	30
13478	1993	WESTERN STAMPIN' BARBIE - WESTERN STAR HORSE* (black - red outfit) *Toys R Us*	40
11591	1994	35th ANNIVERSARY* Brunette *Mattel Festival*	518
11591	1994	35th ANNIVERSARY* Blonde	100
11582	1994	AIRFORCE BARBIE & KEN* (black - Thunderbirds)	50
11581	1994	AIRFORCE BARBIE & KEN* (white - Thunderbirds)	60
11481	1994	BEACH FUN* (Barbie & Ken) *Wholesale Club*	32
12184	1994	BED TIME* *Wholesale Club*	40
—	1994	BED TIME BARBIE W/BED* *Europe & Sam's Club*	45
11589	1994	BIRTHDAY FUN AT *MCDONALDS*	40
12043	1994	DOLLS OF THE WORLD #1* LE 5000 (Dutch, Kenyan, Chinese)	80
12665	1994	HAPPY MEAL STACIE AND WHITNEY* *JCPenney*	30

*indicates cross reference

STOCK NO.	YEAR	DESCRIPTION	NRFB
—	1994	ROLLERSKATING BARBIE & HER ROLL ALONG PUPPY* *Zeller's Canada*	84
13557	1994	WEDDING PARTY* (white) Barbie, Stacie & Todd *Toys R Us*	40
13556	1994	WEDDING PARTY* (black) Barbie, Stacie & Todd *Toys R Us*	32
13181	1995	BARBIE & CHAMPION HORSE RIDING SET* *Europe & Wholesale Club*	72
12371	1995	DENIM 'N RUFFLES* *BJ's Wholesale Club*	50
13939	1995	DOLLS OF THE WORLD #2* (Irish, German, Polynesian)	60
13511/			
11929	1995	HOT SKATIN' BARBIE & MUSTANG DELUXE* *Wholesale Club*	37
14406	1995	*POLLY POCKET* *JCPenney*	30
13742	1995	STROLLIN' FUN BARBIE & KELLY PLAYSET (white)	19
13743	1995	STROLLIN' FUN BARBIE & KELLY PLAYSET (black)	19
14073	1995	TRAVELIN' SISTERS PLAYSET* (Superstar smiling face) *Toys R Us, JCPenney*	47
14073	1995	TRAVELIN' SISTERS (Closed mouth, Mackie face - Japanese)	60
—	1996	BARBIE & KELLY (Philippines - pink)	—
—	1996	BARBIE & KELLY (Philippines - red plaid)	—
16079	1996	BARBIE MILLICENT ROBERTS* 1st (Matinee Today)	94
—	1996	BARBIE Y SU RUESINOR (Europe)	35
15610	1996	BIRTHDAY FUN KELLY* (Barbie, Kelly & Chelsie) *Toys R Us*	35
15283	1996	DOLLS OF THE WORLD #3* (Japanese, Norwegian, Indian)	80
16567	1996	FOAM 'N COLOR* *JCPenney*	30
14879/			
15648	1996	HORSE LOVIN' BARBIE & NIBBLES* *Wholesale Club*	30
16214	1996	OCEAN FRIENDS (Barbie & Keiko) various department stores	27
—	1996	OLYMPIC* *Wholesale Club*	35
15756	1996	SHOPPING FUN (white) Barbie & Kelly	24
15757	1996	SHOPPING FUN (black) Barbie & Kelly	24
15006	1996	*STAR TREK* (Barbie & Ken - 30th Anniversary)	28
13742	1996	STROLLIN' SISTERS (Barbie & Shelly - Europe)	25
63987	1996	SWEET MOMENTS* *Hudson Bay*	60
15645	1996	WINTER HOLIDAY *Ames, JCPenney, Toys R Us, Meijer, FAO, Spiegel, Hills*	40
17116	1997	BARBIE AND GINGER (white)	20
17369	1997	BARBIE AND GINGER (black)	20
17450	1997	BARBIE LOVES ELVIS*	73
17567	1997	BARBIE MILLICENT ROBERTS* 2nd (Perfectly Suited)	69
16708	1997	CHINESE EMPRESS* (Hong Kong Commemorative Edition)	133

indicates cross reference

STOCK NO.	YEAR	DESCRIPTION	NRFB
18547	1997	GAP BARBIE & KELLY* (white)	49
18548	1997	GAP BARBIE & KELLY* (black)	43
17242	1997	GARDENING FUN BARBIE & KELLY* *Toys R Us*	21
17238	1997	HAPPY HALLOWEEN BARBIE & KELLY* *Target*	30
—	1997	HAPPY HALLOWEEN BARBIE & KELLY Brunette - *Children*	—
		Affected by AIDS Foundation, LE	
18726	1997	OLYMPIC SKATER (white)	40
18727	1997	OLYMPIC SKATER (black)	40
17240	1997	PALEONTOLOGIST* (white) *Career Collection, Toys R Us*	18
17241	1997	PALEONTOLOGIST* (black) *Career Collection, Toys R Us*	18
15059	1997	SHOW PARADE w/Star Stampin' Horse* (white) *Toys R Us*	30
15060	1997	SHOW PARADE w/Star Stampin' Horse* (black) *Toys R Us*	30
17350	1997	TALK WITH ME* (white)	30
17370	1997	TALK WITH ME* (black)	30
17243	1997	WEDDING FANTASY* Barbie & Ken *Toys R Us*	30
18187	1998	BALLET RECITAL* (white) Barbie & Kelly	15
21388	1998	BALLET RECITAL* (black) Barbie & Kelly	15
17765	1998	BARBIE SOFTWARE FOR GIRLS PARTY GIFT SET* (Birthday Suprise doll and Party Print 'N Play CD-Rom)	20
19809	1998	CHRISTMAS SISTER'S* Barbie, Stacie & Kelly *Toys R Us*	25
18898	1998	DR. KEN & LITTLE PATIENT TOMMY*	15
18899	1998	DR. KEN & LITTLE PATIENT TOMMY*	15
19014	1998	EASTER EGG HUNT SE * *Target*	39
20649	1998	GOLDEN GREATER QI-PAO* Commemorative Set LE 8888	89
19874	1998	HALLOWEEN PARTY BARBIE & KEN* *Target*	26
—	1998	HAPPY HOLIDAYS BARBIE & KEN GIFT SET* (India)	91
19809	1998	HOLIDAY SISTERS* Barbie, Stacie & Kelly	25
18895	1998	I'M A TOYS R US KID* (white) - 50th Anniversary *Toys R Us*	20
—	1998	I'M A TOYS R US KID* (black) - 50th Anniversary *Toys R Us*	20
19810	1998	KELLY & GINGER*	25
18717	1998	KELLY & TOMMY POWER WHEELS* (white)	20
18718	1998	KELLY & TOMMY POWER WHEELS* (black)	20
19625	1998	LI'L ZOO PALS* Barbie, Stacie & Kelly	25
18976	1998	MIDGE - 35TH ANNIVERSARY* (Senior Prom) *Toys R Us*	48
20377	1998	PHANTOM OF THE OPERA* Barbie & Ken *FAO Schwarz, Select Theatres*	139

indicates cross reference

STOCK NO.	YEAR	DESCRIPTION	NRFB
19791	1998	PINSTRIPE POWER* *Barbie Millicent Roberts*	50
20346	1998	PONY & KELLY GIFT SET*	20
19364	1998	ROMEO & JULIET* *Together Forever Collection*	71
20780	1998	SWEET TREAT GIFT SET	
21524	1998	TOMMY & KELLY POWER WHEELS* (white) *Wal-Mart*	20
19705	1998	WALKING BEAUTY HORSE & HORSE RIDING BARBIE	40
20315	1998	WALT DISNEY VACATION GIFT SET* (Disneyland version - Barbie, Ken, Tommy & Kelly)	48
20221	1998	WALT DISNEY VACATION GIFT SET* (Walt Disney World version - Barbie, Ken, Tommy & Kelly)	48
19850	1998	WINTER RIDE* *Toys R Us, FAO Schwarz*	49
—	1998	WORKIN' OUT* outfits vary *Wholesale*	
19630	1998	X-FILES* Mulder & Scully - Pop Culture (1st version long hair)	80
19630	1998	X-FILES* Mulder & Scully - Pop Culture (2nd version short hair)	48
22953	1999	BARBIE LOVES FRANKIE*	Retail
—	1999	BLAZIN' TRAILS BARBIE AND HORSE	30
21720	1999	EASTER BUNNY FUN BARBIE & KELLY* *Target*	18
24640	1999	FANTASY HORSE & BARBIE	Retail
20333	1999	GIGGLES 'N SWING - Barbie & Kelly* (white)	15
20534	1999	GIGGLES 'N SWING - Barbie & Kelly* (black)	15
23796	1999	HALLOWEEN LI'L FRIENDS OF KELLY GIFT SET	28
23460	1999	HALLOWEEN FUN BARBIE AND KELLY GIFT SET	25
—	1999	HOLIDAY SISTERS	30
22963	1999	KELLY AND TOMMY SOCCER	15
23880	1999	KING ARTHUR & QUEEN GUINEVERE* *Together Forever Collection*	Retail
—	1999	ROYAL ROMANCE (with Horse)	50
20843	1999	WALK AMERICA - MARCH OF DIMES GIFT SET* (white) *K-Mart*	17
20844	1999	WALK AMERICA - MARCH OF DIMES GIFT SET* (black) *K-Mart*	17
22307	2000	BARBIE AND BABY SISTER KRISSY (white)	18
22232	2000	BARBIE AND BABY SISTER KRISSY (black)	18
25502	2000	GENERATION GIRL - Barbie and Lara	15
—	2000	LET'S DRIVE - *Toys R Us* Barbie Skipper*	35
—	2000	RAINBOW HORSE AND PRINCESS BRIDE	30
—	2000	SINGING SISTERS - Barbie - Stacy - Kelly	38
—	2000	THE ADDAMS FAMILY - Pop Culture Series*	63
28395	2000	VICTORIAN HOLIDAY BARBIE AND KELLY*	Retail

BARBIE® ORNAMENTS

STOCK NO.	YEAR	DESCRIPTION	NRFB
		ASHTON-DRAKE (4¾")	
—	1995	ENCHANTED EVENING	12
—	1995	FASHION EDITOR	12
—	1995	GAY PARISIENNE	12
—	1995	ROMAN HOLIDAY	12
—	1995	SATURDAY MATINEE	12
—	1995	SWIMSUIT	12
—	1996	COMMUTER SET	12
—	1996	EASTER PARADE	12
—	1996	EVENING SPLENDOR	12
—	1996	FRATERNITY DANCE	12
—	1996	SILKEN FLAME	12
—	1996	SOLO IN THE SPOTLIGHT	12
		AVON	
—	1997	SUGAR PLUM FAIRY - Porcelain (1st in Series)	25
		CHRISTOPHER RADKO	
—	1997	ALPINE BLUSH BARBIE LE 4½"	45
—	1997	BARBIE BLOCK	40
—	1997	HOLIDAY BARBIE, LE 6½"	50
—	1998	BARBIE STOCKING 5"	38
—	1998	ELEGANT HOLIDAY 10"	35
		ENESCO **also see ENESCO - ORNAMENTS**	
—	1996	1963 HOLIDAY DANCE (4" disc)	15
—	1996	1989 HAPPY HOLIDAYS (3¼" disc)	14
—	1996	1996 HAPPY HOLIDAYS (3¼" disc)	15
182028	1996	BARBIE AS SCARLETT O'HARA 3¼" (green velvet)	12
188867	1996	HAPPY HOLIDAYS 1989 3¼"	15
188824	1996	HAPPY HOLIDAYS 1996 3¼"	15
157724	1996	QUEEN OF HEARTS w/feathers	10
—	1996	QUEEN OF HEARTS (Mackie - heart shaped with red ribbons)	10
—	1996	SCARLETT O'HARA (green velvet - disc) LE	12
—	1996	SUMMER SOPHISTICATE (Spiegel) 3¼" porcelain disc	15

*indicates cross reference

375

BARBIE® ORNAMENTS CONTINUED

STOCK NO.	YEAR	DESCRIPTION	NRFB
		ENESCO (continued)	
—	1997	1990 HAPPY HOLIDAYS	15
260207	1997	BARBIE AS DOROTHY (1st in series)	13
310832	1997	BARBIE AS DOROTHY, KEN A THE LION, KEN AS THE SCARECROW, KEN AS THE TIN MAN 3¼" (3rd in series)	15
284335	1997	BARBIE AS DOROTHY, KEN AS THE LION, KEN AS THE SCARECROW, KEN AS THE TIN MAN plate & ornament set Elite Dealer Exclusive LE 2500 sets*	150
270520	1997	BARBIE AS ELIZA DOOLITTLE (Ascot) 4¼" (1st in series)	12
—	1997	BARBIE AS ELIZA DOOLITTLE (Ascot - disc)	12
274305	1997	BARBIE AS ELIZA DOOLITTLE (Embassy Ball) 4¾"	11
274283	1997	BARBIE AS GLINDA THE GOOD WITCH 3¼" (2nd in series)	14
260177	1997	BARBIE AS SCARLETT O'HARA 3¼" (2nd in series)	13
260223	1997	GODDESS OF THE SUN 4¾"	15
274240	1997	HAPPY HOLIDAYS 1990 3¼"	11
274267	1997	HAPPY HOLIDAYS 1997 3¼"	12
188808	1997	HOLIDAY DANCE 1965 4"	13
260258	1997	MOON GODDESS 3¾"	13
274208	1997	ORNAMENT HOLDER 6"	10
274224	1997	TRIO DISPLAY (plate & ornament)* 15" long	30
260290	1997	WEDDING DAY 1959 3¼"	13
295248	1998	CAMPUS SWEETHEART - heart shaped decal	13
		FAO SCHWARZ	
—	1996	24K GOLD FINISH 2¼"	45
		HALLMARK	
		African-American Holiday Barbie	
—	1998	AFRICAN-AMERICAN HOLIDAY BARBIE* 1st	16
		Barbie Series	
—	1994	35th ANNIVERSARY 1st Blonde Debut (black/white swimsuit)	30
—	1995	SOLO IN THE SPOTLIGHT 2nd	20
—	1996	ENCHANTED EVENING 3rd	18
—	1997	BARBIE & KEN WEDDING DAY SET	30

indicates cross reference

STOCK NO.	YEAR	DESCRIPTION	NRFB
Barbie Series **(continued)**			
—	1997	BARBIE WEDDING DAY 4th	20
—	1998	SILKEN FLAME 5th	18
—	1999	GAY PARISIENNE 6th	18
—	2000	CELEBRATION 1st	16
—	2000	COMMUTER SET	16
Holiday Barbie Series			
—	1993	1993 HOLIDAYS BARBIE 1st	85
—	1994	1994 HOLIDAYS BARBIE 2nd	30
—	1995	1995 HOLIDAYS BARBIE 3rd	25
—	1996	1996 HOLIDAYS BARBIE 4th	15
—	1997	1997 HOLIDAYS BARBIE 5th	15
—	1998	1998 HOLIDAYS BARBIE 6th (white)	15
—	1998	1998 HOLIDAYS BARBIE* (black)	15
Children Collector Series (Springtime)			
—	1997	RAPUNZEL 1st	20
—	1998	LITTLE BO PEEP 2nd	15
—	1999	CINDERELLA 3rd	15
Collectors Club Series			
—	1995	CLUB EDITION 35th ANNIVERSARY, 1959 Debut 1st (brunette in black/white swimsuit)	45
—	1996	CLUB EDITION 1988 HAPPY HOLIDAYS BARBIE 1st	40
—	1997	CLUB EDITION 1989 HAPPY HOLIDAYS BARBIE 2nd	30
—	1998	CLUB EDITION 1990 HAPPY HOLIDAYS 3rd	25
—	1999	CLUB EDITION 1991 HAPPY HOLIDAYS 4th	25
—	2000	PORCELAIN	30
Dolls of the World Ornament Series			
—	1996	NATIVE AMERICAN, Dolls of the World Series 1st	25
—	1997	CHINESE, Dolls of the World Series 2nd	20
—	1998	MEXICAN, Dolls of the World Series 3rd	20
—	1999	RUSSIAN, Dolls of the World Series 4th/final	18

*indicates cross reference

BARBIE® ORNAMENTS CONTINUED

NO.	YEAR	DESCRIPTION	NRFB
Holiday Homecoming Collection			
—	1997	HOLIDAY TRADITIONS 1st	20
—	1998	HOLIDAY VOYAGE 2nd	15
Miniatures			
—	1999	TRAVEL CASE AND BARBIE SET	20
—	2000	SILKEN FLAME BARBIE AND TRAVEL CASE	13
Springtime Barbie Series			
—	1995	SPRINGTIME #1	18
—	1996	SPRINGTIME #2	15
—	1997	SPRINGTIME #3	15
—	1998	SPRINGTIME #4	
Victorian Christmas Collection			
—	1997	VICTORIAN ELEGANCE KEEPSAKE 2 -7/8"	15
—	1998	HOLIDAY MEMORIES, Victorian Collection	15
Miscellaneous			
—	1998	MIDGE 35th ANNIVERSARY	15
—	1999	40th ANNIVERSARY BARBIE	18
—	1999	40th ANNIVERSARY EDITION BARBIE LUNCH BOX	13
—	1999	DREAMHOUSE PLAYHOUSE	15
—	1999	MILLENNIUM PRINCESS (white)	25
—	1999	MILLENNIUM PRINCESS (black)	25
—	2000	ANGEL OF JOY	15
—	2000	HARLEY DAVIDSON	15
—	2000	1962 HATBOX DOLL CASE	10
—	2000	WINTER FUN WITH BARBIE AND KELLY	16
		JCPENNEY	
—	1995	1995 HAPPY HOLIDAY	18
—	1996	WINTER RENAISSANCE 4" decoupage w/stand	18
—	1997	EVENING MAJESTY* 4" decoupage w/stand	18

*indicates cross reference

BARBIE® ORNAMENTS CONTINUED

NO.	YEAR	DESCRIPTION	NRFB
		MATRIX	
—	1996	#1 PONYTAIL IN B/W SS	10
—	1996	1996 HAPPY HOLIDAY 4" decoupage w/wooden stand	15
—	1996	BALLERINA	10
—	1996	DREAM BRIDE 4" decoupage w/wooden stand *Wholesale Club*	15
—	1996	ENCHANTED EVENING	10
—	1996	MY FIRST TEA PARTY	10
—	1996	POODLE PARADE	10
—	1996	PICNIC SET	10
—	1996	RED FLARE	10
—	1996	SOLO IN THE SPOTLIGHT	10
—	1996	SONGBIRD	10
—	1996	WINTER RENAISSANCE* 4" decoupage w/wooden stand *JCPenney*	20
—	1997	1997 HAPPY HOLIDAYS 4" decoupage w/wooden stand	15
—	1997	AMERICAN GIRL W/KEN decoupage	10
—	1997	BLONDE SWIRL IN MIDNIGHT BLUE decoupage	10
—	1997	BRUNETTE BUBBLE CUT IN SILKEN FLAME decoupage	10
—	1997	BRUNETTE PONYTAIL IN GAY PARISIENNE decoupage	10
—	1997	FASHION AVENUE (several versions)	10
—	1998	1998 HAPPY HOLIDAYS 4" decoupage w/wooden stand	15
		MATTEL FESTIVAL	
—	1994	35th ANNIVERSARY BALL	40
		MISCELLANEOUS	
—	1987	OKLAHOMA BARBIE DOLL CLUB	25
—	1987	BARBIE COLLECTORS CONVENTION JUNE 1987 (Mattel Gift)	25
		SPIEGEL	
—	1996	SUMMER SOPHISTICATE 3¼" porcelain disc	15

BARBIE® HOT WHEELS®

DESCRIPTION	YEAR	NRFB
1st EDITION, LE 7000 (#13250)	1994	85
2nd EDITION, LE 8000 (#13250)	1994	50
TOY CLUB PONTIAC STOCKER, LE 7000 (#12873)	1994	25
TOY CLUB CHEVY STEPSIDE, LE 7000	1994	50
HIWAY HAULER, LE 5000	1996	90
TOYS R US 50 YEARS FOREVER FUN SE (4 car set including Barbie Mustang Convertible)	1998	25
BARBIE DODGE CARAVAN	1999	25

❖❖❖❖❖❖❖❖❖❖❖❖❖❖❖

NEWER BOOKLETS/FLYERS

DESCRIPTION	YEAR	NRFB
THE WORLD OF BARBIE	1973	25
WORLD OF BARBIE FASHIONS	1976	8
BARBIE WORLD OF FASHION	1978	8
BARBIE WORLD OF FASHION - Book A	1979	15
BARBIE WORLD OF FASHION - Book B	1979	8
BARBIE WORLD OF FASHION	1980	8
MY FIRST BARBIE	1980	5
BARBIE WORLD OF FASHION	1981	8
BARBIE WORLD OF FASHION	1982	8
BARBIE INTERNATIONAL DOLLS	1983	15
BARBIE WORLD OF FASHION	1983	5
BARBIE WORLD OF FASHION	1984	5
BARBIE WORLD OF FASHION	1985	5
BILLY BOY TOUR BOOKLET (U.S. version)	1985	10
BARBIE WORLD OF FASHION	1986	5
BARBIE WORLD OF FASHION	1987	5
PERFUME PRETTY BARBIE	1987	5
SKIPPER TEEN SCRAP BOOK	1987	5
BARBIE WORLD OF FASHION	1988	5
SKIPPER	1988	5

NEWER BOOKS, COMIC BOOKS & COLORING BOOKS

DESCRIPTION	YEAR	NRFB
BOOKS		
BARBIE - MY VERY OWN DIARY - Help Barbie Write Her Diary	1985	5
BARBIES NEIGHBORHOOD w/45 record included	1992	3
ROCKIN', RAPPIN', DANCIN' Pop-up book	1992	10
WOMEN INVENTORS & THEIR DISCOVERIES by Ethlie Ann Vare and	1993	20
Greg Ptacek (The Oliver Press, Inc.)		
DREAM DOLL Ruth Handler's Autobiography	1994	30
DEAR BARBIE LOOK LOOK® BOOK SET (5 books: Who's the Boss,	1997	15
Riding Champion, The Wonderful Wedding, Too Many Puppies,		
Best Friends)		
COMIC BOOKS		
FASHION FUN & EXCITING ESCAPES January (Marvel)	1990	3
A WINTER WONDERLAND ON THE OUTSIDE February (Marvel)	1991	3
BARBIE 1 January, Fashion Fun & Exciting Escapades (doorknob hanger)	1991	7
BARBIE 2 February, Winter Wonderland on the Outside, Sun & Fun on the Inside	1991	7
BARBIE 3 March, Dancing the Night Away	1991	5
BARBIE 4 April, High Flying Fashion Fun	1991	5
BARBIE FASHION 1 January, Stylish Stories & Rend Setting Tips	1991	7
(Barbie Comic Pink Card)		
BARBIE FASHION 2 February, Barbie	1991	7
BARBIE FASHION 3 March, Barbie	1991	5
BARBIE FASHION 4 April, The Big New York Adventure	1991	5
COLORING BOOKS, STICKER BOOKS & SCRAPBOOKS		
1015 BARBIE & SKIPPER	1973	30
BARBIE AND KEN Coloring Book #1637 (Whitman)	1974	18
BARBIE AND SKIPPER SPORT STARTS Color and Activity Book #1654	1974	14

NEWER BOOKS, COMIC BOOKS & COLORING BOOKS CONTINUED

DESCRIPTION	YEAR	NRFB
COLORING BOOKS, STICKER BOOKS & SCRAPBOOKS (continued)		
BARBIE COLORING BOOK #1670 (Whitman)	1974	12
BARBIE SWEET 16 DOT BOOK - Coloring Book #1280	1974	12
MALIBU CAMPSITE STICKER BOOK (Whitman)	1974	25
MINI POSTERS (14" x 20") (Whitman)	1974	15
QUICK CURL BARBIE Coloring Book #1644(Whitman)	1975	12
BALLERINA BARBIE #1660 (Whitman)	1977	12
SUPERSTAR BARBIE STICKER BOOK (Whitman)	1977	20
WORLD OF BARBIE (Whitman)	1978	12
GREAT SHAPE SLUMBER PARTY PAK STICKER BOOK (Golden)	1985	5
BARBIE AND THE ROCKERS COLOR FORMS (Golden)	1986	7
JEWEL SECRETS (Whitman)	1987	5
BARBIE AND THE ROCKERS (Whitman)	1987	5
BARBIE STICKER ALBUM (Panini)	1989	20
COLOR FORMS, Barbie Holiday	1992	8
COLOR FORMS, Fashion Boutique	1992	8
COLOR FORMS, Hollywood Hair	1993	8
COLOR FORMS, Secret Hearts	1993	8
COLORFORMS, Hollywood Hair Barbie Dress Up Set	1994	9
THE BARBIE PARTY COOKBOOK (Price Stern Sloan)	1994	20

CALENDARS

DESCRIPTION	NRFB
1989 DESIGN LOOK 30th ANNIVERSARY (16 month)	15
1989 GIBSON (8 pictures of Blonde #1 on cover)	10
1990 NOSTALGIC	12
1991 BARBIE SNEAK PREVIEW W/EXTRA DRESS (Mattel) 15 month	12
1991 NOSTALGIC	10
1992 GIBSON	5
1994 FRENCH	5
1994 GERMAN	5
1995 GERMAN	5
1995 HALLMARK Blonde #1 Ponytail in black & white swimsuit	12
1996 HALLMARK - Redhead Bubble Cut, Blonde Ponytail & Brunette Ponytail	15
1997 BARBIE COLLECTIBLES	1
1997 HALLMARK - Blonde TNT Barbie in Live Action outfit	16
1998 HALLMARK	12
1998 HALLMARK BARBIE-A-DREAM WEDDING	12
1999 AT-A-GLANCE (16 month)	10
1999 HALLMARK SPECIAL 40TH ANNIVERSARY EDITION	12
2000 HOMETOWN GRAPHICS (16 month) (4" x 4")	4
2000 HOMETOWN GRAPHICS (16 month) (16" x 16")	6
2000 YEAR-IN-A-BOX (sheet a day)	12
2000 HALLMARK	12

CONVENTION DOLL PACKAGES/ITEMS

DESCRIPTION	YEAR	NRFB
NEW YORK, NY (Beauty Secrets/Banner)	1980	300
TROY, MICHIGAN "Michigan Entertains Barbie" (Eskimo as Indian)	1982	325
PHOENIX, ARIZONA "Barbie's Pow Wow" (Fashion Jeans in Prairie Dress)	1983	350
NEW YORK, NY "Barbie Loves New York" (Loving You in Red Gown)	1984	350
ROMULUS, MICHIGAN "Barbie Around the World Festival"	1985	325
(Japanese Barbie w/banner)		
PHOENIX, ARIZONA "Barbie's Reunion" (Sun Gold in Tan Suit)	1986	300
OKLAHOMA CITY, OKLAHOMA "Christmas w/Barbie"	1987	300
(Astronaut in Nightshirt)		
SEATTLE, WASHINGTON "Rain or Shine" (Sun Gold as Rhododendron)	1988	315
GARDEN GROVE, CALIFORNIA "Barbie Forever Young"	1989	285
(Sensations as Mousekateer)		
DALLAS, TEXAS "Deep in the Heart of Texas" (My First Ballerina as a Cowgirl)	1990	275
OMAHA, NEBRASKA "Barbie Loves a Fairytale"	1991	263
(Dress 'N Play as a Princess w/Ken as Prince Charming)		
NIAGARA FALLS, NY "Wedding Dreams" (Redressed Dream Bride)	1992	225
BALTIMORE, MARYLAND "You've Come a Long Way Barbie"	1993	305
BARBIE CELEBRATES POSTER, LE 500 Catena Lemonakis 15½" x 11½"	1994	30
BIRMINGHAM, ALABAMA "The Magic of Barbie in Birmingham"	1994	275
THE MAGIC OF BARBIE IN BIRMINGHAM POSTER, LE 600	1994	35
Catena Lemonakis 11½" x 14 5/8"		
ALBUQUERQUE, NEW MEXICO "Barbie Olé"	1995	268
PHILADELPHIA, PENNSYLVANIA "Barbie & the Bandstand"	1996	275
BARBIE AND THE BAND STAND AUTOGRAPH BOOK	1996	20
SAN DIEGO, CALIFORNIA "Beach Blanket Barbie" (2 dress versions)	1997	145
Beach ball bag		15
Card catalogs		12
Coin purse		8
Flying disc		4
Magazine		25
Mug		12

CONVENTION DOLL
PACKAGES/ITEMS CONTINUED

DESCRIPTION	YEAR	NRFB
Paper dolls		8
Pen		3
Sunglasses		5
Visor		3
ATLANTA, GEORGIA "A Date With Barbie Doll in Atlanta"	1998	278
Necklace and earring set (includes necklace)		
Black tote bag (canvas)		10
Soiree magazine		2
Makeup case (lipstick, fingernail polish, perfume) black zippered		10
Dress stand		10
Paper dolls (Convention, Midge and Gone With the Wind)		10
Long stem red rose		5
Ornament, Enesco - Campus Sweetheart		15
Miniature Mystery Date game		3
Mug		10
Magnet - Dream Doll		5
Blue coin purse key chain		3
Luggage tag		3
Red rose lapel pin		5
Pink pencil		1
Folder		1
Flyers (Tango in the Night, Getting All Dolled Up, Let's Do Lunch, Mystery Date)		1
Barbie & Ken heart key chain		5
TULSA, OKLAHOMA "Barbie in the Old West"	2000	201

DISNEY CONVENTION EXCLUSIVES

STOCK NO.	YEAR	DESCRIPTION	NRFB HIGH	LOW	AVG
9973	1991	GAY PARISIENNE* Redhead, LE 300 *Porcelain*	706	430	568
9973	1991	GAY PARISIENNE* Blonde, LE 300 *Porcelain*	737	378	558
5351	1992	PLANTATION BELLE* Blonde, LE 300 *Porcelain*	642	416	529
10201	1993	CRYSTAL RHAPSODY* Brunette, LE 250	824	685	755
11099	1993	SILKEN FLAME* Blonde, LE 400 *Porcelain*	651	388	520
13173	1994	EVERGREEN PRINCESS* Redhead, LE 1500	203	108	156
		Winter Princess Collection			
14954	1995	STARLIGHT WALTZ* Brunette, LE 1500 *Ballroom Beauties*	450	225	338
16400	1996	JEWEL PRINCESS* Brunette, LE 1500	140	90	115
18486	1997	MIDNIGHT PRINCESS* Brunette, LE 1500	122	74	98
		Winter Princess Collection			
—	1999	COCA-COLA CAR HOP* Brunette, LE 1500	100	75	88

❖❖❖❖❖❖❖❖❖❖❖❖❖❖

ENESCO - BELLS

STOCK NO.	YEAR	DESCRIPTION	NRFB
174734	1996	HERE COMES THE BRIDE 1966	25

❖❖❖❖❖❖❖❖❖❖❖❖❖❖

ENESCO - CAMEO COLLECTION

STOCK NO.	YEAR	DESCRIPTION	NRFB
162272	1996	GLASS BELL Frosted 5"	20
157570	1996	GLASS BUD VASE Frosted 6"	20
157627	1996	GLASS COVERED BOX Frosted 2"	15
157635	1996	GLASS PICTURE FRAME Frosted	25
157619	1996	GLASS POWDER BOX Frosted 3½"	20
157643	1996	GLASS VANITY TRAY Frosted 6½"	25
157589	1996	PERFUME BOTTLE Frosted 4¼"	20

ENESCO - FIGURINES

❖❖❖❖❖❖❖❖❖❖❖❖❖❖

ENESCO - JEWELRY BOX

❖❖❖❖❖❖❖❖❖❖❖❖❖❖

ENESCO - MUGS

*indicates cross reference

ENESCO - MUSICALS

STOCK NO.	YEAR	DESCRIPTION	NRFB
551538	1994	LET'S GO TO THE HOP *At the Hop* Record Player	125
353752	1994	SOLO IN THE SPOTLIGHT 1960, LE 7500 *Unforgettable*	100
353620	1994	SOME ENCHANTED EVENING 1960, LE 7500 *Enchanted Evening*	100
353639	1994	WEDDING ON THE CHURCH STEPS 1959, LE 7500 *Wedding March* by Mendelssohn	100
113905	1995	BRIDES DREAM 1963, LE 7500 *True Love* 9¼"	100
154199	1995	HAPPY HOLIDAYS BARBIE 1988 *Deck the Halls*	100
154210	1995	HAPPY HOLIDAYS BARBIE 1988 *Deck the Halls* Musical Jewelry Box	100
154202	1995	HAPPY HOLIDAYS BARBIE 1988 *Deck the Halls* Musical Plaque	75
143111	1995	MAGNIFICENCE 1965, LE 7500 *Silver Bells* 10"	100
113891	1995	MIDNIGHT BLUE 1965, LE 7500 *Moon River* Glamour Collection 10½"	100
125776	1995	SENIOR PROM 1963, LE 7500 *All I Have To Do Is Dream* Glamour Collection 10"	100
124370	1995	SENIOR PROM 1963 *Notre Dame Victory March* Austin Healy w/Ken 6"	100
113883	1995	SOPHISTICATED LADY 1963, LE 7500 *Sophisticated Lady* Glamour Collection 10"	100
171107	1996	BARBIE AS SCARLETT O'HARA (green velvet) Wooden Music Box	100
171093	1996	BARBIE AS SCARLETT O'HARA, LE 7500 *Tara's Theme* 10½"	100
185787	1996	ENCHANTED EVENING, LE 2500 *As Time Goes By*	100
274321	1996	HAPPY HOLIDAYS 1996 *Winter Wonderland* 10"	100
188832	1996	HAPPY HOLIDAYS 1989 *Silver Bells* 11"	100
170976	1996	HERE COMES THE BRIDE 1966, LE 7500 *Here Comes the Bride* 10½"	100
157716	1996	QUEEN OF HEARTS *Young at Heart* 5" long wooden	90
157651	1996	QUEEN OF HEARTS, LE 5000 *Young at Heart* Glamour Collection	100
260185	1997	BARBIE AS DOROTHY, LE 5000 *Somewhere Over the Rainbow* (1st in series) 10"	100
270504	1997	BARBIE AS ELIZA DOOLITTLE, LE 5000 *Ascot Gavotte)* (1st in series) 11"	150
274356	1997	BARBIE AS ELIZA DOOLITTLE, LE 5000 *Embassy Ball* 12" I could have danced all night	150
274348	1997	BARBIE AS GLINDA THE GOOD WITCH, LE 5000 *Munchkinland* (2nd in series) 11"	125
233668	1997	BARBIE AS SCARLETT O'HARA, LE 5000 *Tara's Theme* (2nd in series) 10"	125
271616	1997	FRIDAY NIGHT DATE *Rock Around the Clock* Record Action Mini Musical	135
265470	1997	GODDESS OF THE SUN, LE 5000 *Summer Wind* 11"	150
274313	1997	HAPPY HOLIDAYS BARBIE 1990 *Happy Holidays* 11"	100
188786	1997	HOLIDAY DANCE 1965, LE 7500 *I Could Have Danced All Night* 10"	100
265489	1997	MOON GODDESS, LE 5000 *Fly Me to the Moon* 11"	150
260304	1997	MUSICAL CAKE TOPPER *Pachelbel's Canon In D* 5½"	50
260274	1997	WEDDING DAY, LE 2500 *Pachelbel's Canon In D* 9½"	100
295213	1998	CAMPUS SWEETHEART, LE 5000 *Let Me Call You Sweetheart*	100

ENESCO - NIGHT LIGHT

STOCK NO.	YEAR	DESCRIPTION	NRFB
115266	1995	ENCHANTED EVENING 1960	25

❖❖❖❖❖❖❖❖❖❖❖❖❖❖❖

ENESCO - ORNAMENTS
also see BARBIE® ORNAMENTS

STOCK NO.	YEAR	DESCRIPTION	NRFB
—	1996	1963 HOLIDAY DANCE (4" disc)	15
—	1996	1989 HAPPY HOLIDAYS (3¼" disc)	14
—	1996	1996 HAPPY HOLIDAYS (3¼" disc)	15
182028	1996	BARBIE AS SCARLETT O'HARA 3¼" (green velvet)	12
188867	1996	HAPPY HOLIDAYS 1989 3¼"	15
188824	1996	HAPPY HOLIDAYS 1996 3¼"	15
157724	1996	QUEEN OF HEARTS w/feathers - heart shaped w/red ribbons	10
—	1996	SUMMER SOPHISTICATE (Spiegel) 3¼" porcelain disc	15
260207	1997	BARBIE AS DOROTHY (1st in series)	13
310832	1997	BARBIE AS DOROTHY, KEN A THE LION, KEN AS THE SCARECROW, KEN AS THE TIN MAN 3¼" (3rd in series)	15
284335	1997	BARBIE AS DOROTHY, KEN AS THE LION, KEN AS THE SCARECROW, KEN AS THE TIN MAN plate & ornament set Elite Dealer Exclusive LE 2500 sets*	150
270520	1997	BARBIE AS ELIZA DOOLITTLE (Ascot) 4¼" (1st in series)	12
274305	1997	BARBIE AS ELIZA DOOLITTLE (Embassy Ball) 4¾"	11
274283	1997	BARBIE AS GLINDA THE GOOD WITCH 3¼" (2nd in series)	14
260177	1997	BARBIE AS SCARLETT O'HARA 3¼" (2nd in series)	13
260223	1997	GODDESS OF THE SUN 4¾"	13
274240	1997	HAPPY HOLIDAYS 1990 3¼"	15
274267	1977	HAPPY HOLIDAYS 1997 3¼"	12
188808	1997	HOLIDAY DANCE 1965 4"	13
260258	1997	MOON GODDESS 3¾"	13
274208	1997	ORNAMENT HOLDER 6"	10
274224	1997	TRIO DISPLAY (plate & ornament)* 15" long	30
260290	1997	WEDDING DAY 1959 3¼"	13
295248	1998	CAMPUS SWEETHEART - heart-shaped decal	13

❖❖❖❖❖❖❖❖❖❖❖❖❖❖❖

ENESCO - OVAL COVERED BOXES

STOCK NO.	YEAR	DESCRIPTION	NRFB
157562	1996	ENCHANTED EVENING 1960 1¾"	20
157554	1996	SOLO IN THE SPOTLIGHT 1960 1¾"	20
157546	1996	WEDDING DAY 1959 1¾"	20

ENESCO - PLATES*

NO.	YEAR	DESCRIPTION	NRFB
25655112	1994	35th ANNIVERSARY PLATE 1959, LE 5000	45
655058	1994	AFTER FIVE 1962 (mini plate)	12
655074	1994	EASTER PARADE 1959 (mini plate)	12
655104	1994	EVENING SPLENDOR 1959 (mini plate)	12
655066	1994	GAY PARISIENNE 1959 (mini plate)	12
115088	1994	HAPPY HOLIDAYS BARBIE 1994, LE 5000	30
655090	1994	RED FLARE 1962 (mini plate)	12
655082	1994	ROMAN HOLIDAY 1959 (mini plate)	12
154180	1995	HAPPY HOLIDAYS 1988 8½"	30
14354	1995	HAPPY HOLIDAYS 1995 8½"	30
114383	1995	SOLO IN THE SPOTLIGHT 1960	30
174777	1996	1920's FLAPPER, LE 10,000 (2nd in series) 8¼"	30
171069	1996	ARABIAN KNIGHTS SCHEHERAZADE 1964 (mini plate) 4¼"	12
171050	1996	A ROYAL SURPRISE 1964 (Guinevere & King Arthur - mini plate) 4¼"	12
171085	1996	BARBIE AS SCARLETT O'HARA, LE 10,000 8¼"	30
171042	1996	CINDERELLA 1964 (mini plate) 4¼"	12
175587	1996	ENCHANTED EVENING 1960, LE 10,000 8¼"	30
174769	1996	GIBSON GIRL, LE 10,000 (1st in series) 8¼"	30
188859	1996	HAPPY HOLIDAYS 1989 8¼"	30
188816	1996	HAPPY HOLIDAYS 1996 8¼"	35
170984	1996	HERE COMES THE BRIDE 1966 (Oval) 8¼" x 6½"	30
171077	1996	LITTLE RED RIDING HOOD 1964 (mini plate) 4¼"	12
157678	1996	QUEEN OF HEARTS (heart plate) 6½"	30
174785	1997	1950's SOUTHERN BELLE, LE 7500 (3rd in series) 8¼"	30
260193	1997	BARBIE AS DOROTHY, LE 7500 (1st in series) 8¼"	35
284327	1997	BARBIE AS DOROTHY, KEN AS THE LION, KEN AS THE SCARECROW, KEN AS THE TIN MAN, LE 7500 (3rd in Series) 8¼"	35
284335	1997	BARBIE AS DOROTHY, KEN AS THE LION, KEN AS THE SCARECROW, KEN AS THE TIN MAN* plate & ornament set LE 2500 sets Elite Dealer Exclusive	150
270512	1997	BARBIE AS ELIZA DOOLITTLE, LE 7500 (1st in series) 8¼"	30
274291	1997	BARBIE AS ELIZA DOOLITTLE, LE 7500 (Embassy Ball) 8¼"	35
274275	1997	BARBIE AS GLINDA THE GOOD WITCH, LE 7500 (2nd in Series) 8¼"	35
182028	1997	BARBIE AS SCARLETT O'HARA (green dress) LE 10,000 8¼"	35
260169	1997	BARBIE AS SCARLETT O'HARA (red dress) LE 7500 (2nd in Series) 8¼"	35
174793	1997	EGYPTIAN QUEEN, LE 7500 (4th in series) 8¼"	30
174793	1997	EGYPTIAN QUEEN, LE 10,000 8¼"	30
174815	1997	ELIZABETHAN QUEEN, LE 7500 8¼"	30

indicates cross reference   **390**

ENESCO - PLATES* CONTINUED

STOCK NO.	YEAR	DESCRIPTION	NRFB
260215	1997	GODDESS OF THE SUN, LE 7500 8¼"	35
270539	1997	GODDESS OF THE SUN/MOON GODDESS, LE 2500 sets	
		Elite Dealer Exclusive	125
274232	1997	HAPPY HOLIDAYS 1990, LE 7500 8¼"	30
274259	1997	HAPPY HOLIDAYS 1997 8¼"	30
188794	1997	HOLIDAY DANCE 1965, LE 10,000 8¼"	30
174807	1997	MEDIEVAL LADY, LE 7500 (5th) 8¼"	30
260231	1997	MOON GODDESS, LE 7500 8¼"	35
274216	1997	PLATE STAND 7¼" diameter	12
274224	1997	TRIO DISPLAY* (ornament & plate) 15" long	30
260282	1997	WEDDING DAY 1959, LE 7500 8¼"	30
295221	1998	CAMPUS SWEETHEART, LE 7500	30

❖❖❖❖❖❖❖❖❖❖❖❖❖❖

ENESCO - SALT AND PEPPER SHAKERS

STOCK NO.	YEAR	DESCRIPTION	NRFB
113921	1995	BARBIE AND KEN BUS IN CHEF HATS	30

❖❖❖❖❖❖❖❖❖❖❖❖❖❖

ENESCO - VASES

STOCK NO.	YEAR	DESCRIPTION	NRFB
124419	1995	GRADUATION ceramic	25
124397	1995	NURSE	25
124389	1995	SOLO IN THE SPOTLIGHT ceramic	25
124400	1995	SWEET 16 ceramic	25
188913	1996	EVENING SPLENDOR 1959 ceramic	25
157694	1996	QUEEN OF HEARTS ceramic	25

FIGURINES

DESCRIPTION	YEAR	MEDIAN
APPLAUSE - BARBIE STYLE (plastic)		
BALLERINA BARBIE (37010)	1990	20
BEACH BLAST BARBIE (37003)	1990	20
CALIFORNIA DREAM BARBIE (37005)	1990	20
DANCE CLUB BARBIE (37004)	1990	20
DISPLAY FIGURINES (37000)	1990	20
ROMANTIC WEDDING BARBIE (37002)	1990	20
SUPERSTAR BARBIE (37007)	1990	20
DANBURY MINT		
SOLO IN THE SPOTLIGHT	1992	20
BALLERINA	1993	20
BLACK AND WHITE SWIMSUIT	1993	20
BRIDES DREAM	1993	20
FASHION EDITOR	1993	20
FASHION LUNCHEON	1993	20
MIDNIGHT BLUE	1993	20
PAN AM STEWARDESS	1993	20
RED FLARE	1993	20
ENCHANTED EVENING	1994	20
FRATERNITY DANCE	1994	20
DECO PAK		
LONG PINK DRESS (black)	1996	10
LONG PINK DRESS (white)	1996	10
SHORT WHITE DRESS (black)	1996	10
SHORT WHITE DRESS (white)	1996	10
BIRTHDAY BARBIE SET (white) 96093 or 46093	1998	10
BIRTHDAY BARBIE SET (black) 96094 or 46094	1998	10
FOREVER BARBIE MINIATURE COLLECTIBLES (plastic)		
CALIFORNIA DREAM BARBIE 1959	1989	20
EVENING ENCHANTMENT BARBIE 1959	1989	20
HAPPY HOLIDAYS BARBIE 1988 (white dress)	1989	20
SOLO IN THE SPOTLIGHT BARBIE 1959	1989	20
SUPER STAR BARBIE 1989	1989	20
WEDDING PARTY 1959	1989	20
GENERAL MILLS (Cereal Premium)		
COUNTRY WEDDING (black)	1997	5
COUNTRY WEDDING (white)	1997	5

FIGURINES CONTINUED

DESCRIPTION	YEAR	NRFB
GENERAL MILLS (Cereal Premium) continued		
PINK PARTY DRESS (black)	1997	5
PINK PARTY DRESS (white)	1997	5
HALLMARK		
HOLIDAY TRADITIONS, LE 24,500 7½"	1997	35
HOLIDAY VOYAGE - Card Display 8¾" x 6¾"	1998	40
HOLIDAY VOYAGE, LE 24,500 6"	1998	45
LITTLE DEBBIE		
LITTLE DEBBIE, 3 (4 inch) set (Internet Special)	1998	15
MINIATURE BARBIE COLLECTIBLES (plastic)		
BALLERINA BARBIE 1989	1989	20
BATHING BEAUTY BARBIE 1959	1989	20
BEACH BLAST BARBIE 1989	1989	20
COOL TIMES BARBIE 1989	1989	20
DANCE CLUB BARBIE 1989	1989	20
HAPPY HOLIDAYS BARBIE 1988 (pink dress)	1989	20
SENSATIONS BARBIE 1989	1989	20

❖❖❖❖❖❖❖❖❖❖❖❖❖❖❖

NEWER GAMES

DESCRIPTION	YEAR	NRFB
THE MISS AMERICA PAGEANT GAME	1974	15
THE BARBIE GAME (Golden)	1980	30
BARBIE CHARMS THE WORLD (Mattel)	1986	35
WE GIRLS CAN DO ANYTHING	1986	15
BARBIE - JUST US GIRLS	1989	20
QUEEN OF THE PROM	1991	15
BARBIE DREAM DATE	1992	15
BARBIE FOR GIRLS - FUN FASHIONS A MEMORY GAME	1992	10
BARBIE FOR GIRLS DRESS UP GAME	1993	10
BARBIE DRESS UP (Golden)	1994	10
THE BARBIE QUEEN OF THE PROM GAME (35th Anniversary Edition) #410141996		25
BARBIE DRESS UP GAME #7201	1997	10
COOL CAREERS VALUE GAME #41529	1998	10
BARBIE ENCHANTED BALL 3-D GAME #41941	1998	10

NEWER JEWELRY

DESCRIPTION	YEAR	NRFB
NECKLACE, Sweet Sixteen	1974	40
JEWELRY, Barbie Gold Medal Set, ring, chain, picture of Gold Medal Olympic Barbie 75	1975	
BRACELET, charm, Nostalgic Barbie, sterling silver, collectors edition, 8 charms on link chain	1990	125
JEWELRY BOX, Little Treasures Jewelry Box, lacquered pink (Pink Stamp Premium)	1990	16
BRACELET, Dolls of the World *Toys R Us*	1993	15
BRACELET, FAO, 5 charms, Barbie at FAO heart, 14K over sterling silver	1993	100
BRACELET, FAO, 5 charms, Barbie at FAO heart, solid sterling	1993	110
BRACELET, "Barbie" 14K (Michael Anthony)	1994	125
BRACELET, oversized 4 section vintage PT's, Designs from the Deep	1994	—
BRACELET, w/6 gold charms (Mattel Festival) LE 350	1994	175
CHARM, "Barbie" 14K (Michael Anthony)	1994	45
CHARM, "Barbie" heart w/silhouette on reverse 14K (Michael Anthony)	1994	60
CHARM, Glasses 14K (Michael Anthony)	1994	70
CHARM, Mule 14K (Michael Anthony)	1994	70
CHARM, Ponytail silhouette w/"Barbie" 14K (Michael Anthony)	1994	70
CHARM, Purse 14K (Michael Anthony)	1994	70
EARRINGS, blonde Ponytail in b/w swimsuit with dangling clear stone, Designs from the Deep	1994	—
JEWELRY HOLDER, Barbie, Paint Set, 5 pegs	1994	3
PIN, "Barbie" hanger w/3 charms 14K (Michael Anthony)	1994	—
PIN, Festival (Mattel)	1994	30
PIN, Ponytail silhouette w/"Barbie" 14K (Michael Anthony)	1994	—
JEWELRY BOX, FAO Schwarz, decoupage, black or pink w/Nostalgic Barbie images and rhinestones, 5" x 5" x 4½"	1995	100
PIN, 14-Karat gold over sterling silver, 3 charms	1995	50
PIN, sterling silver, 3 charms	1995	50
BRACELET, 6 charms & Barbie logo, 14K gold plated, 7"	1996	85
JEWELRY BOX, Enchanted Evening Musical, lilac colored w/accessory print	1996	25
JEWELRY COLLECTION, FAO Schwarz, child assortment, 10 pieces	1996	25
JEWELRY BOX, Talking, Tara, 12170	1997	8
MINIATURE DOLL, sterling silver	1997	50
OPEN TOE PUMP, sterling silver	1997	30
RING, Sterling Silver, Mule (shoe) Pretty Fab	1997	50
RING, Sterling Silver, Pump (shoe) Pretty Fab	1997	50
SPIKED HEEL PUMP, sterling silver	1997	30
JEWELRY SET, FAO Schwarz, heart shaped (necklace, ring and bracelet)	1998	25
LOCKET NECKLACE, Avon, 16" gold tone chain	1998	13
BRACELET, Barbie Charm (Home Shopping Club exclusive)	—	40
BRACELET, Barbie Charm w/matching ring (T2250)	—	30
CHARM, handcrafted 3D heads (sterling) Ponytail is 14K over sterling	—	125
CHARM, Open Toed Shoe, sterling silver	—	25
CHARM, Sunglasses, sterling silver	—	25
PIN, The Toy Club 35th Exclusive Ponytail Barbie	—	—

PLATES

STOCK NO.	YEAR	DESCRIPTION	MIP
		BRADFORD EXCHANGE	
—	1994	ENCHANTED EVENING	15
—	1994	FOREVER GLAMOROUS	15
—	1994	SOLO IN THE SPOTLIGHT	15
—	1995	ENCHANTED EVENING	30
		DANBURY MINT	
—	1990	BRIDE TO BE	15
—	1990	DEBUTANTE BALL	15
—	1990	HOLIDAY DANCE	15
—	1990	MIDNIGHT BLUE	15
—	1990	SENIOR PROM	15
—	1990	SOLO IN THE SPOTLIGHT	15
—	1990	SOPHISTICATED LADY	15
—	1991	THE 1959 BRIDE-TO-BE	30
—	1992	BARBIE VISITS ENGLAND	15
—	1992	BARBIE VISITS RUSSIA	15
		ENESCO*	
655112	1994	35th ANNIVERSARY PLATE 1959, LE 5000	40
655058	1994	AFTER FIVE 1962 (mini plate)	8
655074	1994	EASTER PARADE 1959 (mini plate)	8
655104	1994	EVENING SPLENDOR 1959 (mini plate)	8
655066	1994	GAY PARISIENNE 1959 (mini plate)	8
115088	1994	HAPPY HOLIDAYS BARBIE 1994, LE 5000	25
14354	1995	HAPPY HOLIDAYS 1995 8½"	25
655090	1994	RED FLARE 1962 (mini plate)	8
655082	1994	ROMAN HOLIDAY 1959 (mini plate)	8
154180	1995	HAPPY HOLIDAYS 1988 8½"	25
114383	1995	SOLO IN THE SPOTLIGHT 1960	25
174777	1996	1920's FLAPPER, LE 10,000 (2nd in series) 8¼"	25
171069	1996	ARABIAN KNIGHTS SCHEHERAZADE 1964 (mini plate) 8¼"	10
171050	1996	A ROYAL SURPRISE1964 (Guinevere & King Arthur - mini plate) 8¼"	10
171085	1996	BARBIE AS SCARLETT O'HARA, LE 10,000 8¼"	25
171042	1996	CINDERELLA 1964 (mini plate) 8¼"	10
175587	1996	ENCHANTED EVENING 1960, LE 10,000 8¼"	25
174769	1996	GIBSON GIRL, LE 10,000 (1st in series) 8¼"	25
188859	1996	HAPPY HOLIDAYS 1989 8¼"	25
188816	1996	HAPPY HOLIDAYS 1996 8¼"	30
170984	1996	HERE COMES THE BRIDE, 1966 (Oval) 8¼" x 6½"	25
171077	1996	LITTLE RED RIDING HOOD 1964 (mini plate) 4¼"	10
157678	1996	QUEEN OF HEARTS (heart plate) 6½"	25

PLATES CONTINUED

STOCK NO.	YEAR	DESCRIPTION	MIP
		ENESCO* (continued)	
174785	1997	1950's SOUTHERN BELLE, LE 7500 (3rd in series) 8¼"	25
260193	1997	BARBIE AS DOROTHY, LE 7500 (1st in series) 8¼"	30
284327	1997	BARBIE AS DOROTHY, KEN AS THE LION, KEN AS THE SCARECROW, KEN AS THE TIN MAN, LE 7500 (3rd in Series) 8¼"	30
284335	1997	BARBIE AS DOROTHY, KEN AS THE LION, KEN AS THE SCARECROW, KEN AS THE TIN MAN* plate & ornament set, LE 2500 sets Elite Dealer Exclusive	125
270512	1997	BARBIE AS ELIZA DOOLITTLE, LE 7500 (1st in series) 8¼4"	25
274291	1997	BARBIE AS ELIZA DOOLITTLE, LE 7500 (Embassy Ball) 8¼"	30
274275	1997	BARBIE AS GLINDA THE GOOD WITCH, LE 7500 (2nd in Series) 8¼"	30
182028	1997	BARBIE AS SCARLETT O'HARA (green dress) LE 10,000 8¼"	30
260169	1997	BARBIE AS SCARLETT O'HARA (red dress) LE 7500 (2nd in Series) 8¼"	30
174793	1997	EGYPTIAN QUEEN, LE 7500 (4th in series) 8¼"	25
174793	1997	EGYPTIAN QUEEN, LE 10,000 8¼"	25
174815	1997	ELIZABETHAN QUEEN, LE 7500 8¼"	25
260215	1997	GODDESS OF THE SUN, LE 7500 8¼"	30
270539	1997	GODDESS OF THE SUN/MOON GODDESS, LE 2500 sets Elite Dealer Exclusive	115
274232	1997	HAPPY HOLIDAYS 1990, LE 7500 8¼"	25
274259	1997	HAPPY HOLIDAYS 1997 8¼"	25
188794	1997	HOLIDAY DANCE 1965, LE 10,000 8¼"	25
174807	1997	MEDIEVAL LADY, LE 7500 (5th) 8¼"	25
260231	1997	MOON GODDESS, LE 7500 8¼"	30
274216	1997	PLATE STAND 7 ¹/4" diameter	10
274224	1997	TRIO DISPLAY* (ornament & plate) 15" long	25
260282	1997	WEDDING DAY 1959, LE 7500 8¼"	25
		FAO	
—	1993	SILVER SCREEN (1st in series) LE 3600	50
—	1995	CIRCUS STAR (2nd in series) LE 3600	35
—	1996	BARBIE AT FAO (Melamine)	15
—	1996	STATUE OF LIBERTY (3rd in series) 8¼"	30
		HALLMARK	
—	1997	HOLIDAY TRADITIONS, LE 24,500	35
—	1997	VICTORIAN ELEGANCE, LE 24,500	30
—	1998	HOLIDAY VOYAGE, LE 24,500	25
—	1998	HOLIDAY MEMORIES, LE 24,500	25
		MATTEL	
—	1994	35th ANNIVERSARY (Mattel Festival)	50

NEWER MAGAZINES, CATALOGS & MARKET REPORTS

DESCRIPTION	YEAR	NRFB
MAGAZINES		
LIFE, Barbie Turns 21	1979	25
BARBIE JOURNAL (various countries)	1980s	3
MATTEL CATALOGUE	1980	40
MATTEL - Barbie Doll Through the Year's	1981	15
MATTEL CATALOGUE	1981	40
MATTEL CATALOGUE	1982	40
MATTEL CATALOGUE	1983	40
BARBIE MAGAZINE FOR GIRLS Winter Premier Issue	1984	15
BARBIE MAGAZINE FOR GIRLS Spring	1984	10
BARBIE MAGAZINE FOR GIRLS Summer	1984	10
BARBIE MAGAZINE FOR GIRLS Fall	1984	10
LIFE, February 1984 (Beatles)	1984	25
MATTEL CATALOGUE	1984	40
PLAYTHINGS MAGAZINE February-Ad for 25th Birthday	1984	15
BARBIE MAGAZINE FOR GIRLS Fall	1985	8
MATTEL CATALOGUE	1985	35
BARBIE MAGAZINE FOR GIRLS Spring	1986	8
BARBIE MAGAZINE FOR GIRLS Summer	1986	8
BARBIE MAGAZINE FOR GIRLS Fall	1986	8
BARBIE MAGAZINE FOR GIRLS Winter	1986	8
MATTEL CATALOGUE	1986	35
BARBIE MAGAZINE FOR GIRLS Winter	1987	8
MATTEL CATALOGUE *Department Store Special*	1987	10
BARBIE MAGAZINE FOR GIRLS Spring	1989	5
BARBIE MAGAZINE FOR GIRLS Summer	1989	5
BARBIE MAGAZINE FOR GIRLS Fall	1989	5
BARBIE MAGAZINE FOR GIRLS Winter	1989	5
MATTEL CATALOGUE	1989	20
SMITHSONIAN MAGAZINE December	1989	15
BARBIE JOURNAL (various countries)	1990s	3
30th ANNIVERSARY w/outfit	1990	10
30th ANNIVERSARY w/out outfit	1990	5
BARBIE MAGAZINE FOR GIRLS Spring	1990	5
BARBIE MAGAZINE FOR GIRLS Summer	1990	5
BARBIE MAGAZINE FOR GIRLS Fall	1990	5
BARBIE MAGAZINE FOR GIRLS Winter	1990	5
BARBIE MAGAZINE FOR GIRLS Spring	1991	5
BARBIE MAGAZINE FOR GIRLS Summer	1991	5
BARBIE MAGAZINE FOR GIRLS Fall	1991	5
BARBIE MAGAZINE FOR GIRLS Winter	1991	5
MATTEL BARBIE CATALOGUE (70 pages of All Barbie)	1991	20
BARBIE MAGAZINE FOR GIRLS Spring	1992	5
BARBIE MAGAZINE FOR GIRLS Summer	1992	5
BARBIE MAGAZINE FOR GIRLS Fall	1992	5

DESCRIPTION	YEAR	NRFB
MAGAZINES (continued)		
BARBIE MAGAZINE FOR GIRLS Winter	1992	5
BARBIE MAGAZINE FOR GIRLS Holiday Special Issue	1992	5
BARBIE MAGAZINE (Italian - magazine, comic book, puzzle, punchouts)	1993	10
BARBIE MAGAZINE FOR GIRLS January/February	1993	5
BARBIE MAGAZINE FOR GIRLS March/April	1993	5
BARBIE MAGAZINE FOR GIRLS May/June	1993	5
BARBIE MAGAZINE FOR GIRLS July/August	1993	5
BARBIE MAGAZINE FOR GIRLS September/October	1993	5
BARBIE MAGAZINE FOR GIRLS November/December	1993	5
BARBIE MAGAZINE FOR GIRLS Winter	1993	5
MATTEL GERMAN CATALOGUE (76 pages)	1993	25
BARBIE MAGAZINE FOR GIRLS January/February	1994	5
BARBIE MAGAZINE FOR GIRLS March/April	1994	5
BARBIE MAGAZINE FOR GIRLS May/June	1994	5
BARBIE MAGAZINE FOR GIRLS July/August	1994	5
BARBIE MAGAZINE FOR GIRLS September/October	1994	5
BARBIE MAGAZINE FOR GIRLS November/December	1994	5
MATTEL TIMELESS CREATIONS	1994	30
BARBIE MAGAZINE FOR GIRLS January/February	1995	5
BARBIE MAGAZINE FOR GIRLS March/April	1995	4
BARBIE MAGAZINE FOR GIRLS May/June	1995	4
BARBIE MAGAZINE FOR GIRLS July/August	1995	4
BARBIE MAGAZINE FOR GIRLS September/October	1995	4
BARBIE MAGAZINE FOR GIRLS November/December	1995	4
COLLECTING BARBIE Vol. 1, No. 1, September	1995	10
(was included in Today's Parent and Chatelaine Magazines) Canada		
MATTEL TIMELESS CREATIONS	1995	25
BARBIE MAGAZINE FOR GIRLS January/February	1996	4
BARBIE MAGAZINE FOR GIRLS March/April	1996	4
BARBIE MAGAZINE FOR GIRLS May/June	1996	4
BARBIE MAGAZINE FOR GIRLS July/August	1996	4
BARBIE MAGAZINE FOR GIRLS September/October	1996	4
MATTEL - BARBIE COLLECTIBLES	1996	25
MATTEL - BARBIE COLLECTIBLES	1997	10
HALLO BARBIE - MATTEL GERMANY	1998	5
MATTEL - BARBIE COLLECTIBLES	1998	10
MILLER'$		
MILLER'$ Price Guide & Collector's Almanac June/July Premier Issue	1992	40
MILLER'$ Price Guide & Collector's Almanac August/September	1992	20
MILLER'$ Price Guide & Collector's Almanac October/November	1992	20
MILLER'$ Price Guide & Collector's Almanac December/January	1992/93	20
MILLER'$ Price Guide & Collector's Almanac February/March	1993	20
MILLER'$ Price Guide & Collector's Almanac April/May	1993	20

NEWER MAGAZINES, CATALOGS & MARKET REPORTS CONTINUED

DESCRIPTION	YEAR	NRFB
MILLER'$ (continued)		
MILLER'$ Price Guide & Collector's Almanac June/July	1993	20
MILLER'$ Price Guide & Collector's Almanac August/September	1993	20
MILLER'$ Price Guide & Collector's Almanac October/November	1993	20
MILLER'$ Price Guide & Collector's Almanac December/January	1993/94	20
MILLER'$ Price Guide & Collector's Almanac February/March	1994	20
MILLER'$ Price Guide & Collector's Almanac April/May	1994	20
MILLER'$ Barbie Collector June/July Premier Issue-Full Size	1994	45
MILLER'$ Barbie Collector August/September	1994	15
MILLER'$ Barbie Collector November	1994	15
MILLER'$ Scarlett Special Collectors Reference Edition Infomercial Edition	1994	15
MILLER'$ Barbie Collector January/February	1995	15
MILLER'$ Barbie Collector Spring	1995	15
MILLER'$ Barbie Collector Summer	1995	15
MILLER'$ Barbie Collector Fall	1995	15
MILLER'$ Pocket Annual	1995	8
MILLER'$ Barbie Collector Spring	1996	15
MILLER'$ Summer (includes The Barbie Collector's Anthem CD) 2 cover versions	1996	30
MILLER'$ Fall	1996	15
MILLER'$ Winter	1996/97	15
MILLER'$ Spring	1997	15
MILLER'$ Summer	1997	15
MILLER'$ Fall	1997	10
MILLER'$ Winter	1997/98	15
MILLER'$ Price Guide Pocket Annual	1996/97	8
MILLER'$ Fashion Doll Magazine (Premiere Issue) July	1998	8
MILLER'$ Fashion Doll Magazine September	1998	8
MILLER'$ Fashion Doll Magazine November (2 cover versions)	1998	8
MILLER'$ Price Guide Pocket Annual	1998	10
MILLER'$ Fashion Doll Magazine January	1999	8
MILLER'$ Fashion Doll Magazine March	1999	6
MILLER'$ Fashion Doll Magazine May	1999	6
MILLER'$ Fashion Doll Magazine July	1999	6
MILLER'$ Fashion Doll Magazine September	1999	6
MILLER'$ Fashion Doll Magazine November	1999	6
MILLER'$ Fashion Doll Magazine January	2000	6
CATALOGUES		
MATTEL CATALOGUE (ALL TOYS FOR 1978)	1978	20
MATTEL BARBIE DOLL THROUGH THE YEARS	1981	15
MATTEL SPRING PROGRAM CATALOGUE	1985	25
MATTEL CATALOGUE	1986	25
MATTEL CATALOGUE	1987	25
MATTEL ANNUAL REPORT ('89 Superstar & '62 Ponytail on cover)	1988	5

DESCRIPTION	YEAR	NRFB
CATALOGUES (continued)		
MATTEL TOY CATALOGUE (all toys offered in '88)	1988	12
MATTEL TOY CATALOGUE (all toys offered in '90)	1988	12
MATTEL CATALOGUE	1989	25
MATTEL COLLECTOR CLASSICS	1989	15
MATTEL CATALOGUE w/67 pages of Barbie	1990	25
MATTEL GIRLS CATALOGUE (shows all girls toys in 1990)	1990	15
MATTEL BARBIE CATALOGUE	1991	20
MATTEL TIMELESS CREATIONS	1991	20
MATTEL TOY CATALOGUE (all toys offered in '91)	1991	10
MATTEL TIMELESS CREATIONS	1992	20
BARBIE COLLECTIBLES BARBIE CATALOGUE	1993	5
MATTEL BARBIE CATALOGUE	1993	25
MATTEL BARBIE CATALOGUE (German)	1993	25
MATTEL TIMELESS CREATIONS	1993	20
MATTEL TOY CATALOGUE (all toys offered in '93)	1993	12
MATTEL TOY CATALOGUE (girl toys offered in '93)	1993	10
MATTEL TIMELESS CREATIONS	1994	25
MATTEL TOY CATALOGUE (girl toys offered in '94)	1994	8
MATTEL ANNUAL REPORT	1995	5
MATTEL TIMELESS CREATIONS	1995	15
SEARS BARBIE CATALOGUE	1995	2
MATTEL BARBIE COLLECTIBLES (formerly Timeless Creations)	1996	30
JCPENNEY BARBIE CATALOGUE	1996	2
MATTEL BARBIE COLLECTIBLES	1997	20
MARKET REPORTS		
MILLER'$ Market Report May Premier Issue	1995	15
MILLER'$ Market Report June	1995	5
MILLER'$ Market Report July	1995	5
MILLER'$ Market Report August	1995	5
MILLER'$ Market Report September	1995	5
MILLER'$ Market Report October	1995	5
MILLER'$ Market Report November	1995	5
MILLER'$ Market Report December	1995	5
MILLER'$ Market Report January	1996	5
MILLER'$ Market Report February	1996	5
MILLER'$ Market Report March	1996	5
MILLER'$ Market Report April	1996	5
MILLER'$ Market Report May	1996	5
MILLER'$ Market Report June	1996	5
MILLER'$ Market Report July	1996	5
MILLER'$ Market Report August	1996	5
MILLER'$ Market Report September	1996	5
MILLER'$ Market Report October	1996	5

NEWER MAGAZINES, CATALOGS &
MARKET REPORTS CONTINUED

DESCRIPTION	YEAR	NRFB
MARKET REPORTS (continued)		
MILLER'$ Market Report November	1996	5
MILLER'$ Market Report December	1996	5
MILLER'$ Market Report January	1997	5
MILLER'$ Market Report February	1997	5
MILLER'$ Market Report March	1997	5
MILLER'$ Market Report April	1997	5
MILLER'$ Market Report May	1997	5
MILLER'$ Market Report June	1997	5
MILLER'$ Market Report July	1997	5
MILLER'$ Market Report August	1997	5
MILLER'$ Market Report September	1997	5
MILLER'$ Market Report October	1997	5
MILLER'$ Market Report November	1997	5
MILLER'$ Market Report December	1997	5
MILLER'$ Market Report January	1998	5
MILLER'$ Market Report February	1998	5
MILLER'$ Market Report March	1998	5
MILLER'$ Market Report April	1998	5
MILLER'$ Market Report May	1998	5
MILLER'$ Market Report June	1998	5
MILLER'$ Market Report July	1998	5
MILLER'$ Market Report August	1998	5
MILLER'$ Market Report September	1998	5
MILLER'$ Market Report October	1998	5
MILLER'$ Market Report November	1998	5
MILLER'$ Market Report December	1998	5
MILLER'$ Market Report January	1999	5
MILLER'$ Market Report February	1999	5
MILLER'$ Market Report March	1999	3
MILLER'$ Market Report April	1999	3
MILLER'$ Market Report May	1999	3

McDONALDS®

DESCRIPTION	YEAR	NRFB
TEST MARKET JULY 1990 SAVANNAH, GEORGIA		
DISPLAY - BARBIE - HOT WHEELS	1990	350
FIGURINE - IN CONCERT (SOLO IN THE SPOTLIGHT) W/PAPER THEATRE ENTRANCE	1990	—
FIGURINE - MOONLIGHT BALL W/PAPER BALLROOM	1990	—
FIGURINE - MOVIE STAR W/PAPER DRESSING ROOM	1990	—
FIGURINE - TEA PARTY (ENCHANTED EVENING) W/PAPER DINING ROOM	1990	—
HAPPY MEAL BOX - BARBIE IN CONCERT	1990	—
HAPPY MEAL BOX - MOVIE STAR/ROAD RACE	1990	—
DISTRIBUTION AUGUST 2-28, 1991		
BUTTON "ASK ME ABOUT TODAY'S BARBIE OR HOT WHEELS"	1991	8
DISPLAY - BARBIE - HOT WHEELS	1991	200
FIGURINE - ALL AMERICAN #1	1991	6
FIGURINE - COSTUME BALL #2	1991	6
FIGURINE - LIGHTS/LACE #3	1991	6
FIGURINE - HAPPY BIRTHDAY #4	1991	6
FIGURINE - HAWAIIAN FUN #5	1991	6
FIGURINE - WEDDING DAY MIDGE #6	1991	6
FIGURINE - ICE CAPADES #7	1991	6
FIGURINE - MY FIRST BARBIE #8	1991	6
FIGURINE - COSTUME BALL (under 3)	1991	5
FIGURINE - WEDDING DAY MIDGE (under 3)	1991	5
HAPPY MEAL BOX - AT HOME	1991	3
HAPPY MEAL BOX - ON STAGE	1991	3
TRANSLITE - CHOOSE HOT WHEELS OR BARBIE HAPPY MEAL	1991	30
DISTRIBUTION AUGUST 7-SEPTEMBER 3, 1992		
DISPLAY - BARBIE OR MINI-STREET HAPPY MEAL	1992	100
FIGURINE - BIRTHDAY SURPRISE	1992	4
FIGURINE - MY FIRST BALLERINA	1992	4
FIGURINE - RAPPIN' ROCKIN'	1992	4
FIGURINE - ROLLERBLADE	1992	4
FIGURINE - ROSE BRIDE	1992	4
FIGURINE - SNAP 'N PLAY	1992	4
FIGURINE - SPARKLE EYES	1992	4
FIGURINE - SPARKLE EYES (under 3)	1992	5
FIGURINE - SUN SENSATION	1992	4
HAPPY MEAL BOX - BEACHFRONT FUN	1992	2
HAPPY MEAL BOX - MAGICAL WORLD	1992	2
TRANSLITE - BARBIE OR MINI-STREET HAPPY MEAL	1992	10
DISTRIBUTION AUGUST 6-SEPTEMBER 2, 1993		
DISPLAY - BARBIE OR HOT WHEELS HAPPY MEAL	1993	85
FIGURINE - BIRTHDAY PARTY	1993	4
FIGURINE - HOLLYWOOD HAIR	1993	4
FIGURINE - MY FIRST BALLERINA	1993	4
FIGURINE - PAINT 'N DAZZLE	1993	4
FIGURINE - ROMANTIC BRIDE (also used as the under 3)	1993	4
FIGURINE - SECRET HEARTS	1993	4
FIGURINE - TWINKLE LIGHTS	1993	4
FIGURINE - WESTERN STAMPIN'	1993	4

McDONALDS® CONTINUED

DESCRIPTION	YEAR	NRFB
DISTRIBUTION AUGUST 6-SEPTEMBER 2, 1993 (continued)		
HAPPY MEAL BAG - BARBIE/HOT WHEELS	1993	2
TRANSLITE - BARBIE WITH HAIR YOU CAN STYLE OR	1993	10
HOT WHEELS HAPPY MEAL		
DISTRIBUTION DECEMBER 10, 1993-JANUARY 6, 1994		
DISPLAY - TOTALLY TOY HOLIDAY W/SNOW DOME	1993	175
FIGURINE (RECALLED) - HOLIDAY BARBIE - SNOW DOME	1993	110
TRANSLITE - TOTALLY TOY HOLIDAY PICTURES SNOW DOME	1993	10
DISTRIBUTION AUGUST 5-SEPTEMBER 8, 1994		
DISPLAY - BARBIE AND FRIENDS HAPPY MEAL - WORLD OF HOT WHEELS	1994	85
FIGURINE - BICYCLIN' BARBIE #1	1994	3
FIGURINE - JEWEL/GLITTER SHANI #2	1994	3
FIGURINE - CAMP BARBIE #3	1994	3
FIGURINE - CAMP TERESA #4 (blue sunglasses/blue patch on pants)	1994	3
FIGURINE - CAMP TERESA #4 (yellow sunglasses)	1994	3
FIGURINE - LOCKET SURPRISE #5 (black)	1994	3
FIGURINE - LOCKET SURPRISE #5 (white)	1994	3
FIGURINE - LOCKET SURPRISE KEN #6 (black)	1994	3
FIGURINE - LOCKET SURPRISE KEN #6 (white)	1994	3
FIGURINE - JEWEL/GLITTER BRIDE #7	1994	3
FIGURINE - BRIDESMAID SKIPPER #8	1994	3
HAPPY MEAL BAG - BARBIE AND FRIENDS	1994	2
TOY - BARBIE BALL (under 3)	1994	3
TRANSLITE - BARBIE AND FRIENDS HAPPY MEAL - WORLD OF HOT WHEELS	1994	8
DISTRIBUTION OCTOBER 28-DECEMBER 1, 1994		
DISPLAY - HAPPY BIRTHDAY HAPPY MEAL	1994	125
FIGURINE (RECALLED) BALLERINA BARBIE	1994	15
NOTICE - TOY SAFETY NOTICE TO PARENTS	1994	3
TRANSLITE - HAPPY BIRTHDAY HAPPY MEAL	1994	8
DISTRIBUTION AUGUST 1-AUGUST 28, 1995		
DISPLAY (with 16 premiums)	1995	50
CREW POSTER	1995	5
CREW REFERENCE SHEET	1995	3
FIGURINE - HOT SKATIN' BARBIE #1	1995	3
FIGURINE - DANCE MOVES BARBIE #2	1995	3
FIGURINE - BUTTERFLY PRINCESS TERESA #3	1995	3
FIGURINE - COOL COUNTRY BARBIE #4	1995	3
FIGURINE - LIFEGUARD KEN #5 (black)	1995	5
FIGURINE - LIFEGUARD KEN #5 (white)	1995	5
FIGURINE - LIFEGUARD BARBIE #6 (black)	1995	5
FIGURINE - LIFEGUARD BARBIE #6 (white)	1995	5
FIGURINE - BLUE ANGEL BARBIE #7	1995	3
FIGURINE - ICE SKATIN' #8	1995	3
HAPPY MEAL BAG	1995	1
TOY (under 3)	1995	3
TRANSLITE	1995	10

McDONALDS® CONTINUED

DESCRIPTION	YEAR	NRFB
DISTRIBUTION JULY 12-AUGUST 15, 1996		
CREW POSTER	1996	5
CREW REFERENCE SHEET	1996	3
DISPLAY (with 10 premiums)	1996	50
FIGURINE - DUTCH BARBIE #1	1996	2
FIGURINE - KENYAN BARBIE #2	1996	2
FIGURINE - JAPANESE BARBIE #3	1996	2
FIGURINE - MEXICAN BARBIE #4	1996	2
FIGURINE - CANADIAN (gymnast) #5	1996	5
FIGURINE - U.S.A. (gymnast) #5	1996	4
HAPPY MEAL BOX (2 versions)	1996	1
TOY (under 3) BARBIE - SQUARE WINDOW SLIDE	1996	3
TRANSLITE	1996	10
DISTRIBUTION OCTOBER 24-NOVEMBER, 1997		
CREW POSTER	1997	5
CREW REFERENCE SHEET	1997	3
DISPLAY (with 10 premiums)	1997	40
FIGURINE - WEDDING RAPUNZEL #1	1997	2
FIGURINE - RAPUNZEL #2	1997	2
FIGURINE - ANGEL PRINCESS #3	1997	2
FIGURINE - HAPPY HOLIDAYS #4	1997	2
FIGURINE - BLOSSOM BEAUTY (black) #5	1997	2
TRANSLITE	1997	8
DISTRIBUTION AUGUST 14-SEPTEMBER 10, 1998		
CREW POSTER	1998	5
CREW REFERENCE SHEET	1998	3
DISPLAY (with 4 Barbie premiums)	1998	35
FIGURINE - TEEN SKIPPER	1998	2
FIGURINE	1998	2
FIGURINE	1998	2
FIGURINE	1998	2
UNDER 3 TOY	1998	3
DISTRIBUTION DECEMBER 31st 1999 - JANUARY 27 2000		
Once In A Lifetime Collection"		
MILLENIUM PRINCESS #1	1999	2
1959 #1 BARBIE #2	1999	2
SOLO IN THE SPOTLIGHT #5	1999	2
HOLLYWOOD NAILS #6	1999	2
MALIBU #9	1999	2
SUPER GYMNAST #10	1999	2
TOTALLY HAIR #13	1999	2
SIT IN STYLE #14	1999	2
WORKING WOMAN #17	1999	2
CHIC #18	1999	2

NEWER MISCELLANEOUS

DESCRIPTION	YEAR	NRFB
ACTIVITY BOX, Barbie, 6 drawers, includes stamps, crayons, parer & beads	1995	15
ADDRESS BOOK, Nostalgic Barbie, 6 ring binder, *FAO Schwarz*	1996	15
ART STUDIO, Barbie Jumbo Art Studio, *FAO Schwarz*	1993	20
BACKER CARD, Little Theatre, Enesco, Foam Core 14"	1997	10
BAG, Book, Barbie Style Print, Mattel	1990	10
BASEBALL CAP, denim (fits ages 7-14), *FAO Schwarz*	1996	10
BASEBALL CAP, pink (fits ages 7-14), *FAO Schwarz*	1996	10
BASEBALL CAP, white (fits ages 7-14), *FAO Schwarz*	1996	10
BOXER SHORTS, blue, adult, flannel, *FAO Schwarz*	1993	15
BOXER SHORTS, pink, adult, flannel, *FAO Schwarz*	1993	15
BUNNY, Barbie Easter promotion, 36" pink w/Barbie bow	1995	45
BUTTON, Barbie Collectibles, Enesco, 3" diameter	1997	1
CABOODLE, Barbie includes Barbie-size caboodle	1993	10
CAFE, Barbie #10134 from Italy through *JCPenney* catalog	1993	40
CAKE PAN, Barbie (Wilton Industries)	1996	5
CAMERA, Barbie & Me Camera & Glitter Glasses, comes w/Barbie size camera/glasses	1993	15
CAMERA, Barbie photo fun camera set, 110 film, *FAO Schwarz*	1995	15
CAMERA, Polaroid Barbie	1998	20
CANDY, Barbie Bubble Gum w/stickers (Canada)	1995	1
CANDY, Barbie Candy Bank (Canada)	1993	5
CANDY, Barbie Heart Pop (Canada)	1993	1
CANDY, Barbie Milk Chocolate Bars (Canada)	1996	6
CANDY, Barbie Milk Chocolate Coated Nougat/Caramel Bar (Canada)	1996	6
CANDY, Barbie Milk Chocolate small bars w/premium (Canada)	1996	5
CANDY, Barbie Real Fruit Snacks (Canada)	1992	5
CANDY, Barbie Solid Milk Chocolate (Canada)	1992	5
CANDY, Barbie Sweet Lips – Strawberry (Canada)	1995	3
CANDY, Barbie Taffy Pops (Canada)	1995	3
CANDY, Barbie Tin Full of Popcorn (Canada)	1995	8
CAR, Corvette, ages 2-5, 6V battery, white, *FAO Schwarz*	1992	250
CAR, Lamborghini, child size, pink, talking phone, power wheels	1994	125
CARD, boxed trio, Hallmark Barbies	1997	10
CARD, greeting, Mattel Public Relations	1981	15
CARD, Hallmark, 12 "vintage look" versions	1994	4
CARD, Hallmark Glamour Dream Collection (1st)	1994	15
CARD, Hallmark Glamour Dream Collection (2nd)	1995	15
CARD, Hallmark Holiday Christmas Collection (2nd)	1995	15
CARDS, Holiday, 20, Barbie Collectibles promotion	1998	15
CARDS, Barbie for Girls Playing Cards #42265	1998	5
CARRY ALL, Barbie Style Print, Mattel	1990	10
CASE, Display, Hexagon (pink or black base) #67660	1997	10
CASE, Display, Mattel #67660	1998	15
CASE, Circus Star, *FAO Schwarz*	1995	40
CASE, Madison Avenue, *FAO Schwarz*	1992	50

DESCRIPTION	YEAR	NRFB
CASE, Silver Screen, *FAO Schwarz*	1994	45
CASE, Statue of Liberty, *FAO Schwarz*	1996	25
CASE, Barbie and Friends, *JCPenney*	1995	20
CASSETTE PLAYER, AM/FM cassette player, pink (Pink Stamp Premium)	1990	20
CASSETTE PLAYER, AM/FM Cool Tunes cassette deck, pink (Pink Stamp Premium)	1990	35
CD PLAYER, Barbie Disc Girl, 32 songs on 4 CD's, included Barbie for Girls	1994	20
CD-ROM, Barbie Cool Looks, Fashion Designer #17768	1998	20
CD-ROM, Barbie Cool Looks, Fashion Designer Refill Kit #17769	1998	10
CD-ROM, Barbie Cut ' Grow #26339	2000	Retail
CD-ROM, Barbie Digital Makeover #23465	2000	Retail
CD-ROM, Barbie Fashion Designer #16379	1996	15
CD-ROM, Barbie Fashion Designer (MacIntosh version) #18953	1997	30
CD-ROM, Barbie Iron-On Designer #23018	1998	20
CD-ROM, Barbie Jewel Designer and Nail Designer Refill Kit #22346	1998	10
CD-ROM, Barbie Jewelry Designer #20462	1998	20
CD-ROM, Barbie Magic Fairy Tales, Barbie as Rapunzel #16378	1997	20
CD-ROM, Barbie Magic Hair Styler #16376	1997	20
CD-ROM, Barbie Nail Designer #20463	1998	15
CD-ROM, Barbie Ocean Discovery – Adventures with Barbie #17764	1997	20
CD-ROM, Barbie Party Print 'N Play #17765	1997	10
CD-ROM, Barbie Pet Rescue #26341	2000	Retail
CD-ROM, Barbie Photo Designer Digital Camera & CD-Rom #20779	1998	50
CD-ROM, Barbie Photo Designer World in Motion #22474	1999	20
CD-ROM, Barbie Print 'N Play #16538	1997	10
CD-ROM, Barbie Print 'N Play #22340-0970	1998	8
CD-ROM, Barbie Riding Club #20460	1998	20
CD-ROM, Barbie Screen Styler #18052	1997	10
CD-ROM, Barbie Software for Girls Party Gift Set* #17765 (Birthday Surprise Barbie and Party Print 'N Play CD-Rom)	1998	20
CD-ROM, Barbie Sports #22473	1998	20
CD-ROM, Barbie Sticker Designer #23752	1998	20
CD-ROM, Barbie Story Maker #16377	1997	20
CD-ROM, Barbie Totally Tattoos #23017	1998	20
CD-ROM, Body Art Designer #23017	1998	25
CD-ROM, Detective Barbie #20461	1998	25
CD-ROM, Mattel Media #21394	1998	20
CEREAL, Breakfast with Barbie (Ralston) 4 versions	1989	15
CLOCK, plate clock, decoupage, 12" diameter, 5 FAO Barbies w/rhinestones, pink or black, *FAO Schwarz*	1993	110
CLOCK, round, pink w/Barbie & accessories, Designs from the Deep	1996	40
CLOCK, Solo in the Spotlight	1995	40
CLOCK, Solo in the Spotlight, Premier Edition, LE 10,000 Hope	1995	90
CLOCK RADIO, Austin Healey, AM-FM	1996	40
CLOCK RADIO, Barbie, FM or Barbies voice, Barbie for Girls	1994	20

DESCRIPTION	YEAR	NRFB
CLUB, Barbie Fan Club Kit, welcome letter, autographed picture of Barbie, membership card, iron on, "I'm a Barbie Fan" patch, coloring poster, sun visor, quarterly issue of Barbie Fan Club News	1981	30
CLUB, Barbie Pink Stamp Club Kit, poster, doll t-shirt, Fashion Fun Guide	1992	5
CLUB, Pink Stamp Club Membership Kit	1990	20
CLUB, Pink Stamp Club Membership Kit	1991	15
CLUB, Rose Collector Club (England)	1993	10
COCA-COLA Soda Fountain #26980	2000	150
COIN, 30th Anniversary, Evening Enchantment, one troy ounce silver	1989	80
COIN, George Washington LE 1000, *FAO Schwarz*	1997	65
COIN, Statue of Liberty, LE 1000, .999 Silver, *FAO Schwarz*	1996	70
COIN PURSE, vinyl Ponytail, keychain (4" x 4½"), *FAO Schwarz*	1996	8
COIN PURSE, Pyramid	1997	4
COMPACT, Barbie, Double mirrored, Katherine Baumann Barbie Collection *FAO Schwarz*	1996	150
COMPACT, decoupage Enchanted Evening Compact, *FAO Schwarz*	1996	40
COMPACT, decoupaged mirrored, 2½" metal frame, Barbie icons and Austrian crystal, pink or black, *FAO Schwarz*	1995	45
COOKIE CUTTERS, Wilton Enter. (4 cutters)	—	—
COOKIES, Barbie Cookies Biscuits, Christie Brown & Co. (Canada)	1992	5
COSMETIC KIT, travel case & toiletries, *FAO Schwarz*	1993	30
COSTUME TRUNK, includes Secret Hearts, Hollywood Hair and Wedding Fantasy costumes, *FAO Schwarz*	1993	70
COSTUME, Circus Star, child size, *FAO Schwarz*	1995	50
COSTUME, Silver Screen (gown, bag & gloves), *FAO Schwarz*	1993	50
COSTUME, Statue of Liberty Barbie w/crown, child size, *FAO Schwarz*	1996	50
DIARY, Barbie, pink flowers w/key	1995	12
DIARY, BD1000 – Flying Colors	1997	5
DIARY, Barbie at FAO, *FAO Schwarz*	1996	12
DISH SET, Deluxe Cook 'N Serve - Service for 4	—	—
DISH SET, Barbie Melamine, *FAO Schwarz*	1993	20
DISPLAY, Beauty Secrets Store Display, LE	1980	180
DISPLAY, Dream House, Enesco, cardboard/vinyl	1997	15
DISPLAY, Solo in the Spotlight, 5'-5" Cardboard Lifesize Barbie, Enesco	1997	35
DOLLAR, Barbie, Collectors Edition, Meijer, $1.00 premium	1993	10
DOME, Black Wooden Base, Enesco, 7" (glass & wood)	—	20
DRESS, child size, hot pink w/gold accents/Barbie signature (Hickory Hills Industries)	1991	15
DRESS, child size, purple/hot pink w/gold accents/Barbie signature (Hickory Hills Industries)	1991	15
DRESSER SET, Barbie 3-piece set w/paper doll on back of box	1979	25
EASEL CARD, Barbie Collectibles, Enesco, 11 x 8½"	1997	6
EGG CUP, Porcelain, Barbie	1997	25
FASHION PLAY CARDS, Barbie (6 different packs) 10 cards per pack The River Group	1994	5

NEWER MISCELLANEOUS CONTINUED

DESCRIPTION	YEAR	NRFB
FILE, Barbie Style Print, Applause	1990	10
FOLIO, Abbeville Publishing Group	1994	10
FOLIO, leather, black, Nostalgic Barbie, *JCPenney*	1996	40
FOOTSTOOL, pink, multiple Barbie pictured, Designs from the Deep	1996	40
FORK & SPOON SET, Melamine, *FAO Schwarz*	1993	5
FUN FIXIN' SETS, 10 versions	1997	5
FURNITURE, Barbie Table and Chairs Set, child size, American Toy & Furniture Co.	1983	30
FURNITURE, Gourmet Kitchen, child size, American Toy & Furniture Co.	1983	30
FURNITURE, Kitchen Stool, child size, American Toy & Furniture Co.	1983	20
FURNITURE, Night Stand & Vanity, child size, American Toy & Furniture Co.	1983	30
GAME, hand held computer, Skate Away, Barbie for Girls – Konami	1993	20
GAMEBOY, Barbie Ocean Discover #22991	1999	20
GAMEBOY, Back Pack Games #26338	2000	Retail
GOWN, child size, red/gold – Barbie Dress Up for Girls (Rubies Costume Co.)	1994	25
GUITAR, Barbie for Girls, Electronic keyboard, 8 keys	1993	50
HANDBAG, vinyl Ponytail, zipper closure (8½" x 12"), *FAO Schwarz*	1996	30
HANDBAG, vinyl, Snips 'N Scraps by Ponytail, *FAO Schwarz*	1998	40
HELMET, Barbie for Girls, bicycle helmet, pink	1993	30
JACKET, Black wool w/ buff leather sleeves, "Barbie & B" applique on front, Barbie & Ken in sportscar applique on back	1995	200
JACKET, Embroidered denim, adult	1995	95
JACKET, Embroidered denim, child	1995	85
JACKET, Handmade leather, white, zippered wrists, *FAO Schwarz*	1996	400
JACKET, leather, reversible, bomber style, *FAO Schwarz*	1995	325
JOURNAL, Nostalgic Barbie (6¼" square), *FAO Schwarz*	1996	15
KEY RING, 35th Anniversary, black & purple vinyl	1994	10
KEYCHAIN, Barbie, Katherine Baumann Barbie Collection, *FAO Schwarz*	1996	30
KEY CHAIN, 40th Anniversary Gala Bumble Bee (Canadian Gift)	1999	10
KIT, Holiday Decorating Kit	1998	10
KITCHEN, Gourmet, American Toy Furniture (ATF), range, oven, dishwasher, sink	—	—
KNEE & ELBOW PADS, Barbie for Girls, pink/purple	1993	8
LAMP, Nostalgic Barbie Night Lamp, porcelain bisque w/removable faux fur 8"	1995	50
LIGHT, Barbie Enchanted Evening Night Light w/fake fur wrap	1995	75
LIMOGES, Barbie Hatbox, Bloomingdale's (1st in Series)	1996	200
LIMOGES, Bloomingdale's, Barbie Fashion Designer Portfolio	1997	200
LIMOGES, Bloomingdale's, Barbie Phonograph	1997	170
LIMOGES, Barbie Hatbox	1998	25
LIMOGES, Barbie Portfolio w/sketches	1998	25
LIMOGES, Barbie Record Play w/records	1998	25
LIPSTICK CASE, Mirror inside, Katherine Baumann, *FAO Schwarz* Barbie Collection	1996	295
LUNCH BOX, pink metal "Lunch Kit", *FAO Schwarz*	1996	25
LUNCH BOX, Barbie Lunch Kit, vinyl, black	1997	20
LUNCH BOX, Barbie Lunch Kit, vinyl, pink	1997	20
LUNCH BOX, Barbie (3/4 size) *Hallmark* N.E.	1999	11

NEWER MISCELLANEOUS CONTINUED

DESCRIPTION	YEAR	NRFB
MAGNETS, 2 set versions, City Gal or Country Weekend (Caryco)	1998	20
MAGNETS, set of 4, 2", Matrix	1996	10
MASK, Barbie Halloween, child size, Italy	1988	30
MASKS, 5 versions, by Florian – Nova Rico, Italy	1985	—
MEDALLION, 30th Anniversary Official Commemorative silver, 1 troy ounce, LE 25, 000 Pink Jubilee	1989	55
MINAUDIERE, Barbie, Katherine Baumann Barbie Collection, LE 75, *FAO Schwarz*	1996	1875
MIRROR, hand mirror, 12" decoupage, pink or black, *FAO Schwarz*	1993	80
MIRROR, hand, pink, pictures Barbies & accessories, Designs from the Deep	1996	30
MIRROR, heart shaped, pink, pictures various Barbies, Designs from the Deep	1996	30
MIRROR AND COMB SET, Blonde Living	1974	20
MIRROR AND COMB SET, Brunette TNT	1974	20
MUG, Nostalgic Barbie, "Clay Art," Blonde Ponytail	1991	25
MUSIC BOX, Circus Star Barbie "Over the Waves", *FAO Schwarz*	1995	50
MUSIC BOX, Heart Shaped, SOLO IN THE SPOTLIGHT, "Unforgettable"	1995	30
MUSICAL, Carousel Wal-Mart	1998	30
MUSICAL, Holiday Carriage, Barbie and Ken #26401 *Wal-Mart*	1998	30
MUSICAL, Holiday Dance, Christmas Ballroom plays 30 songs,*Wal-Mart*	1997	30
NICOLE MILLER, Backpack, 11" x 4" x 14", accessories print	1996	40
NICOLE MILLER, Box, round covered, porcelain/fabric, Nostalgic Design 7"	1997	25
NICOLE MILLER, Boxer shorts	1994	30
NICOLE MILLER, Camp shirt	1994	90
NICOLE MILLER, Camp shirt, silk, 35th Anniversary print	1995	90
NICOLE MILLER, Doll case, oval shape, zippered, pink lining holds 2 dolls	1996	40
NICOLE MILLER, Fanny pack "Silhouette"	1996	40
NICOLE MILLER, Fanny pack, silk, 35th Anniversary print	1995	55
NICOLE MILLER, Purse, Austin Healy - PT in various outfits, *FAO Schwarz*	1993	45
NICOLE MILLER, Frame, Nostalgic Design, porcelain/fabric 5½" h.	1997	15
NICOLE MILLER, Hand mirror, Nostalgic Design, porcelain/fabric 9½"	1997	30
NICOLE MILLER, Jacket, zippered silk, Solo print, adult sizes	1995	150
NICOLE MILLER, Large umbrella, Nostalgic print, 40" open	1995	50
NICOLE MILLER, Mini Umbrella w/case, "Silhouette"	1996	50
NICOLE MILLER, Necktie, adult, Austin Healy – PT in various outfits	1993	50
NICOLE MILLER, Night shirt	1994	60
NICOLE MILLER, Organizer/Eyeglass Bag "Silhouette"	1996	45
NICOLE MILLER, Overnight Duffel Bag "Silhouette"	1996	75
NICOLE MILLER, Queen of the Prom Scarf, silk (36" x 36")	1996	70
NICOLE MILLER, Scarf "Silhouette" (43" x 43")	1996	70
NICOLE MILLER, Scarf, 43" x 43", Austin Healy – PT in various outfits	1993	80
NICOLE MILLER, Sunglasses, 1486, with silk hard case, sterling, smoke lenses	—	—
NICOLE MILLER, Tie "Silhouette"	1996	45
NICOLE MILLER, Tote Bag, zippered sild, 35th Anniversary print	1995	140
NICOLE MILLER, Travel Cosmetic Case "Silhouette"	1996	35
NICOLE MILLER, Umbrella, child, fold up, pouch case, accessories print	1996	45

DESCRIPTION	YEAR	NRFB
NICOLE MILLER, Umbrella, child, pink handle, accessories print	1996	20
NICOLE MILLER, Vase, Nostalgic Design, porcelain/fabric 8" h.	1997	30
NICOLE MILLER, Vest, adult, Austin Healy – PT in various outfits	1993	85
NICOLE MILLER, Vest, child size, Austin Healy – PT in various outfits	1993	70
NICOLE MILLER, Vest, Solo in the Spotlight theme, adult	1995	90
NICOLE MILLER, Vest, Solo in the Spotlight theme, child	1995	70
NIGHT SHIRT, child size, includes Barbie size night shirt Hollywood Hair	1993	15
NIGHT STAND, American Toy, Wood & Hardboard 20 x 16 x 25	1983	30
PAGER, BE110, Super Talking	1997	13
PAJAMAS, blue striped, adult, flannel, *FAO Schwarz*	1993	50
PAJAMAS, pink striped, adult, flannel, *FAO Schwarz*	1993	50
PAJAMAS, Nostalgic Barbie, pink/white/black, adult size	1994	25
PAPERWEIGHT, Waterford, *Bloomingdale's*	1996	75
PARTY GOODS, cups, Hallmark, b/w striped accent w/ blonde PT	1994	4
PARTY GOODS, invitations, Hallmark, b/w striped accent w/ blonde PT	1994	3
PARTY GOODS, napkins 2 sizes, Hallmark, b/w striped accent w/ blonde PT	1994	4
PARTY GOODS, tablecloth, Hallmark, b/w striped accent w/ blonde PT	1994	4
PARTY GOODS, plates 2 sizes, Hallmark, b/w striped accent w/ blonde PT	1994	3
PENCIL CASE, pictures, Barbie and Ken dancing with people dancing in background (ADI)	1983	20
PENCIL CASE, pictures, Barbie in bathtub with kitten popping bubbles (ADI)	1983	20
PHONE CARD, Giamaica ATW, Paniniphone calling card	1998	10
PHONE CARD, Hallmark, oval shaped, Solo in the Spotlight, 10 minutes	1995	20
PHONE, Barbie, Super Talking phone & answering machine plays thousands of messages in Barbies voice	1996	45
PHONE, Solo in the Spotlight "The Busy Buzz"	1993	70
PHOTO ALBUM, Coldtone (holds 24, 4" x 6" photos), *FAO Schwarz*	1996	40
PHOTO SET, camera, opera glasses, film photo album	1996	20
PICTURE FRAME, black 5 x 7, Designs from the Deep	1996	15
PICTURE FRAME, Decoupage, LE 200, Mattel Festival (Designs from the Deep)	1994	145
PICTURE FRAME, 4" x 5" photo, decoupage, Nostalgic with rhinestones, black, *FAO Schwarz*	1993	115
PICTURE FRAME, 4" x 5" photo, decoupage, Nostalgic with rhinestones, pink, *FAO Schwarz*	1993	1115
PICTURE FRAME, Coldtone (3" x 5" photo), *FAO Schwarz*	1996	40
PICTURE FRAME, Poodle Parade (#790113), *FAO Schwarz*	1996	40
PICTURE FRAME, Winter Renaissance (and jewelry box set), *JCPenney*	1996	30
PICTURE FRAME, Nostalgic Barbie, "Clay Art," Blonde Ponytail full length, sunglasses and "Barbie"	1991	25
PICTURE FRAME, pink 4" x 6", Designs from the Deep	1996	25
PICTURE FRAME, Poodle Parade (4" x 6" photo)	1996	15
PICTURE FRAME, Summer Sophisticate, 5" x 7", decoupage, *Spiegel*	1996	18
PILL BOX, Barbie, Heart shaped, Katherine Baumann Barbie Collection, *FAO Schwarz*	1997	250

DESCRIPTION	YEAR	NRFB
PLACE SET, Ballerina Barbie, plate, bowl & cup (Zak Designs)	1996	12
PLAYHOUSE, Barbie Garden Party, Fisher Price™, 53" x 50" x 51"	1995	300
POG™, Barbie Milkcap, 7 pogs & 1 WPF™ Kini, Barbie for Girls	1995	—
POG™, set of 70, Canada	1995	—
POSTCARDS, American Postcard Co. NY, NY	1989	2
(Hollywood California, Beverly Hills, Surfs Up, California Dream)		
POSTCARDS, American Postcards	1994	—
POSTCARDS, Barbie "A Postcard Book" Forever Barbie, 30 postcards	1992	15
POSTCARDS, Nostalgic Barbie Book (30 postcards)	1990	25
POSTER, Trading Card Poster, 1st Edition	1990	10
POSTER, Trading Card Poster, 2nd Edition	1991	25
POSTER, 40th Anniversary Commemorative	1999	8
PREMIUM, Mousepad, Barbie Software for Girls (Target)	1998	5
PREMIUM, sunglasses & purse set, Fashion Ave. promotion	1998	10
PROMOTION, Barbie "My First Fashion" #10735 (Canada)	1993	—
PROMOTION, Barbie Family Tree (Canada)	1996	5
PROMOTION, Bedtime Barbie Nightgown, child size, Canada	1996	10
PROMOTION, Coronet Paper Towels, purple, heart base 4"	1997	5
PROMOTION, Crimped Hair with beads & Hair Bow, for Cut 'N Style Barbie (Canada)	1995	5
PROMOTION, Figurines, Little Debbie, set of 3 - 3½"	1998	10
PROMOTION, Kool-Aid Barbie LE 3000 (Canada)	1996	—
PROMOTION, Kool-Aid fashion included with Wacky Warehouse doll (Canada)	1994	—
PROMOTION, Life Size Barbie Poster (Canada)	1995	—
PROMOTION, Magic Jeans outfit for Barbie (Canada)	1994	—
PURSE, Bob Mackie, Gold Sensation, includes .4 oz. parfum purse spray	1993	100
PURSE, Bob Mackie, Mackie Jewels, includes .4 oz. parfum purse spray	1993	100
PURSE, Barbie Evening Purse, Cabochon clasp (5" diameter), *FAO Schwarz*	1996	1450
PURSE, Decoupage Enchanted Evening Mini Purse, *FAO Schwarz*	1996	150
PURSE, mini purse, 6" x 4" decoupage, pink or black, *FAO Schwarz*	1993	175
PURSE, mini, pink box w/clear handle, pictures Nostalgic Barbies	1996	40
Designs from the Deep		
PURSE, Barbie Superstar Purse Set	1977	40
RAINCOAT, Hollywood Hair, vinyl raincoat, tote & Barbie-size tote, child size, *FAO Schwarz*	1993	35
RADIO, AM/FM– 9V – Powertronic by Nasta	1985	25
RECORD, Dance Party, LP (Disco Barbie & Ken on cover)	1981	50
RECORD ALBUM, Phono Picture Disc, LE KPD 6003, Collector Series	1981	50
RECORDER, BE265 – Talking Voice, Kids Designs	1997	13
SAFE, Fur & Jewels, BD1	1978	—
SCARF, Silk, LE 100, Mattel Festival (43 x 43)	1994	50
SHIRT, denim, embroidered, adult, *FAO Schwarz*	1996	40
SHIRT, denim, embroidered, child, *FAO Schwarz*	1996	35
SHOES, 13 varieties of clogs, sneakers & shoes, Pagoda Trading Company	1994	—

DESCRIPTION	YEAR	NRFB
SHOES, black canvas high tops with accessories on side	1994	15
SHOES, black loafers, girls sizes, gold charms on gold chain, Pagoda	1993	15
SHOES, pink sneakers with Ponytail silouhette	1994	15
SHOES, white sneakers with 4 accessories on top	1994	15
SHOPPING BAG, Nicole Miller, Nostalgic Design, porcelain/fabric, 11¼" h.	1997	25
SHOPPING BAG, Nicole Miller, Nostalgic Design, porcelain/fabric, 6" h.	1997	15
SIGN, Barbie Collectibles, Enesco, 20½" x 29"	1997	7
SKATES, In-Line, Barbie for Girls, white	1993	30
SLEEPSHIRT, adult, Barbie Nights, large accessories on white cotton, *FAO Schwarz*	1993	30
SLEEPSHIRT, Solo in the Spotlight, 100% cotton, adult, *FAO Schwarz*	1995	25
SPECIAL COLLECTION, Holiday Present Gift Set #20203	1998	10
SPECIAL COLLECTION, Horse Care Set #18438	1998	10
SPECIAL COLLECTION, Living Assortment, Bath set #19697	1998	10
SPECIAL COLLECTION, Living Assortment, Desk set #19700	1998	10
SPECIAL COLLECTION, Living Assortment, Gardening Set #19698	1998	10
SPECIAL COLLECTION, Living Assortment, Teen-Scene #19699	1998	10
SPECIAL COLLECTION, Special Occasion Assortment, Beautiful Dining set #18444	1998	6
SPECIAL COLLECTION, Special Occasion Assortment, Birthday Surprise set #18440	1998	6
SPECIAL COLLECTION, Wedding Set #18296	1998	7
SPECIAL COLLECTION, Beach Fun Kelly #18433	1999	6
SPECIAL COLLECTION, Camping Fun	1999	6
SPECIAL COLLECTION, Desk	1999	6
SPECIAL COLLECTION, Ken Toolbox set #21275	1999	8
SPECIAL COLLECTION, School's Cool	1999	6
SPECIAL COLLECTION, Sport Gear #21274	1999	6
SPECIAL COLLECTION, Teen Scene	1999	6
SPECIAL COLLECTION, Tropical Trip	1999	6
SPOON, "Barbie Doll Memories" Pewter, 4 inches	1998	25
STAMP & STICKER SET, Barbie at FAO, *FAO Schwarz*	1996	15
STAMP AND STICKER STORY SET, Barbie	1995	15
STAMP KIT, Rubber Stamp Workshop, "Let's Stamp", *FAO Schwarz*	1993	35
STAMPER SET, Butterfly Princess, 17320, Tara	1995	5
STAMPER SET, 18610, mini stamper set	1997	8
STAMPER SET, 18630, 16 piece, Tara	1997	15
STATIONARY, Barbie at FAO, *FAO Schwarz*	1996	10
STATIONARY, Nostalgic Barbie (6" x 9" folio), *FAO Schwarz*	1996	15
STOCKING HANGER, Hallmark 1994 Happy Holiday	1995	20
STOCKING HANGER, Hallmark 1995 Happy Holiday	1996	20
STOCKING, Hallmark 1995 Happy Holiday Christmas Stocking	1995	20
STOOL, Barbie, pink and white, American Toy Furniture (ATF)	1983	45
STYLING HEAD, Hollywood Hair	1993	20
STYLING HEAD, Jewel hair Mermaid (white, black or Hispanic)	1996	20
SUITCASE, Barbie Hollywood, Ero Industries	1993	15
SWEATSHIRT, "Barbie at *FAO Schwarz*" adult, *FAO Schwarz*	1995	35

DESCRIPTION	YEAR	NRFB
SWEATSHIRT, "Barbie at *FAO Schwarz*" child, *FAO Schwarz*	1995	35
SWIMWEAR, mask, snorkel and fin set	1993	15
SWITCH PLATE, black, Designs from the Deep	1996	20
TABLE, decoupaged wooden, heart shaped	1995	150
TABLE AND CHAIR SET, American Toy, wood & hardboard	1983	60
TABLE AND 2 CHAIRS, pink and white, steel frame, American Toy Furniture (ATF)	1983	60
TABLEWARE, acrylic, chip 'n dip platter (15"), *FAO Schwarz*	1996	20
TABLEWARE, acrylic, frosty mug, *FAO Schwarz*	1996	12
TABLEWARE, acrylic, ice bucket with tongs, *FAO Schwarz*	1996	25
TABLEWARE, acrylic, pitcher, *FAO Schwarz*	1996	14
TABLEWARE, acrylic, serving tray (13" x 20"), *FAO Schwarz*	1996	20
TABLEWARE, tumbler set, *FAO Schwarz*	1996	15
TAKE ALONG, holds 6 dolls and accessories, *FAO Schwarz*	1997	35
TAKE ALONG, holds 6 dolls and accessories	1997	25
TAKE ALONG, Barbie Pullman Trunk, Tara Toy Corp.	1995	25
TALK ALONG, pictures FAO exclusive including Statue of Liberty, *FAO Schwarz*	1996	35
TALKING VIEW MASTER, Barbie's Around the World Trip #AVB500 (Gaf - box dated 1965)	1974	—
TALKING VIEW MASTER, Barbie's Great American Photo Race #AVB576 (Gaf – box dated 1973)	1974	—
TELEPHONE, 2 piece, pink (Pink Stamp Premium)	1990	20
TELEPHONE, Battery Inter-com, pink w/purple push buttons	1976	—
TELEVISION, 5" black & white, pink (Pink Stamp Premium)	1990	60
THIMBLE, "Memories - Year 1959" Pewter, Nicholas Gish	1998	25
THROW, Barbie, Triple Woven, (50" x 60")	1996	40
TIARAS, 3 gold toned w/inset crystals in black velvet box (Barbie Collectibles)	1998	10
TOOTHBRUSH, 4 color versions (Colgate, Palmolive)	1996	3
TOOTHBRUSH, talking in Barbie's voice, battery operated Janex division of MJL	1994	—
TOWEL, "On the Go" Avon Exclusive	1998	25
TRADING CARDS, 300 cards plus 20 extra	1991	45
TRADING CARDS, 321 cards	1990	25
TRADING CARDS, Tempo "Barbie Goes Wild" LE 36 Australia	1996	20
TRADING CARDS, Tempo (card showing #3 PT & 1995 Barbie/Kelly) Australia	1996	40
TRADING CARDS, Tempo "Ken & Barbie" and "Happy Birthday" 3 card set Australia	1996	18
TRADING CARDS, Tempo "The Beginning" 5 card insert set Australia	1996	25
TRADING CARDS, Tempo (Barbie Bride Pop-up Cards) Australia	1996	20
TRADING CARDS, Tempo Redemption Card Australia	1996	80
TRADING CARDS, Tempo, World of Barbie Collector Cards Australia	1996	5/pkg.
TRADING CARDS, Tempo, World of Barbie Collector Cards Australia	1996	3/pkg.
TRADING CARDS, Vinyl Binder, Tempo Australia	—	—
TRAY, silver tray, invitation for VIP's to Lincoln Center, LE 500 30th Anniversary	1989	400
TRINKET BOX, Circus Star, Laquered, *FAO Schwarz*	1995	25
TRINKET BOX, Poodle Parade (#790121), *FAO Schwarz*	1996	—
TRINKET BOX, Poodle Parade (5½" x 4") 3 compartments	1996	25

NEWER MISCELLANEOUS CONTINUED

DESCRIPTION	YEAR	NRFB
TRINKET BOX, Summer Sophisticate, round 5¼", *Spiegel*	1996	25
UMBRELLA, Hollywood Barbie, Barbie for Girls	1993	20
VANITY, American Toy, wood & hardboard 29 x 21 x 38	1983	35
VANITY, Barbie My Very Own Vanity, includes vanity, mirror & chair #16964	1997	101
VIDEO, Mail Order, "The Secret of How Barbie dolls are Made"	1993	25
VIDEO, The World of Barbie Collecting – Mattel	1993	10
VIDEO, Barbie Birthday Party (Epcot 94 WDW) Mattel	1994	10
VIDEO, Dance Workout with Barbie, Buena Vista Home Video	1994	15
VIDEO, The Fabulous Vintage Fashion Show, Starring Barbie	1998	25
VIDEO GAME, Barbie Shakin' Pinball, Barbie for Girls Video	1995	20
VIDEO GAME, Barbie Super Model, Sega & Nintendo, Hi Tech Expressions	1994	—
VIDEO GAME, Barbies Beach Patrol Adventure, heart shaped	1996	25
VIDEO GAME, Barbies Birthday Surprise, heart shaped	1996	25
VIDEO GAME, Barbies Design Studio, IBM-Tandy Compatible High Tech Expressions	1993	20
VIDEO GAME, Barbies Hearts and Stars, heart shaped	1996	25
VIDEO GAME, Barbies In-Line Skating, heart shaped	1996	25
VIDEO GAME, Barbies Shopping Adventure, heart shaped	1996	25
VIDEO GAME, Barbies Soccer, heart shaped	1996	25
VIDEO GAME, Gamegirl Barbie	1993	20
VIDEO GAME, Genesis, Barbie Super Model	1993	30
VIDEO GAME, Nintendo, "A Glamorous Quest" High Tech Expressions	1993	20
VIEW, Barbies Great American Photo Race, GAF – #B576	1973	15
VIEW MASTER, Superstar Barbie, GAF – J70	1978	15
VIEW MASTER, Barbie and the Rockers #2327 (Gift Set)	1986	25
VIEW MASTER, Barbie and the Rockers #2327 (reels only)	1986	12
VIEW MASTER, Barbie #4093	1986	15
VIEW MASTER REELS, Barbie and the Rockers	1986	10
VOUCHER, Happy Holidays open package	1995	10
VOUCHER, Happy Holidays open package	1996	10
WAGON, Barbie for Girls, 34" steel w/vinyl pad	1993	40
WALKIE TALKIE, Cordless-style, includes Barbie-sized set, pink	1993	30
WALKIE TALKIE, Telephone Set, by Power Tronic	1983	22
WALLET, 2-in-1 Wallet 'N Watch Pink Stamp Club Premium	1990	17
WALLET, vinyl, black, Snips 'N Scraps by Ponytail, FAO Schwarz	1998	14
WATER, Bottled Alpine Spring, Barbie, Buykin Collectibles, Mattel Toy Club Dallas – Fort Worth	1998	5

NEWER TRANSPORTATION

DESCRIPTION			YEAR	NRFB
8669	1973	BARBIE GOIN' CAMPING SET Breeze Buggy with tent and trailor		80
7738	1973	BARBIE GOING BOATING SET *Sears Exclusive*		75
8639	1973	Barbie United Airlines – Friendship		75
—	1973	Dune Buggy (metallic purple w/black seats)		25
7777	1974	Barbies 10-Speeder		25
7805	1974	Barbies Beach Bus		45
7232	1975	BARBIES DREAM BOAT (Chris Craft™)		70
—	1975	BARBIE SPRUCE GREEN MERCEDES, dark cream colored seats, black steering wheel – Irwin Sears		175
—	1975	RED BOAT red w/ ivory seat, blue trim & blue engine that partially shows Sears		60
9612	1976	BARBIE CLASSY CORVETTE (yellow) DSS		35
9106	1976	BARBIES SUNSAILER – Catamaran		40
—	1977	BARBIE STAR VETTE (red) SuperStar		35
—	1977	KEN DREAM VETTE blue *Toys R Us*		35
—	1978	BARBIE MOTORCYCLE ATC "Big ATV" Made in West Germany		30
—	1979	SUPER CORVETTE metallic wine		25
—	1981	SNOW PRINCESS SLED (Scandinavia)		300
—	1982	BARBIE STAR CYCLE		35
—	1983	BARBIE 10-SPEED BICYCLE		15
5493	1983	BARBIE DREAM CARRIAGE w/2 horses (Canada)		150
5493	1983	BARBIE DREAM CARRIAGE no horses (Europe)		100
—	1983	BARBIE TRAVELIN' TRAILER off road vehicle and horse trailer (DSS)		35
—	1984	BARBIE CRYSTAL Corvette silver		20
4853	1984	BARBIE MOTOR BIKE realistic motor noise		35
2784	1985	ULTRAVETTE pinkish-purple		50
—	1987	BARBIE AND THE ROCKERS, ROCKIN' CYCLE remote control		37
—	1989	BARBIE '57 CHEVROLET BEL AIR CONVERTIBLE light blue		72
3561	1991	BARBIE '57 CHEVROLET BEL AIR CONVERTIBLE pink		50
—	1991	BARBIE FERRARI (328) red		40
—	1991	BARBIE FUN RIDER white open sport vehicle		25
—	1991	BARBIE MAGICAL MOTORHOME pink		30
—	1992	BARBIE AROUND TOWN SCOOTER pink		15
—	1992	BARBIE PORSCHE pink		20
—	1993	BARBIE CRYSTAL HORSE AND CARRIAGE (Europe)		45
—	1993	BARBIE GOLDEN DREAM MOTORHOME pink/white/blue		60
—	1993	BARBIE MUSTANG pink		25
—	1993	BARBIE PORSCHE 911 Cabriolet white		25
—	1993	BARBIE SEA HOLIDAY™ CRUISE SHIP FAO Schwarz		125
—	1993	PAINT 'N DAZZLE CONVERTIBLE		25
7981	1993	SHANI CORVETTE *Toys R Us*		41
—	1994	BARBIE CAMP SUN CRUISER pink		25
—	1994	BARBIE JAGUAR XJS pink metallic		25

DESCRIPTION			YEAR	NRFB
—	1994	BARBIE SWIM 'N DIVE SPEEDBOAT pink & white		30
—	1994	BARBIE STARLIGHT MOTORHOME pink		40
—	1994	BARBIE TRAILER/CAMPER WITH HORSE pink		70
—	1995	BARBIE BAYWATCH REMOTE CONTROL RESCUE CRUISER yellow		45
—	1995	BARBIE BAYWATCH RESCUE BOAT yellow & white		30
—	1995	BARBIE BAYWATCH RESCUE WHEELS yellow		25
—	1995	BARBIE BUTTERFLY PRINCESS ATV		50
11929	1995	BARBIE MUSTANG red		20
67486	1995	BARBIE SPARKLE BEACH SCOOTER		15
—	1995	BARBIE SPORTS CRUISER light blue *FAO Schwarz*		40
—	1995	PRANCING HORSE & CARRIAGE SET		65
67053-91	1996	BARBIE BIKING FUN		10
13185	1996	BARBIE MINI-VAN white/lilac/pink		50
67413-91	1996	BARBIE OCEAN FRIENDS SPEEDBOAT		20
67486-91	1996	BARBIE SCOOTER FUN		15
14862	1996	BARBIE SONGBIRD HORSE & CARRIAGE SET		70
60-1157	1996	BARBIE SPARKLE BEACH SUN RIDER, wire controlled *Radio Shack*		25
—	1996	BARBIE SWEET MAGNOLIA HORSE & CARRIAGE SET *Wal-Mart*		38
—	1996	CORVETTE pink		15
—	1996	FORD EXPLORER, radio controlled Eddie Bauer, 11½" dolls, pink w/brown		50
		seats & wheel wells, *Spiegel*		
67596	1997	BARBIE & KELLY BIKIN' FUN BICYCLE		12
67560	1997	BARBIE COUNTRY RIDE BIKE		10
16544	1997	BARBIE CRUISIN' CAR		30
67544	1997	BARBIE FUN FOR 4 CAR		15
67532	1997	BARBIE HOT DRIVIN' SPORT CAR		25
67708	1997	BARBIE MOTOR SCOOTER		18
14614	1997	BARBIE MOTORHOME		50
7005	1997	BARBIE REMOTE CONTROL CITY NIGHTS CYCLE		35
67557	1997	BARBIE SUN WHEELER (Splash 'N Color)		22
67786	1998	BARBIE SPORTS CAR		25
67790	1998	BARBIE COOL CONVERTIBLE		14
67342	1998	BARBIE SPORTWAGEN (purple convertible) Europe		35
—	1998	HARLEY DAVIDSON MOTORCYCLE, Maisto-1200C Sportster		
		Custom LE 15,000		50
18549	1998	BARBIE PORSCHE BOXSTER SPORTS CAR		35
22007	1999	BARBIE AIRPLANE		40
21736	1999	BARBIE SPEEDBOAT		30
67707-91	1999	BARBIE SPLASH 'N FUN PLAYSET (Wetbike)		10
26132	2000	BARBIE HARLEY FAT BOY *Toys R Us* – Harley Dealership		100
24936	2000	KELLY PRINCESS CARRIAGE		Retail
—	2000	VOLKSWAGON BEETLE "Bugs" Assorted Colors		50

NEWER BARBIE® WATCHES

STOCK NO.	YEAR	DESCRIPTION	MEDIAN
—	1980	THE OFFICIAL WRIST WATCH - Barbie Bradley Time	25
—	1981	BARBIE FAN CLUB PROMOTIONAL white w/white plastic sleeve case	75
—	1986	BARBIE & THE ROCKERS digital (Armitron)	20
—	1989	ARMITRON BARBIE'S 30th ANNIVERSARY WRISTWATCH (white vinyl envelope)	90
—	1992	MADISON AVENUE WATCH, LE *FAO Schwarz*	125
26517	1994	1959 BARBIE black strap *Hope*	30
—	1994	35th ANNIVERSARY FOSSIL WATCH, LE 20,000	125
—	1994	CHARMING BARBIE FOSSIL WATCH, LE 20,000	90
—	1994	GLAMOUR & STYLE green strap *Hope*	30
26512	1994	GLAMOUR & STYLE pink strap *Hope*	30
26514	1994	HEART SHAPE BARBIE black strap *Hope*	30
26515	1994	HEART SHAPE BARBIE pink strap *Hope*	30
26516	1994	NOSTALGIC ICONS purple strap *Hope*	30
—	1994	PRETTY & PINK FOSSIL WATCH, LE 20,000	80
—	1994	SILVER SCREEN WATCH FOSSIL, LE 5000 *FAO Schwarz*	105
26519	1994	TRAVEL USA black strap Hope	30
26518	1994	TRAVEL USA pink strap Hope	30
—	1995	BARBIE OLé black band, Convention Hostess Gift, LE 70	—
—	1995	BARBIE WATCH rotating accessories on face w/pink band *QVC*	75
L1-1400	1995	BLACK PIANO FOSSIL WATCH, LE 1000 Sterling Silver	150
—	1995	CIRCUS STAR FOSSIL, LE 5000 *FAO Schwarz*	110
—	1995	PEPPERMINT PRINCESS WATCH FOSSIL, LE 5000 *Macy's*	115
L1-1296	1995	PINK PIANO FOSSIL WATCH, LE 10,000	90
—	1995	RED FLARE WATCH Fossil Relic *Sears*	55
—	1995	STARLIGHT WALTZ WATCH, LE 10,000 Fossil Relic *JCPenney*	70
26547	1996	45 RPM plastic strap *Hope-Hyde Park*	35
—	1996	ACCESSORIES compact, mule purse, sunglasses on face w/ accessories, pink plastic band	35
—	1996	AMERICAN GIRL pink plastic strap, Poodle Parade *Hope-Hyde Park*	35
—	1996	BANDSTAND BEAUTY BARBIE black band, Philadelphia Convention	25
26532	1996	BLACK/WHITE striped rectangular dial, gold rectangular case, black suede band	45
—	1996	BLONDE PONYTAIL head facing front, dots instead of numbers, on face Barbie on face, black plastic strap w/ accessories *Hope-Hyde Park*	40
—	1996	BLONDE PONYTAIL profile w/pearl necklace, gold/silver woven interlocking mesh band	60
—	1996	ENCHANTED EVENING "COLLECTOR'S WATCH" in book & ribbon tie *QVC*	70
—	1996	ENCHANTED EVENING POWDER PUFF WATCH Fossil Relic *JCPenney*	65
26524	1996	HEART SHAPED FACE w/gold ponytail, head profile, black leather strap	50

STOCK NO.	YEAR	DESCRIPTION	MEDIAN
		Hope-Hyde Park	
—	1996	OVAL DIAL w/blonde PT silhouette and pink Barbie, gold oval case, black shiny band	45
26545	1996	PICNIC red, pink & white checkered face, purple rectangle w/opaque green, red, white & blue plastic band w/ Barbie in gone fishing	35
		Hope-Hyde Park	
26531	1996	PINK DIAL w/blonde PT profile and pink Barbie, gold curved rectangular case, black band	55
26541	1996	PINK PROFILES small pink silhouette pink Barbie, numbers on face are each spelled out, (black, white, purple & 2 shades of pink face), purple case, pink plastic band, small Barbie & small silhouette *Hope-Hyde Park*	35
26533	1996	PINK/WHITE striped rectangular dial, gold rectangular case, pink suede band	45
—	1996	PONYTAIL head profile on gold face w/purple in round case, purple leather band	40
26544	1996	PONYTAIL Blonde head profile plastic black strap w/picnic set & red flare outfits *Hope-Hyde Park*	30
26536	1996	PONYTAIL head profile, no numbers on face, white pearl necklace, black leather strap *Hope-Hyde Park*	40
—	1996	POODLE PARADE, LE 1000 gold	125
—	1996	POODLE PARADE, LE 10,000 pink	95
26526	1996	RECTANGULAR FACE w/small gold Barbie profiles & gold Barbies, black leather strap *Hope-Hyde Park*	50
26526	1996	RECTANGULAR FACE w/small gold Barbie profiles & gold Barbies, brown leather strap *Hope-Hyde Park*	50
26543	1996	SOLO IN THE SPOTLIGHT plastic strap Hope-Hyde Park	30
—	1996	STAR TREK – 30TH ANNIVERSARY – BARBIE/KEN	25
—	1996	STATUE OF LIBERTY FOSSIL, LE 5000 *FAO Schwarz*	95
—	1996	SUMMER SOPHISTICATE FOSSIL, LE 5000 *Spiegel*	70
—	1996	WINTER RENAISSANCE Fossil Relic *JCPenney*	70
—	1997	AVON BARBIE WATCH	25
—	1997	BARBIE HOLIDAY WATCH Relic	30
—	1997	BEACH BLANKET BARBIE black band, Convention Hostess Gift	40
—	1997	GEORGE WASHINGTON FOSSIL, LE *FAO Schwarz*	70
—	1997	LIMITED HOLIDAY EDITION Girls Barbie Wristwatch, Relic	35
96056	1998	CHEERLEADER, pink strap, rotating accessories, Relic	35
96057	1998	pink strap, inset stones, Relic	35
98571	1999	TIMEX BARBIE	27
88651	1999	TIMEX BARBIE	27
88601	1999	TIMEX BARBIE	27
88841	1999	TIMEX BARBIE	27

NEWER PAPER DOLLS

STOCK NO.	YEAR	DESCRIPTION	MEDIAN
1971	1973	BARBIE & PJ – A CAMPING ADVENTURE (book)	20
4347	1973	BARBIE COUNTRY CAMPER & PAPER DOLL (box)	20
1983	1973	BARBIE COUNTRY CAMPER DOLL BOOK	20
1990	1973	BARBIE COUNTRY CAMPER DOLL BOOK (book)	25
1947	1973	BARBIES BOUTIQUE	20
1974-1	1973	BARBIES BOUTIQUE (reprint with price change)	30
1954	1973	BARBIES BOUTIQUE (book)	30
1954	1973	BARBIES BOUTIQUE (reprint with price change)	30
1996-1	1973	BARBIES BOUTIQUE	30
1996	1973	BARBIES FRIENDSHIP PAPER DOLLS	25
4322	1973	BARBIES MAGIC PAPER DOLLS (box)	20
1982	1973	FRANCIE WITH GROWIN' PRETTY HAIR (book)	35
1982	1973	FRANCIE WITH GROWIN' PRETTY HAIR (folder)	40
1969	1973	HI! I'M SKIPPER PAPER DOLL FASHIONS	30
1955	1973	MALIBU FRANCIE DOLL BOOK (book)	20
1945-2	1973	MALIBU SKIPPER	20
1952	1973	MALIBU SKIPPER (book)	25
1952	1973	MALIBU SKIPPER (reprint)	25
1952	1973	MALIBU SKIPPER (reprint with price change)	25
1952	1973	MALIBU SKIPPER (book, reprint with encircled price)	20
1978	1973	MISS AMERICA PAPER DOLL	20
1984	1973	QUICK CURL BARBIE & HER PAPER DOLL FRIENDS (book, six pages)	30
1984	1973	QUICK CURL BARBIE & HER PAPER DOLL FRIENDS (reprint, four pages)	30
4336	1974	BARBIE & KEN – NEWPORT (box)	20
1951	1974	BARBIE GOIN' CAMPING	20
1951	1974	BARBIE GOIN' CAMPING (reprint with price change)	20
1961	1974	BARBIE GOIN' CAMPING	20
—	1974	BARBIE MINI POSTER SET SHOWS SKIPPER HOLDING SWEET 16 BARBIE POSTER	10
1981	1974	BARBIES SWEET 16 PAPER DOLLS	20
4338-7420M	1974	SUN VALLEY BARBIE & KEN (box)	20
1981	1975	BARBIE & HER FRIENDS ALL SPORTS TOURNAMENT	15
2352	1975	BARBIE SPORT TOURNAMENT FASHION SET (book)	20
1644	1975	QUICK CURL BARBIE (book)	15
4399	1975	QUICK CURL BARBIE (box)	20
1956	1975	YELLOWSTONE KELLEY PAPER DOLLS	15
4391	1976	BALLERINA BARBIE (box)	20
4392-7411	1976	BARBIE & FRANCIE (box)	20
4389	1976	BARBIE & KEN - ALL SPORTS TOURNAMENT (box)	15
1989	1976	BARBIE FASHION ORIGINALS PAPER DOLL	20

NEWER PAPER DOLLS CONTINUED

STOCK NO.	YEAR	DESCRIPTION	MEDIAN
1996	1976	BARBIES BEACH BUS PAPER DOLLS	15
1996-1	1976	BARBIES BEACH BUS PAPER DOLLS (reprint with price change)	15
1990	1976	GROWING UP SKIPPER PAPER DOLLS	20
4393-7420	1976	MALIBU FRANCIE – 21 piece Wardrobe (box)	20
4395-7420	1976	SKIPPER (box)	20
1993	1977	BALLERINA BARBIE PAPER DOLLS	20
1993-1	1977	BALLERINA BARBIE PAPER DOLLS	20
1983	1977	SUPERSTAR BARBIE PAPER DOLL	15
1983-2	1977	SUPERSTAR BARBIE PAPER DOLL (reprint with price change)	15
1982-32	1978	FASHION PHOTO BARBIE & PJ	20
1982-32	1978	FASHION PHOTO BARBIE & PJ (reprint with price change)	20
1997	1978	FASHION PHOTO BARBIE & PJ	20
1997-1	1978	FASHION PHOTO BARBIE & PJ	20
1997-21	1978	FASHION PHOTO BARBIE & PJ (reprint)	15
7413-D	1978	SUPERSTAR BARBIE (box)	15
4328-20	1979	BARBIES DESIGN-A-FASHION PAPER DOLL KIT (box)	15
1997-21	1979	FASHION PHOTO BARBIE & PJ	15
1976-3	1979	MISS AMERICA PAPER DOLL	20
4329-21	1979	SKIPPERS DESIGN-A-FASHION PAPER DOLL KIT (box)	15
1836	1980	BARBIE & SKIPPER CAMPSITE AT LUCKY LAKE PLAYBOOK	15
1836-31	1980	BARBIE & SKIPPER CAMPSITE AT LUCKY LAKE PLAYBOOK (reprint #1836)	15
1836-41	1980	BARBIE & SKIPPER CAMPSITE AT LUCKY LAKE PLAYBOOK (reprint #1836)	20
1836-41	1980	BARBIE &SKIPPER CAMPSITE PLAYBOOK (reprint #1836 with price change)	15
7410	1980	PRETTY CHANGES BARBIE (box)	20
1980-1	1980	SUPER-TEEN SKIPPER PAPER DOLL	15
1980-3	1980	SUPER-TEEN SKIPPER PAPER DOLL	15
1982-33	1980	SUPER-TEEN SKIPPER PAPER DOLL (reprint #1980-3)	15
1982-34	1981	PRETTY CHANGES BARBIE PAPER DOLL	20
1982-42	1981	PRETTY CHANGES BARBIE (reprint #1982-34)	20
1982-42	1981	PRETTY CHANGES BARBIE (reprint #1982-34 with cover & price change)	20
4328-21	1982	BARBIE DESIGN-A-FASHION PAPER DOLL KIT (box)	10
1983-43	1982	GOLDEN DREAM BARBIE PAPER DOLL	10
7408C	1982	GOLDEN DREAM BARBIE (box)	10
7408-E	1982	MALIBU BARBIE (box)	10
4329-21	1982	SKIPPER DESIGN-A-FASHION PAPER DOLL KIT (box)	15
1982-43	1982	WESTERN BARBIE PAPER DOLL	15
7408-H	1982	WESTERN BARBIE (box)	20

NEWER PAPER DOLLS CONTINUED

STOCK NO.	YEAR	DESCRIPTION	MEDIAN
1982-45	1983	ANGEL FACE BARBIE PAPER DOLL	10
1944	1983	BARBIE & SKIPPER (book)	15
7407-E	1983	BARBIE PAPER DOLL ANGEL FACE (box)	10
1838-45	1983	PAPER DOLL PLAYBOOK – Pink & Pretty Barbie (book)	15
7411-B	1983	PINK & PRETTY BARBIE (box)	10
1983-44	1983	PINK & PRETTY BARBIE PAPER DOLL	13
1936-43	1983	PINK & PRETTY BARBIE PAPER DOLL PLAYBOOK	10
1982-44	1983	SUNSATIONAL MALIBU BARBIE PAPER DOLL	10
1982-46	1983	TWIRLY CURLS BARBIE PAPER DOLL	10
7411-C	1983	WESTERN SKIPPER (box)	10
1527	1984	BARBIE & KEN PAPER DOLL	12
1985-51	1984	BARBIE & KEN PAPER DOLL (reprint #1527)	12
1731	1984	BARBIE CHRISTMAS TIME PAPER DOLL	20
1982-47	1984	BARBIE FANTASY PAPER DOLL	10
7407-B	1984	CRYSTAL BARBIE (box)	10
1983-46	1984	CRYSTAL BARBIE PAPER DOLL	13
1982-49	1984	GREAT SHAPE BARBIE PAPER DOLL	10
1985-51	1984	GREAT SHAPE BARBIE PAPER DOLL (reprint #1982-49)	10
1521	1985	DAY-TO-NIGHT BARBIE PAPER DOLL	10
1982-48	1985	DAY-TO-NIGHT BARBIE PAPER DOLL (reprint #1521)	15
1522	1985	GREAT SHAPE BARBIE PAPER DOLL	10
1525	1985	GREAT SHAPE BARBIE PAPER DOLL	10
1982-49	1985	GREAT SHAPE BARBIE PAPER DOLL	10
1985-51	1985	GREAT SHAPE BARBIE PAPER DOLL	10
1525	1985	PEACHES 'N CREAM BARBIE PAPER DOLL	10
1983-48	1985	PEACHES 'N CREAM BARBIE PAPER DOLL	10
1528	1986	BARBIE AND THE ROCKERS PAPER DOLLS	15
1528-1	1986	BARBIE AND THE ROCKERS PAPER DOLLS (reprint #1528)	10
1523	1986	TROPICAL BARBIE PAPER DOLLS	10
1523-1	1986	TROPICAL BARBIE PAPER DOLLS (reprint #1523)	10
1537	1987	JEWEL SECRETS BARBIE PAPER DOLLS	12
1537-1	1987	JEWEL SECRETS BARBIE PAPER DOLLS	12
1500	1988	PERFUME PRETTY PAPER DOLLS	10
1537-3	1989-91	BARBIE PAPER DOLL (reprint #1537-2)	10
1537-2	1989	SUPERSTAR BARBIE PAPER DOLL (2 cover versions)	12
1502	1990	BARBIE PAPER DOLL	10
1502-1	1990	BARBIE PAPER DOLL	10
1502-2	1990/91	BARBIE PAPER DOLL (reprint #1502)	10
1523-2	1990	BARBIE PAPER DOLL	10
1502-5	1990	BARBIE PAPER DOLL	10

STOCK NO.	YEAR	DESCRIPTION	MEDIAN
1502-5	1990-93	BARBIE PAPER DOLL (reprint #1502-1)	10
1532-3	1990	BARBIE PARIS PRETTY FASHION (book)	10
1690	1990	DELUXE PAPER DOLL BARBIE	10
1690-1	1990	DELUXE PAPER DOLL BARBIE	10
1690-1	1990/91	DELUXE PAPER DOLL BARBIE (reprint #1690)	10
5522	1991	BARBIE (box)	10
1695	1991	DELUXE PAPER DOLL BARBIE	10
1695-1	1991	DELUXE PAPER DOLL BARBIE	10
1502-3	1992	BARBIE PAPER DOLL	10
2371	1992-94	BARBIE PAPER DOLL DELUXE EDITION (reprint #1695-1)	10
2389	1992-94	BARBIE PAPER DOLL DELUXE EDITION (reprint #1690-2)	10
1690-2	1992	DELUXE PAPER DOLL BARBIE	10
1502-4	1993	BARBIE PAPER DOLL	10
5559	1993	BARBIE PAPER DOLL (box)	10
5570	1993	BARBIE PAPER DOLL (box)	10
2748	1993-94	BARBIE PAPER DOLL DELUXE EDITION	10
2381	1994	BARBIE (book)	10
2018	1994	BARBIE PAPER DOLL DELUXE EDITION	10
		PECK GANDRÉ AND PECK AUBRY	
—	1989	NOSTALGIC BARBIE PAPER DOLL Blonde #1 Ponytail	20
—	1989	NOSTALGIC BARBIE PAPER DOLL Brunette #5 Ponytail	20
—	1989	NOSTALGIC KEN PAPER DOLL	20
—	1994	The 1959 (Number One) BARBIE PAPER DOLL	10
—	1994	The 1961 (Bubble Cut) BARBIE PAPER DOLL	10
—	1994	The 1964 (Swirl Ponytail) BARBIE PAPER DOLL	10
—	1995	The 1965 (American Girl) BARBIE PAPER DOLL	10
—	1996	The 1966 (Color Magic) BARBIE PAPER DOLL	10
—	1996	The 1967 (Twist 'N Turn) BARBIE PAPER DOLL	10
—	1997	The 1959 (Number One) BARBIE & THE 1964 SWIRL *Avon*	10
		PRICE STERN SLOAN	
—	1991	BARBIE AND THE BEAT ON TOUR PLAY SET	15

NEWER PATTERNS, SEWING & CRAFTS

DESCRIPTION	YEAR	MINT UNCUT & COMPLETE
7277 SEW MAGIC ADD ONS	1974	15
7723 SEW MAGIC ADD ONS	1974	15
CROCHETED FASHION DOLL CLOTHES, Leaflet 268	1983	5
FASHION DOLL FANTASY CROCHET BOOKLET Annies Pattern Club	—	10
SIMPLICITY CRAFTS, MY SIZE BARBIE	—	12
BURDA PATTERNS		
9723 BARBIE, KEN & FRANCIE	1975	50
9724 BARBIE, KEN, FRANCIE & SKIPPER	1975	50
3886 BARBIE & KEN	1994	20
3887 BARBIE & KEN	1994	20
E437 BARBIE & KEN	1995	30
BUTTERICK		
6664 OR 224 BARBIE	1978	20
4687 OR 257 BARBIE	1980	20
6170 OR 295 BARBIE	1984	20
4329 OR 436 BARBIE	1986	15
5925 OR 464 BARBIE	1987	15
6495 OR 481 BARBIE	1988	15
5569 BARBIE & KEN	1989	15
4533 OR 122 BARBIE & KEN	1989	15
5014 OR 145 BARBIE	1990	15
5061 BARBIE	1997	10
5865 BARBIE	1998	12
6110 BARBIE	1999	10
6469 BARBIE (Reproduction of 9993)	1999	10
McCALL'S		
4716 BARBIE & KEN	1975	25
McCALL'S DOLL FASHIONS VOLUME 1, NO.1, BARBIE, KEN & FRANCIE	1976	35
6317 BARBIE, KEN & SUPERSIZE BARBIE	1978	20
7774 BARBIE, KEN & SUPERSIZE BARBIE	1978	20
8181/627 BARBIE	1983	20
8727/696 BARBIE	1983	20
9283/750 BARBIE	1984	20
9316/757 BARBIE & KEN	1984	20
2207/789 BARBIE & KEN	1985	20
2686/823 BARBIE	1986	20
3281/869 BARBIE	1987	20
3880 BARBIE	1988	20
4400/632 BARBIE	1989	20
4906/662 BARBIE	1990	20

DESCRIPTION	YEAR	MINT UNCUT & COMPLETE
McCALL'S (continued)		
5171/679 BARBIE	1991	20
5462/701 BARBIE & KEN	1991	20
5738/730 BARBIE & KEN	1992	20
6316 BARBIE (HAPPY TO BE ME, TOO!)	1993	20
6317 BARBIE & KEN	1993	20
6876/874 BARBIE	1994	15
7400 BARBIE & KEN	1994	15
7932 BARBIE & KEN	1995	15
8140 BARBIE-SCALE BEDROOM SUITE	1995	15
8552 BARBIE	1996	15
8825 BARBIE-SCALE LIVING ROOM & DINING ROOM SUITE	1997	14
9115 BARBIE	1997	14
SIMPLICITY		
6697 BARBIE	1974	20
7210 BARBIE	1975	20
7737 BARBIE & KEN	1976	20
8281 BARBIE	1977	20
9194 BARBIE (12½" Mego Dolls such as Cher, Farrah, Diana Ross, Wonder Woman, too!)	1979	20
5356 BARBIE	1981	15
5637 BARBIE	1982	15
5807 BARBIE & KEN	1982	15
6097 BARBIE	1983	15
6363 BARBIE	1983	15
6369 BARBIE	1983	15
6507 BARBIE	1984	15
6967/309 BARBIE & KEN	1985	15
7582 BARBIE, KEN & HEART FAMILY-SIZED KIDS	1986	15
7928 BARBIE & KEN	1986	15
8333 BARBIE	1987	15
8377 BARBIE & KEN	1987	15
100 BEGIN TO SEW WITH BARBIE & SIMPLICITY	1987	15
101 BEGIN TO SEW WITH BARBIE & SIMPLICITY	1987	15
102 BEGIN TO SEW WITH BARBIE & SIMPLICITY	1987	15
103 BEGIN TO SEW WITH BARBIE & SIMPLICITY	1987	15
104 BEGIN TO SEW WITH BARBIE & SIMPLICITY	1987	15
105 BEGIN TO SEW WITH BARBIE & SIMPLICITY – KEN	1987	15
106 BEGIN TO SEW WITH BARBIE & SIMPLICITY – KEN	1987	15
107 BEGIN TO SEW WITH BARBIE & SIMPLICITY – KEN	1987	15
9334 BARBIE	1989	15
0076 DESIGN DEBUT same as 9334 (Sewing Store Promotional Give-Away)	1989	15

DESCRIPTION	YEAR	MINT UNCUT & COMPLETE
7046 BARBIE	1990	15
7122, 7125 BARBIE GIRL™	1991	8
7130, 7314 BARBIE GIRL™	1991	8
7362 BARBIE & KEN	1991	15
7600 SKIPPER	1991	15
7603 KEN (M.C. HAMMER, TOO!)	1991	15
7601 BARBIE	1991	15
7270 BARBIE & KEN	1991	15
7712 BARBIE	1991	15
8157 BARBIE	1992	15
8158 BARBIE-SCALE LIVING ROOM & BEDROOM SUITE	1992	15
8388 LITTLE GIRL & BARBIE	1993	15
8389 LITTLE GIRL & BARBIE	1993	15
8518 BARBIE & KEN	1993	15
8566 LITTLE GIRL & BARBIE	1993	15
8581 LITTLE GIRL & BARBIE HALLOWEEN COSTUMES	1993	15
8633 LITTLE GIRL & BARBIE	1993	15
8682 LITTLE GIRL & BARBIE	1993	15
8797 BARBIE & KEN	1994	15
8817 MY SIZE BARBIE	1994	15
9838 BARBIE	1996	12
7952 BARBIE	1997	12
7959 BARBIE	1997	12
8369 BARBIE	1998	10
8457 BARBIE	1998	10
8481 BARBIE	1998	10
9062 BARBIE	1999	10
VOGUE		
9531 BARBIE	1995	12
9686 BARBIE – ORIGINAL VINTAGE WARDROBE	1996	12
9669 BARBIE	1996	12
9759 BARBIE – PAST PERFECT!	1997	12
9834 BARBIE – VINTAGE BRIDAL TROUSSEAU	1998	12
9867 BARBIE – VISIONS FROM VERSAILLES	1998	12
9894 BARBIE – OUT ON THE TOWN	1998	12
9964 BARBIE – SISTERS!	1998	12
9917 BARBIE – MAKING HISTORY	1998	12
9985 BARBIE – WEDDING BELLE!	1998	12
7070 BARBIE & KEN		
VIRGINIA LAKIN BOOKLETS		
DOLL KNITTING & CROCHETING, Book 14	1973	10

PETS

STOCK NO.	YEAR	DESCRIPTION	MIP
1157	1971	DANCER (horse)	90
—	1976	DANCER (horse) Europe re-issue – lighter brown	70
—	1976	HATATITLA (horse) Germany – Karl May	50
—	1976	THUNDER (horse) Germany – Big Jim's Buckskin horse cream colored	50
—	1977	EQUESTRIENNE BARBIE AND HER HORSE DANCER (Canadian exclusive)	150
1018	1980	BEAUTY (afghan dog)	30
3312	1981	DALLAS (horse)	40
—	1981	DALLAS (horse) Europe – jointed	50
5019	1982	BEAUTY AND PUPPIES	35
—	1982	MIDNIGHT (stallion)	35
5524	1983	FLUFF (kitten)	20
—	1983	HONEY (Skippers pony)	35
—	1984	DIXIE (Dallas' colt)	30
—	1984	PRANCER (horse)	35
7928	1985	PRINCE (Poodle)	35
2064	1985	TAHITI (bird w/cage)	20
—	1988	BLINKING BEAUTY (horse)	25
—	1988	GINGER (giraffe)	30
—	1988	ZIZI (zebra)	30
6252	1989	MR. BOBBIE (dog) Germany	35
—	1990	SNOWBALL (dog) Arco	35
9961	1990	SUN RUNNER (horse)	30
—	1991	ALL AMERICAN (horse)	32
—	1991	CHAMPION (horse)	35
—	1991	SNOW FLAKE	30
—	1992	HONEY (kitten)	10
4041	1992	ROSEBUD (horse)	30
—	1992	SACHI (puppy)	10
—	1992	STAR STEPPER (Arabian horse)	35
3352	1992	TAG ALONG TIFFY (kitten)	15
3335	1992	TAG ALONG WAGS (puppy)	15
7273	1992	TURQUOISE (Collie dog)	15
—	1993	BUTTERFLY (pony)	20
—	1993	CHELSIE (pony)	20
—	1993	PRANCING HORSE (FAO – batteries required)	50
—	1993	STOMPER (horse)	25
—	1993	WESTERN STAR (horse)	20
11766	1994	BARBIE PRANCING HORSE	25
12271	1994	COUNTRY STAR HORSE (*Wal-Mart* exclusive)	25
—	1994	HIGH STEPPER (horse)	35
—	1994	HIGH STEPPER (horse & carriage)	80
11069	1994	MITZI MEOW (cat)	10
11079	1994	PUPPY RUFF (dog)	10
14265	1995	FLYING HERO (horse)	25
12436	1995	TROPICAL SPLASH SEA HORSE	20

STOCK NO.	YEAR	DESCRIPTION	MIP
—	1996	CALICO (cat)	12
67573	1996	MOMMY AND TWIN POODLES	10
14879	1996	NIBBLES (horse)	25
—	1996	OCEAN FRIENDS KEIKO (whale)	20
—	1997	CANDIE (brown)	10
—	1997	GINGER (white)	10
—	1997	HONEY (grey)	10
—	1997	MANDY (yellow)	10
—	1998	STABLE FRIENDS FAMILIES	12
17718	1998	WALKING BEAUTY HORSE	25
17970	1998	WALKING PONIES – Sassy Pony	12
18498	1998	WALKING PONIES – Baby Pony	12
18497	1998	WALKING PONIES – Sweetie Pony	12
67572-91	1999	BARBIE PETS Yorkie	5
20848	1999	DALMATIAN Pet Lovin'	10
—	1999	DELUXE PETS – Sheep Dog (barks)	8
—	1999	DELUXE PETS – Collie (barks)	8
21726	1999	ENGLISH POINTER Pet Lovin'	10
20848	1999	GOLDEN RETRIEVER Pet Lovin'	10
20847	1999	ST. BERNARD Pet Lovin'	10
25998	2000	GLAM 'N GROOM – Poodle	10
25998	2000	GLAM 'N GROOM – Cat	10
25998	2000	GLAM 'N GROOM – Afghan	10
25998	2000	GLAM 'N GROOM – Irish Setter	10
25998	2000	GLAM 'N GROOM – Cocker Spaniel	10
—	2000	RAINBOW HORSE	25
9403		SNOW DANCE (horse)	30

❖❖❖❖❖❖❖❖❖❖❖❖❖❖❖

NEWER PUZZLES

DESCRIPTION	YEAR	NRFB
BARBIE SITTING IN FRONT OF MIRROR (Milton Bradley – 100 piece)	1976	5
HAPPY HOLIDAYS	1988	15
HAPPY HOLIDAYS	1989	15
HAPPY HOLIDAYS	1990	15
NOSTALGIC (Features 35 Barbie & Ken's – 550 piece)	1990	20
HAPPY HOLIDAYS	1991	15
JEWEL	1993	15
JEWEL	1994	15
NOSTALGIC (9 photos of Barbie) Western Publishing – Golden	1994	20
JEWEL	1995	15
JEWEL	1996	15
BARBIE 25-piece puzzle assortment (4 variations) #41659	1998	3
Barbie STICKER/GLITTER PUZZLE ASSORTMENT (two styles) #41647	1998	3

NEWER RECORDS & MUSIC RELATED

DESCRIPTION	YEAR	NRFB
BARBIE DISCO RECORD PLAYER	1976	150
BARBIE & HER FRIENDS KID STUFF, LE, KPD 6003 Collector Series	1981	65
Phono Picture Disc		
BARBIE COUNTRY FAVORITES RECORD, Kid Stuff Records	1981	20
BARBIE LOOKING GOOD FEELING GREAT EXCERCISE ALBUM	1982	35
(Free exercise poster) Kid Stuff Records		
BARBIE & THE BANDSTAND CONVENTION "60'S STYLE" CD	1996	15
BARBIE SINGS Autograph and Beehive 45rpm record, Barbie and the	1996	25
Bandstand Convention		
BARBIE TUNE TOTE, black vinyl case, Barbie and the Bandstand Convention	1996	30
"I'M STILL HERE" (Steve Gideon) The Barbie Collector's Anthem CD	1996	10
Barbie Music Cassette "THE LOOK" Rincon Recordings	1991	15
Barbie Music CD "THE LOOK" Rincon Recordings	1991	20
Aquarium - Aqua MCA Records CD	1997	10
"BARBIE GIRL" Aqua MCA Records maxi CD	1997	10
"BARBIE GIRL" Aqua MCA Records single CD	1997	6
"BARBIE GIRL" Aqua MCA Records 55393 4 versions	1997	12
"BARBIE GIRL" Aqua Universal Music (Made in Germany) 4 versions	1997	12
"BARBIE GIRL" Velva Blue Waxworks Collectables CDS 5051-2	1997	6
BARBIE - Here in Nashville	—	20

❖❖❖❖❖❖❖❖❖❖❖❖❖❖

NEWER TEA SETS

DESCRIPTION	YEAR	NRFB
BARBIE FOR GIRLS		
MUSICAL TEAPOT SET - plays *I'm a Little Teapot*	1994	10
CHILTON-GLOBE, INC.		
PORCELAIN BARBIE TEA SET	1980	90
17 PIECE TEA SET	1992	20
35th ANNIVERSARY *JCPenney Exclusive*	1994	45
35th ANNIVERSARY MINIATURE NOSTALGIC TEA SET (17 piece)	1994	45
FAO Schwarz, LE		
HOLIDAY TEA SET - green velour box w/4 cups, 4 saucers, 4 napkins	1994	32
showing '88,'89,'90 & '91 Holiday Barbies		
HOLIDAY TEA SET - green velour box w/4 cups, 4 saucers, 4 napkins	1994	30
showing '92,'93,'94 & '95 Holiday Barbies		
SOLO IN THE SPOTLIGHT (Miniature tea set) *JCPenney, FAO Schwarz*	1995	50
ENCHANTED TEA SET	1996	25
MATTEL		
MATTEL FESTIVAL '94, LE 150 (Chilton-Globe)	1994	150

Gene Dolls

STOCK NO.	YEAR	DESCRIPTION	HIGH	LOW	AVG
96403	1995	MONACO 2nd (Timothy Alberts)	195	125	160
96401	1995	PREMIERE 1st (Tim Kennedy)	995	595	795
96402	1995	RED VENUS 3rd (Tim Kennedy)	95	60	78
93503	1996	BLUE GODDESS	95	59	77
93507	1996	PIN UP (Tim Kennedy)	95	65	80
94397	1997	BIRD OF PARADISE (William Ivey Long)	175	80	128
94396	1997	ICED COFFEE (Laura Meisner)	90	60	75
93525	1997	THE KING'S DAUGHTER, Special LE 5000 (Michelle Gutierrez)	350	216	283
93550	1997	MIDNIGHT ROMANCE, *NALED Exclusive* (Timothy Alberts)	185	159	172
—	1997	NIGHT AT VERSAILLES 1st, LE 5000 *FAO Schwarz Exclusive*	240	155	198
94394	1997	SPARKLING SEDUCTION (Shelley Rinker)	110	65	88
94395	1997	WHITE HYACINTH (Doug James)	150	80	115
94662	1998	CHAMPAGNE SUPPER	100	80	90
94664	1998	COVENT GARDEN, *NALED Exclusive*	140	70	105
94685	1998	CREME DE CASSIS (Tim Alberts)	95	75	85
94667	1998	DAUGHTER OF THE NILE	90	70	80
94656	1998	DESTINY *1st Annual Edition Series*	105	80	93
94657	1998	HELLO HOLLYWOOD, HELLO	90	70	80
94659	1988	INCOGNITO	95	65	80
94666	1998	MIDNIGHT GAMBLE 1st, LE 9500 *1st Retailer Exclusive doll*	140	100	120
—	1998	ON THE AVENUE 2nd, LE 5000 *FAO Schwarz Exclusive*	250	159	205
—	1998	HOLIDAY BENEFIT GALA LE 25 (Mark Middendorf)	265	265	265
94663	1998	WARMEST WISHES *FAO Schwarz Exclusive*	199	100	149
—	1999	AN AMERICAN COUNTESS *NALED Exclusive,* LE 7500	80	80	80
76074	1999	BREATHLESS *2nd Retailer Exclusive doll*	100	100	100
76063	1999	LOVE, PARIS	80	80	80
73529	1999	LUCKY STRIPE	80	80	80
76064	1999	SAVANNAH	80	80	80
76062	1999	SHE'D RATHER DANCE	80	80	80
93526	1999	SIMPLY GENE Redhead	50	50	50
93527	1999	SIMPLY GENE Blonde	50	50	50
93528	1999	SIMPLY GENE Brunette	50	50	50
76065	1999	SONG OF SPAIN *2nd Annual Edition Series*	100	100	100
76066	1999	TEATIME AT THE PLAZA *FAO Schwarz Exclusive*	100	100	100
76061	1999	USO	80	80	80
—	2000	BON VOYAGE - 3rd Retailer exclusive, LE 3500	100	100	100
—	2000	DANCE WITH ME		85	
—	2000	ENCORE	100	100	100
—	2000	I DO		85	
—	2000	LOVE AT FIRST SIGHT		85	
—	2000	MOOD MUSIC		Retail	
—	2000	ON THE SET		Retail	
—	2000	PRICELESS		Retail	
—	2000	SANTA FE CELEBRATION		Retail	
—	2000	SHOOTING STAR		85	

STOCK NO.	YEAR	DESCRIPTION	NRFB HIGH	LOW	AVG
—	2000	SIMPLY GENE PLATINUM	55		
—	2000	SPOTTED IN THE PARK	Retail		
—	2000	TWILIGHT RUMBA - 3rd Annual Edition Series	100		
—	2000	UNFORGETTABLE	Retail		

❖❖❖❖❖❖❖❖❖❖❖❖❖❖❖

Gene Costumes

STOCK NO.	YEAR	DESCRIPTION	NRFB HIGH	LOW	AVG
96404	1995	BLOND LACE (Tim Kennedy)	55	40	50
96409	1995	BLUE EVENING (Timothy Alberts)	40	30	35
93502	1995	CRIMSON SUN (Doug James)	40	30	35
93501	1995	GOOD-BYE NEW YORK (Doug James)	40	30	35
96410	1995	THE KISS (Tim Kennedy)	40	30	35
96406	1995	LOVE'S GHOST (Doug James)	40	30	35
96405	1995	PINK LIGHTNING (Tim Kennedy)	75	30	53
96407	1995	STRIKING GOLD (Timothy Alberts) 2 shawl versions	40	30	35
96408	1995	USHERETTE (Tim Kennedy)	40	30	35
93508	1996	AFTERNOON OFF (Doug James)	75	30	53
93505	1996	CRESCENDO (Doug James)	60	40	50
93506	1996	EL MOROCCO (Timothy Alberts)	30	30	30
94392	1996	HOLIDAY MAGIC LE 2000 *1st Retail Exclusive costume*	475	250	363
93544	1997	BLOSSOMS IN THE SNOW, LE 5000 *2nd Retail Exclusive costume* (Tim Kennedy)	195	130	163
93543	1997	MANDARIN MOOD (Tim Kennedy)	45	35	40
93542	1997	PERSONAL SECRETARY (Tim Kennedy)	35	35	35
93541	1997	PROMENADE (Tim Kennedy)	75	40	57
93546	1997	SEA SPREE (Tim Kennedy)	40	35	38
93545	1997	TANGO (Tim Kennedy)	45	40	43
94655	1998	CAMEO	35	30	33
94652	1998	EMBASSY LUNCHEON	50	32	41
94653	1998	FORGET-ME-NOT (Tim Alberts)	50	30	40
94686	1998	MY FAVORITE BOW - Gold Sensation	50	40	45
94669	1998	HI-FI	35	29	32
94658	1998	LOVE AFTER HOURS	35	35	35
94674	1998	MIDNIGHT ANGEL	40	40	40
94675	1998	RAIN SONG	30	25	27
94676	1998	RANSOM IN RED, LE 7500 *3rd Retail Exclusive costume*	95	55	75
94673	1998	SAFARI (African)	40	40	40
94687	1998	SMART SET	40	29	35

STOCK NO.	YEAR	DESCRIPTION	NRFB HIGH	LOW	AVG
76084	1999	AT HOME FOR THE HOLIDAYS *4th Retail Exclusive cosutme*	50	50	50
76085	1999	AVANT GARDE	40	40	40
76088	1999	BLACK RIBBON	40	40	40
76069	1999	BRIDGE CLUB	35	35	35
76086	1999	COGNAC EVENING	45	45	45
76067	1999	FAREWELL, GOLDEN MOON	45	45	45
93524	1999	HONEYMOON	45	45	45
76068	1999	ON THE VERANDA NALED Exclusive	50	50	50
76077	1999	PICNIC IN THE COUNTRY	40	40	40
76078	1999	POOLSIDE	35	35	35
76068	1999	PRESS CONFERENCE	45	45	45
93523	1999	SECRET SLEUTH	40	40	40
93522	1999	SOMEWHERE SUMMER	45	45	45
76070	1999	STAND UP AND CHEER	45	45	45
93521	1999	SUNDAY AFTERNOON	40	40	40
76076	1999	SUNSET CELEBRATION	40	40	40
—	2000	BAKING COOKIES, LE 5000		35	
—	2000	BOLERO, LE 5000		40	
—	2000	CROQUET, ANYONE?, LE 5000		35	
—	2000	DON'T FENCE ME IN, LE 5000		35	
—	2000	FIRST CLOSE-UP, LE 5000		40	
—	2000	FIRST STOP: CHICAGO, LE 5000		45	
—	2000	HACIENDA, LE 5000		45	
—	2000	HEART'S AFIRE, LE 5000		45	
—	2000	IT'S A WRAP, LE 5000		33	
—	2000	JAZZ NOTE, LE 5000		45	
—	2000	KISS ME, GENE, LE 5000		45	
—	2000	LITTLE BLACK DRESS, LE 5000		45	
—	2000	LOVE LETTERS, LE 5000		35	
—	2000	SHORTS STORY, LE 5000		33	
—	2000	SPELLBOUND, LE 5000		50	
—	2000	ST. MORITZ, LE 5000		50	
—	2000	TABLE FOR TWO, LE 5000		35	
—	2000	THE PERFECT GIFT, LE 5000		45	
—	2000	THE SPIRIT OF TRUTH, LE 5000		45	
—	2000	WILL YOU MARRY ME?, LE 5000		45	

Gene Conventions

DESCRIPTION	NRFB HIGH	LOW	AVG
1996 1ST ANNUAL EAST COAST GENE CONVENTION			
PACKAGE	1000	1000	1000
ATLANTIC CITY BEAUTY OUTFIT (1st Convention) non A.D.	800	695	750
1997 2ND ANNUAL EAST COAST GENE CONVENTION			
PACKAGE	1500	1200	1350
MY FAVORITE WITCH DOLL, LE 350 (Masquerade)		910	
PRETTY KITTY OUTFIT (New Jersey) non A.D.		Retail	
TRUNK w/accessories		Retail	
PROGRAM (includes paper doll w/3 outfits)		Retail	
GIFT BAG w/3" button, collector cards (32 - 4" x 6")		Retail	
MY FAVORITE WITCH SKETCH		Retail	
SWEATSHIRT		Retail	
BLACK TOTE BAG		Retail	
PIN		Retail	
1998 1ST ANNUAL WEST COAST HOLLYWOOD GENE CONVENTION			
PACKAGE	750	475	613
DREAM GIRL OUTFIT LE 250 (non Ashton-Drake costume by D.A.E.)		Retail	
COSTUME SKETCH		Retail	
ASHTON-DRAKE HAT BOX w/accessories		Retail	
BLACK TOTE BAG		Retail	
PROGRAM "HELLO HOLLYWOOD"		Retail	
PATTERN GLAMOUR GAL		Retail	
KEY CHAIN		Retail	
BUTTON "SHARE THE DREAM"		Retail	
PROMOTIONAL PHOTO		Retail	
CONVENTION TRUNK w/stickers		Retail	
MILLER'$ 1997 MAGAZINE		Retail	
1998 3RD ANNUAL EAST COAST GENE CONVENTION			
PACKAGE	910	450	680
BROADWAY MEDLEY DOLL		255	
TOTE BAG		Retail	
FOLDER WITH STRETCH		Retail	
TWO PINS (B.M. and Share the Dream)		Retail	
PEN		Retail	
HATBOX		Retail	
PERFUME BOTTLE		Retail	
PHOTO CARDS		Retail	
TWO MAGNETS (B.M. and My Favorite Witch)		Retail	
NY TIMES MINATURES		Retail	
TRUNK		Retail	
WORKSHOP KITS		Retail	
1999 WEST COAST CONVENTION		268	
PACKAGE		300	
MOOD MUSIC DOLL		203	
SKETCH		Retail	
TOTE		Retail	
PINS		Retail	
PROGRAM		Retail	
2000 PARIS FASHION DOLL FESTIVAL			
DOLL		390	

Gene Accessories

STOCK NO.	YEAR	DESCRIPTION	NRFB HIGH	LOW	AVG
—	1996	CARD PACK	10	10	10
94390	1996	DRESS FORM	20	19	20
94391	1996	HAT BOX, SE (turquoise w/Gene printed, black satin card)	20	15	18
93504	1996	WARDROBE TRUNK	70	50	60
94398	1997	CHRISTMAS TREE (Mel Odom) white w/colored ball ornaments	80	25	53
93548	1997	HOT DAY IN HOLLYWOOD Accessory Set	35	35	35
93547	1997	OUT FOR A STROLL "Dottie" & "Dashiell" Dogs, Accessory Set (Etta Foran)	30	30	30
—	1998	BUTTON, Share the Dream from the Asthon-Drake Galleries (head only)	15	15	15
—	1998	BUTTON, Share the Dream from the Ashton-Drake Galleries (3/4 length) Iced Coffee	15	15	15
95121	1998	CARD PACK	10	10	10
—	1998	GENE LAPEL PIN w/Swarovski Crystals	35	20	28
—	1998	RIALTO THEATRE	70	70	70
76079	1999	BIRTHDAY PARTYPACK	30	30	30
76080	1999	DIRECTOR'S CHAIR	30	30	30
76073	1999	DRESSER	80	80	80
—	1999	GENE LINE COLLECTOR POSTER	10	10	10
92938	1999	JEWELRY SET	35	35	35
92931	1999	MAGNETIC PAPER DOLL SET 1	13	13	13
92932	1999	MAGNETIC PAPER DOLL SET 2	13	13	13
93321	1999	MUSIC CD, MENU FOR ROMANCE	15	15	15
93323	1999	MUSIC VIDEO, MENU FOR LOVE	15	15	15
94679	1999	PATIO SET	50	50	50
9049	1999	PATTERN - Simplicity	10	10	10
76087	1999	SWAN BED	90	90	90
94677	1999	USO PACKAGE	35	35	35
—	2000	CHAISE LOUNGE	75	75	75
—	2000	CROQUET SET	50	50	50
—	2000	DARK SHOES	20	20	20
—	2000	DRESSING SCREEN	45	45	45
—	2000	GAZEBO	45	45	45
—	2000	GENE FAN - Appreciation Weekend Ornament	30	15	22
—	2000	HALL TABLE	35	35	35
—	2000	HANGER SET	15	15	15
—	2000	HAT STAND	15	15	15
—	2000	HAT AND PURSE SET 4 versions	45	45	45
—	2000	HEARTS AND FLOWERS	35	35	35
—	2000	PANTHER LAMP	Retail		
—	2000	RIBBON SHOES	20	20	20

Gene Accessories *continued*

STOCK NO.	YEAR	DESCRIPTION	NRFB HIGH	LOW	AVG
—	2000	SHOE SET 2 versions	45	45	45
—	2000	SWAN LAMP	50	50	50
—	2000	UNDERCOVER STORY	30	30	30
—	2000	WARDROBE RACK	45	45	45

❖❖❖❖❖❖❖❖❖❖❖❖❖❖

Signing Items

DESCRIPTION	YEAR	NRFB HIGH	LOW	AVG
CLASSIC ELEGANCE COSTUME/TWO DAYS IN PARADISE	1998	425	150	288
LE 100 (Mark Middendorf) Mel Odom signing in Sarasota, Florida				

❖❖❖❖❖❖❖❖❖❖❖❖❖❖

Madra Lord

STOCK NO.	YEAR	DESCRIPTION	NRFB HIGH	LOW	AVG
		DOLLS			
—	2000	FIRST ENCOUNTER	110	110	110
—	2000	BLACK WIDOW		Retail	
		COSTUMES			
—	2000	CAT WALK	40	40	40
—	2000	DEVIL MAY CARE	50	50	50
—	2000	DRESSED TO KILL	45	45	45
—	2000	HEARTLESS	45	45	45
—	2000	PINK WITH ENVY	45	45	45
—	2000	SO EVIL MY LOVE	50	50	50
		ACCESSORIES			
—	2000	DOG ACCESSORIES	50	50	50

Tyler Wentworth Collection

STOCK NO.	YEAR	DESCRIPTION	NRFB
—	1999	**DOLLS**	
	1999	Tyler Wentworth, redhead	80
	1999	Tyler Wentworth, blonde	80
	1999	Tyler Wentworth, brunette	80
	1999	Party of the Season, LE 2,500	170
	1999	Toast of the Party, LE 1,000 (Corbett's Exclusive)	190
	2000	Casual Luxury, LE 3,000	170
	2000	Esme	80
	2000	Esme Cover Girl, LE 3,000	150
20800	2000	Something Sleek	70
20806	2000	White House Dinner, LE 3,000	170
	2000	Opera Gala, LE 3,000	170
		FASHIONS	
99810	1999	Cashmere Noire, LE 2,500	85
99811	1999	Collection Premiere, LE 2,500	70
99814	1999	Wake Up Call, LE 2,500	50
99813	1999	Fragrance Launch, LE 2,500	60
99812	1999	Gallery Soiree, LE 2,500	65
99815	1999	Fashion Design Weekly Awards, LE 2,500	80
20831	2000	Sweet Indulgence	60
20820	2000	Champagne Bubble, LE 3,000	80
20822	2000	Shakespeare In The Park, LE 3,000	90
20830	2000	Madison Avenue Afternoon	60
20832	2000	Beverly Hills Chic	60
	2000	Market Week, LE 1,000	100
	2000	Russian Renaissance, LE 3,000	60
	2000	Manhattan Music Award, LE 3,000	60
	2000	Weekend Retreat, LE 3,000	60
		ACCESSORIES	
		Fall Sportswear Pattern	12
99850		Evening Separates Pattern	12
9985		Resort Separates Pattern	12
99890		Tyler's Dress Form	70

INDEX TO VINTAGE PIECES

VINTAGE DOLLS

VINTAGE DOLLS

VINTAGE DOLLS

INDEX TO VINTAGE PIECES

VINTAGE DOLLS

VINTAGE DOLLS

VINTAGE FASHIONS

INDEX TO VINTAGE PIECES

VINTAGE FASHIONS

INDEX TO VINTAGE PIECES

INDEX TO VINTAGE PIECES

VINTAGE FASHIONS

441

INDEX TO VINTAGE PIECES

VINTAGE FASHIONS

442

INDEX TO VINTAGE PIECES

VINTAGE FASHIONS

VINTAGE FASHIONS

INDEX TO VINTAGE PIECES

VINTAGE FASHIONS   VINTAGE FASHIONS

INDEX TO VINTAGE PIECES

INDEX TO VINTAGE PIECES

VINTAGE FASHIONS

VINTAGE FASHIONS

GENERAL INDEX, BY CATEGORY

GENERAL INDEX, BY CATEGORY